Prototype and Scriptaculous
in Action

Prototype and Scriptaculous in Action

DAVE CRANE
BEAR BIBEAULT
with TOM LOCKE

MANNING
Greenwich
(74° w. long.)

Manning Publications Co.   Copyeditor: Andy Carroll
Sound View Court 3B   Typesetter: Gordan Salinovic
Greenwich, CT 06830   Cover designer: Leslie Haimes

ISBN 1-933988-03-7

Second, corrected printing, July 2007
Printed in the United States of America

2 3 4 5 6 7 8 9 10 – MAL – 11 10 09 08 07

To Vesta,
the goddess of tidy housekeeping,
and every coder's best friend

brief contents

contents

ix

foreword

Niceness is key.

Web development is traditionally centered around finding workarounds for problems when implementing something that looks easy enough to do on paper. Probably the most sinister and seemingly magical part of all is the web browser. Besides the fact that the major browsers all have various bugs and don't completely support what is stated in the specs, you'll quickly run into basic limitations, like missing user interface controls, unnecessarily complicated coding in Java-Script, and, of course, the dreaded cross-browser differences.

Well, forget about all that. This book will show you how to use Prototype and Scriptaculous to concentrate on what's really important: implementing your ideas.

The simple premise of how to achieve this goal is *niceness*. The concept of niceness permeates both libraries, on all levels. First off, the libs are nice to you, as a developer. Most of the time, you can write a short line of code, and it just works. They also follow a consistent style throughout, so you don't have to learn lots of stuff when you use a function for the first time. The source code is optimized to be very readable—just give it some time! The net effect is that you can create rich user interactivity in a very short time, extending this niceness directly to the user. You'll actually get to make little tweaks to improve the user interface, instead of having to worry about how to get the underlying technology to work. This way, you can set up a productive "rinse and repeat" development cycle that easily allows you to get both designers and users on board early in the process (yes, "beta" is not just a hollow word).

Prototype and Scriptaculous didn't invent this approach—they both were born out of and borrow heavily from the Ruby on Rails web development framework. Many things will be quite familiar if you have worked with Rails—and if you haven't, you should try it!

Niceness goes a long way. It applies to all aspects of developing websites, from the underlying back end to seeing the user smile. To quote a Scriptaculous user, "The puff effect made me cry. They were tears of joy." While you might not react quite like this, there are many ways to enjoy these libraries. Perhaps the most important one is being able to get home on time—because you finished early.

So have fun creating the next nice thing on the Web, and, if you like, give back to the community what you've learned by joining IRC channels and mailing lists. Or, even nicer, write patches and do bug fixes, or create your own open source extensions for Prototype and Scriptaculous!

THOMAS FUCHS
CTO, wollzelle
Creator of Scriptaculous

A couple of years ago, JavaScript was generally looked down on as something that one did when one couldn't be bothered doing proper programming. The advent of Ajax has given the language a smart new set of clothes, and it's almost respectable to describe oneself as a JavaScript programmer. I've followed this transition myself, from doing JavaScript here and there because I had to, to figuring out some fairly neat tricks that just couldn't be accomplished any other way.

I even started to dig into the language itself, and was pleasantly surprised to find out that, although it wasn't really that much like Java at all, it had a style and logic of its own. I got my head around prototype chains and started writing Java-Script objects. I was very pleased with myself the day I figured out how closures worked in JavaScript, and congratulated myself on achieving a certain level of mastery. Pride comes before the fall.

I picked up Sam Stephenson's Prototype library somewhere along the way, and copied a few lines of code written by someone else who had used it, and found that it provided shortcuts that speeded up my typing. It wasn't long before curiosity got the better of me and I wanted to know how it worked. When I first read the source code for Prototype, I thought I'd stumbled across some arcane dialect of Perl. This didn't look like the JavaScript that I was accustomed to writing, and I did the only thing a brave and seasoned programmer could do—I ran away and hid.

I couldn't keep away for long, though, and each time I looked, the coding style made more sense. I was kicking the tires of this new scripting language called

Ruby at the same time and I started to make a few connections between the two, and gradually a pattern began to emerge. Along the way, I realized that Sam had forgotten more about closures, prototype chains, and all the other things that make JavaScript such a fun language, than I had learned in the first place. A lot of thought had gone into building up the library the way it was, so that a few well-placed lines of code early on could be exploited again and again elsewhere.

Thomas Fuchs's Scriptaculous library takes the same approach, building larger constructs out of well-designed parts, and then, with a flourish, wraps the whole thing up so that the novice can exploit all the power and grace of these libraries in a few lines of code. When I teach Ajax courses, the day on which we unwrap Scriptaculous and create singing, dancing, drag-and-dropping interactive user interfaces (OK, so I lied about the singing and dancing) often feels a bit like Christmas, as my students achieve things with a few lines of code and a couple of hours that look slicker and smarter than what they thought they could turn out in a week.

You can use this book to find out how to harness the power of these libraries in a few lines of code, quickly. Prototype and Scriptaculous let you do the easy things easily, so that you can get on with the business side of your work, unencumbered by cross-browser worries or the burden of supporting your own libraries. You can also use the book to develop a deeper understanding of how these libraries work, and, as a consequence, how JavaScript works.

For me, using Prototype and Scriptaculous has made JavaScript coding more fun. I hope that fun is catching. Enjoy.

DAVE CRANE

acknowledgments

We would like to express our thanks and gratitude to the many people who contributed to make this project a reality and to turn our ideas into the book that you are now reading.

To the reviewers who gave us feedback on the manuscript in its various stages of development and helped make it a much better book. They include Philip Hallstrom, Christopher Haupt, Derek Lakin, Jon Tirsen, Deepak Vohra, Jeff Cunningham, Christopher Bailey, Scott Shaw, Mark Eagle, and Benjamin Gorlick. Special thanks to Deepak Vohra who did a thorough technical proofread of the book just before it went to press.

To the readers of Manning's Early Access Program who helped ferret out many last-minute errors and inconsistencies in our draft chapters.

To everyone at Manning Publications, especially publisher Marjan Bace and our editors Mike Stephens and Cynthia Kane, as well as the production team of Andy Carroll, Dottie Marisco, Gordan Salinovic, Elizabeth Martin, and Mary Piergies.

To Thomas Fuchs for agreeing to write the foreword and to Tom Locke for contributing the chapter on Rails. Our sincere thanks for lending your names and efforts to our endeavor.

DAVE CRANE

Above all, I'd like to thank Sam Stephenson and Thomas Fuchs for creating these remarkable libraries, and to the Prototype core development team—Justin Palmer, Andrew Dupont, Dan Webb, Scott Raymond, Mislav Marohnic, Christophe Porteneuve, Tobie Langel, and Seth Dillingham—for keeping the ball rolling at such dizzying speed while staying on course.

I'd like to thank my colleagues Simon Warrick, Tim Wilson, Susannah Ellis, Simon Crossley, Rob Levine, and Miles Wilson at Historic Futures for their support for this project, and to Wendy, Nic, Graeme, and the team at Skillsmatter.com—and all my talented students—for helping to shape my thoughts on how this book should be written.

And thanks to Bear and Tom for their invaluable help and insight in getting this book into shape.

Finally, and by no means least, I'd like to thank the rest of the Crane family—Chia, Ben, and Sophie—for putting up with me while I wrote yet another book, my Mum and Dad, and my cats, for being so patient and understanding about not always getting fed quite on time.

BEAR BIBEAULT

I'd like to thank my friends at javaranch.com, who encouraged me to put pen to paper (rather, fingers to keyboard) and to "Go for it!" when I expressed an interest in writing. They include, but are not limited to, Ernest Friedman-Hill, Eric Pascarello, Ben Souther, Max Habibi, Mark Herschberg, and Kathy Sierra.

I'd like to thank Paul Wheaton, owner of javaranch.com, for creating such a wonderful place to linger, learn, and help others.

I'd like to thank Dave Crane and Michael Stephens for putting their trust in me and for giving me the opportunity to contribute to this work.

I'd also like to thank my dogs Gizmo and Little Bear, whose visages appear in some of the screen captures in these pages, without their written consent, and who provided companionship by lying on my feet as I typed away.

And I'd like to thank my partner Jay, who put up with all the long nights, the rants regarding Word, the moaning and groaning about browser idiosyncrasies, and who introduced me to the Mac all those years ago.

about this book

Prototype and Scriptaculous are both, like most software libraries, productivity tools. Coding in a web browser is a curious experience—it is much freer and more expressive than any desktop GUI toolkit, yet it is also lacking in some of the most basic facilities. I know of few desktop developers who tried to maintain their own drag-and-drop library or drop-down list widget as part of a product, and several DHTML/Ajax developers who did. This type of feature is rarely the raison d'être of a software project, but rather is a means to an end. Guddling around with the low-level code required to enable those means is, at best, a distraction, and at worst, a burden that can sink a project.

Audience

This book is aimed at JavaScript coders with a clear purpose behind what they're doing, who need to express their business ideas and concepts elegantly and to spend their time improving user workflow and satisfaction, or developing cool new features. Prototype and Scriptaculous let you express your code fluidly and elegantly, and you get to lead a full and rewarding life outside your programming job. If you like futzing around developing your own coordinate system, or reimplementing commonplaces in modern computing, such as tree widgets, sorting algorithms, and event listeners from scratch, then you're out of luck here. Although, come to think of it, Prototype and Scriptaculous could certainly help you to do that faster, and better...

Our second intended audience are the experienced Ajax programmers who want to improve their understanding of why these libraries work the way they do. We present most of the features in these libraries as straightforward recipes that anyone can use, but we also take the time to look at the internal workings of the key components and functions. Perhaps even more importantly, we have tried to pay attention to the bigger pattern, and to how the various pieces fit together into a relatively harmonious whole.

Whether you're simply looking to get the job done effectively, or want to hone your JavaScript skills to the next level, we hope that this book has something for you.

Roadmap

We've divided the book into four parts, in order to provide some structure to our discussions. Part 1 concentrates on the centerpiece of the recent upsurge of interest in web-based clients, namely the asynchronous request. Ajax is a small piece of functionality with a big impact on many aspects of application design, and Prototype provides a lot of power in assisting us in doing that.

Chapter 1 provides a general introduction to the Prototype and Scriptaculous libraries and their place in the modern Ajax landscape. Chapter 2 introduces our main sample application, a web-based image viewer called QuickGallery. In chapters 3 and 4, we use QuickGallery to explore the different styles of Ajax supported by Prototype, from the basic components required to make an Ajax request, through to the more sophisticated helpers developed in recent versions of Prototype, which address architectural issues in the way an application manages its HTTP traffic.

Part 2 turns to the Scriptaculous libraries, devoting a chapter to each of the key components. Chapter 5 looks at the Effects subsystem, and takes us from the one-line instant gratification of invoking our first special effect, through customizing and composing effects, on to writing our own effect types.

Chapter 6 examines the Controls subsystem, which provides out-of-the-box Ajax-enabled components for use on web pages. Again, we run the full gamut from one-line deployment to a thorough understanding of customization and composition of these components. We also show how to hook these up to processes on the server side, in order to deliver a highly interactive workflow.

Chapter 7 looks at the drag-and-drop subsystems of Scriptaculous. In Scriptaculous, drag and drop is layered, with relatively simple objects providing the basic capabilities, and sophisticated drag-and-drop UI components being built on top of these. We describe both how these systems work, and how to use them in your own projects.

Part 3 is intended mainly for the language aficionados. JavaScript is a malleable language and Prototype molds it into some very interesting, and useful, structures. We step through the various new capabilities that Prototype provides to the core object types, and illustrate each feature with a small practical example. In order to achieve maximum coverage of all the new features, we've adopted a snippet-based approach to this part of the book and we provide an interactive interpreter program that will execute these snippets for us.

Chapter 8 looks at the JavaScript Object, the base class upon which all other JavaScript objects are founded. We show how to create new objects, and reusable types of objects, and how to work with JavaScript's prototype-based system of inheritance. We then describe how the Prototype library has simplified these techniques, and show you how to create your own object hierarchies using Prototype.

Chapter 9 looks at JavaScript functions and the related concept of closures. This is a small but powerful chapter, covering one of the most misunderstood and useful features of the JavaScript language. Closures can be difficult to work with, but Prototype provides a simpler approach.

Chapter 10 looks at JavaScript arrays. It's no overstatement to say that Prototype completely changes the way one works with Arrays, adding over thirty new methods. We cover each of these in depth, and look at how the magical new facilities can even be extended to objects other than bona fide arrays, such as collections of DOM elements and plain old JavaScript objects.

In chapter 11, we look at Prototype's support for the web browser environment, namely the Document Object Model and HTML forms. The functionality that we cover here greatly improves the experience of creating cross-browser user interfaces and it provides a useful low-level counterpart to the pyrotechnics of the Scriptaculous library that we described in part 2.

Part 4 concludes our exploration of these libraries with a couple of advanced topics. Chapter 12 returns to the QuickGallery application that we described in part 1 and applies the knowledge garnered in parts 2 and 3 of the book to rapidly add new features to the app. This illustrates the process of using these libraries in real-world settings.

Chapter 13 looks at the integration between Scriptaculous and Prototype and the Ruby on Rails framework, and shows how Rails builds upon these libraries to deliver even more elegance and ease of use.

HTTP underlies everything we do on the Web, and when we're using Ajax, we get a bit more control over how we use it. With great power comes great responsibility, as they say. Appendix A covers the basics of the protocol, and appendix B details the techniques we use in this book to profile the HTTP traffic from an app.

The main examples in this book rely on PHP and Java on the server. Not all of our readers will be familiar with these technologies, so appendices C and D provide a step-by-step setup guide for the most popular operating systems, for the Java Tomcat web server and PHP/Apache respectively.

The focus of this book is on JavaScript code and the server-side code that we present in these examples is, on the whole, quite simple. We do, however, use a few server-side tricks that are only likely to find use with Ajax. In appendix E, we provide a quick conversion guide on how to master these tricks in some of the popular sever-side languages that we don't cover in detail in the main examples.

Code conventions

The code examples that we present in this book cover a number of programming languages, including JavaScript, Java, JSP, Ruby, and PHP. We present the longer pieces of code in these languages as "listings" with their own headers. Smaller bits of code are simply run inline with the text. In all cases, we present the code using a `monospaced font`, to differentiate it from the rest of the text. Many longer listings have numbered annotations that we refer to in the text, and, in several cases where we're looking at incremental changes to a piece of code, we have highlighted the modified parts in **bold**.

In chapters 8 through 11, we deal with the lower-level language features of the Prototype library, and so are dealing almost exclusively with small fragments of code. Rather than present all the example code inline, we've given these examples the status of "snippets." These are similar to listings, with the important distinction that they can be run inside the interactive interpreter (the Scratchpad application) that we introduce in chapter 8 and use throughout these chapters. This interpreter allows us to visualize the nonvisual effects of the code we're discussing, and each snippet is accompanied by a screenshot showing its output in the interpreter.

Code downloads

The complete example code for the book can be downloaded from the Manning website page for this book, at http://www.manning.com/crane3. This includes the interactive interpreter required to run the snippets, and the larger examples for the other chapters. Some of these require a Java web server or Apache/PHP setup to run them. We step through the business of setting these up to run the examples in appendices C and D.

What's next?

Our book should give you a thorough grounding in Prototype and Scriptaculous, but we can't cover every question that might arise within these pages. Manning provides an online forum for talking to the authors of every book that it publishes, and you can reach Dave, Bear, and Tom at the Author Online forum for this book at http://www.manning-sandbox.com/forum.jspa?forumID=276.

Prototype and Scriptaculous have a vigorous online presence beyond our involvement in the book, of course. Prototype's official documentation site can be found at http://www.prototypejs.org/. Scriptaculous is documented mainly via Wiki at http://wiki.script.aculo.us. General questions about both libraries can also be addressed to the Ruby on Rails Spinoffs group, which can be found at http://groups.google.com/group/rubyonrails-spinoffs?hl=en. Despite the name, the group isn't exclusively used by Ruby coders, and serves the wider constituency of Prototype and Scriptaculous users.

We look forward to hearing from you!

Author Online

Purchase of *Prototype and Scriptaculous in Action* includes free access to a private web forum run by Manning Publications where you can make comments about the book, ask technical questions, and receive help from the authors and from other users. To access the forum and subscribe to it, point your web browser to http://www.manning.com/crane3. This page provides information on how to get on the forum once you are registered, what kind of help is available, and the rules of conduct on the forum.

Manning's commitment to our readers is to provide a venue where a meaningful dialogue between individual readers and between readers and the authors can take place. It is not a commitment to any specific amount of participation on the part of the authors, whose contribution to the book's forum remains voluntary (and unpaid). We suggest you try asking the authors some challenging questions, lest their interest stray!

The Author Online forum and the archives of previous discussions will be accessible from the publisher's website as long as the book is in print.

about the title

By combining introductions, overviews, and how-to examples, the *In Action* books are designed to help learning and remembering. According to research in cognitive science, the things people remember are things they discover during self-motivated exploration.

Although no one at Manning is a cognitive scientist, we are convinced that for learning to become permanent it must pass through stages of exploration, play, and, interestingly, re-telling of what is being learned. People understand and remember new things, which is to say they master them, only after actively exploring them. Humans learn in action. An essential part of an *In Action* book is that it is example-driven. It encourages the reader to try things out, to play with new code, and explore new ideas.

There is another, more mundane, reason for the title of this book: our readers are busy. They use books to do a job or solve a problem. They need books that allow them to jump in and jump out easily and learn just what they want just when they want it. They need books that aid them in action. The books in this series are designed for such readers.

about the cover illustration

The figure on the cover of *Prototype and Scriptaculous in Action* is an "Ichlogan," or an inhabitant of Turkey dressed in a regional costume. The illustration is taken from a collection of costumes of the Ottoman Empire published on January 1, 1802, by William Miller of Old Bond Street, London. The title page is missing from the collection and we have been unable to track it down to date. The book's table of contents identifies the figures in both English and French, and each illustration bears the names of two artists who worked on it, both of whom would no doubt be surprised to find their art gracing the front cover of a computer programming book...two hundred years later.

The collection was purchased by a Manning editor at an antiquarian flea market in the "Garage" on West 26th Street in Manhattan. The seller was an American based in Ankara, Turkey, and the transaction took place just as he was packing up his stand for the day. The Manning editor did not have on his person the substantial amount of cash that was required for the purchase and a credit card and check were both politely turned down. With the seller flying back to Ankara that evening the situation was getting hopeless. What was the solution? It turned out to be nothing more than an old-fashioned verbal agreement sealed with a handshake. The seller simply proposed that the money be transferred to him by wire and the editor walked out with the bank information on a piece of paper and the portfolio of images under his arm. Needless to say, we transferred the funds the next day, and we remain grateful and impressed by this unknown person's trust in one of us. It recalls something that might have happened a long time ago.

The pictures from the Ottoman collection, like the other illustrations that appear on our covers, bring to life the richness and variety of dress customs of two centuries ago. They recall the sense of isolation and distance of that period—and of every other historic period except our own hyperkinetic present.

Dress codes have changed since then and the diversity by region, so rich at the time, has faded away. It is now often hard to tell the inhabitant of one continent from another. Perhaps, trying to view it optimistically, we have traded a cultural and visual diversity for a more varied personal life. Or a more varied and interesting intellectual and technical life.

We at Manning celebrate the inventiveness, the initiative, and, yes, the fun of the computer business with book covers based on the rich diversity of regional life of two centuries ago, brought back to life by the pictures from this collection.

Part 1

Getting Started

This book is intended as an in-depth introduction to the Prototype and Scriptaculous libraries. When documenting libraries, it is important to present a feature-by-feature account of the details, but also to present the libraries in context, and show how they fit into the bigger picture. This part of the book deals with the bigger picture.

Chapter 1 provides an introduction to both libraries and concludes with a quick example of how they can be made to work for us. Prototype and Scriptaculous are designed to make the development of Ajax web applications simpler and easier, and to remove a lot of the repetitive drudge work. We therefore present the same application twice, first with and then without the help of these powerful libraries.

We devote the rest of this part of the book to exploring a more detailed example application—an image browser called QuickGallery. We introduce the vanilla, non-Ajax version of the app in chapter 2, and discuss some of the limitations of traditional web applications. In chapters 3 and 4, we set about resolving these issues by introducing a variety of techniques for Ajax-enabling the QuickGallery app.

The real purpose of chapters 3 and 4 is not to show you how to make a better image browser. Throughout these chapters, we explore Prototype's Ajax helper classes and examine not only how they work, but what they can do to improve the workflow of a web application. We conclude by evaluating the various styles of Ajax that Prototype enables.

Introducing Prototype and Scriptaculous

3

Ajax is growing up fast. One of the signs of that growth is the appearance, and widespread adoption, of a number of third-party libraries that make it easier to work with Ajax, and the web technologies that support it, such as DOM, CSS, and, above all, JavaScript. This book covers two related JavaScript libraries in depth: Prototype and Scriptaculous. Prototype provides many small-scale features that make it easier to work with Ajax applications. Scriptaculous leverages these features to build a number of higher-level user interface components. Together, they can give your Ajax development the edge, making it easy to express your ideas in JavaScript, and ridiculously easy to make your user interface sing.

In this chapter, we'll set the scene for the Prototype and Scriptaculous libraries, describing how they relate to the bigger picture of Ajax development, and why we thought it useful to write a book about them. We understand that Manning readers are typically a practical bunch, so we'll also take the libraries out for a quick spin in this chapter, using them to turbocharge a plain old Ajax application by cutting out a lot of unnecessary low-level code, and making it easy to create a fluid, pleasant user interface. In subsequent chapters, we'll drill down into the details of the libraries, and provide all the details you'll need to turbocharge your applications in a similar way.

In part 1 of this book, we'll concentrate on Ajax; that is, the business of communicating between the browser and the server without causing the full page to refresh. By the end of part 1, you'll be able to make use of Prototype's support for Ajax in a variety of ways. From there, we'll move on to look at Scriptaculous in more detail in part 2, and at Prototype's support for JavaScript and the DOM in part 3. In part 1, we'll also introduce an example application, which we'll return to in part 4 of the book to apply what we've learned. We'll begin, though, with a brief review of Ajax, in order to set the context in which Prototype and Scriptaculous work.

1.1 A brief history of Ajax

Ajax is a recently coined term used to describe the business of programming highly interactive web-based interfaces using nothing more than HTML, Cascading Style Sheets (CSS), and a good dose of JavaScript. People have been writing this sort of application for several years, but Jesse James Garrett only christened the practice in February 2005, and it has since gone on to become one of the hot tech topics.

The adoption of Ajax by the web community has been rapid, and the landscape has changed considerably. Prototype and Scriptaculous are in the thick of these changes, and it's useful to see where they're coming from. So, let's briefly put our tech-archaeologist hats on and dig through the history of Ajax.

1.1.1 Prehistory

If the history of Ajax began with Garrett's article in 2005, then the discipline has a rich prehistory, in which the techniques behind Ajax were being explored without a name around which to rally the various practitioners. Ajax was first made possible by the invention of an ActiveX component called XMLHttpRequest. This component allowed web applications to contact the web server without refreshing the entire page, but rather passing the response to a script for processing. These hidden requests for data are generally referred to as *asynchronous*, a term that provides the first "A" in Ajax. Browsers had long been able to manipulate the user interface programmatically using the Document Object Model (DOM) and CSS, but without the ability to fetch anything new from the server; full-page refreshes were still frequent. Adding XMLHttpRequest into the mix made it possible for an entire application workflow to be encapsulated within a single web page, which simply reorganized itself in response to asynchronous requests for data made while the user was working.

Technologically, this was a cool new toy to play with. In usability terms, it offered a major breakthrough, because it allows the user to continue working while the browser waits for the server to respond to a request. Without Ajax, web-based apps are characterized by frequent periods of inactivity while a new page is requested, and this stop-start pattern is unsuitable for any serious application. Nonetheless, web-based apps are beloved of tech support departments because they don't need to be installed on the user's machine, and can be upgraded instantly. The tension between these two factors is resolved by Ajax, making Ajax-powered web apps a compelling alternative to desktop apps and thick clients in a wide variety of applications.

XMLHttpRequest was made available with Internet Explorer 5, in 2000. However, the adoption of Ajax didn't happen then. Everyone who saw Microsoft Exchange Web Mail thought it was pretty neat, but few rushed in to copy it. Maybe the fact that it relied on ActiveX, and was therefore limited to Microsoft operating systems was seen as too great a drawback. Maybe broadband penetration wasn't sufficiently advanced to consider providing apps that required a constant connection to the server. Maybe it just looked too complicated or different. Whatever the case, the capability wasn't exploited by many, and it would take several years before widespread interest in the techniques developed and the barrier imposed by the stop-start workflow was finally lifted.

1.1.2 *The pioneer phase*

In these days of Ajax prehistory, a few hardy individuals—Eric Costello, Erik Hatcher, and Jim Ley, to name but three—explored the possibilities of communicating asynchronously with the server, and they even published descriptions of the techniques that they developed, sometimes using XMLHttpRequest and sometimes falling back on other browser features such as IFrames to enable asynchronous traffic. As well as these publicly visible efforts, several corporate or private developers (including ourselves) were also discovering the techniques and putting them to use internally.

Another group of pioneers deserves a mention in this section. These are the people who were exploring the JavaScript language and the browser environment in which JavaScript commonly sits. Doug Crockford did pioneering work on object-oriented JavaScript techniques back when it was generally regarded as a toy for script-kiddies. Piers-Paul Koch explored the intricacies of cross-browser behavior, and Dan Steinberg and Mike Foster developed entire frameworks for cross-browser DOM manipulation, some of which even predated XMLHttpRequest's first appearance. JavaScript is the glue that holds Ajax applications together, and the work of these four has done a great deal to inform current thinking on Ajax web development.

When Ajax became a household name, there was already a rich seam of work by Crockford, Koch, and others waiting to be discovered. However, communication between these efforts was limited, given the low profile of the subject prior to 2005, and the early Ajax landscape consisted largely of roll-your-own solutions and makeshift frameworks. With more eyes on the subject of developing large, robust JavaScript applications, though, the amount of effort in this area intensified.

1.1.3 *The settlers arrive*

The year 2005 saw an explosion in the number of Ajax and JavaScript frameworks, helper libraries, and other projects aimed at assisting in the development of Ajax apps. *Ajax in Action* (by Dave Crane and Eric Pascarello with Darren James) included a list of over forty frameworks, and several were certainly left out. The pioneers were being followed by a wave of settlers, staking out territory and busily setting up small settlements. Inevitably, some of these withered, and others grew into small towns. Over the next year or two, we can expect to see a reduction in completely hand-coded Ajax applications, as best practices and the results learned from other people's mistakes crystallize into frameworks and utilities.

Prototype and Scriptaculous are two of the more successful of these JavaScript frameworks, and they have grown quite a community in a short time. (In fact, according to the Ajaxian.com 2006 frameworks and libraries survey, Prototype and Scriptaculous dominated the field at 43 and 33 percent adoption respectively.) A large part of their design is focused on making Ajax development faster, easier, and more enjoyable. The impact of these, and other, frameworks on the nature of Ajax development is likely to be considerable.

1.1.4 Civilization

That brings our history of Ajax development up to the present day. The phase that we'd consider analogous to "civilization" hasn't happened yet. (We won't even stop to consider the subsequent descent into barbarism that tends to plague real-world empires!) There are still many ways to get the job done using Ajax, and many of these ways are only partly compatible. In this book, you'll learn the details of one particular way, but we'll also look at how Prototype and Scriptaculous can interact with other popular frameworks.

And so, without any further ado, let's start to unpack Prototype and Scriptaculous, and see what they're capable of.

1.2 What is Prototype?

We'll look at Prototype first, because it is the more fundamental of the two libraries. Prototype provides a set of language extensions for JavaScript, for the browser environment, and for the XMLHttpRequest object. Scriptaculous (and other libraries, such as Rico) build on Prototype's foundations to create widgets and other end-user "stuff."

It might seem odd to state that a JavaScript library can extend the language in which it was written, but that's exactly what Prototype does. JavaScript provides a mechanism known as prototype-based inheritance (from which this library derived its name). In fact, several scripting languages provide features for extending the base objects of the language. Ruby does it, and many of the extensions provided by Prototype are borrowed from Ruby. Once could describe Prototype's goal as making JavaScript feel more like Ruby.

The good news for most of us is that it isn't necessary to understand everything that's going on under the hood in order to get the benefits of Prototype. We will look under Prototype's hood in part 3 of the book, but if you simply want to get the job done without worrying about extending the extensions yourself, parts 1 and 2 will explain everything in detail.

Right now, though, we'll run through the features that Prototype does provide, in order to give a more concrete sense of its scope and the issues it is designed to address. We'll group these into features that address the core language, and those that are designed specifically for web browsers.

1.2.1 JavaScript language features

JavaScript is a general-purpose programming language. As an Ajax developer, you'll generally be using Prototype inside a web browser, but certain parts of it, such as objects, features, arrays, strings, and numbers, are designed to enhance the JavaScript language itself.

The JavaScript Object class

At the core of most JavaScript programming is the base class Object. Creating an Object in JavaScript can be accomplished in as few as two characters:

```
var myObject = {};
```

myObject is endowed with a number of useful features and methods, such as a toString() method, the prototype-based inheritance mechanism, and the ability to absorb new properties and methods on the fly. We'll look in more detail at the JavaScript Object in chapter 8.

Using the prototype property of Object, it is possible to create proper object-oriented hierarchies of object types similar to those that a Java or C# programmer would be used to. That is, it's possible, but it is rather cumbersome. Prototype adds useful features to the Object that make it a lot easier and more natural to develop object type hierarchies. We'll see these capabilities in action as we examine other parts of Prototype, and Scriptaculous, which make heavy use of these functions.

JavaScript functions

JavaScript Function objects represent pieces of code that one can call, passing arguments into them, and that will return a result. In this, they're very similar to the methods that OO-programmers attach to objects.

A JavaScript function, unlike a Java or C# method, is a first-class citizen in the language. It can be referenced directly, passed as an argument to other functions, and even attached to arbitrary objects. This freedom gives the JavaScript programmer the opportunity to indulge in all sorts of strange and clever hacks. For the more practical among us, understanding JavaScript Function objects is important because the browser event model relies upon them. Prototype comes to our rescue here again, making it easier to bind Function objects to JavaScript objects in the way that the event model commonly calls for. We'll examine functions in detail in chapter 9.

JavaScript arrays

In JavaScript, arrays are expandable, numerically indexed lists of variables. The base language supports accessing array members using square braces notation, like this:

```
var element = myArray[3];
```

Iterating through the members of an array is generally done using a `for()` loop, like this:

```
for (var i=0;i<myArray.length;i++){
  alert(myArray[i]);
}
```

The Ruby programming language has a much richer way of interacting with arrays, based on an Enumeration type. Prototype has ported this concept over to JavaScript, and enhanced the native arrays with a similar functionality. If you're used to working with Ruby's Enumerable types, Prototype offers a home away from home. And even if you don't know Ruby, Prototype's array extensions are easy to pick up, and will soon become a powerful addition to your repertoire. Chapter 10 provides the details.

JavaScript strings and numbers

The String and Number classes in JavaScript allow methods to be attached to the language primitives directly. Functions attached to strings can be called directly from the primitive:

```
"abcdefghijklm".substring(4,10)
```

This line will evaluate to the string "efghij", for example. With numbers, it is necessary to reference the number as a variable first:

```
var x=123456789; x.toExponential()
```

This evaluates to the string "1.23456789e+8".

The standard methods on JavaScript primitives mostly relate to formatting and some helpers for generating HTML content. Prototype extends both String and Number with some useful utilities that make it easier to work with HTML colors, that support internationalized text, and provide other useful features.

That wraps up the features of Prototype that affect the core JavaScript language. Let's look now at what Prototype can do specifically within the web browser.

1.2.2 Web browser features

More lines of JavaScript code have been written for use inside web browsers than for any other environment. When coding in such an environment, various parts of the web browser are exposed to the JavaScript interpreter, and Prototype offers support for the web coder in various ways. We'll map out the territory here; these topics will be covered in detail in chapter 11.

The Document Object Model

The Document Object Model (DOM for short) is the mechanism by which the visual elements of a web page are exposed to the JavaScript interpreter. When we hide or show on-screen elements in response to a mouseclick or keypress, build a DHTML navigation menu, or create a browser-based animation, we're using the DOM. Programming the DOM used to be a major exercise in cross-browser workarounds and tricks, but the major browser vendors have, in recent years, converged around the W3C standards, and cross-browser DOM programming is no longer the problem that it was. However, the W3C model is rather verbose and unwieldy, and writing code against it can become an exercise in stamina.

Prototype provides a few helper methods that ease some of the strain of DOM programming, and we'll look at these in chapter 11. For now, let's continue our quick tour of Prototype's features.

HTML forms

HTML forms are a mainstay of web application development, and, in the pre-Ajax era, presented the only serious way to elicit information from a user. With Ajax, other input mechanisms, such as drag and drop, can be used as part of a conversation between the browser and the server, but forms still have a very important role to play. Prototype provides a set of utilities for working with HTML forms, which we'll cover in chapter 11.

JavaScript events

Event handling is central to the Ajax user interface. Although the major browsers have converged in their DOM-manipulation APIs, the event models of the Internet Explorer and Mozilla browsers still differ considerably, in both the calling semantics and the implementation details. Prototype provides some excellent cross-browser support when coding events, and it extends the Function object to make it easy to work with event handling, as we noted earlier.

Ajax utilities

The final feather in Prototype's cap is its support for Ajax. All major browsers support a version of the XMLHttpRequest object that makes Ajax possible, either as an ActiveX component or as a native JavaScript object. XMLHttpRequest, however, exposes the HTTP protocol at a very low level, which gives the developer a lot of power, but also requires her to write a lot of code in order to do simple things.

Prototype uses its own object inheritance system to provide a hierarchy of Ajax helper objects, with generic base classes being subclassed by more focused helpers that allow the most common types of Ajax requests to be coded in a single line. By making Ajax this easy, Prototype provides even more value to web developers.

1.3   What is Scriptaculous?

Prototype provides an extremely solid foundation for developing complex, well-structured code, but on its own does little beyond that. The onus of developing the functionality that the end user will see still rests firmly with the developer.

Scriptaculous is a library that makes use of Prototype to deliver a rich set of high-level functionality that the developer can put to work directly in creating polished interactive user interfaces. On its own, Prototype smoothes out many of the wrinkles of Ajax development. When used with Scriptaculous, it transforms the way in which we approach the web user interface, by making features such as animation and dragging and dropping as simple as a few lines of code.

Like Prototype, Scriptaculous covers several distinct areas. Let's look at each briefly in turn.

1.3.1   Visual effects

It is common when writing any computer application to wish to draw the user's attention to some part of the interface, in order to provide visual feedback. A button may wish to announce that it is clickable when the mouse moves over it. Lists of items may wish to notify the user when new items arrive or old ones vanish, particularly if it is the result of a background process. It's easy to overdo this type of functionality and end up with a user interface that distracts users or gets in their way, but such effects, if well done, can make an application more pleasant to use. In the world of web applications, in which a user may go elsewhere with a few keystrokes, making an application easy to use is imperative.

Scriptaculous makes it easy to create visual feedback of this type through its Effects library. This library is remarkable not only for the quality and range of effects that it enables, but for the high quality of the underlying design of the code, which makes it easy to compose multiple effects, run arbitrary code before, during, and after the effect, and synchronize effects with one another. Needless to say, this good design is made possible by the language features provided by Prototype.

In addition to being directly available to the coder, the Effects package is used within Scriptaculous to add visual feedback to the other main packages. Let's look at them now.

1.3.2 Drag and drop

Before Ajax, clicking on hyperlinks or submitting HTML forms could only initialize requests to the server. Now that requests can be fired programmatically, other types of user interaction can be used to trigger requests too, so a wider range of user interaction techniques are finding their way into web applications.

Dragging and dropping is a common user interface metaphor in desktop applications, and in many cases it provides the most convenient and intuitive way of interacting with a computer. The DOM has no direct support for drag-and-drop events, and implementing drag and drop in JavaScript means relying on nothing more than mouse click and movement events.

The good news is that Scriptaculous implements a feature-complete drag-and-drop system that can be applied to most types of DOM elements with relatively little code. The look and feel of the interaction can be customized using the Effects library, and custom event handlers provide callbacks for all stages of the drag-and-drop event.

1.3.3 Components

The features that we've discussed so far are frameworks that can be used to enhance a coder's application. Scriptaculous also provides a number of complete widgets, in the Components library. At the time of writing, the Components library contains two components: the AutoCompleter can attach a predictive drop-down element to any text field, which can endow an ordinary HTML Form element with features similar to Google Suggest; the in-place editor allows any DOM element to transform itself into a text input field and back again.

In addition to these high-level components, Scriptaculous provides a few helpers and utilities of its own. We'll conclude our initial review of the library with a look at these.

1.3.4 *Utilities and testing frameworks*

Scriptaculous provides some further extensions to the core JavaScript objects and DOM that are mainly concerned with easier manipulation of the user interface. These build on top of the extensions defined by Prototype.

In addition, Scriptaculous provides a complete unit-testing framework that runs inside the browser. This is designed mainly for internal use by the Scriptaculous development team, as the entire library is well covered by tests, but it can be used as a standalone testing library too.

This concludes our initial review of the Prototype and Scriptaculous libraries. Before we look in more detail at the features of each in subsequent chapters, we'll quickly demonstrate what Prototype and Scriptaculous can do to help an ordinary Ajax application.

1.4 *Applying Prototype and Scriptaculous*

Writing Ajax applications by hand requires an intimate knowledge of JavaScript's language features, many of which are rather exotic to those of us coming to Ajax from server-based web coding, familiar with languages such as Java, PHP, and C#. Worse, we will need to master the subtleties of cross-browser incompatibilities. Prototype and Scriptaculous have many language and cross-browser features built in, and they can help to ease the pain a great deal.

In this section, we'll look at a simple Ajax application that allows a user to assign a rating to an article (or a tune, picture, or anything else). We'll show how to code the app by hand, and then refactor it using Prototype and Scriptaculous to simplify a few knotty bits of JavaScript and add a few quick wins too. So, without further ado, let's have a look at the Ratings application.

1.4.1 *Introducing the Ratings example*

The Ratings example is a simple widget built using Ajax and DHTML techniques that can be easily inserted into a web page to show an interactive display of the rating that the user has assigned to an item. Figure 1.1 shows the widget's visual components.

Operating the widget is simple enough. The user can increase or decrease the rating by clicking on the blue arrow buttons with the mouse, and the number of stars is incremented or decremented, within the range of zero to five. When the user changes the rating, the widget also makes an asynchronous call to the server to update the central records. We won't worry for now about what the server does with that information, or what the response is.

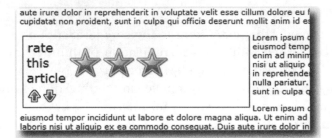

Figure 1.1   Ratings widget embedded in a web page. The small arrow icons are buttons allowing the user to increase or decrease the number of stars assigned to an item—in this case an article. (Icons are from the "Nuvola" icon set by David Vignoni, http://www.icon-king.com.)

That's our brief, then. As coders, we're more interested in getting under the hood and seeing how the implementation is done. Let's run through a few highlights of the code now. The complete code for the app is available for download at http://www.manning.com/crane3.

Using the component

We have striven to follow best practices in writing the app, and we tried to make it simple for designers to use without having to write a lot of JavaScript themselves, or to prepare a complex HTML template. As a result, the Ratings app creates all of its user interface programmatically, and the designer need only specify an empty HTML element within which it will sit. Needless to say, we've separated our various resources out nicely, providing a .js file containing all the code, a CSS stylesheet, and a set of images.

To incorporate the widget into a page, then, the designer needs to add a few lines of code in the header of the page:

```
<link rel=stylesheet                          Import CSS
  type="text/css" href="css/ratings.css">  ◁┘ stylesheet
<script type='text/javascript'               Import
  src='scripts/ratings.js'></script>  ◁┘     JavaScript library
<script type='text/javascript'>
  window.onload=function(){          Create Rating
    new Rating(                   ◁┘ object
      "myRating","rate this article"
    );
  }
</script>
```

The Rating object is defined in the JavaScript library, which we'll look at shortly. The constructor for the object takes two arguments: the ID of the HTML element in which it will render itself, and a caption to be displayed. We've specified a target element called myRating, so we'll define this in the HTML like so:

```
<div id='myRating'>
```

That's everything that our design team needs to do to use the widget. Let's see what goes on behind the scenes, when the widget is activated.

Initializing the user interface

The constructor function for the Rating object is relatively simple, taking a note of the main arguments and then delegating to a second function updateUI(). Listing 1.1 shows the code for these functions.

Listing 1.1   User interface code for Rating object

```
function Rating(divId,data){                              ◁──┐   Define
  this.body=document.getElementById(divId);          ❶  constructor
  this.title=data;
  this.rating=1;
  this.updateUI();
}

Rating.prototype={
  updateUI:function(delta){
    if (!delta){ delta=0; }
    if (delta>0){
      this.rating++;
    }else if (delta<0){
      this.rating--;
    }
    var inner="<table border='0'><tr><td width='42'>"
      +"<span class='title'>"+this.title+"</span></td>"
      +"<td>";
    for (var i=0;i<this.rating;i++){
      inner+="<img src='images/star.png'/>"
    }
    inner+="</td></tr><td>"
      +"<img src='images/up.png' id='plus_"+this.title+"'/>"
      +"<img src='images/down.png' id='minus_"+this.title+"'/>"
      +"</td><td>"
      +"<div id='message_"+this.name+"' class='message'></div>"
      +"</td></tr></table>";
    this.body.innerHTML=inner;      ◁──── ❷ Assign HTML to target
    var rating=this;                ◁──── ❸ Make reference for closure
    this.plusButton=document
      .getElementById("plus_"+this.title);        ❹ Reference
    this.minusButton=document                        button widgets
      .getElementById("minus_"+this.title);
```

```
this.body.onclick=function(event){
    var e=(event) ? event : window.event;
    var target=(e.target) ?
      e.target : e.srcElement;
    if (target.id==rating.plusButton.id
      && rating.rating<5){
      rating.updateUI(1);
    }else if (target.id==rating.minusButton.id
      && rating.rating>0){
      rating.updateUI(-1);
    }
  }
  this.tellServer();
},
```

5 Assign event handler

6 Inform server

There is quite a lot going on here, so let's pick through it piece by piece. The updateUI() method takes an optional argument delta, which we'll ignore when we initially call it in the constructor **1**. It then proceeds to build up a set of HTML markup as a string, defining the UI that we saw in figure 1.1 as an HTML table. This string is then assigned to the target element using the innerHTML property **2**.

We go on to assign event handlers to the buttons. The next line looks quite strange—we are defining a variable called rating that is a direct reference to this **3**. The reason for this is rather arcane. We are going to create a closure when we define the event handler, and the special variable this cannot be passed in to a closure. We create rating as a copy in order to pass it in.

In the next few lines we're back on fairly safe ground. We've added unique IDs to our buttons in the big innerHTML string that we just wrote, so now we can programmatically reference the button elements **4**.

Adding event handlers

We go on to define an event handler for the entire widget (**5** in listing 1.1). This is an anonymous function, defined inline. Because of the way the JavaScript event model works, when the function is called, the variable this will no longer refer to the Rating object, but to the HTML element that fired the event. We refer to the variable rating, which is bound to the function as part of the closure, in order to see the Rating object inside the event-handling code.

It's a common mistake to refer to this inside event handlers, and writing this code took a few goes to straighten all the ratings and thises out, but we've done it. When the buttons are pressed, we re-render the entire UI by calling updateUI() again, this time with the delta argument to indicate that the rating is going up or down.

Finally, we tell the server that the rating for this item has changed ❻. We'll be using core Ajax techniques to do this, and we'll look at these in a minute. First, let's review what we've done in order to get our two buttons up and running. We've visited a number of unusual language features in JavaScript, including the ability of Function objects to be called with arbitrary contexts (i.e., the variable that evaluates to this within the function), and the ability of Function objects to create closures implicitly. Both of these require quite a deep understanding of the language, which is fine if we like collecting unusual programming languages, but if we're a Java or PHP coder seconded into doing a bit of Ajax work, it's quite a lot to take on board.

We'll soon see how Prototype and Scriptaculous can help to keep the language out of our hair. First, let's have a look at the Ajax code.

Making an asynchronous HTTP call

We're going to use the XMLHttpRequest object to contact the server whenever the user clicks one of the buttons. As we noted earlier, XMLHttpRequest confers the ability to work with the HTTP protocol at quite a low level, and it is consequently not very straightforward to use for extremely simple tasks. There are several wrappers for the XMLHttpRequest available now, and we'll see the one provided by Prototype in a minute. To emphasize the difference, though, we're going to use the raw XMLHttpRequest in this example. Listing 1.2 shows the code required to do so.

Listing 1.2 Ajax call code for Rating object

```
tellServer:function(){
  if (window.XMLHttpRequest){
    this.request=new XMLHttpRequest();        ❶ Obtain XHR
  } else if (window.ActiveXObject){              object
    this.request=new
      ActiveXObject("Microsoft.XMLHTTP");
  }
  if (!this.request){
    this.showMessage("no Ajax support");
  }
  try{                        ❷ Make reference
    var rating=this;             for closure
    var params="name="
      +encodeURI(this.name)      ❸ Create encoded
      +"&rating="                   querystring
      +encodeURI(this.rating);
    this.request.onreadystatechange
      =function(){
```

```
            rating.onReadyState();        ←———  Create closure
        };                              ④    implicitly
    this.request.open(
     "POST","updateRating.php",true
    );
    this.request.setRequestHeader(
      'Content-Type',
      'application/x-www-form-urlencoded'
    );
    this.request.setRequestHeader(
      "Content-Length",
      params.length
    );                                 ⑤ Send
    this.request.send(params);    ←———    request
  }catch (err){
    this.onAjaxError(err.msg);
  }
},
onReadyState:function(){
  var req=this.request;          ⑥ Check request
  var ready=req.readyState;   ←—    readystate
  if (ready==4){
    var httpStatus=req.status;
    if (httpStatus==200 || httpStatus==0){  ⑦ Call success
      this.onAjaxLoad.call(this);   ←—         handler
    }else{
      this.onAjaxError.call(        ←———  Call error
        this,"HTTP code "+httpStatus  ⑧  handler
      );
    }
  }
},
onAjaxLoad:function(){
  this.showMessage(
    "server OK "+this.request.responseText
  );
},
onAjaxError:function(msg){
  this.showMessage(
    "server error"+( (msg) ? " - "+msg: "")
  );
},
showMessage:function(str){
  document.getElementById
    ("message_"+this.name)
    .innerHTML=str;
  }
};
```

Again, the code required to do the job isn't that small. Let's pick through the main points. First, we need to get hold of an XMLHttpRequest object. In some browsers it's a native object, and in others it's an ActiveX component, and we try to account for all the possibilities ❶. By luck, we've got it the right way around here, testing for a native object first. Internet Explorer 7 has arrived upon the scene, and it supports a native XMLHttpRequest, as well as ActiveX for backward compatibility. If we'd tested for ActiveX first, we would have ended up using ActiveX unnecessarily under IE 7, and potentially blocking browsers where ActiveX controls have been locked down, but our Ajax code would otherwise have worked. We could have supported older versions of IE by checking for alternative ActiveX types too, but that's a lot of background knowledge required to implement a simple rating widget, so users of IE 5.5 are maybe out of luck with our app.

The second point to note is that strange closure trick again. We define the variable `rating` ❷ and refer to it inside the event handler ❹. In this case, the event handler is simply a one-line call to another function, which might leave us wondering why the `onReadyState()` function wasn't assigned directly if we didn't understand the intricacies of implicit closures in JavaScript.

We're calling a server-side process that talks in terms of standard querystring key-value pairs. Almost every server-side language provides automatic parsing of querystrings, but with XMLHttpRequest, we need to build up the string manually ❸, remembering to call `encodeURI()` for each value. We then need to set a few crucial HTTP headers before we're ready to send out our request ❺. It's a little-known fact that the convenience methods we're used to on the server, such as Java Servlet's `request.getParameter()` and PHP's `$_GET` array, will only be populated if the request has a content type of `application/x-www-form-urlencoded`. HTML forms fill this in for us automatically, but with XMLHttpRequest, we need to do it ourselves.

Once the request goes out, our callback handler is busy. Rather than being called once when the request completes, it is notified at various stages in the lifecycle of the request, which is great for implementing progress bars, but something of an overhead for us here. A readystate value of 4 corresponds to a completed request, so we simply check for that ❻ and call either the success handler ❼ or the error handler ❽ depending on the HTTP code of our response.

Let's review what we've been through here. Once more, everything is done, and it works, but we've gone to rather a lot of effort, and we've needed rather an intimate knowledge of the HTTP protocol, particularly concerning how querystrings are encoded in requests and are only decoded on the server if the right set of HTTP headers is applied. Furthermore, we've had to get our heads around closures once again.

After writing this application, I refactored the code to use Prototype and Scriptaculous features in a few places, to make it easier to work with. Let's look at how it simplified things.

1.4.2 Adding Prototype and Scriptaculous

We can see the first advantage of using Prototype and Scriptaculous before we open the files. The main code file, ratings.js (see listing 1.3), is roughly 20 percent smaller as a result of our work, which certainly suggests that these libraries can help our productivity. However, that in itself doesn't tell us very much. Let's step through the refactoring and look at the details.

DOM helper methods

Prototype comes equipped with a range of helper methods that make it easier to work with the DOM. The simplest of all is a function named simply $() (and, yes, that is a valid name for a variable in JavaScript). In our original code, we've been looking up DOM elements by their IDs, like this:

```
this.body=document.getElementById(divId);
```

Prototype allows us to rewrite this as simply as this:

```
this.body=$(divId);
```

For now, it's enough to know that we've saved ourselves from some tedious typing. In fact, $() is a lot more powerful than document.getElementById(), as we'll see in chapter 11, but for now, let's leave it at that, and look at the next item.

Event handlers

In the original version of the code, we had to get our heads around closures and function contexts when writing the event handler for the buttons (see ❺ in listing 1.1). This had two practical consequences. First, we had to define the event-handler code inline as an anonymous function, in order to get the closure to work. Sometimes it's good to use anonymous inline functions, but here we did it because we had no choice. Second, we had to refer to the Rating object as rating rather than this inside the event-handler code, which felt a bit odd.

While writing the event handler, we also had to write some cross-browser code to handle the different ways of obtaining the event object and its target element. Prototype can relieve us of all these chores with a single call. Function.bindAsEventListener() wraps an ordinary function up as an event handler, creating the closure for us, sorting out the function context issues, and presenting us with a robust, cross-browser event object whose target element we can readily access. Listing 1.3 shows the modified code, with changes shown in bold.

Listing 1.3   Modified event-handler code

```
updateUI:function(delta){
  if (!delta){ delta=0; }
  if (delta>0){
    this.rating++;
  }
  var inner="<table border='0'><tr><td width='42'>"
    +"<span class='title'>"+this.title+"</span></td>"
    +"<td>";
  for (var i=0;i<this.rating;i++){
    inner+="<img src='images/star.png' id='ratingstar_"+i+"'/>"
  }
  inner+="</td></tr><td>"
    +"<img src='images/up.png' id='plus_"+this.title+"'/>"
    +"<img src='images/down.png' id='minus_"+this.title+"'/>"
    +"</td><td>"
    +"<div id='message_"+this.name+"' class='message'></div>"
    +"</td></tr></table>";
  this.body.innerHTML=inner;
  var rating=this;
  this.plusButton=$("plus_"+this.title);
  this.minusButton=$("minus_"+this.title);
  Event.observe(           Bind event to
    this.body,          ❶ DOM node
    "click",
    this.clickHandler            Create event
      .bindAsEventListener(this)  ❷ handler
  );
  this.tellServer();
},                          Define
clickHandler:function(event){ ❸ handler code
  var target=Event.element(event);
  if (target==this.plusButton          Get event
    && this.rating<5){          ❹ target
    this.updateUI(1);
  }else if (target==this.minusButton
    && this.rating>0){
    this.updateUI(-1);
  }
},
```

We're using two event-handler features to get around differences in the cross-browser event models here. Event.observe() ❶ allows us to attach multiple handler functions to an HTML element safely. Function.bindAsEventListener() ❷ turns an ordinary function into an event handler, supplying it with a cross-browser event object, and passing in the first argument as the event context. Here, we've passed our Rating object in, which means that we can define our event-handling code as an ordinary member function of the Rating prototype ❸.

The clickHandler() function that we define contains the same logic as its anonymous predecessor but is certainly easier to read. We can access the HTML element that fired the event in a single line of code ❹, and we refer to the member variables of the object in a natural way using this.

There is an even bigger win to be made, though, when sending the Ajax request to update the server. Let's look at that next.

Ajax requests made easy

Coding the Ajax request required not just a detailed knowledge of JavaScript language internals, but of the HTTP protocol too. Knowledge is good, but we were in a hurry, and figuring out the details slowed us down rather a lot.

Prototype provides a utility object, the Ajax.Request, which encapsulates a lot of this complexity so that we don't have to in a simple case like this (but we still can when we're in HTTP power-coding mode!). Listing 1.4 shows the revised Ajax code.

Listing 1.4   Modified Ajax request code

```
tellServer:function(){
  var params=$H(
    {name:this.name,              ❶ Create
     rating:this.rating}             querystring
  ).toQueryString();
  new Ajax.Request(               ❷ Create Ajax.Request
    "updateRatings.php",            object
    {
      method:"post",
      parameters: params,
      onSuccess:
        this.onAjaxLoad
          .bind(this),            ❸ Declare callback
      onFailure:                    handlers
        this.onAjaxError
          .bind(this)
    }
  );
},
onAjaxLoad:function(transport){
  this.showMessage
    ("server OK "+transport.responseText);
},
onAjaxError:function(transport){
  this.showMessage
    ("server error ["+transport.httpStatus+"]");
},
```

When writing our own Ajax call, we had to manually encode and create a querystring (see ❸ in listing 1.2). Here, we're using Prototype's $H() function (yes, these guys like short names!) to create a Hash object out of an ordinary JavaScript object ❶. We'll look at Hashes in more detail in chapter 10; for now, suffice it to say that Hash has a predefined toQueryString() method that will create our parameters for us. The syntax may look a little odd at first, especially if you don't realize that $H() is just a JavaScript function, but once you get it, it saves a lot of trouble in remembering to call encodeURI() every time you create a querystring.

Now on to the biggest improvement in the coding—making the request. The Ajax.Request object takes two arguments in its constructor ❷. The first is the URL on the server, and the second is a JavaScript object stuffed full of optional arguments. (We'll see this idiom a lot throughout this book, in the predefined objects and in our own code.) We specify the HTTP method as POST, and pass in our querystring. Details such as MIME type will be taken care of for us.

We also add in two callback handlers. Ajax.Request allows us to define suitably high-level callbacks, for success and failure of the request ❸. Note that we're using Function.bind() here. Like bindAsEventListener(), this simply ensures that when the callback is invoked, it will have the context object that we want it to have.

We no longer need to write a callback that will be invoked multiple times during the request, because in this simple case, we don't need to. Prototype handles all that and the HTTP response codes for us. Compared to listing 1.2, tellServer() has shrunk by at least 50 percent, and we've gotten rid of onReadyState() altogether.

We could rest on our laurels right now, but let's make one final change to the application before we wrap up this chapter, and show off one of Scriptaculous's useful features.

Adding polish to the user interface

Our refactored app is matching the original version feature for feature with less effort. While coding up the original app, we thought of several "nice to have" features that there just wasn't time to implement. Well, we've saved ourselves a little bit of time now, so let's have a look at one of them.

When the user modifies the rating, there is no visual feedback beyond the star disappearing. A little animation might make the app more satisfying to use, and might ultimately increase uptake of the project. This sort of benefit is hard to gauge, though, so we don't want to spend too much effort on it, lest it distract us from more serious matters.

Using Scriptaculous's Effects library, we can animate the adding and removing of stars in only a few lines of code, as shown in listing 1.5. (We've reproduced the entire function here—the new code is highlighted in bold).

Listing 1.5 Adding effects to the Ratings app

```
updateUI:function(delta){
  if (!delta){ delta=0; }
  if (delta>0){                      ❶ Increment
    this.rating++;                       rating
  }
  var inner="<table border='0'><tr><td width='42'>"
    +"<span class='title'>"+this.title+"</span></td>"
    +"<td>";
  for (var i=0;i<this.rating;i++){
    inner+="<img src='images/star.png'"
      +"id='ratingstar_"+i+"'/>"        ❷ Provide
  }                                          image IDs
  inner+="</td></tr><td>"
    +"<img src='images/up.png' id='plus_"+this.title+"'/>"
    +"<img src='images/down.png' id='minus_"+this.title+"'/>"
    +"</td><td>"
    +"<div id='message_"+this.name+"' class='message'></div>"
    +"</td></tr></table>";
  this.body.innerHTML=inner;
  var rating=this;
  this.plusButton=$("plus_"+this.title);
  this.minusButton=$("minus_"+this.title);
  Event.observe(this.body, "click",
   this.clickHandler.bindAsEventListener(this));
  this.tellServer();
  if (delta<0){
    new Effect.DropOut("ratingstar_0");    ❸ Animate and
    this.rating--;                             decrement
  }else if (delta>0){
    new Effect.Pulsate                         Animate
      ("ratingstar_"+(this.rating-1));    ⊲⎯┘ addition
  }
},
```

In the previous versions of the application, we always corrected the rating score before rendering. In this case, when we decrement, we want to initially draw in one extra star, and then get rid of it, so we correct the rating beforehand only if the score has gone up ❶. After everything has rendered, we then set up the effects and decrement the score if necessary ❸.

The effects themselves are ridiculously easy to use, requiring only the ID of the element to operate upon. We therefore need to provide ID attributes for our images ❷, but that's a minor hardship. The constructors can, like Ajax.Request, also accept an object full of options, but we'll leave that for a more detailed look in chapter 5.

By adding these few lines of code, a newly improved rating will flash on and off briefly to announce its presence, and a reduced rating will see the leftmost star drop off the bottom of the page. It's hard to present this as a still picture in a book, unfortunately, but you can download the code and see it for yourself.

That concludes our first taste of what these libraries can do for us. In subsequent chapters, we'll dig more methodically into this rich seam.

1.5 *Summary*

In this chapter, we looked at the development of Ajax technologies. As long ago as the late 1990s, preliminary explorations of asynchronous communication between the browser and server were being undertaken, mostly in isolation. In early 2005, the coining of the name Ajax provided a much-needed focal point for these explorations. Since then, there has been a major drive toward increasing the ease of development of Ajax, in which frameworks and libraries are playing an important part. It is no longer sufficient to be able to make an Ajax app work; we now need it to work smoothly and robustly, and it must be easy to develop and maintain.

We introduced Prototype and Scriptaculous, two best-of-breed JavaScript and Ajax libraries, and we looked at their main purposes and constituent pieces. Prototype is a relatively low-level library, providing additional language features and facilities. Scriptaculous makes use of Prototype to provide a number of higher-level widgets and components, mostly aimed at creating user interfaces.

Both libraries use a number of advanced JavaScript techniques internally, and even introduce new advanced features of their own. However, using these libraries in the most straightforward way does not require a detailed understanding of these capabilities. We introduced a simple Ajax example app and refactored it using Prototype and Scriptaculous. Internally, the libraries are complex, and reading their source code, one might suppose that a degree in rocket science is necessary to understand them. However, our refactoring showed this not to be the case, and we firmly believe that the average coder can make quick wins by using these libraries. We'll continue to explore the libraries in more depth throughout this book, and demonstrate how you can benefit from their raw power.

Introducing QuickGallery

2

In this chapter

- Introducing the QuickGallery web app
- Evaluating the classic web app model

Prototype and Scriptaculous are designed to make Ajax quicker and easier to work with. Ajax's core function is to dispatch asynchronous requests to the server, and in the previous chapter we saw how Prototype's Ajax.Request class could simplify making an asynchronous request (see listing 1.4). In the next three chapters, we'll look at Prototype's support for Ajax in more detail, and show how it can support the requirements of more complex applications. We'll examine Ajax.Request in detail in chapter 3; in this chapter, we'll set the scene for our examination of Ajax and several of the other features that we'll use throughout the book.

As we progress through the various parts of Prototype and Scriptaculous, we'll want to see how they can be used in a moderately complex, real-world situation. In this chapter, we'll also introduce the example application that we will develop throughout the rest of this part of the book, and then pick up again in chapter 12. It's a web-based image gallery application called QuickGallery. (Every application needs a name, and most web applications have slightly silly names!) The version that we'll develop in this chapter is simple and unremarkable. It doesn't make use of Ajax, and is designed simply as a starting point for exploring the benefits of Ajax when we do apply them to the application in chapters 3 and 4. The final version of QuickGallery is introduced in chapter 12, where we will add a raft of new features to demonstrate the full capabilities of Prototype and Scriptaculous in a real-world setting.

So don't expect any fireworks in this chapter! If you're in a hurry, you might like to skip to chapter 3, and refer back here when you need to get up to speed on the implementation details of QuickGallery.

2.1 Design and implementation

We have two things to cover. First, we need to describe how QuickGallery works, from usability and technical perspectives. Second, we need to look at the shortcomings of the classic web application model. Specifically, we need to see how it affects QuickGallery, so that we can identify where there is potential for improvement as we introduce Ajax in chapters 3 and 4.

In this section, we'll provide a tour of QuickGallery. We'll start by looking at the requirements for the application, and what we want it to do.

2.1.1 Application requirements

The application that we're going to work with in this book is an image gallery viewer, capable of displaying images within a subtree of the server's filesystem, both in thumbnail view and close up. Initially, our requirements are fairly straightforward.

We want to be able to view the images in a folder as a set of thumbnails that can be clicked on to see the full image. We also want to be able to drill down into subfolders and navigate back up the folder tree. We've therefore divided the screen into three areas, as shown in figure 2.1.

A "breadcrumb trail" along the top allows us to navigate back up the tree, and a list down the left side details subfolders. The remaining space is given over to displaying either thumbnails or the close up version of the selected image.

Thumbnail images are small copies of images that can be downloaded and rendered quickly, allowing the user to preview the images. Images produced by modern digital cameras are too large to download in bulk, and scaling down a large number of them might give your user's web browser indigestion. Instead, the gallery will create the thumbnail images on demand.

The application has been implemented on the back end using PHP. We chose PHP because it's a simple, ubiquitous language. The server-side functionality is relatively simple, so porting the app to other server languages should be straightforward. The server-side code for an Ajax app mostly relies on similar techniques to those found in non-Ajax apps. There are a few differences, though, and we've run through how to implement these techniques in the most popular sever-side languages (PHP, Java, .NET, and Ruby on Rails) in appendix E.

Figure 2.1   The QuickGallery application, showing the contents of a folder with navigation aids to subfolders (along the left side) and to parents (along the top), as a "breadcrumb trail"

Out in the real world, there are two kinds of Ajax projects: the new development and the conversion of legacy web apps to Ajax. Although QuickGallery was written specifically for this book, we've invented a short history for it as a classic web app, to simulate the experience of converting a classic web app to use Ajax.

Our QuickGallery application begins life as a classic web application, in which any user interaction resulted in a full-page refresh. The back-end implementation consists of a single PHP file for generating the view and a PHP include file containing the logic behind the application. Let's start off by looking at the business logic.

2.1.2 *Navigating the filesystem*

The first thing we need to establish is which part of the filesystem our application will be able to access. In the interests of simplicity, we'll assume that all our images are stored under a single folder, and we will specify this folder path in our configuration. We will also specify a partial URL path to be used when writing the image URLs, which will reflect the way our web server has been set up.

Our demonstration server is an unmodified Apache 2.0 running on Ubuntu Linux, with the server root pointing at /var/www/. We've created a folder /var/www/dave/album in which to store Dave's QuickGallery files, and added a symbolic link to Dave's home directory called "sites," pointing to /var/www/dave. So our configuration for the gallery looks like this:

```
$basedir='/home/dave/sites/album/images';
$img_pre_path='/dave/album/images';
```

We'll use this information in several ways. In order to navigate the filesystem successfully, the first thing we need to know is where we are within this tree. We'll pass a request variable to the application, specifying the path relative to the base directory. If no path is specified, we'll start at the top level. The code for this is straightforward:

```
if (isset($_GET['path'])){
  $path=$_GET['path'];
  $fulldir=implode('/',array($basedir,$path));
}else{
  $path="";
  $fulldir=$basedir;
}
```

The implode() function in PHP simply joins together the elements of an array with the specified delimiter. The $path variable provides the location of the user within the image directory, and $fulldir maps that to the actual filesystem.

Now that we know where we are, we can start to generate some navigation information.

Examining the folder contents

Our first task is to examine the current directory for images and subfolders. This task is handled by the list_dir() function, which is given here:

```
function list_dir($dir,$path){
  $dirs=array();
  $imgs=array();
  $others=array();
  $d=dir($dir);
  while (false != ($entry = $d->read())){        ❶ Iterate through
    if (is_dir(implode('/',array($dir,$entry)))){     folder
      if (($entry!='.') && ($entry!='..')){
        $dirs[]=$entry;                          ❷ Record
      }                                             subfolder
    }else if (is_image_file($entry,$path)){
      $bits=explode('.',$entry);
      $imgs[]=$bits[0];          Record
    }else{                    ❸ image file
      $others[]=$entry;
    }
  }
  $results=array(
    'dirs' => $dirs,
    'imgs' => $imgs,
    'others' => $others
  ); #4
  return $results;
}              ❹ Assemble results
```

The function takes two arguments: the absolute path to the directory and the notional path from the user's perspective. We only need the absolute path directly in this function, but we will use the notional path when we come to generate the thumbnail images later.

The list_dir() method basically iterates through the current folder using PHP's filesystem functions ❶ and records each item in one of three categories: subfolder ❷, image ❸, and everything else. The results are then assembled as an array and returned ❹. We can test for subfolders using PHP's built-in is_dir() method. Note that we explicitly ignore the special folders . and .., which represent the current location and its immediate parent respectively. The breadcrumb trail will handle navigation up the tree, and we're already at the current location.

We determine whether a file is an image simply by examining its name. To keep things simple, we're going to work with only JPEG images for now. The is_image_file() function does the work here:

```
function is_image_file($entry,$path){
  $is_image=false;
  $bits=explode('.',$entry);
  $last=count($bits)-1;
  if ($bits[$last]=='jpg'){
    $is_image=($bits[$last-1]!='thumb');
    if ($is_image){
      ensure_thumbnail($bits[0],$path);
    }
  }
  return $is_image;
}
```

PHP's explode() function is the opposite of implode(), breaking a string into an array along the specified delimiter. We use it here to extract the file extension; if it ends with ".jpg", we take it to be an image. There is an exception—if the file ends with ".thumb.jpg", we don't count it as an image, because we assume that it's a thumbnail image that we've already generated. If we're satisfied that we have got a bona fide image, we return true, but before doing so, we check to make sure that we have a thumbnail image ready.

We'll look at how we create the thumbnails shortly, but first, let's wrap up the navigation functionality by generating the breadcrumb trail.

Creating the breadcrumb trail

The breadcrumb trail will allow users of our app to quickly climb back up the directory tree, and it will provide contextual information on where they are now. Creating the breadcrumb trail is simply a matter of splitting the user's path into its constituent folders:

```
function get_breadcrumbs($path){
  $bits=split('/',$path);
  $crumbs=array();
  $tmp_path='/';                    ❶ Add top-level
  $crumbs[]=array(         ⤶            crumb
    'name' => 'home',
    'path' => $tmp_path
  );
  foreach ($bits as $i => $value){
    if (strlen($value) > 0){
      $tmp_path.=$value.'/';        ❷ Add crumb
      $crumbs[]=array(      ⤶          for folder
        'name' => $value,
```

```
        'path' => $tmp_path
      );
    }
  }
  return $crumbs;
}
```

First, we add a breadcrumb to represent the top-level folder ❶. We then iterate through the elements on the path, creating a breadcrumb item for each ❷. For each breadcrumb that we create, we want to record two things: the name to be displayed, and the path that it represents, which is simply an accumulation of the path elements that preceded it. Finally, we return the data as an array of arrays.

Now that we've generated all the navigation data, let's have a quick look at the thumbnail generation.

2.1.3 Generating the thumbnail image

When we identified a file as an image, we made a call to ensure that a thumbnail image existed. Generating a thumbnail image entails opening a potentially large image and performing a scaling algorithm on it. Compared to the usual HTML generation, this is a relatively expensive operation, so we want the method that checks for thumbnails to undertake it only if necessary. Let's see how we accomplish that.

```
function ensure_thumbnail($base_name,$path){
  global $basedir,$thumb_max;
  $thumb_name=join('/',
    array($basedir,$path,
    $base_name.'.thumb.jpg')
  );
  if (!file_exists($thumb_name)){        ❶ Check for
                                            thumbnail
    $source_name=join('/',
      array($basedir,$path,$base_name.'.jpg')
    );
    $source_img=imagecreatefromjpeg        ❷ Read
      ($source_name);                         image file
    $source_x=imageSX($source_img);
    $source_y=imageSY($source_img);
    $thumb_x=($source_x > $source_y) ?
      $thumb_max :
      $thumb_max*($source_x/$source_y);
    $thumb_y=($source_x < $source_y) ?
      $thumb_max :
      $thumb_max*($source_y/$source_x);
    $thumb_img=ImageCreateTrueColor($thumb_x,$thumb_y);
    imagecopyresampled(
      $thumb_img,$source_img,           Create
                                        thumbnail  ❸
```

```
      0,0,0,0,
      $thumb_x,$thumb_y,
      $source_x,$source_y        ❹  Copy thumbnail
    );                                 data
    imagejpeg($thumb_img,$thumb_name);        Save
    imagedestroy($source_img);             ❺  thumbnail
    imagedestroy($thumb_img);
  }
}
```

The first thing we do in this function is check whether a thumbnail image already exists ❶. If it does, we simply bail out and don't do any hard work. If we can't find a thumbnail, we create one.

There is a final bit of configuration associated with the app now—we need to specify how large we want the thumbnails to be. Not all images have the same aspect ratio, so we do this by specifying a single dimension, which the thumbnail's largest dimension will be scaled to. This ensures that all thumbnails will line up nicely within the square tiles defined by the CSS when we display them (see figure 2.1).

Thumbnails are generated using functions provided by GD, the de facto standard for PHP image manipulation. GD was an optional module in PHP prior to version 5.2, at which point it was absorbed into the core distribution. On our test Linux system, we had to install the php-gd module separately after installing Apache and PHP. Your mileage may vary depending on your distribution or ISP. In appendix D, we show how to get PHP with GD running for Windows, Mac, and Linux systems. If you're porting the app to a different server language, you'll need to research the image manipulation libraries for that language, but the principles will be similar.

Once GD is up and running, we can create the thumbnail in the following stages. First, we read in the source image ❷. Next, we create a new blank image ❸, scaled to match our maximum thumbnail dimension. We then scale the source image down to match the thumbnail size ❹. Finally, we save the thumbnail image ❺, using the simple naming scheme that we described earlier, of replacing ".jpg" with ".thumb.jpg".

We've now covered all the elements required to generate our gallery. The final step in the app's business logic is simply orchestrating these functions, so let's cover that now.

2.1.4 *Putting the pieces together*

We know where we are, and how to generate all the navigational data that we need in order to move around. We can create thumbnails for our image files on demand, and keep them ready for future use. Pulling things together is now very straightforward. The final bit of code in our app works out which of these functions to call, as shown here:

```
$crumbs=get_breadcrumbs($path);
$cc=count($crumbs);
if ($cc > 0){
  $closeup=is_close_up($crumbs[$cc-1]['name']);
}else{
  $closeup=false;
}
if ($closeup==false){
  $listings=list_dir($fulldir,$path);
  $subdirs=$listings['dirs'];
  $imgs=$listings['imgs'];
  $others=$listings['others'];
}
```

First, we get the breadcrumb data. If we have any breadcrumbs, we then check whether we're examining a folder or a single image in close-up. If we're looking at a folder, we go ahead and list the contents of the folder.

We determine whether we're looking at a single image simply by testing whether the name of the final breadcrumb ends with ".jpg". If it does, we assume that our path points directly to an image. This is the code for this function:

```
function is_close_up($name){
  $result=false;
  $bits=explode('.',$name);
  $last=$bits[count($bits)-1];
  if ($last=='jpg'){ $result=true; }
  return $result;
}
```

Once again, we're simply using PHP's explode() method to dissect the filename information. This system isn't foolproof, and would be easy to corrupt by creating a folder whose name ends with ".jpg", for example, but if we don't manually interfere with our images directory, it will work well enough.

That concludes the business logic for our application. By way of a summary, the full listing for the include file is given in listing 2.1. Note that the paths defined in the first two lines of code may vary on your system. Section 3 of appendix D describes how to configure QuickGallery.

Listing 2.1   Business logic for QuickGallery (images.inc.php)

```php
<?php
$basedir='/home/dave/sites/album/images';
$img_pre_path='/dave/album/images';
$thumb_max=120;

function list_dir($dir,$path){
  $dirs=array();
  $imgs=array();
  $others=array();
  $d=dir($dir);
  while (false != ($entry = $d->read())){
    if (is_dir(implode('/',array($dir,$entry)))){
      if (($entry!='.') && ($entry!='..')){
        $dirs[]=$entry;
      }
    }else if (is_image_file($entry,$path)){
      $bits=explode('.',$entry);
      $imgs[]=$bits[0];
    }else{
      $others[]=$entry;
    }
  }
  $results=array(
    'dirs' => $dirs,
    'imgs' => $imgs,
    'others' => $others
  );
  return $results;
}

function is_image_file($entry,$path){
  $is_image=false;
  $bits=explode('.',$entry);
  $last=count($bits)-1;
  if ($bits[$last]=='jpg'){
    //ignore the thumbnails we've already made!
    $is_image=($bits[$last-1]!='thumb');
    if ($is_image){
      ensure_thumbnail($bits[0],$path);
    }
  }
  return $is_image;
}

function ensure_thumbnail($base_name,$path){
  global $basedir,$thumb_max;
  $thumb_name=join('/',array($basedir,$path,$base_name.'.thumb.jpg'));
  if (!file_exists($thumb_name)){
    $source_name=join('/',array($basedir,$path,$base_name.'.jpg'));
```

```php
    $source_img=imagecreatefromjpeg($source_name);
    $source_x=imageSX($source_img);
    $source_y=imageSY($source_img);
    $thumb_x=($source_x > $source_y) ?
      $thumb_max :
      $thumb_max*($source_x/$source_y);
    $thumb_y=($source_x < $source_y) ?
      $thumb_max :
      $thumb_max*($source_y/$source_x);
    $thumb_img=ImageCreateTrueColor($thumb_x,$thumb_y);
    imagecopyresampled(
      $thumb_img,$source_img,
      0,0,0,0,
      $thumb_x,$thumb_y,
      $source_x,$source_y
    );
    imagejpeg($thumb_img,$thumb_name);
    imagedestroy($source_img);
    imagedestroy($thumb_img);
  }
}

function get_breadcrumbs($path){
  $bits=split('/',$path);
  $crumbs=array();
  $tmp_path='/';
  $crumbs[]=array(
    'name' => 'home',
    'path' => $tmp_path
  );
  foreach ($bits as $i => $value){
    if (strlen($value) > 0){
      $tmp_path.=$value.'/';
      $crumbs[]=array(
        'name' => $value,
        'path' => $tmp_path
      );
    }
  }
  return $crumbs;
}

function is_close_up($name){
  $result=false;
  $bits=explode('.',$name);
  $last=$bits[count($bits)-1];
  if ($last=='jpg'){ $result=true; }
  return $result;
}

if (isset($_GET['path'])){
```

```
    $path=$_GET['path'];
    $fulldir=implode('/',array($basedir,$path));
}else{
    $path="";
    $fulldir=$basedir;
}
$crumbs=get_breadcrumbs($path);
$cc=count($crumbs);
if ($cc > 0){
    $closeup=is_close_up($crumbs[$cc-1]['name']);
}else{
    $closeup=false;
}
if ($closeup==false){
    $listings=list_dir($fulldir,$path);
    $subdirs=$listings['dirs'];
    $imgs=$listings['imgs'];
    $others=$listings['others'];
}
?>
```

Once this include file has been executed, we will have assembled all the data that we need to populate our HTML. In fact, by separating out the behind-the-scenes processing in this way, we've done ourselves a favor. This file makes no assumptions about presentation of the data to the web browser, so it should be easy to reuse in an Ajax application, where we may be sending text, HTML, XML, or other types of data to the browser, rather than a complete HTML page. We'll revisit this code in chapters 3 and 4, but we won't need to modify it very much.

We will, however, need to modify the other half of our application, which is concerned with presentation. In the next section, we'll look at how we create the HTML pages from the data generated by our business logic code.

2.1.5 Creating the HTML

The bulk of the work for our application has been done for us in the include file, which has included all the data that we need. Writing the HTML is relatively straightforward now, and is simply a matter of defining a few <DIV> tags to house the main user-interface elements, positioning them on the page using CSS stylesheets, and iterating over the arrays of data that we have created. Listing 2.2 shows the main PHP file for our app.

Listing 2.2   Generating the HTML for QuickGallery (index.php)

```php
<?php
require('images.inc.php');          Include
?>                                  business logic ❶
<html>
<head>
<link rel='stylesheet' type="text/css" href="images.css">
</head>
<body>

<div id='title' class='box'>                    Iterate over ❷
<?php foreach ($crumbs as $i => $value){ ?>     breadcrumbs
   &gt; 
  <a href="images.php?path=<?php echo $value['path'] ?>">
  <?php echo $value['name'] ?>
  </a>
<?php } ?>
</div>
                            Render close- ❸
<?php if ($closeup){ ?>     up view

<div id='closeup' class='box'>
<img src='<?php echo $img_pre_path.$path ?>'>
</div>
<?php }else{ ?>  ❹  Render folder view

<?php if (count($subdirs)>0){ ?>
<div id='folders' class='box'>              Iterate over ❺
<?php foreach ($subdirs as $i => $value){ ?> subfolders
<div>
  <a href="images.php?path=<?php
    echo implode('/',array($path,$value))
  ?>">
    <?php echo $value ?>
  </a>
</div>
<?php } ?>
</div>
<?php } ?>
                            Iterate over ❻
<?php if (count($imgs)>0){ ?>  images
<div id='images' class='box'>
<?php foreach ($imgs as $i => $value){
    $full_img=implode('/',array($path,$value));
?>                                          Generate ❼
<div class='img_tile'>                      image tile
  <a href="images.php?path=<?php echo $full_img ?>.jpg">
  <img border='0'
    src="<?php echo $img_pre_path.$full_img ?>.thumb.jpg"/>
  </a>
```

```
    <br/>
    <?php echo $value ?>
    </a>
</div>
<?php } ?>
</div>
<?php } ?>

<?php } ?>

</body>
</html>
```

In the business logic, we were working with a single, solid block of PHP. Here, we're interweaving PHP snippets with HTML, in a way that should be familiar to JSP or ASP programmers.

The first thing that we do is include the business logic ❶. We then iterate over the breadcrumbs ❷, which we will want to render regardless. We then need to choose between rendering an image in a close-up ❸ or folder view ❹. If the latter, we iterate over subfolders ❺ and images ❻, rendering each image as a tile ❼.

This is essentially a structural definition of the document. That is, we're defining the parent-child relationships between elements on the page. For example, we're placing the thumbnail images inside the element with an ID `images`. We don't define much visual styling in the HTML—stating exactly how big the elements are, or how they occupy the space on the page—as we delegate that to a CSS stylesheet. The contents of the CSS file is shown in listing 2.3.

Listing 2.3   CSS for QuickGallery (images.css)

```
*{
  font-face: Arial, Helvetica;
}                                    ❶ Common
.box{                                   styling rule
  position: absolute;
  border: solid #adf 1px;
  background-color: white;
  padding: 4px;
}
#title{                  Specific
  top: 5px;          ❷  positioning rules
  left: 5px;
  height: 18px;
  font-size: 14px;
  color: #8af;
}
```

```
#folders{            ◁——————————┐
   top: 35px;                    │
   left: 5px;                    │
   width: 150px;                 │
}                         ❷  Specific
#images{             ◁————————┤  positioning rules
   top: 35px;                    │
   left: 180px;                  │
}                                │
#closeup{            ◁———————————┘
   top: 35px;
   left: 180px;
}                       ❸  Thumbnail
.img_tile{           ◁——┘  image tile
   float: left;
   width: 160px;
   height: 160px;
}
```

The stylesheet is principally concerned with layout. Each of the main elements on the page has a CSS class of box, which is defined here in terms of simple border styling, and, importantly, an absolute position ❶. The various elements also each have their own CSS rule matching their ID ❷, defining their positions on the page. Finally, we define a rule for the image tiles containing the thumbnails ❸, which uses the CSS float property to lay them out neatly in folder view, regardless of the size of the browser window.

Together, the PHP page that generates the HTML (listing 2.2) and the stylesheet (listing 2.3) define the look of the application as a single monolithic page. Whenever we want to change what is on the page, we recreate the entire page and re-render all elements on it. That's the nature of web applications, at least up until Ajax arrived on the scene. In the next section, we'll take up this issue in more detail.

That concludes our tour of the classic pre-Ajax QuickGallery application. We haven't presented anything astounding or original here, but it does give us a solid base on which to start working our Ajax magic. It's also worth noting that we've gone to some effort to separate out the different aspects of the application, containing all the business logic in one file, and separating the view into structure (the HTML) and presentation (the CSS). As we'll see, these practices will stand us in good stead when we come to factor Ajax into the equation. In the following section, we'll look at how Ajax will influence the design of the app, and see what it can buy us.

2.2 Evaluating the classic web app model

As we stated at the outset of this chapter, we're going to start our exploration of Ajax by developing a simple non-Ajax web application, so that we can assess the limitations of the approach. This will help us identify where Ajax can really help, rather than simply introducing Ajax for its own sake. Now that we've described how QuickGallery works, we're going to take a look at the way in which the classic web app approach has shaped it.

2.2.1 Links, forms, and full-page refresh

As we noted in the previous section, the user interface of a classic web application is defined as a single page of HTML. This page may contain several secondary elements, such as CSS stylesheets and images, but, at the top level, the server will generate a single, monolithic page.

The user can interact with the page in two ways, namely by clicking hyperlinks and by filling out HTML forms. In both cases, these will generate a request to the server, to which the response will be a complete new page. As we noted in chapter 1, this leads to a stop-start pattern of user interaction, in which any contact with the server mandates a period of inactivity while the user waits for the response to come back. This situation is summarized visually in figure 2.2.

Time is moving from left to right in this diagram. The upper band represents the web browser—the user is only able to use the application when the server is idle and not processing a request. While waiting for a request, the browser has nothing to display but the previous page, which may already be out of date as a

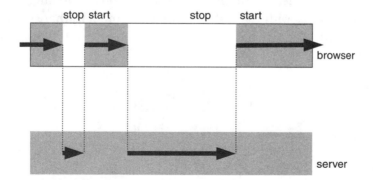

Figure 2.2   Stop-start pattern of user interaction in a classic web application

result of the user's interaction. The more interactive an application is, the more frequent, and frustrating, these periods of inactivity will be.

Now that we have a grasp on the generic problem, let's see how it manifests for QuickGallery.

2.2.2 *The classic web app and QuickGallery*

In QuickGallery, we're interacting solely with hyperlinks. We interact with the server in two ways: to change directory (either via the subfolders list or the breadcrumb trail) and to request a full-sized view of an image from a thumbnail. Let's take a look at each of these interactions in turn.

Changing directory

The images being presented in the gallery are arranged in a tree structure, based on their location in the server's filesystem. We provide navigation around this tree by providing a breadcrumb trail along the top of the image storage area, and as a list of subfolders down the left side. Thus, there are three regions on the screen in our application, and whenever we interact with these three regions, all of them get refreshed, as illustrated in figure 2.3.

We've shaded in the various elements on the right side to indicate whether or not content inside them has changed (gray indicates a change, white no change). In this case, almost every element has changed, so the fact that we've refreshed the entire screen is not too inefficient. The one exception is the breadcrumb trail. Depending on how far up or down the trees we're moving, some of the content will be repeated. We've represented areas that are re-rendered by the server's response, but contain identical content, with the diagonal hatching pattern. These are the problem areas with the full-screen refresh model, where we're creating extra network traffic and visual jerkiness as the screen refreshes.

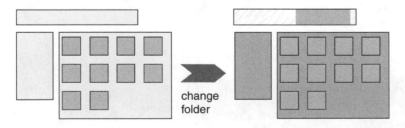

Figure 2.3   The effect of changing directory on the visual layout of QuickGallery

Now let's look at what happens when we click on a thumbnail and retrieve the close-up image.

Viewing an image in close-up mode

When we view an image in close-up mode, we replace the thumbnail region with the close-up image. The subfolder list remains the same, as does the breadcrumb trail, apart from having the image name appended to it. This allows us to return to thumbnail viewing mode by clicking on a subfolder or breadcrumb link. Figure 2.4 illustrates the transitions associated with going in and out of close-up mode.

When we enter close-up mode, we perform an unnecessary refresh on the breadcrumb and subfolder lists. (We haven't actually changed the current folder this time, merely drilled down to a closer look at its contents.) So, again, the full-page refresh approach that we're using is suboptimal. More interestingly, when we move back out to the thumbnail view, we're serving up an entire page of content that the user has already seen (unless the contents of the folder have changed since the user's last visit). The only exception to this is if the user is drilling down into a previously unvisited subfolder directly from the close-up view. The inability to maintain any information about the previous state of the application on the client is costing us dearly in this case, in both network load and responsiveness of the application.

So, we can see that the classic web application model has a problem when we want to build interactive, responsive applications. Further, QuickGallery suffers from that problem. We'll pick up this thread in chapters 3 and 4, when we introduce Ajax to QuickGallery and evaluate a number of solutions.

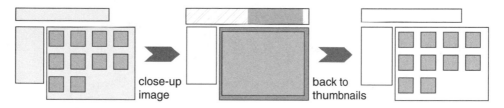

Figure 2.4   The effect on the screen layout of entering and leaving close-up mode

2.3 *Summary*

In this chapter, we've introduced the main features of our gallery application in its pre-Ajax incarnation in order to set the stage for the transformations that are to follow. QuickGallery is a simple application that does what it's tasked with doing in a straightforward fashion. From our discussion of the classic web interaction model, we can see that it suffers from a certain clunkiness, and that most classic web applications are likely to experience this problem in one form or another.

Introducing Ajax as a solution to this problem may seem a daunting prospect, but with the help of Prototype and Scriptaculous, we hope to show you how painless it can be to deliver some quick wins. We'll commence that job in the next chapter, when we move away from full-screen refreshes toward Ajax-based communications with the server.

Simplifying Ajax
with Prototype

3

This chapter covers

- Redesigning QuickGallery for Ajax
- Using XML and Ajax
- Using JSON and Ajax

At the heart of Ajax is the ability to make asynchronous requests to the server, and thereby separate communications from the user interface. The impact of this on usability can't be overstated. It allows the user to get on with the job while the web app gets on with its own housekeeping duties, without the two coming into conflict. Increasing usability not only makes the current round of web apps easier to use, it extends the reach of the web app to far more demanding usage scenarios, right up to the mission-critical apps that are used intensively, day-in, day-out.

In chapter 1, we saw how complicated dealing with the XMLHttpRequest object could be, and we offered a sneak preview of how Prototype's Ajax helper classes could make it that much easier to work with. In this chapter, we'll unpack Prototype's support for Ajax more comprehensively, and examine the full range of options that it offers. (This and the next chapter deal with Prototype. We'll start to work with Scriptaculous in chapter 5.) Once you've mastered the contents of this chapter, you'll not only be able to improve the usability of your apps by an order of magnitude, you'll get to stay sane and go home on time.

In chapter 2, we introduced the QuickGallery application that we're going to use as a test-bed for Prototype's Ajax capabilities. As we left it at the end of chapter 2, QuickGallery was able to function without Ajax, but it suffered from a lack of responsiveness owing to the need to refresh the entire page every time we made a request to the server. We'll pick up from there in this chapter, and illustrate how to go about separating the communication from the presentation, and get rid of those pesky full-page refreshes.

3.1 Redesigning for Ajax

Our QuickGallery application has fairly basic functionality now, and it does what we've asked it to do. In its current form, it doesn't look very beautiful, but we've separated the presentation out into a stylesheet, and we're confident that our design team can take care of the look of the application, whether that's a professional design team down the corridor, or ourselves on a Friday afternoon!

When using the app, we've noticed that it is a bit slow to use in some cases, particularly when generating large numbers of thumbnails for the first time. We also made a few experiments at building it into a larger page alongside other content, and found the continual full-page refreshes to be even more distracting. Further, while working on it and using it, we've drawn up a long list of functionality that we'd like to add. This includes the ability to browse more than one folder side by side, to update the thumbnail list automatically when the server's contents change, and to filter the images we're viewing by date, name, and possibly other tags that we attach to them. We'd also like to be able to reorganize the images—to move them between folders, to delete them, and to upload new images through the Web.

We realize that this is a lot of work, and we've heard that Ajax can fix some of the clunkiness for us. We also recognize that some of the more interactive features will change the nature of the conversation between the application and the user, making the stop-start nature of the traditional web app even harder to deal with. The classic web application model has just about coped with the basic functionality that we developed in chapter 2, but it is unlikely to support everything we want to do with the app. So we commit to developing the next version of QuickGallery as an Ajax application. As with most projects, the first step in Ajax-enabling a web app is to reimplement the existing functionality using Ajax. We'll do that in this and the next chapter, and we'll return to QuickGallery in chapter 12 to implement some new features, once we've figured out all the fine details of Prototype and Scriptaculous.

Having made this commitment, we're faced with a number of choices. Ajax incorporates many technologies that can be combined in different ways. We need to choose which method we are going to adopt, so let's take a look at our options.

3.1.1 *Designing the asynchronous request*

As we've already noted, the core function of Ajax is the process of making an asynchronous request. That is, we communicate with the server in the background, while the user is working, rather than forcing the user to stop while the entire page refreshes. One major choice that we're faced with is what our server is going to respond to the request with. In broad terms, there are three choices.

First, it can respond with HTML content. In this case, we wouldn't be returning an entire web page, but a fragment of content that can be stitched into the existing page. We refer to this as a content-centric approach to Ajax. The second option is to return a piece of generated JavaScript, which the web browser then evaluates. We call this a script-centric solution. The third option is to return data, which the client-side code parses using custom code, and then executes. This is a data-centric solution.

We should also note that there are other ways of making asynchronous requests that don't use the XMLHttpRequest object at all. Some of these, such as loading data into hidden iframes, can still be classified into content-, script-, and data-centric patterns, but others, such as dynamically changing the `src` attribute of images, are entirely different.

Each approach has its pros and cons. In moving from content- through script- to data-centric solutions, we are handing over more responsibility to the client-side code, and therefore simplifying the server side at the expense of increasing complexity on the client side. Let's look at each of our options briefly.

Content-centric Ajax

In a content-centric solution, we generate HTML and insert it dynamically into our page using JavaScript. This has a big advantage when moving a classic web app over to Ajax, because our classic app (the version of QuickGallery that we presented in chapter 2) was also generating HTML. We can use either the official DOM methods, or the innerHTML property. DOM methods have the advantage of being a formal standard, but they are rather clumsy to work with. The innerHTML property is not part of any standard, but it is simple to use and is available in all major browsers. We'll follow the majority of Ajax developers in this case, and go with innerHTML.

At its simplest, we return one piece of HTML, which we then assign as the innerHTML for a single DOM element. Unfortunately, the design of our QuickGallery app requires us to update no less than three areas of the screen at once when showing a folder—the breadcrumbs, the subfolder list, and the thumbnail images. We could issue three separate calls to the server, but this introduces a number of new problems. First, we would be adding network overhead. Second, we'd need to execute our business logic more than once, as we currently create the subfolders and images lists as part of the same iteration. Third, we'd introduce the possibility of the three areas of the screen getting out of sync with one another. Therefore, if we want to adopt a content-centric approach, we'll need to figure out a way of sending three sets of content back as a single response, and unpacking them on the client.

We'll return to the content-centric approach soon, but first let's move on to the next of our options.

Script-centric Ajax

In a script-centric approach, we generate JavaScript and send that back to the client. The JavaScript can then be executed using the eval() function built into the language.

A script-centric approach offers more flexibility as far as updating multiple areas of the screen is concerned. On the downside, we're going to have to change our server-side code more, in order to generate JavaScript rather than HTML. If we do go down this route, we'd do well to read up on code generation best practices, and generate code that talks to a high-level API rather than directly generating low-level code. This will simplify the code that has to be generated, and it will also decrease the coupling between the client and server code bases.

Tight coupling of code is a general problem in any type of software development. Two pieces of code are said to be tightly coupled when one makes calls into the implementation details of the other. In loosely coupled code, only a few methods or functions in each piece of code are marked as publicly available, and any communication between the two pieces of code goes through those methods. The advantage of loose coupling is that each piece of code can be modified and improved independently of the other without fear of breaking interactions with other pieces of code. In a complex piece of software composed of many parts, tight coupling can lead to gridlock and stagnation.

So, if we plan to follow a script-centric approach, we ought to define a JavaScript API in the static client code (that is, the handwritten JavaScript in the .js files), and generate calls to that API. Before we consider this option any further, let's take a look at the final option that we have available to us.

Data-centric Ajax

A data-centric Ajax application receives raw data back from the server. The format of the data can be anything that we like, so long as it can be represented as text. The two most popular choices are XML and JSON.

XML is an industry-standard format, widely supported by server languages and frameworks, and, indeed, by nearly all programming environments these days. Further, the XMLHttpRequest object that enables asynchronous requests in Ajax has special support for XML, automatically parsing the incoming response data and allowing us to interact with it as a set of objects rather than just plain text. The downside of this facility is that we interact with the parsed XML data using DOM manipulation methods, which, as we have noted, are rather cumbersome.

Prototype does provide some relief here, in the form of extra DOM helpers (see chapter 11) and support for DOM pseudo-arrays (see chapter 10), but even so, JSON is commonly seen as a lighter alternative to XML. JSON stands for JavaScript Object Notation, and it allows us to represent complex objects in a format that can be easily parsed by the JavaScript interpreter. Once parsed, these objects can be interacted with as ordinary JavaScript objects, with much less overhead than their XML counterparts. The downside of using JSON is that it is only understood by JavaScript interpreters, and therefore few server-side systems will have the ability to speak JSON easily. Thus, generating the data on the server will typically involve more overhead.

Whichever format of data we choose, adopting a data-centric approach will require us to write some extra code to parse the response and decide what to do with it.

Those, then, are our three options. While making our decision to rewrite QuickGallery as an Ajax app, however, we also heard that the Prototype library makes Ajax easier to work with. So before we make our choice, let's take a look at what Prototype can offer us.

3.1.2 *Prototype's Ajax classes*

We've considered three different flavors of Ajax in the previous section. Which of these does Prototype support? The short answer is "all of them," but it doesn't support all of them as well as one another. Let's unpack Prototype's Ajax support classes and see what conclusions we can reach.

Prototype provides not one, but four Ajax helper objects. These are organized in a class hierarchy, using Prototype's own support for class definitions. We don't need to worry about the implementation details of this for now, as we'll explain those in chapter 8 when we look under the hood of Prototype. For now, we simply need to understand that Prototype provides several Ajax helper objects, in much the way that car manufacturers provide several models. The most basic of the Prototype Ajax helpers will get us where we want to go smoothly and without fuss. The deluxe versions provide extra convenience and features. We'll start with the most basic Ajax objects in this chapter, and work through to the specialty objects in chapter 4.

Ajax.Base

The common ancestor of all Ajax helper classes is the Ajax.Base class. In object-oriented terminology, this is an abstract or virtual class; that is, it isn't designed to be used directly, but rather to serve as a common foundation for more complete classes.

Ajax.Base provides the ability to instantiate an XMLHttpRequest object, referred to as the transport by Prototype, and to determine whether or not a request made via that transport was successful. It also provides hooks for passing in common configuration parameters, namely the HTTP verb, CGI parameters, and one indicating whether or not the request is made asynchronously. (If any of these terms aren't familiar, have a look at appendix A, our primer on the HTTP protocol.)

That's about all there is to the base class, so let's move on to the first really useful Ajax class.

Ajax.Request

The Ajax.Request class extends the Ajax.Base class by providing a mechanism for making a request to a server-side resource, as represented by a URL. It also provides a fuller implementation of handling the response from the server, defining high-level callback functionality. We saw how to use the Ajax.Request object in listing 1.4, which was considerably shorter than its code-from-the-ground-up counterpart, in listing 1.2.

The Ajax.Request object requires two arguments when created. The first is the URL of the server-side resource to which the request is made. The second is a JavaScript object used to contain an arbitrary number of options. (JavaScript objects can be treated rather like associative arrays—we'll discuss this feature in detail in chapters 8 and 10.) When an Ajax.Request object is created, the options argument can be omitted altogether, or it can be provided, with some or all of the options defined. Any option that isn't explicitly defined will fall back to a sensible default value. So, we can create an Ajax.Request object very simply, like so:

```
var request=new Ajax.Request("ajax/myData.jsp");
```

More commonly, we would provide a few optional arguments. Typically, we will define our options inline. If we were to provide some CGI parameters to the request and a function to be invoked when the request is complete, our invocation might look like this:

```
var request=new Ajax.Request(
  "ajax/myData.jsp",
  {
    parameters: "id=1234",
    onComplete: parseData
  }
);
```

The second argument (yes, there are only two arguments being passed in!) is an object that we have defined inline. This notation, known as JSON, is shorthand that creates an instance of an object and specifies its properties. This can also be termed an object literal. This type of parameter is a standard part of the Prototype and Scriptaculous house coding style. As this is the first time we've come across it, let's take a small detour to look at it in detail.

An aside on the Prototype.js coding style

In many scripting languages, such as Ruby, Python, and Visual Basic, it's possible to provide named arguments to a function. This can be helpful if a function is capable of accepting a wide range of arguments but will generally be called with only one or two. Named arguments allow a function to provide sensible defaults for the casual user, and a fine degree of control for the power user.

JavaScript doesn't support named arguments, but Prototype.js has adopted a coding idiom that is almost as simple. Ajax.Request's constructor function uses this idiom, so let's look at an example of how it works.

In the course of creating the Ajax.Request object, we invoked the constructor with only two arguments, the second of which was rather complex. We defined this argument inline using JSON. The previous notation might also have been written like this:

```
var xyz = new Object();
xyz.parameters = "id=1234";
xyz.onComplete = parseData;
var request=new Ajax.Request("ajax/myData.jsp",xyz);
```

Using JSON is obviously less wordy, and once you get used to it, it's a lot easier to scan quickly.

You might wonder why Prototype and Scriptaculous chose to pass options in this manner. After all, JavaScript allows the passing of optional parameters. Why not just define the functions with all the options as parameters?

For illustrative purposes, let's assume that a function takes seven parameters, only the first of which is required. That means that parameters two through seven are optional and need not be specified at all if they come at the end of the parameter list.

A call to this function specifying only the required parameter is incredibly simple:

```
someFunction('something');
```

It's easy for code in the body of the function to check for the existence of a parameter, since a simple null check will tell the code whether the parameter exists. If the function signature was defined as

```
function someFunction(required, opt1, opt2, opt3,
                      opt4, opt5, opt6) {
```

then a test such as

```
if (opt1) alert( 'opt1 exists!' );
```

could be made to check for the existence of an argument.

That's all well and good for the author of the function, but what about the poor sap who has to call the function? Let's say that a function user wishes to call it with the fourth and last optional parameters specified. The call might look like this:

```
someFunction('something',null,null,null,'a value',
             null,'another value');
```

Ick!

Because we need to keep the parameters in order, nulls must be specified for any non-trailing optional parameters that we don't want to supply values for. This not only makes the code rather messy and hard to scan, it forces the user to rely heavily on the documentation or function source whenever the function call needs to be understood. Simply looking at such a call to the function doesn't tell us much about the nature and meaning of the parameters. We could really do with named arguments here.

Let's take our call to the Ajax.Request object. Without the use of the anonymous object, the call might have looked like this:

```
new Ajax.Request('ajax/myData.jsp', "id=123", parseData);
```

Quick, determine which parameter is the post body value? Which is the callback? There's no way to know for sure, without looking at the function source or documentation.

And even worse, those aren't the only options to the object. So without the anonymous object mechanism, a call to the object might be even more horrendous:

```
new Ajax.Request('ajax/myData.jsp',null, null, "id=123", null, parseData);
```

The advantage that the anonymous object technique brings to the table is twofold:

- Only options that are to be explicitly specified need be included. No nulls are required to serve as ordinal placeholders.

- Each option is explicitly named, making it trivial to determine which value is being supplied for which option.

Once you get over the initial strangeness of the notation, you'll begin to wonder how you ever got along without it. And before long, you'll find yourself using it in your own functions that take complex parametric input.

We'll discuss the JSON syntax in more detail in chapter 8. For now, let's look at the options we've passed in.

Optional parameters for Ajax.Request

The first option we're passing to our example Ajax.Request object is a simple querystring that will be exposed as POST variables on the server. The second is a callback function, which will be invoked when the server returns a response, allowing us to parse the data. We've passed a reference to a predefined function object here, but we'll commonly see functions being defined inline within these arrays, which can make the invocation of a constructor function quite lengthy. Indentation is usually the key to maintaining readability.

The practice of passing in an options object is powerful and concise, but it does have a downside. Even with the source code available, it can be quite difficult to determine the full range of options that an object supports. To this end, we'll tabulate the options available to the Prototype and Scriptaculous objects when we come across them. Table 3.1 lists the options that can be set when creating an Ajax.Request object, along with their default values.

Table 3.1 Optional properties of the Ajax.Request object

Name	Default value	Comments
method	'post'	The HTTP method or verb used to send the request. Most commonly 'get' or 'post' (note that Prototype expects these in lower case). See appendix A for more details. Used by Ajax.Base.
asynchronous	true	Value indicating whether sending the request will block the thread of execution until the response comes (if set to false), or if the thread of execution will return immediately, and the arrival of the response will trigger a callback (if set to true). Because the JavaScript interpreter is single-threaded, synchronous requests tend to block the entire user interface, making the browser freeze up; they are therefore not recommended. Used by Ajax.Base.
parameters	' '	A parameter string passed to the server, as either a URL querystring for GET requests, or as the request body for POST requests. GET requests should follow the querystring format, but POST requests may send XML, JSON, or any type of text body. Alternatively, this may be an array, from which a querystring will be constructed. Used by Ajax.Base.
postBody	null	A synonym for parameters, but applicable only to POST requests.
requestHeaders	null	An array of data that may be applied to the request as extra HTTP headers. HTTP headers are described in detail in appendix A. Typical uses include setting the MIME type of the request.
onLoading	null	A callback function to be called when the XMLHttpRequest object reaches the loading state (readyState=1). Although the Ajax.Request object supports callbacks for all readyState transitions of the underlying XMLHttpRequest object, there isn't usually a good use case for this option.

Table 3.1 Optional properties of the Ajax.Request object *(continued)*

Name	Default value	Comments
onLoaded	null	A callback function to be called when the XMLHttpRequest object reaches the loaded state (readyState=2). Although the Ajax.Request object supports callbacks for all readyState transitions of the underlying XMLHttpRequest object, there isn't usually a good use case for this option.
onInteractive	null	A callback function to be called when the XMLHttpRequest object reaches the interactive state (readyState=3). When loading a large resource in Mozilla browsers, this callback will be handled multiple times, allowing implementation, for example, of a simple progress bar. In Internet Explorer, however, this callback is invoked only once, however large the file.
onComplete	null	A callback function to be called when the XMLHttpRequest object reaches the complete state (readyState=4). The response is fully loaded at this point and can be parsed as XML if appropriate.
onSuccess	null	A more specific version of the onComplete handler, which will be called only when the HTTP status of the response lies in the range 200–299, indicating a successful response. This is the most common callback to provide when using the Ajax.Request object.
onException	null	A callback to be invoked when the handling of a response encounters a JavaScript exception.
onFailure	null	A more specific version of the onComplete handler, which will be called only when the HTTP status of the response lies outside the range 200–299, indicating an unsuccessful response. HTTP response statuses are described in appendix A. Note that many server-side frameworks report internal server errors by sending 'success' HTTP responses (code 200) containing error messages marked up as HTML. These responses will be caught by the onSuccess handler function, not onFailure.

We'll see Ajax.Request in use in the QuickGallery app in a minute, but first, Prototype also provides us with a couple of more specific Ajax helper classes, known as the Ajax.Updater and the Ajax.PeriodicalUpdater. We won't be using these until the next chapter; we'll return to them in more detail later.

We've outlined the three basic flavors of Ajax and the four Ajax helper objects that Prototype provides. Now let's put them to use and breathe some new life into the QuickGallery application that we presented in chapter 2. The app underwent a full-page refresh whenever we switched to a different folder, or when we viewed an image in close-up view. We're going to use Ajax now to eliminate those full-page refreshes. Our first problem is deciding which type of Ajax to use, out of our three categories: data-, script-, and content-centric.

We've already identified pros and cons to each approach. Rather than indulge in further discussion, we're going to roll up our sleeves and start to implement using two of the three approaches, the data- and content-centric ones. We won't explicitly start off a script-centric implementation yet, but we will also find ourselves employing that approach in one of our solutions.

We won't take either implementation very far yet, but the experience of working with each approach will add some fuel to our decision-making when we do decide which avenue to go down further. So, enough talk. We'll start off by implementing a data-centric redesign of the app.

3.2 *Using XML and Ajax*

We've heard that the x in Ajax stands for XML, and that a lot of Ajax projects have had success with generating XML data on the server in response to a request and then parsing it. Parsing XML seems like a good fit for the XMLHttpRequest object, because of its native XML parsing ability. In this section, we're going to develop an Ajax-enabled version of QuickGallery that uses XML as the communication medium, so let's see what's necessary to make it work. The most important (and frequent) page transitions in the app occur when the user moves to a new folder, and when the app displays a close-up of an image. The folder is the more complex of the two, so let's concentrate on that first.

When a new folder is displayed, we update all three elements of the user interface—the breadcrumb trail, the list of subfolders, and the thumbnail images (see figure 2.1). If we're sending back a response as XML, we'll need to include all this information.

3.2.1 *Designing the XML response*

Before we look at how we are going to generate the XML data that our server will respond with, and that our client code will parse, we need to define what the data format is. XML is, after all, a general-purpose format for transferring structured data, so we need to decide what set of tags we are going to use, and how they relate to each other. And that depends on what information we are trying to convey.

We need to transmit three pieces of information: the path within the image directory, the immediate subfolders, and the contents of the current folder. The path can be sent to the client as a single value, but the subfolders and image lists are best treated as collections of elements. Listing 3.1 provides an example of the XML that our process might generate.

Listing 3.1 Sample XML data generated by Ajax QuickGallery

```
<gallery path='/plants/trees'>     ◁——❶  Path attribute
  <folders>                        ◁         List of
    <folder>forest</folder>        ❷         subfolders
    <folder>bark close-ups</folder>
  </folders>
  <images>                         ◁         List of
    <image>dscn0034</image>        ❸         images
    <image>dscn0037</image>
    <image>dscn0187</image>
  </images>
</gallery>
```

We define a top-level `<gallery>` element with a path attribute ❶ from which we can establish where we are in the image folder. Two elements are nested within, listing subfolders ❷ and images ❸ respectively. Both are optional, although we'd expect every folder to contain at least one of the two. Note that the image names are returned without the file type suffix. As before, we're assuming that all images are in JPEG format, and that the names end with the suffix ".jpg". Omitting the suffix makes it easy to generate the thumbnail image names too.

Defining the XML format is a useful starting point, as it serves as the glue between our client and server code. Now let's see how it affects the implementation of the server and client code bases.

3.2.2 Modifying the server-side code

In the pre-Ajax version of the QuickGallery app, the response returned from the server took the form of an HTML document. Here, we want to return the response as pure XML, as illustrated in listing 3.1. Fortunately, the pre-Ajax app was developed in a clean, modular fashion, with a clear separation of logic (see listing 2.1) and presentation (see listing 2.2). Now we want to present the same basic information—breadcrumbs, subfolders, and image list—in a different form. Hence, we only need to modify the presentation template to generate XML rather than HTML. The XML-generating template file is shown in listing 3.2.

Listing 3.2   dataXML/images.php generating XML

```php
<?php
header(                                          ①  Set MIME
   "Content-type: text/xml; charset=utf-8"         type
);
require('../config.php');        ②  Include business
require('images.inc.php');          logic
?>
<gallery                        ③  Path
   path="<?php echo $path ?>"       attribute
   pre="<?php echo $img_pre_path ?>">
<?php if (count($subdirs)>0){ ?>
<folders>                                        ④  List of
<?php foreach ($subdirs as $i => $value){ ?>        subfolders
<folder><?php echo $value ?></folder>
<?php } ?>
</folders>
<?php } ?>
                                ⑤  List of
<?php if (count($imgs)>0){ ?>       images
<images>
<?php foreach ($imgs as $i => $value){ ?>
<image><?php echo $value ?></image>
<?php } ?>
</images>
<?php } ?>
</gallery>
```

Before we generate the XML, we need to do a couple of important pieces of housekeeping. First, we need to set the MIME type of the response to a value that the browser will understand as being XML ①. The XMLHttpRequest object has a native XML parser that exposes the response as an XML document, and we will use this capability in our client-side code to parse the data. However, this capability is only activated if the response MIME type indicates that the response body is XML. In PHP, we use the built-in `header()` function to set the MIME type. Other server-side languages have similar mechanisms—JSPs would use a page directive or `ServletResponse.setContentType()` directly. ASP/.Net programmers would set `Response.ContentType` directly. Ruby on Rails users would modify the `headers[]` array inside the Controller class code. See appendix E for details.

The second piece of housekeeping is to include the business logic file ②, as we did with our HTML template. This will populate the variables used by the template to fill in the blanks in the XML.

Once that is done, the remainder of the template simply follows the XML spec that we defined in listing 3.1, defining a path attribute ❸ and a collection of sub-folders ❹ and images ❺.

We should point out that using the JSP as a template to directly handwrite the XML, as we have done here, is rather simplistic. For a small document like this one it works well enough, but for larger documents, manually mapping start and end tags and escaping variable values would become burdensome. In production, we strongly recommend the use of a library that allows XML to be constructed automatically from an object model. In this book, though, our emphasis is on the client, and these libraries tend to be specific to particular server technologies, so we've erred on the side of simplicity to keep things clear.

As you can see, porting the server-side code across to use Ajax is relatively straightforward. Before we decide that this whole Ajax thing is a piece of cake, though, let's remember that we've only tackled one side of the problem so far. Our server knows how to send back XML to the browser, but we still need to write the JavaScript code to handle that response. In the next section, we'll take a look at the changes we need to make to the client side.

3.2.3 *Writing the client code*

The pre-Ajax QuickGallery didn't have any client-side code as such. An HTML user interface was generated on the server, containing hyperlinks that provided the only form of user interaction. The entire workflow (if that isn't too grand a term for browsing an image gallery!) was defined on the server. Now, however, we're sending a stream of raw data back from the server, so we need to have some client-side intelligence to parse it. Because we're no longer refreshing the page every time the user does something, we also need to define a simple outline of a page upon which the client-side code can operate.

The good news is that defining the page outline is very simple. We don't even need to use PHP (or any other dynamic server-side system) to generate the page for us. Because it initially contains no content, plain old HTML is good enough. Listing 3.3 shows the outline page for our XML-based Ajax QuickGallery.

Listing 3.3 Outline page for Ajax QuickGallery (dataXML/index.html)

```
<html>
<head>
<link rel='stylesheet'
  type="text/css" href="images.css"/>
<script type='text/javascript'                    ❶ Include
  src='lib/prototype/prototype.js'></script>  ⤶     prototype
```

```
<script type='text/javascript'
  src='lib/images_datacentric.js'></script>      ◁─┐   ❷  Include
</head>                                                   client code
<body>
                                              ❸  Define
<div id='title' class='box'>      ◁─┘            titlebar
</div>
                                              ❹  Define close-
<div class='box' id='closeup'>    ◁─┘            up image
<img id='closeup_img'></img>
</div>
                                              ❺  Define
<div id='folders' class='box'>    ◁─┘            subfolder list
</div>
                                              ❻  Define image
<div id='images' class='box'>     ◁─┘            list
</div>

</body>
</html>
```

The HTML file itself is little more than a statement of the structure of the document, which is as it should be. We delegate the actual layout and positioning to a CSS stylesheet and the behavior to client-side JavaScript. First we include the Prototype library ❶, and then our own client-side code ❷, which we'll look at in detail shortly. The various visual elements—the titlebar ❸, the close-up image ❹, the folders list ❺, and the thumbnail images list ❻—are initially devoid of content and styled via the CSS file by having class attributes assigned to them. Note also that we include all visual elements on the page at once here. The close-up image and the thumbnails list will never be visible at the same time, but we'll hide and show the elements programmatically as needed.

Implementing the client-side logic isn't so simple. The JavaScript needs to take care of making the Ajax requests, parsing the XML response, and then rendering the various parts of the user interface. We need to provide code to handle each of these steps.

The first step is sending the request to the server, so let's start off by looking at that.

Requesting data from the server

We can make a request to the server quite easily, using Prototype's Ajax.Request class, which we discussed in section 3.1.2. We'll wrap the creation of the request up in a function, like so:

```
function load(path){
  new Ajax.Request(
    "images.php?path="+path,
    {
      method: "get",
      onSuccess: parseAjaxResponse
    }
  );
}
```

Our server-side process requires a single parameter, the path to the current folder, so we'll pass that in as an argument to our function. The Ajax.Request object has a large number of options that can be passed to it when it is created, but for now we'll simply specify the HTTP verb and a reference to the callback function that will handle the response when it comes in.

We're using the underlying XMLHttpRequest object in asynchronous mode here. Using a callback handler is slightly more complicated than simply waiting for the response to come back, but it is much more flexible and user friendly. Some browsers will lock the entire user interface while waiting for a synchronous request to complete. Most production Ajax code uses asynchronous requests, and the Ajax.Request object assumes it by default.

Unpacking the response

This is a data-centric implementation of Ajax, so the response will consist of raw data. Once the response comes in, we need to parse the data that it contains, so we'll deal with that next. Because this is a simple example, we'll define a global variable to hold the various pieces of data. This is simply an empty JavaScript object, which we'll add some data to in a minute.

```
var data={}:
```

When we created the Ajax.Request object, we referenced a parseData function that would act as a callback handler when the response comes in. With Ajax, remember, we need to provide code to deal with the response when it comes back. Within that function, we'll fill out the data object, as shown here:

```
function parseAjaxResponse(transport){
  var response=transport.responseXML;
  var docRoot=response.getElementsByTagName('gallery')[0];
  data.path=docRoot.attributes.getNamedItem("path").value;
  data.pre=docRoot.attributes.getNamedItem("pre").value;
  data.folders=parseChildNodes(docRoot,"folders","folder");
  data.images=parseChildNodes(docRoot,"images","image");
  showDir();
}
```

```
function parseChildNodes(node,parentTag,childTag){
  var results=[];
  try{
    var children=$A(
      node.getElementsByTagName(parentTag)[0].
      getElementsByTagName(childTag)
    );
    results=children.collect(
      function(value,index){
        return value.firstChild.data;
      }
    }
  }catch(e){
  }  return results;
}
```

We've defined two functions to parse the data in the response. The first, parseAjaxResponse(), is the callback that we referenced when we created the request. The XMLHttpRequest object is referred to by the Prototype Ajax classes as the underlying transport mechanism, and it is passed to our callback function as the transport variable. Retrieving the response as a structured XML document is easy, but wading through the document using the DOM methods is best described as tedious, and we need to write quite a lot of code to retrieve attributes and child nodes from the data.

A couple of DOM methods are worth highlighting here. The first is getElementsByTagName(). This returns a collection of all child nodes underneath the current element whose tag name matches the argument. We're using it here to find the first child of the document. While it might be easier to write node.firstChild than node.getElementsByTagName(tag)[0], it is less reliable to do so. DOM nodes come in several flavors, including text nodes and element type nodes. Mozilla browsers will translate whitespace in an XML markup into text nodes, so the firstChild in a nicely formatted XML document is often a text node representing a carriage return and a few tabs or spaces of indentation.

The second method is what we use to fetch attribute values from the DOM elements. The DOM element property attributes returns a collection of all attributes, which in itself returns Attribute objects using the getNamedItem() method. Attribute objects possess a property value that refers to the attribute value. We hope to have convinced you by this point that working with the DOM methods directly is somewhat tedious.

Parsing the lists of subfolders and the list of images from the XML is done essentially the same way, so we define a parseChildNodes() helper method to handle both problems. We're using Prototype's array extensions in this method twice. The `$A()` function converts DOM collection classes (such as the ones returned by `getElementsByTagName()`) into JavaScript Array objects, and the `Array.collect()` method is provided by Prototype too, as a concise way to perform an operation on every element of an array and collect the results as a second array.

We'll look at the Prototype Array methods in more detail in chapter 10. For now, let's move on to see how we use the data once we've parsed it.

Displaying the new data

When we show the contents of a new directory, we perform three tasks: rendering the breadcrumbs, showing subfolders, and displaying the thumbnail contents of the current folder. We'll provide a top-level method that breaks the work down into these three tasks:

```
function showDir(){
  showBreadcrumbs();
  showFolders();
  showThumbnails();
}
```

We'll also define a global variable to keep a reference to all the user interface components, much like the data variable that stored all the behind-the-scenes state. Once again, our use of a global variable here keeps things simple while we get started, but we'll refactor it away later. We need to initialize the user interface variable `ui` inside the `window.onload()` event, because at that point we are guaranteed that all the DOM nodes in the page have been fully loaded:

```
var ui={};

window.onload=function(){
  ui.title=$('title');
  ui.closeup=$('closeup');
  ui.closeupImg=$('closeup_img');
  ui.folders=$('folders');
  ui.images=$('images');
  Element.hide(ui.closeup,ui.folders);
  load('/');
}
```

We make good use of Prototype's `$()` function to find all the DOM elements by their ID attributes. We also use the Prototype Element object, which provides various helper classes for working with DOM elements. The `hide()` method, and its counterpart `show()`, are simple wrappers around the programmatic interface to the CSS styling of an HTML element that makes them visible or invisible. Initially, we hide both the close-up image and the subfolders view. We then call the `load()` method on the root of our path to make the first Ajax request and populate our gallery.

Rendering the breadcrumb trail

So far, so simple. We've made the request and parsed it into our data structure on the browser. To complete the process, we now need to write the code to update the user interface with this new data. As we already noted, the user interface for QuickGallery consists of several components, namely the breadcrumb trail, the subfolder list, and the main viewing area. Let's look at the first of these, rendering the breadcrumbs.

The server has provided the path to the current folder as a single string, so we'll need to break it up into the individual breadcrumbs on the client. For each folder in the path, we need to extract both the name of that folder and the cumulative path up to that point. (In the hypothetical path /here/are/my/files, for example, the third breadcrumb would have a name my, and would represent the cumulative path /here/are/my.) Here is the code for rendering the breadcrumb trail:

```
function showBreadcrumbs(){
  var crumbHTML=" &gt; <span onclick='load(\"\")'>home</span>";
  var crumbs=data.path.split("/");
  for(var i=0;i<crumbs.length;i++){
    var crumb=crumbs[i];
    if (crumb.length>0){
      var path=subpath(data.path,"/",i);
      crumbHTML+=" &gt; <span onclick='load(\""+path+"\")'>"+crumb+"</span>";
    }
  }
  ui.title.innerHTML=crumbHTML;
}
```

We could generate this as a set of data, but we instead take the path of least resistance here and assemble a long string of HTML, which we then assign to the relevant user interface element using the `innerHTML` property. We've delegated the hard work of generating the cumulative path for each breadcrumb node to the `subpath()` method. Let's look at the implementation of that now.

```
function subpath(str,delim,ix){
  var all=str.split(delim);
  var some=all.findAll(
    function(v,i){
      return (i<=ix);
    }
  );
  return some.join(delim);
}
```

Once again, we've found a good use for Prototype's array helper methods. The findAll() method applies a test to all the elements of an array, returning a result array of only those elements that pass the test. The test function has access to both the value and the numerical index of each element, and here we use the numerical index to compute which elements belong in the subpath.

That's the breadcrumb trail generated. Now let's have a look at the rendering of the subfolders list.

Rendering the subfolders list

Rendering the subfolders is quite straightforward. It's simply a matter of iterating through the elements and creating a link to our load() function for each one. Here's the code:

```
function showFolders(){
  if (data.folders.length==0){
    Element.hide(ui.folders);
  }else{
    var links=data.folders.collect(
      function(value,index){
        var path=[data.path,value].join("/");
        return "<div onclick='load(\""+path+"\")'>"+value+"</div>";
      }
    );
    Element.show(ui.folders);
    ui.folders.innerHTML=links.join("");
  }
}
```

For each subfolder, we know the display name. We calculate an absolute path to that folder by adding on the base path provided by the data that we've collected from the server response. Again, we're using Prototype's Array.collect() method to simplify the generation of the HTML, including simple event handlers, which we then apply using the innerHTML property.

Rendering thumbnail images

Finally, creating the thumbnails is very similar to rendering the subfolder list. The code required to achieve that is shown here:

```
function showThumbnails(){
  Element.hide(ui.closeup);
  if (data.images.length==0){
    Element.hide(ui.images);
  }else{
    var links=data.images.collect(
      function(value,index){
        var imgUrl=data.pre+data.path+"/"+value+".thumb.jpg";
```

```
        return "<div class='img_tile'>"
          +"<img onclick='showCloseup(\""
          +value
          +"\")' src='"
          +imgUrl
          +"'/>"
          +"<br/>"
          +value
          +"</div>";
      }
    );
    Element.show(ui.images);
    ui.images.innerHTML=links.join("");
  }
}
```

Structurally, showThumbnails() and showFolders() are almost identical, so we won't go over the details again here. The only point to note is that we've referred to a showCloseup() method in the onclick event handler for the thumbnails. The code for that function is as follows:

```
function showCloseup(imgSrc){
  Element.hide(ui.images);
  Element.show(ui.closeup);
  ui.closeupImg.src=imgSrc;
}
```

Displaying a close-up image is simply a matter of rearranging the user interface elements using Prototype's Element.hide() and Element.show() methods and setting the source of the image object appropriately. Note that we are fetching a resource asynchronously from the server without refreshing the page, so technically we are using Ajax, although no XMLHttpRequest object is required. In fact, the canonical Ajax application, Google Maps, uses the same method to update its interface, and makes little use of XMLHttpRequest objects.

Putting it all together

That completes our data-centric implementation of the QuickGallery application. Looking back, most of the heavy lifting required to make it work was on the client side, and Prototype came to our assistance in several ways.

The Ajax helper objects made fetching the XML data much simpler than it might otherwise have been. We were able to provide high-level callback functions to the Ajax.Request, unlike the low-level callbacks of the XHR object, which require us to worry about ready states and HTTP statuses. We were able to supply an HTTP verb as a configuration option. The DOM helper classes, such as the $() function and Element object, were made use of more than once, as were the extensions to the Array object. Without Prototype to help us along, we would have had to write much more JavaScript ourselves. Nonetheless, in putting it all together we still had to write quite a lot of JavaScript.

We've done our best to structure the client-side code in several ways. Let's review the design briefly. We declared a couple of global variables to hold all the application state: one for user interface elements, and another for background data. We've initialized each of these at the appropriate times: the user interface when the DOM has loaded, and the data after making the asynchronous call to the server using the Prototype helper classes. We parsed the XML data that the server returned using the raw DOM methods, and we broke down the task of updating the user interface into a set of subtasks, one for each on-screen component. As we move forward and add new features, the code should be easy enough to maintain and refactor.

There is, however, a niggling doubt. We've had to write a lot of code to get the job done, and although Prototype streamlined the business of making the request, we still had to parse the response by hand. The `parseAjax()` method, in particular, is big and ugly-looking.

We've heard that there's a more lightweight alternative to XML out there, going by the name of JSON. Migrating our XML solution to JSON won't require too many changes, so let's give it a try and see if it really does make things easier for us.

3.3 *Using JSON and Ajax*

In section 3.2, we implemented an Ajax-driven version of QuickGallery using XML as the communication medium. We're still exploring the options available to us as Ajax programmers, and JSON seems to be an intriguing alternative to XML. JSON, as we have said, stands for JavaScript Object Notation. It's a markup for data structures, just as XML is, but it follows the conventions of the JavaScript language. We'll look at the structure of JSON in more detail in chapter 8, when we examine JavaScript objects.

When we communicate using JSON, we're still using the same Ajax mechanisms, so we can still use Prototype's Ajax.Request to make that part of the implementation easy. The difference will lie in how we parse the response. The big advantage of using JSON is that when the response arrives the JavaScript interpreter will parse it for us.

Using JSON, we're still following a data-centric approach, so we can adapt our XML-based solution very easily. The only things that we need to modify are the generation of the data on the server, and the parsing of the response. Let's look at each in turn.

3.3.1 Modifying the server code

We still want to generate a data structure that lists the path information and the lists of subfolders and images. Listing 3.4 shows us a typical piece of JSON data that the server might produce.

Listing 3.4 Sample JSON data generated by Ajax QuickGallery

```
{
  path:'/plants/trees',          Path
                                 attribute
  folders: [                     List of
    "forest",                    subfolders
    "bark close-ups"
  ],
  images: [                      List of
    "dscn0034",                  images
    "dscn0037",
    "dscn0187"
  ]
}
```

Comparing this with the sample XML that we presented in listing 3.1, we can see that the differences are purely syntactic. Generating the JSON data, then, is simply a matter of modifying our PHP template. Listing 3.5 shows the modifications that we've made.

Listing 3.5 dataJSON/images.php generating JSON

```php
<?php
header("Content-type: text/javascript");
require('../config.php');
require('images.inc.php');
?>
{
 path:"<?php echo $path ?>",
 pre: "<?php echo $img_pre_path ?>"
<?php if (count($subdirs)>0){ ?>
 ,folders:["<?php echo join($subdirs,'","'); ?>"]
<?php } ?>
<?php if (count($imgs)>0){ ?>
 ,images:["<?php echo join($imgs,'","'); ?>"]
<?php } ?>
}
```

Because the JSON output is less verbose than XML, we've been able to use PHP's join() method to assemble the lists of folders and images. Apart from that, the code is very straightforward. A typical piece of JSON generated by this code is as follows:

```
{
 path:"",
 pre: "/album/images"
 ,folders:["animals","buildings","landscape","plants","things"]
}
```

We're using a simple, and arguably crude, templating approach here, writing out the JSON by hand and inserting variables and control loops directly into the markup. If we were to get serious about using JSON, there are libraries available for most programming languages that let us assemble the data as a nested set of arrays and objects, from which the JSON markup is generated automatically. As with our XML generation in the previous section, we've resisted the temptation of employing them here because we want to keep the server-side code as simple as possible, so that we can concentrate on the client-side code. The interesting thing for us here, after all, is to find out what the impact of JSON will be on the client tier, so let's look at that next.

3.3.2 *Modifying the client code*

The server is generating some nice-looking JSON for us now, and we need to write a callback function to parse it, much as we did with the XML. Let's take a look at how we consume JSON. The entry point on the client will be the callback function that we supply to the Prototype Ajax.Request object. The code for this method is as follows:

```
function parseAjaxResponse(transport){
  var response=transport.responseText;
  var jsonObj=eval("("+response+")");
  data.path=jsonObj.path;
  data.pre=jsonObj.pre;
  data.folders=jsonObj.folders || [];
  data.images=jsonObj.images || [];
  showDir();
}
```

The first thing to note is that we're reading the responseText property of the XHR object, rather than the responseXML. This will return a string to us, containing all the JSON data. In the next line, we then simply evaluate the JSON expression, and get back a JavaScript object. The remainder of the function is simply concerned with populating our global data object with the parsed data before we invoke the `showDir()` method to display the content. Compared to the parsing of the XML data, using JSON is certainly a lot easier to write, and read.

And that's it! Our gallery now works with JSON as the communication medium.

That concludes our exploration of JSON as an alternative to XML. It has made things a little easier for us on the client side, because we don't need to use the DOM to parse our data. XML, of course, has big advantages in some situations, because most server-side technologies will speak XML with a high degree of fluency. In our case, the data being generated was trivial enough that we could easily switch to JSON.

3.4 Summary

We looked at Prototype's support for Ajax through the Ajax.Request object in this chapter, and we put the Ajax.Request through its paces. By the end of the chapter, we had two working Ajax versions of our gallery application: one using XML and the other JSON as transport media.

Looking back on the experience, we've succeeded in our goal of Ajax-powering the gallery app, but there's still a niggling doubt about the amount of code that we've had to write, particularly to support the user interface. Furthermore, when we looked at Prototype's Ajax support classes earlier, we saw several nifty-looking subclasses that made Ajax even easier. Here we only used the Ajax.Request class. Surely there's meant to be a better way?

We're currently at the early prototyping stage (no pun intended!) of adding Ajax features to our QuickGallery application, so now is a good time to listen to such doubts. We identified three broad types of Ajax communication earlier—data-centric, script-centric, and content-centric—and we have tried the data-centric approach so far with mixed results. Prototype's Ajax.Updater classes look to offer further support for what we called a content-centric approach, so in the next chapter we'll reimplement the gallery using that style and see what differences it makes.

Using Prototype's
Advanced Ajax Features

This chapter will conclude our examination of the different styles of Ajax, of what Ajax can bring to a web application, and how Prototype makes Ajax development easy. In chapter 2, we introduced the QuickGallery application, a non-Ajax web app that we were going to convert to use Ajax, in order to eliminate the full-page refresh associated with every request made to the server and change the stop-start pattern of user interaction. In chapter 3, we developed two Ajax-powered versions of the QuickGallery application, using XML and JSON. Both transmitted updates from the server as structured data, with the client-side JavaScript containing all the logic for parsing this data and generating updates to the user interface. In terms of the types of Ajax that we identified in section 3.1.1, the implementations that we presented in chapter 3 clearly fitted the content-centric model.

In this chapter, we're going to rework QuickGallery, still using the content-centric approach to Ajax, to see if we can cut down on the amount of client-side code we have to write. That is, the server will generate updates as fragments of HTML directly, relieving the client-side code of the burden of parsing data and generating HTML markup in one fell swoop. All we have to do is read the response data and stitch it into the document using the innerHTML property.

In fact, we don't even need to do that. In section 3.1.2, we alluded to "deluxe models" of the Ajax helper class in the Prototype library. As we will see, Prototype provides us with a special helper class, the Ajax.Updater, that will make working with Ajax even easier. We'll begin this chapter, then, by looking at the Ajax.Updater and related classes. We'll then move on to develop an implementation of Quick-Gallery that makes use of these classes, and conclude by evaluating and comparing the various styles of Ajax that we've encountered in chapters 3 and 4.

4.1 Prototype's advanced Ajax classes

In the previous chapter, we looked at the Ajax.Request class supplied by Prototype.js. Ajax.Request provides an easy-to-use wrapper around the XMLHttpRequest object, but it still leaves the developer with the job of writing code to make sense of the response. Prototype.js also provides us with a pair of more advanced Ajax helper classes, specifically designed to support content-centric Ajax. In this section, we'll look at these classes in more detail before making use of them in our QuickGallery application.

4.1.1 Ajax.Updater

Ajax.Updater extends Ajax.Request in a very convenient way. When using the content-centric approach to Ajax that we described earlier, we will generally want to read the server response as a string, and then apply it as the `innerHTML` property of a DOM element somewhere on the page. Ajax.Updater saves us the trouble of doing this manually every time. When we create the object, we specify a URL as an argument, as before, but also a container element to be populated by the response. The container argument may be either a single DOM element, or a pair of DOM elements, one of which will be populated if the response is successful, the other if it is unsuccessful.

Because Ajax.Updater extends Ajax.Request, we can still access all the configuration options of the parent class when using the Ajax.Updater, as outlined in table 3.1. In addition to these, some additional configuration options are provided, as listed in table 4.1.

Table 4.1   Optional properties of the Ajax.Updater object

Name	Default value	Comments
`insertion`	`null`	A Prototype.js Insertion object (see chapter 11) that, if present, will be used to insert the response content into the existing markup for the target element. If omitted, the response replaces any existing markup.
`evalScripts`	`false`	When a DOM element's content is rewritten using innerHTML, `<script>` tags present in the markup are ignored. The Ajax.Updater will strip out any `<script>` tags in the response. If `evalScripts` is set to `true`, the content of these scripts will be evaluated.
`onComplete`	`null`	Supplied by Ajax.Request-see table 3.1. Programmatic callbacks can still be used with the Ajax.Updater. These will be executed after the target's content has been updated.

Ajax.Updater neatly encapsulates a commonly used way of working with Ajax. We'll make use of this object in our QuickGallery application too, and look at its advantages and disadvantages compared with direct use of the Ajax.Request.

4.1.2   Ajax.PeriodicalUpdater

The Ajax.PeriodicalUpdater helper class adds a final twist to the Prototype Ajax classes, once again automating a commonly used Ajax coding idiom. Ajax.PeriodicalUpdater extends Ajax.Updater by managing a timer object, so that the request for fresh content is made automatically with a given frequency. Using this object, an automatically updating stock ticker or news feed, for example, can be created with a minimum of fuss. The Ajax.PeriodicalUpdater class is a direct descendant of Ajax. Updater, and, as such, has access to all of its configuration options. New options provided by Ajax.PeriodicalUpdater are shown in table 4.2.

Table 4.2 Optional properties of the Ajax.Updater object

Name	Default value	Comments
frequency	2	Frequency of automatic update of the content, measured in seconds.
decay	1	Decay in frequency of updates when the received response is the same as the previous response. Set to a value less than 1 to increase the frequency on successive polls, or greater than 1 to decrease the frequency (i.e., increase the length of time between updates).

The Ajax.PeriodicalUpdater class also introduces two useful methods, stop() and start(), which will pause and resume the automated polling of the server.

Ajax.PeriodicalUpdater is useful for situations where regular updates from the server are required. It should be noted, though, that it makes it extremely easy to increase both the amount of HTTP traffic that an application generates, and the load on the server. It should therefore be used with caution.

As you can see, Prototype provides us with some very useful tools for content-centric Ajax. In the next section, we'll put them to use in our QuickGallery application. First, though, we'll round off our tour of the Ajax helper classes provided by Prototype with a quick mention of a recently added feature.

4.1.3 Ajax.Responders

In version 1.5 of Prototype, a new Ajax feature was added to the library. We've already seen in chapter 3 how to attach callback handler functions to an Ajax.Request object by specifying an onComplete, onSuccess, or onFailure option in the options passed to the constructor. These functions will be triggered only when a specific response comes in. In most cases, this is exactly what we need, but in a few cases, we might also want to be notified whenever any Ajax response comes in.

The Ajax.Responders object looks after this requirement for us. It maintains a list of objects that will automatically be notified whenever any Ajax request is made. We'll see the Ajax.Responders object in action later in this chapter.

That's enough of an introduction for now. In the next section, we'll return to the QuickGallery example and see how these extra Ajax helper classes operate.

4.2 Using HTML and Ajax

In this section, we'll develop the third Ajax-based version of QuickGallery. We originally applied Ajax to QuickGallery in order to get rid of unnecessary full-page refreshes in the app, and both of the implementations in chapter 3 succeeded on that score. However, we had to develop a lot of JavaScript code to handle the response data and manually update the user interface. On first glance,

Ajax.Updater looks like it will make things much simpler for us on the client. All we need to do is tell it which DOM node we want to update, and generate the request as we did previously.

In this section, we'll put those first impressions to the test and see how much added convenience Ajax.Updater really offers us.

4.2.1 *Generating the HTML fragment*

Let's get started, then. The most complex part of the user interface in QuickGallery is the thumbnail images, so we'll begin by generating HTML fragments for that. Because our server-side code is well-factored, we don't need to even touch our business logic, but simply alter the template that generates the response. Listing 2.2 presented the original template for the pre-Ajax application, and listing 3.2 the modified template for our XML-powered version of the app. Listing 4.1 shows how we've modified the template to generate a fragment of HTML.

Listing 4.1   contentUpdate/images.php

```php
<?php
require('../config.php');
require('images.inc.php');              ❶ Import
                                          business logic
if (count($imgs)>0){
  foreach ($imgs as $i => $value){
    $full_img=implode('/',array($path,$value));    ❷ Render
?>                                                    image tile
<div class='img_tile'>
  <img border='0'
    src="<?php echo $img_pre_path.$full_img ?>.thumb.jpg"
    onclick="showCloseup('<?php echo $img_pre_path.$full_img ?>.jpg')"/>
  <br/>
  <?php echo $value ?>
  </a>
</div>
<?php
  }
}
?>
```

The template is very straightforward. We simply import the business logic code ❶ that generates the data on thumbnails, subfolders, etc., for the current folder, and then iterate over the list of images, outputting a bit of HTML for each one ❷. So far, so good. Now let's take a look at the client.

4.2.2 *Modifying the client-side code*

On the client side, our task is equally simple. In the `load()` function, we create an Ajax.Updater object rather than an Ajax.Request, and pass it a reference to the DOM element that we want to receive the content. The code required to do this is as follows:

```
function load(newPath){
  if (newPath!=null){ currPath=newPath; }
  new Ajax.Updater(
    "images",
    "images.php?path="+currPath,
    {
      method: "get",
      onComplete: function(){
        Element.hide(ui.closeup);
      }
    }
  );
}
```

Creating the Ajax.Updater looks pretty familiar after our work with Ajax.Request, but there is an extra argument present in our call to the constructor. Let's stop and look at the arguments we passed into Ajax.Updater. The first is the name of the DOM element, in this case images. We've passed in a string here, but Ajax.Updater will also accept a reference to the DOM element itself. Most Prototype functions and objects that work with DOM nodes provide this flexibility, because the `$()` function makes it so simple to resolve either as a programmatic reference to the element itself.

The second argument is the URL to our server-side resource, and the third argument is the collection of options. Ajax.Updater inherits all of the functionality of the Ajax.Request class, so it understands all of the options that Ajax.Request does (see table 3.1), and it operates on the same defaults. It also understands a few more options of its own, as we saw in table 4.1. For now, all we need to do is pass in the HTTP method that we're going to use, and a small function that we'll execute when the request completes, to ensure that the close-up DOM element is hidden from view (otherwise we might not be able to see our refreshed thumbnail view, as the two share the same portion of the screen).

So, Ajax.Updater has made life a lot easier for us. The server-side code is no more complex than before, and the client-side code is markedly simpler. However, in the case of our application, there is a catch. We'll look at the problem—and solutions—in the next section.

4.2.3 *Updating multiple DOM elements*

The code we've presented so far is admirably simple, but we have a problem. When we navigate to a new folder, we need to update the breadcrumb trail, the subfolders list, and the thumbnails. We've laid these out as three separate DOM elements on the page, but so far we've only updated one of them. The limitation of Ajax.Updater without evaluating scripts in the response is that the class updates only one element in an Ajax request.

Outlining the problem

So what are our options? We could create three Ajax.Updater objects, one for each element, but this would be extremely inefficient in several ways.

First, we'd be generating three HTTP requests. HTTP requests contain considerable bandwidth overhead in terms of the headers in the request and response, so we'd be adding to the bandwidth use of our app (see appendix A for more details of the HTTP protocol and appendix B for techniques for measuring HTTP traffic).

Second, on the server side, we'd need to execute our business logic three times, once for each request. In our case, that's three hits to the filesystem, and in other applications it might translate to three hits to the database, to some other network resource, or three runs of an expensive calculation. Either way, we're increasing the server load significantly. We could do the calculations once and store the results in session, but this would require us to write some tricky synchronization logic to ensure that the session gets tidied up at the right time. Remember, we're going down this route to make our client-side coding simpler. We don't want to simply trade it for more complex server-side code.

Finally, we'd need to account for the fact that the network is unpredictable and unreliable. We don't know in what order our requests will be processed or the responses will be returned. We don't want to update each element as the response returns, because it leaves the user interface in an inconsistent state. When we consider that we run the risk of some requests failing while others succeed, we face the problem of this inconsistency persisting indefinitely.

So, we've persuaded ourselves that we need to update all elements of the user interface in a single request. We could regenerate the entire page as a single top-level DOM element, but that would take us back to a full-page refresh. Our UI is pretty sparse at the moment, but if we had dressed it up a bit more, we'd be back in the world of flickering pages and clunky stop-start interactions, only with more code to maintain! Another dead end.

Fortunately, there is more than one way out for us that conveniently allows us to introduce some of Prototype's more advanced Ajax features. We'll see how it's done in the next section.

Attaching scripts to the response

Our first solution continues to use the Ajax.Updater object. Ajax.Updater allows us to attach script content to the response. Both the subfolder list and the breadcrumb trail are very simple in terms of the HTML behind their user interfaces, and if we're willing to put up with generating those interfaces in the JavaScript, we can pass the necessary data up with our request.

Here's how it works. When we add markup to the DOM using `innerHTML`, any `<script>` tags in the HTML text will be ignored by the browser. However, Ajax.Updater has a mechanism that allows it to extract the content of these script tags and evaluate them immediately after updating the DOM element. We can use this to generate calls to update the breadcrumbs and subfolders list, and achieve our aim of updating all user interface elements with a single request. Let's see what we need to do to make it work.

Our first job is to switch the feature on when we create the Ajax.Updater object. This is accomplished simply by passing in an extra option to the constructor, as follows (changes from the previous versions of this code, presented in section 3.2.3, are in bold):

```
function load(newPath){
  if (newPath!=null){ currPath=newPath; }
  new Ajax.Updater(
    "images",
    "images.php?path="+currPath,
    {
      method: "GET",
      evalScripts:true,
      onComplete: function(){
        Element.hide(ui.closeup);
      }
    }
  );
}
```

The `evalScripts` option simply tells the updater to execute any scripts that it extracts from the response.

Now that we've told it to do that, we need to generate the scripts. Listing 4.2 shows the modified PHP template, which corresponds to images.php in the contentScript directory.

Listing 4.2   images.php with added script tags

```php
<?php
require('../config.php');
require('images.inc.php');
$folder_list="";          ◁——❶ Compute folder list
if (count($subdirs)>0){
 $folder_list='"'.implode('","',$subdirs).'"';
}
?>
<script type='text/javascript'>  ◁——❷ Generate script tag
  showBreadcrumbs();
  showFolders([<?php echo $folder_list ?>]);
  imgCount=<?php echo count($imgs)?>;
  if (imgCount>0){
    Element.show(ui.images);
  }else{
    Element.hide(ui.images);
  }
</script>

<?php
if (count($imgs)>0){
  foreach ($imgs as $i => $value){
    $full_img=implode('/',array($path,$value));
?>
<div class='img_tile'>
  <img border='0'
    src="<?php echo $img_pre_path.$full_img ?>.thumb.jpg"
    onclick="showCloseup('<?php echo $img_pre_path.$full_img ?>.jpg')"/>
  <br/>
  <?php echo $value ?>
  </a>
</div>
<?php
  }
}
?>
```

The script that we've generated ❷ simply collates the list of subfolders as a string ❶ and calls two JavaScript functions that we've defined statically. The showBread-crumbs() function needs no arguments because the client-side code already knows the destination folder's path, having passed it down in the request. The second function, showFolders(), takes a JavaScript array as an argument, which we populate with the list of subfolders that we generated earlier. The line

```
showFolders([<?php echo $folder_list ?>]);
```

will generate code looking like this:

```
showFolders(["trees","foliage","flowers"]);
```

Or, if no subfolders are present, it will simply look like this:

```
showFolders([]);
```

We need to support the generated script by providing the functions that it calls in our static JavaScript. Fortunately, we've already written them when we developed the XML-based version of our Ajax app, so we need only repeat that here. The show-Breadcrumbs() method can be reused unaltered from listing 3.2. The showFolders() method needs a little bit of tweaking, as shown here (changes in bold, again):

```
function showFolders(folders){
  if (folders.length==0){
    Element.hide(ui.folders);
  }else{
    var links=folders.collect(
      function(value,index){
        var path=[data.path,value].join("/");
        return "<div onclick='load(\""+path+"\")'>"+value+"</div>";
      }
    );
    Element.show(ui.folders);
    ui.folders.innerHTML=links.join("");
  }
}
```

In the data-centric approach, we assigned the global value data.folders when we parsed the response, and iterated over that. Here, we're simply using the locally scoped variable passed in as an argument.

The astute reader will have noticed at this point that we've slipped from a purely content-centric approach to a mixture of content-centric and script-centric. That is, we're generating a mixture of HTML markup and client-side code. We noted in our earlier discussion of script-centric Ajax, in section 3.1.1, that this approach presents a danger of introducing tight coupling between the client- and server-side code bases. We also noted that the best way to avoid this was to define a high-level API in the static client code, and simply call that API in the generated code. This is what we've done here.

In addition to reducing coupling, keeping generated code to a minimum makes the application easier to maintain. Static JavaScript is easier to debug than dynamically generated code, and it is also more amenable to testing. We have also reduced the size of the response by abstracting out the common logic into a static API that needs be downloaded only once.

We've now implemented the complete QuickGallery app in a mostly content-centric way, with a bit of script-centric Ajax thrown in. The Ajax.Updater class looked at first like it was going to eliminate most of our code, and in a simpler application it might have done just that. Our requirement to simultaneously update more than one DOM element made us dig into some of the more advanced features of the Ajax.Updater object, but, even so, we've managed to simplify our client-side code base considerably.

Happily, Ajax.Updater has shown that it is capable of addressing the problem of updating multiple elements from a single response. Only one element can be updated as pure content, but we can pass additional instructions in the response as JavaScript.

Before we leave this topic of multiple-element refreshes, though, we should note that there's a second approach that we can take to solving this problem, using a different set of features from Prototype's Ajax support classes. We'll take a look at that in the next section.

Responding to custom headers

As an alternative to adding script tags to the response body, we can encode the additional information in the HTTP headers of the response. Recent builds of Prototype have added support for this, using the compact JSON syntax that we saw in the previous chapter. There are two parts to this approach, so let's take each in turn.

First, if a response contains a header called X-JSON, Prototype's Ajax classes will try to parse it and pass it to the callback functions as an extra parameter. In order to generate this header, we need to modify our PHP script, contentJSON/images.php, as follows (changes shown in bold, again):

```php
<?php
require('../config.php');
require('images.inc.php');
$folder_list="";
if (count($subdirs)>0){
 $folder_list='"'.implode('","',$subdirs).'"';
}
$json='{ folders:['.$folder_list.'], count:'.count($imgs).'}';
header('X-JSON: '.$json);
?>
<?php
if (count($imgs)>0){
  foreach ($imgs as $i => $value){
    $full_img=implode('/',array($path,$value));
?>
```

```
<div class='img_tile'>
  <img border='0'
    src="<?php echo $img_pre_path.$full_img ?>.thumb.jpg"
    onclick="showCloseup('<?php echo $img_pre_path.$full_img ?>.jpg')"/>
  <br/>
  <?php echo $value ?>
  </a>
</div>
<?php
  }
}
?>
```

When the response comes back, the body will now contain only the HTML for the main panel, and an additional header looking something like this:

```
X-JSON: { folders: ["trees","foliage"], count: 6 }
```

In this case, we're indicating that the current folder contains six images and has two subfolders, called "trees" and "foliage".

The second part of the solution involves picking this header up on the client and unpacking the data. Prototype will handle the evaluation of the JSON expression for us—the first thing we'll see of it is the parsed object appearing as an argument to our callback function. We could parse the JSON object within our main callback handler, but instead we're going to define a separate responder to handle it, using the Ajax.Responders object. This will give us the option of updating the subfolders list whenever we make an Ajax call, and not only when we're changing directory.

To set this up, we need to register a responder. The Ajax.Responders object provides a register() method for us, to which we pass our responder object. The responder can define any of the callbacks available to the Ajax.Request object. Here, we'll simply provide an onComplete() method. Let's look at the code now.

```
Ajax.Responders.register(
  {
    onComplete:function(request,transport,json){
      showBreadcrumbs();
      showFolders(json.folders);
      if (json.count!=null){
        if (json.count>0){
          Element.show(ui.images);
        }else{
          Element.hide(ui.images);
        }
      }
    }
  }
);
```

The `onComplete()` callback takes three arguments. The first is the Ajax.Request object that has received the response, the second is the underlying XHR transport, and the third is the parsed X-JSON header. This object contains all the information we need, so we can then call our existing API to update the breadcrumb trail and the folders list as before.

The Ajax.Updater object, then, is capable of combining ease of use with flexibility in handling multiple elements, and it can do so in more than one way. We've now completed implementations of QuickGallery using a variety of different Ajax techniques. We'll compare these in section 4.3, but first we're going to look at the final Ajax helper object that Prototype provides.

4.2.4 *Automatically updating content*

We've now solved the issue of updating multiple elements within a content-based approach in two ways, by using `<script>` tags and JSON-formatted headers. Along the way, we've seen practical use of two of the three advanced Ajax helpers that we introduced in section 4.1. Before we move on to compare content- and data-centric Ajax, we'll briefly take a look at the third of the advanced Ajax helpers, the PeriodicalUpdater.

There are a number of use cases in which it is desirable for the server to be able to notify the browser of updates. HTTP is not built to support this model of interaction—all interactions must be initiated by the browser. A common workaround is for the browser to poll the server at regular intervals for updates. (This is not the only way of implementing a push of data from server to client, but that's outside the scope of our discussion here.)

Let's suppose that we want the images in the current folder to automatically update at regular intervals, so that we can see new images posted to the site. Using plain JavaScript, we'd need to start creating timer objects using `setTimeout()`, but Prototype wraps all this up for us in the Ajax.PeriodicalUpdater object.

To make the QuickGallery poll the server for updates, we only need to alter a couple of lines of code. Using Ajax.Updater, our `load()` method read as follows:

```
function load(newPath){
  if (newPath!=null){ currPath=newPath; }
  new Ajax.Updater(
    "images",
    "images.php?path="+currPath,
    {
      method: "get",
      evalScripts: true,
```

```
      onComplete: function(){
        Element.hide(ui.closeup);
      }
    }
  );
}
```

To make our Updater poll the server, we simply need to replace Ajax.Updater with Ajax.PeriodicalUpdater, as shown here:

```
function load(newPath){
  if (newPath!=null){ currPath=newPath; }
  if (updater){
    updater.stop();
  }
  updater=new Ajax.PeriodicalUpdater(
    "images",
    "images.php?path="+currPath,
    {
      method: "get",
      evalScripts: true,
      frequency: 10,
      onComplete: function(){
        Element.hide(ui.closeup);
      }
    }
  );
}
```

We also added a frequency value in the options object. This specifies the time between receiving a response and sending out the next request, in seconds. Here, we've set a ten-second delay. Tuning this parameter is very application-specific, and it boils down to a trade-off between responsiveness and server load.

That's all there is to the Ajax.PeriodicalUpdater object. We don't have a desperate need for automatic updates in our gallery app, so we won't be carrying this change forward as we develop the app further, but hopefully we've demonstrated how easy it is to add that functionality if needed. We'll get back on track now, and return to the debate between content- and data-centric Ajax.

We've now implemented no less than four Ajax-based versions of the Quick-Gallery application that we described in chapter 2, each of which reproduces the functionality of the original application completely. In chapter 3, we developed two data-centric versions, in which the client-side code parsed raw data sent by the server, in the form of XML and JSON. In this chapter, we developed two content-centric implementations of the app, in which the server updated the main panel by directly generating the HTML, and updated secondary elements by adding extra <script> tags, or by passing JSON data in the header.

Before we go on to add any new functionality, which we'll do in chapter 12, we have a decision to make: we must decide whether to follow the data-centric or content-centric approach. We'll compare the two approaches in the following section, with an eye to seeing which will make life easiest for us as we begin to add new features.

4.3 Comparing data- and content-centric Ajax

We've implemented two versions of the application using Ajax, each with two variations, and now we face a difficult choice. We can easily draw up a long wish-list of new features for the QuickGallery application, and can envisage several additional months of development work implementing them all. In order for this development to be effective, we need to opt for either a data-centric or a content-centric approach. How are we going to make this decision?

There are several criteria that we can take into consideration, such as ease of development, support for the approach by our toolset, the efficiency and performance of the application, and how future-proof each solution is as our requirements expand. Breaking down our assessment in this way won't get us off the hook entirely—we'll still have a difficult decision to make at the end of the day, but at least it will be an informed decision. So let's consider each of our criteria in turn.

4.3.1 Considering ease of development

Ease of development cannot be measured in a hard and fast way, as it is ultimately subjective. Let's begin with the assumption that all code is difficult to write, and therefore the less code written, the easier the project is. It isn't as simple as that in reality, of course, and we'll unpack some of the nuances shortly, but this approach allows us to put forward some numbers to start the discussion.

Table 4.3 lists the total size of the files of each type in our three solutions in bytes, as reported by the Unix `ls` command. Numbers in parentheses indicate files reused without modification by an Ajax project from the non-Ajax project. The total for JavaScript files excludes the size of the Prototype libraries, as it took us negligible effort to download them and start using them.

The first thing we can see from these numbers is that all three Ajax projects required more code to be written than their non-Ajax counterpart. While the server-side code became simpler, we added a lot of client-side JavaScript. Of the two Ajax projects, the data-centric one required almost twice as much code as the content-centric one.

Table 4.3 Size of the QuickGallery projects by file type (in bytes)

Solution	PHP	HTML	JavaScript	Total
non-Ajax	4175	0	0	4175
content-centric Ajax	3841 (3122)	421	1659	5936
data-centric Ajax (XML)	3599 (3122)	433	3218	7250
data-centric Ajax (JSON)	3451 (3122)	421	2738	6610

As we already noted, not all code is equally difficult to write, either. Simply by virtue of using two programming languages instead of one, we've presumably ramped up the difficulty level by introducing Ajax. We haven't had to write very much additional PHP, and what we did write was simple template stuff, but looking forward we still have to maintain our existing business logic code. So the main extra burden comes from the JavaScript.

But we knew that already. Our immediate concern is the difference between content-centric and data-centric Ajax. The content-centric Ajax required less code. When we look at the extra code required by the data-centric approach, we see a lot of involved user interface generation, and unpleasant DOM manipulation routines in the XML case too. If we accept that not all JavaScript code is equally difficult to write, the content-centric approach is even more of a clear winner here.

Let's note another point in the content-centric solution's favor. If we compare the two PHP templates that we had to write, the one for the content-centric solution is largely a direct cut and paste of PHP from the non-Ajax code. It isn't elegant reuse, but it is easier to write than the XML- or JSON-based templates, both of which required us to figure out a new data format.

Is the content-centric solution always the clear winner, then? There is one final point that we ought to consider. Our PHP template for the content-centric approach benefited from the fact that our legacy app was HTML-based. In another situation, we might have inherited an XML document format, in which case the data-centric Ajax solution might require very little work on the server. Reuse is king as far as ease of development is concerned, and reuse is highly context-dependent. If we're "Ajaxifying" a straightforward HTML-based web application, we'll find more scope for reuse in the content-centric option. In an enterprise setting, the XML data-centric solution might hold its own.

However, all in all, the content-centric approach seems to have won this round. Let's move on to our next criterion.

4.3.2 *Fitting the tools*

Ease of development in itself is a good thing. When considering which style of programming to use in a project, though, it's also useful to look at any supporting libraries that we're making use of, and ask ourselves which styles they favor. This ties in closely to ease of use, but it also gives an indication of how the library might develop in the future. If we're having to fight against the library to achieve our ends, and work around the recommended usage of that library or use undocumented features, future versions of the library might break those workarounds. Being left to rely on an old, unsupported version of a library is not a comfortable situation.

The main library we've used so far is Prototype.js. Prototype is very much geared toward doing things in a content-centric way. The specialist Ajax helper classes that we saw in this chapter are all geared toward the content-centric approach. Further, so is the entire Ruby on Rails development movement, both in the design of the framework and in the opinions expressed by leading Rails developers. We don't need to be using Rails for this to be a consideration. Prototype's main author, Sam Stephenson, is a core Rails committer, and its a fair bet that Prototype will continue to evolve to support the content-centric way of doing Ajax. Recent developments in Prototype (and in Ruby on Rails) are exploring script- and data-centric approaches, but only as complements to the core content-centric approach.

So, round two goes to the content-centric approach too. The next criterion that we put up for consideration was the performance of the app, so let's look at that.

4.3.3 *Comparing performance*

While it is important to work in a style that makes development easy, it's also important that our methodology produces code that runs efficiently. After all, we'd rather pay the price of difficult development once than the price of poor performance continually.

There has been a lot of debate about whether Ajax increases or decreases the efficiency of an application. Tuning in to this debate, we've heard good things about the reduction in traffic that comes from not continually sending boilerplate markup over the wire, and concerns expressed about the increased network traffic resulting from too many little messages being exchanged between the client and the server. Being cautious types, we aren't going to believe either argument until we've seen some hard numbers, and fortunately, there are a number of tools out there that can help us get those numbers.

We've defined a simple methodology for analyzing live HTTP traffic from any web application running in any web browser. We describe all the technical details in appendix B, but as this is the first time we've used our analysis toolkit, let's run through the procedure right now, before we look at the numbers.

The bandwidth that an application consumes is unlikely to be regular. All the time that the user is interacting with the app, there will be traffic between the browser and the server. Because we're interested in the overall impact on the network of our app, we're going to have to define a test script to represent a typical session with the server. Our test script for working with the QuickGallery application is quite straightforward and is outlined in table 4.4. In order to write the test script, we created a sample set of images to be viewed by the QuickGallery, taken from Dave's copious collection of photos that sit on his computer doing nothing. (I knew they'd come in useful one day!)

Table 4.4   Script used for monitoring the performance of QuickGallery

Step	Description
1	Browser starts on the home page
2	User navigates into the "animals" folder, which contains 8 images
3	User clicks on the first thumbnail to view close-up
4	User returns to the home folder by the breadcrumb trail
5	User navigates to the "plants" folder, which contains 38 images
6	User navigates into the "foliage" subfolder (only 2 images)
7	User returns to the "plants" folder
8	User navigates into the "trees" subfolder, which holds 7 images
9	User clicks the first thumbnail in "trees" to view close-up

Because our three versions of the Ajax app have identical functionality at this point, we can apply the same script to all our tests. The test will be executed manually, so we kept it fairly short and made sure to flush the browser's cache in between runs. While running the test script, we recorded all the traffic, in this case using the LiveHttpHeaders plug-in for Mozilla. We then saved the HTTP session data as a text file and ran it through our script to generate a data file that could be read by a spreadsheet. We then used the spreadsheet to analyze the traffic and create a few pretty graphs. The nitty-gritty on how to achieve all these steps is given in appendix B.

Here and now, we want to see what the different flavors of Ajax have done for the performance of our application, so let's have a look at the results. Figure 4.1 compares the total HTTP traffic generated by three of the QuickGallery applications, namely the non-Ajax version from chapter 2, the XML version from chapter 3, and the content-centric version from this chapter.

The first thing to notice is that viewing the close-up images takes by far the biggest toll on the network. The images weigh roughly 700 KB each. They dominate the traffic so much, in fact, that we've modified the scale of the vertical axis, in order to be able to see what's going on in the other steps of the script.

One reason often cited for not adopting Ajax—and Ajax frameworks in particular—is the weight of the additional code. As we can see in figure 4.1, the initial loading of the home page is far greater for the two Ajax apps, largely because we're loading roughly 40 KB of Prototype.js. (This data was recorded against Prototype version 1.4. Version 1.5 has grown to a little over 50 KB.) However, viewed against the traffic as a whole, it isn't making much of a difference.

In subsequent steps of the test script, we can see that the Ajax apps are making a small positive difference, with the data-centric approach typically consuming a little less bandwidth than the content-centric version. The most notable difference is in step 7, in which the non-Ajax app consumes over 100 KB, whereas the Ajax apps

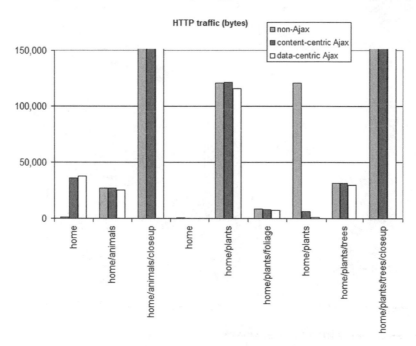

Figure 4.1 HTTP traffic generated at each step of the test script, for non-Ajax, content-centric, and data-centric Ajax versions of the QuickGallery app

consume practically nothing. Looking at the details of the logs, we can see that this is due to not having to refetch the thumbnail images for the "plants" folder.

In order to get a clearer picture of the contributions to overall traffic levels from the various types of data being sent, we've also plotted the traffic breakdown by MIME type in figure 4.2.

The pie charts in the lower half of the figure show the contribution from all media types, excepting the two large close-up images, which we've omitted again in order to make the other details show up. Even so, 90 percent or more of the total traffic comes from images. It's instructive to note how small the program-

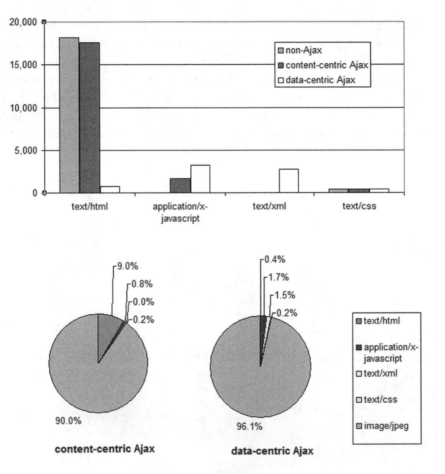

Figure 4.2   Breakdown of HTTP traffic by MIME type

matic elements of the Ajax app are in the face of broadband-sized media such as high-resolution images, videos, and audio.

The bar chart in the top half of figure 4.2 shows the relative makeup of the three apps' traffic, once we've taken the images out of the equation. It's interesting to note that our content-centric Ajax application generates almost as much HTML as the non-Ajax app, although we might expect a larger difference if the design of the application weren't so spartan. Certainly, comparing the HTML generated by the content-centric app against the XML generated by the data-centric app, we can see that the data-centric app is making more efficient use of the network when transmitting the navigational information. In order to do so, it requires roughly twice as much JavaScript code as the content-centric app.

So, in terms of overall impact on the network, how do the three solutions stack up? Figure 4.3 plots the cumulative HTTP traffic for each application.

The clear take-home message from this picture is that Ajax is good for the network. Our simple nine-step test script equates to only a minute or so of use of the

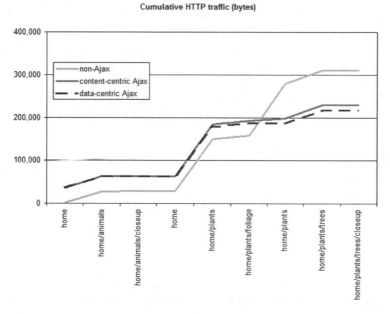

Figure 4.3 Cumulative use of bandwidth by the Ajax and non-Ajax QuickGallery applications

QuickGallery application, and we've already made a significant net saving in bandwidth by step 7. Remember, at that point, the non-Ajax application reloaded all the thumbnail images, whereas the Ajax apps didn't. If we've been looking for a clear signal to adopt Ajax as we take our development forward, this is it.

As we said earlier, there is plenty of folklore about Ajax network performance floating around on the Internet. Looking at the numbers for ourselves, we've established that Ajax is good for bandwidth in our particular application. We've also confirmed the story that data-centric solutions make more efficient use of the network than content-centric solutions (see figure 4.2). However, we can also see from figure 4.3 that in the overall picture, these savings aren't worth a great deal. This also sheds some light on the often-quoted adage that XML is a nasty, bloated data format. We aren't saying that it isn't bloated, but the bloat doesn't figure much in the overall scheme of things.

So, do we have a clear winner in terms of bandwidth performance? It seems not—we have to call this round a tie, or a very narrow victory for the data-centric version of QuickGallery at the best.

Before we move on, we ought to stress that this is a verdict about the QuickGallery application, not about data- and content-centric Ajax in general. We don't wish to add to the folklore that's out there, and we urge you to measure your own application's performance using the tools that we describe in appendix B and take things from there. Now let's move on to the final criterion for comparing the different styles of Ajax, so that we can arrive at a decision as to which one we'll use when we develop extra functionality into the QuickGallery app.

4.3.4 *Looking for future-proof solutions*

We've seen how our current content-centric and data-centric Ajax apps stack up against the non-Ajax app, and against each other, but we have to bear in mind that these are little more than prototypes of the all-singing, all-dancing QuickGallery that we want to go on to create. We have big plans for our app, and a to-do list as long as your arm, so we need to consider whether the two types of Ajax will be able to grow with us.

Our requirements are somewhat vague at the moment, but we do know that we want to be able to attach metadata to our images and sort the folder contents using this metadata. We also want to loosen the mapping between the navigation of the images and the underlying filesystem, so that we can display "virtual folder" contents based on search criteria. We also might want to be able to show more than one folder's contents side by side. Storing the metadata and running the searches are mostly server-side issues, but we want to be able to edit the metadata and rearrange folder contents in the browser. To satisfy these requirements, we can see that it would be useful to have some sort of model of the folder tree held in the JavaScript layer. The data-centric approach lends itself more readily to maintaining such a model, so we find ourselves leaning in that direction when we consider this issue.

This sort of discussion can be very open-ended, and it can be hard to determine how easy or difficult the unimplemented features will be, based on choices that we might make. We can, however, look at our experience in getting this far. The content-centric application was certainly easier to write, but we already ran into issues with wanting to update multiple DOM elements from a single Ajax request. While we found a workaround by updating the sidebar and breadcrumb trail using scripts, this was something of a kludge, and it only worked because the content of the secondary DOM elements was so simple. If we implement the ability to view multiple folders at once, we might want to update several thumbnail windows at once. Prototype's Ajax helpers solve the multiple update problem in simple cases, but only by falling back on script- or data-centric Ajax for the secondary updates.

All other considerations—ease of use, fit to the Prototype.js library, and performance of the network traffic—have either pointed us toward the content-centric model or come out neutral. This is the only major obstacle to adopting a content-centric approach as we go forward, so can we see a way of getting around these problems? One possibility is to extend Ajax.Updater to support refreshing multiple DOM elements from a single response. While this will entail some extra development work, Prototype.js provides a very good mechanism for extending existing objects, so the overhead shouldn't be too large.

So we have a decision. For this project, we're adopting the content-centric approach. The decision was fairly close, and our aim here is not to promote content-centric Ajax as the only solution for all problems. Rather, we hope we've shown the process by which we've made the decision, and the range of factors that we've taken into account.

4.4 *Summary*

In this chapter, we looked at Prototype's advanced Ajax classes and their support for the content-centric style of Ajax. We also explored some of the features that provide secondary script- and data-centric support. We applied these classes to our QuickGallery application and noticed a significant improvement in developer productivity over the data-centric approach that we used in chapter 3.

In deciding which approach to use as our application development goes forward, we looked at a range of criteria. By analyzing the HTTP traffic, we were able to see significant improvements over the non-Ajax application. The data-centric approach came first in only one category: performance of HTTP traffic. However, although the data-centric application made better use of the network than the content-centric one, the overall impact for our application was insignificantly small, leaving the content-centric approach as the clear way forward.

It's important to stress again that we reached this decision for this specific application. Rather than remembering the conclusion that we came to, we urge you to remember our decision-making process, and follow it in order to reach your own conclusions.

This concludes our review of Prototype.js's Ajax helper classes. In the next section of the book, we're going to look at the Scriptaculous library, and the ways in which it can enhance the usability of our application.

Part 2

Scriptaculous Quickly

This part of the book provides an in-depth look at Scriptaculous. Although Scriptaculous is built on top of Prototype, we've chosen to present Scriptaculous first because it presents a number of quick wins for the web app developer, and it can be used without a detailed knowledge of Prototype. To a newcomer to these libraries, we believe that this is the most likely entry point for learning these libraries. Scriptaculous provides plenty of instant gratification, whereas Prototype's power is more low-key, and better learned slowly. This is not to say that Scriptaculous doesn't contain complex code too, and, for each of the topics covered in this part of the book, we will walk you through from the one-line first encounter to mastery of the details of the library.

Chapter 5 examines the Effects library, which provides a dazzling range of animations and special effects to liven up your web pages. As well as showing you how to create these effects, we also provide some guidance on when to use them, so as to improve the usability of your app without sinking it under a barrage of fireworks!

Chapter 6 looks at the Scriptaculous Controls library, and, again, discusses how to make use of these widgets in your applications, as well as explaining how they work and how to configure them.

Chapter 7 describes the drag-and-drop system in Scriptaculous, and shows how to use a single line of code to do everything from making it possible to drag an image across the page to creating sets of sortable lists on a page.

Scriptaculous Effects 5

This chapter covers

- Obtaining and setting up Scriptaculous
- Using Scriptaculous core and combination effects
- Customizing Scriptaculous effects

Special effects can add pizzazz and excitement to any feature movie from the Hollywood film machine. But if overdone, poorly executed, or used in lieu of essential elements like plot and characterization, effects can also lead to the utter ruin of an action flick. Just take a look at what's in the dollar DVD bin of your local discount store if you need convincing. Likewise, adding animation effects to your web application is a double-edged sword that must be wielded carefully.

Animation effects can reinforce a message, clarify a user interface paradigm, and even entertain. But they can just as easily cloud the interaction, distract the user, and annoy your visitors. Properly utilized, animation effects should emphasize the message of the site, clarify or reinforce the user interaction, or mildly entertain (bearing in mind that something that's mildly entertaining on first viewing might become stupefyingly tedious after that).

Take the Ratings component example of the first chapter (listing 1.5). In its final, polished form, animation effects were added to punctuate the interaction that occurred whenever a rating was changed. When a star was added to the rating, it pulsated for a few seconds as it was added to the component. This effect serves to ensure that the user doesn't miss the fact that a star was added if they were to blink or momentarily look away. If the new star appeared instantaneously, a distracted user might be left wondering "did it change the rating or not?"

Even more apropos is the animation effect that occurs when a rating is lowered, causing a star to appear to "drop off" the component. This effect again underscores the interaction, and unequivocally informs the user that the rating has been lowered.

Imagine that rather than dropping out, the star turned various colors, whirled in place a few times, and then spiraled around the page before disappearing. While perhaps mildly entertaining on first viewing (and probably incredibly tedious after that), all that activity has absolutely nothing to do with the interaction that has occurred. No part of that effect conveys any additional information to the user about the nature of the interaction. In fact, it might even distract the user to the point where she is left not even noticing that a star has been removed from the component and instead is left wondering, "what just happened?" How counterproductive!

In this chapter, we'll see how Scriptaculous makes adding effects to your web applications easy and fun. But this ease should not be taken as a license to take a holiday from common sense. Use this newly found power responsibly, and you will be rewarded with spectacular user interfaces that not only are fun to write, but enjoyable and easy for visitors to use.

5.1 Quick win: adding an effect with only one line

If you read through the entire example in chapter 1, you've already seen how easy it is to add an effect with Scriptaculous, but let's work through another small example.

Let's say that we have some running text in which a famous quote is embedded. Perhaps something along these lines:

```
<body>
  <p>Someone famous once said:<p>
  <blockquote id="theQuote">
    Necessity never made a good bargain. &mdash; Ben Franklin
  </blockquote>
  <p>And I believe him.
</body>
```

We've used a `<blockquote>` element to add visual emphasis to the quote, but we want to add that little "something extra" to make it pop. So we've decided to make the quote fade into view as the visitor reads the first paragraph.

We'll address how to set up and include the Scriptaculous library shortly, but for now we'll do a bit of hand-waving and simply add this effect to our page by adding this single line to the page's `onload` handler:

```
new Effect.Opacity('theQuote',{duration:1.5,from:0.0,to:1.0});
```

It's that easy. In Scriptaculous, an effect is created by the act of instantiating one of the effect objects, passing it the information regarding the element to which the effect is to be applied as well as some optional values that specify how the effect is to be applied.

Again, how easy is that? The code for the entire page is shown in listing 5.1.

Listing 5.1 A quick win with Scriptaculous

```
<html>
  <head>
    <title>Quick Win!</title>                        ❶ Import Prototype
    <script type="text/javascript"                      and Scriptaculous
          src="../scripts/prototype.js"></script>
    <script type="text/javascript"
          src="../scripts/scriptaculous.js?load=effects"></script>
    <script>
      window.onload = function() {        ❷ Apply
          new Effect.Opacity(                effect
            'theQuote',
            {duration:1.5, from:0.0, to:1.0});
      }
```

```
      </script>
   </head>

   <body>
      <p>Someone famous once said:</p>
      <blockquote id="theQuote">     <----
        Necessity never made a good bargain. &mdash; Ben Franklin
      </blockquote>
      <p>And I believe him.</p>
   </body>
</html>
```

**Define effect
target**

One of the first things we do on our page is import the Prototype and Scriptaculous libraries ❶. Scriptaculous is built upon Prototype, and whenever you import the Scriptaculous JavaScript library, you'll also need to include Prototype. Not that that's an issue. We've already seen how useful Prototype can be, and we wouldn't want to be without it in any case! We'll learn more about setting up Scriptaculous in section 5.2.

In the window's onload handler, we apply the effect by instantiating an effect object ❷. Inspecting the parameters passed to the constructor for the Effect.Opacity object, we can readily deduce that the first parameter is the ID of the target element to which the effect is to be applied; in this case, the <blockquote> element to which we assigned the ID of theQuote.

The second parameter ... well, that's a little more complex. Like the Prototype library upon which it is built, and which had a heavy influence on its design, Scriptaculous makes extensive use of hashes (also known as associative arrays) created as anonymous objects to pass optional parameters. We've already seen this sort of mechanism at work in the constructor for the Ajax.Request object in chapter 3. Check out section 3.1.2 if you want to refresh your memory.

In this example, that second parameter specifies that the effect is to last for 1.5 seconds, and that during that time the opacity is to be adjusted from the value 0.0 (invisible) to 1.0 (fully opaque).

5.2 *Setting up Scriptaculous and the examples*

If you haven't yet downloaded the sample code for this book, now would be a good time. The material in this and other chapters is much easier to grasp with concrete code examples to read and execute.

Within this sample code, you will find a folder for the chapter 5 sample applications. You can either inspect the folders and load files individually, or you can display the index.html page for chapter 5 in your browser. This page displays a "control panel" for the code of this chapter, as shown in figure 5.1. Note that this page contains links to all the sample application pages that we'll be discussing in this chapter, including the Quick Win example.

Scriptaculous is already set up within the code examples, but when it comes time to write your own code, you'll need to obtain a copy of Scriptaculous and set it up in your own web applications. As such things go, Scriptaculous is extremely easy to set up.

5.2.1 *Getting Scriptaculous*

As we write this, the Scriptaculous download is available at

```
http://script.aculo.us/downloads
```

Given the nature of the URL, it's unlikely to change by the time you read this, but the web being what it is, you never know! The download is available as a compressed tar file for Unix-based systems, and as a zip file for Windows. Users of Mac OS X, comfortable with either format, can choose either.

Once the download is unpacked, you will find the expected read me, change log, and license files. You will also find a folder named lib, which contains the version of Prototype that you should use with the Scriptaculous files.

Under a folder named src, you will find the Scriptaculous .js files. Scriptaculous divides itself among a number of .js files so that, if desired, you can pick and choose which parts are to be loaded. This allows you to better control the

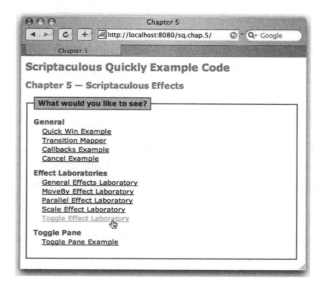

Figure 5.1
The chapter 5 control panel page

download footprint of your pages. Section 5.2.2 will discuss how to control which libraries are loaded.

Copy all the .js files from the src folder, as well as the Prototype file from the lib folder, to a convenient location within your web application. In our sample code for this chapter, we placed them in a scripts folder rooted at the base of the chapter 5 folder. The files should include builder.js, controls.js, dragdrop.js, effects.js, scriptaculous.js, and slider.js.

It is imperative that you place all of the files from the src folder into the same target folder. The library loading mechanism of Scriptaculous will not work if you spread the files out across multiple folders.

Now we're ready to load Scriptaculous into our pages.

5.2.2 *Loading the Scriptaculous libraries*

The easiest way to load Scriptaculous into a page is to simply import the scriptaculous.js file, as we did in our Quick Win example:

```
<script type="text/javascript"
        src="scripts/scriptaculous.js"></script>
```

This causes the Scriptaculous loading mechanism to automatically import all the remaining script files. For our small example page, that probably wasn't the smartest thing we could do. Within that page, we only employed the Effects library, so loading everything was a bit of a waste of bandwidth.

Scriptaculous provides a loading mechanism that allows us to specify which libraries to load via a query parameter that we place on the reference to the scriptaculous.js file. If the parameter is omitted, all the libraries are loaded, but if provided, it is a comma-delimited list of the libraries to load.

If we wanted to put our Quick Win page on a bit of a bandwidth diet, limiting the script loading to just the Effects library, we could change our script import line like this:

```
<script type="text/javascript"
        src="scripts/scriptaculous.js?load=effects"></script>
```

This tells Scriptaculous to only load the Effects library.

Note that you are never expected to use a script import on any file except the master scriptaculous.js file itself. Other files are automatically imported using the Scriptaculous loading mechanism from the master script.

If you are curious as to how Scriptaculous accomplishes this, take a look inside the surprisingly short scriptaculous.js file. But you may want to wait until you've got a little more Prototype expertise under your belt, as the loading mechanism makes heavy use of some of the wonderful tools Prototype provides.

Now we're ready to actually use the Scriptaculous effects, so let's have a look at them in more depth.

5.3 *Types of Scriptaculous effects*

Scriptaculous divides its effects into two categories: core effects and combination effects. The core effects primarily consist of some basic animations, which the combination effects build upon to create more complex animations.

The effects, both core and combination, are listed in table 5.1 with brief descriptions. We'll get up-close and personal with them in the next section.

Table 5.1   The core and combination effects

	Effect	Description
Core effects	Opacity	Adjusts the opacity of the target element.
	Highlight	Adjusts the background color of the target element.
	Scale	Adjusts the size of the target element.
	MoveBy	Adjusts the position of the target element.
	Parallel	Allows multiple effects to be executed smoothly in parallel (see section 5.9). Although listed as an effect, Parallel is actually a wrapper.
Combination effects	Appear	Adjusts the opacity of the target element after revealing it.
	Fade	Adjusts the opacity of the target element and then hides it.
	Puff	Expands the target element while adjusting its opacity.
	DropOut	Moves the target element down the page while fading its opacity.
	Shake	Moves the target element left and right a few times.
	SwitchOff	Flickers the opacity of the target element, and then collapses and hides it (emulating switching off a television).
	BlindUp	Progressively hides the target element from the bottom up.
	BlindDown	Progressively reveals the element from top to bottom.
	SlideUp	Slides the target element up until it is hidden.
	SlideDown	Slides the target element down until it is fully revealed.
	Pulsate	Adjusts the opacity of the target element multiple times through a range.
	Squish	Reduces the target element in size (toward the top left) until it is hidden.

Table 5.1   The core and combination effects *(continued)*

	Effect	Description
Combination effects *(continued)*	Fold	Reduces the target element in size from top to bottom, then right to left, until it is hidden.
	Grow	Reveals the target by scaling it from zero to full size in a specified direction.
	Shrink	Hides the target element by scaling it from full size to zero in a specified direction.

5.4   *Understanding the effects*

In this section we will take a look at each effect in detail. We will learn how each effect works, and how the `duration`, `from`, and `to` common options are applied (or not; some effects will ignore the common options). If the effect accepts effect-specific parameters or effect-specific options, they will also be described.

It would be difficult to show the animation effects in any meaningful way on printed pages, so extensive sample pages have been provided within the example code for this book. If you have yet to download the code for this book, now would be good time to take the time to grab it at http://www.manning.com/crane3. The material covered in this chapter is much easier to follow if you can load and interact with the provided pages.

One important example page is the Effects Lab page (lab-general.html), located in the "labs" subfolder. This file implements an effects laboratory that we will use to experiment with the various effects in order to demonstrate their operation.

5.4.1   *The effects laboratory*

The purpose of the Effects Lab page is to allow us to see the Scriptaculous effects in action, and to observe the consequences that various options have upon the effect.

When initially displayed in a browser, the Effects Lab page appears as shown in figure 5.2.

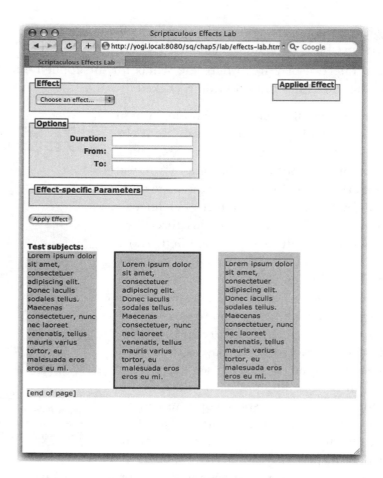

Figure 5.2   The Effects Lab page can help you understand how the effects operate

The page is fairly simple in layout and use. At the top is a form containing five sections:

- A drop-down list that allows you to choose a Scriptaculous Effect to apply.

- Input controls for the options that will be applied to the effect. If the effect allows options specific to itself to be applied, they are displayed here when the effect is chosen from the drop-down list.

- Input controls for any extra parameters that the effect takes. Only the Scale and MoveBy effects take extra parameters, so if one of those effects is chosen, input controls for the effect-specific parameters will be displayed.

- An Apply Effect button that applies the specified effect with the options and parameters specified by the input elements.

- An Applied Effect display area where the syntax for the applied effect will be shown after the Apply Effect button is clicked.

Note that in order to keep the page fairly simple, little in the way of error checking is performed on the input elements. So, if an option, such as duration, expects a numeric value, be sure to specify a valid one or you will receive JavaScript errors. Feel free to make the page more robust using your JavaScript skills if you feel so inclined.

The bottom section of the page contains three "test subjects" upon which the effects will be applied, and a horizontal bar indicating the end of the page. The significance of this marker will be explained shortly.

Expanding the drop-down list at the top of the page shows the effects that can be chosen, as shown in figure 5.3.

All of the Scriptaculous effects, both core and combination, are included in this drop-down list save for the Parallel effect, which isn't really an effect at all (see section 5.9). To experiment with the operation of each effect, we will choose it from the drop-down list, specify options and any parameters, and click the Apply Effect button. The effect will be applied to the test subjects, and the syntax for the applied effect will be displayed.

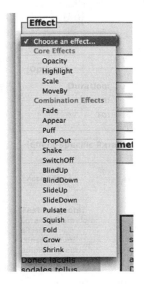

Figure 5.3 The Effects drop-down list gives you easy access to the core and combination effects

For now, bring up the Effects Lab page and run through the various effects leaving the option fields blank so that their defaults will apply. For effects that take parameters, fill in some test values (what the parameters represent should be fairly obvious even at this point).

You will note that some effects, like Opacity, don't do anything at all with the options defaulted. Others, such as Appear, don't have any effect when the element is already displayed. But apply the Appear effect after applying the Fade effect, and you will see it at work.

While you are applying the various effects, note the behavior of the end-of-page bar while the effect is in progress and after it has finished. It is a good indication of the display status of the test subject elements. As the elements change size, the bar will usually cinch up or move down to accommodate the new element size. Other times it will immediately jump up so that it is just below the Apply Effect button as the test elements are removed from the flow of the document (for example, with the Puff effect).

With that introduction under our belts, let's take a look at the options that are common to all effects.

5.4.2 *The common effects options*

The common options are shown in table 5.2 and will be explored in detail in the sections that follow. Even though these are considered the "common" options that are applicable to all effects, not all effects honor the settings of these options. When we explore the individual effects, we will make note of those that ignore any common option settings.

Table 5.2   The common effect options

Option	Description
duration	Specifies the length of time that an effect is to take. The default is usually 1 second.
from	Defines the starting point of an effect. Its exact semantics depend on the effect to which it is applied. The default is usually 0.0.
to	Defines the ending point of an effect. Its exact semantics depend on the effect to which it is applied. The default is usually 1.0.
transition	Specifies a callback function that controls the progression of the effect. The default function provides a smooth progression.
fps	Specifies the frames-per-second value. The default is 25.
sync	Synchronizes effects when applied in parallel.
queue	Sets the queuing position for effect queues.

The following sections explore the common options in greater detail. Most of these options can be observed in action by playing around with the Effects Lab except for sync and queue, which it does not expose. Examine the actions of these common options until you get a good handle on how they affect the effects.

Setting the duration of an effect

The duration option sets the time, in seconds, that the effect is to span. Some effects, such as Shake and SwitchOff, ignore this option and proceed at their own pace. Most effects, however, will spread the animation of the effect over the time span specified. For effects that pay attention to the setting of duration, the default value is 1.0.

To see how duration affects an effect (say that fast three times!), bring up the Effects Lab page, set the duration to 5 seconds (a long time by effect standards), and apply the various effects to see how they react to the longer-than-default time span.

Controlling the starting and ending points

The from and to options set the starting and ending points of the effect. They generally default to values of 0.0 and 1.0. Some effects, such as Opacity, must have at least one of these options explicitly set to operate, but most happily accept the defaults.

Figuring out how the from and to values affect the effects is where the Effects Lab page really shines. You can try setting the values of these options to various values, each of which is expected to be between 0.0 and 1.0 inclusive. For some effects, the values can be put to good use in controlling the operation of the effect. For others, the outcome is sometimes not so pleasing, and it's best to leave these at the default values. You can even get some interesting, though sometimes less-than-charming, behavior by making the to value lower than the from value. The Effects Lab can show you which is which—try it out.

Affecting the drawing of frames

The fps (frames per second) option affects how many frames Scriptaculous attempts to draw while it is animating the effect.

Generally, the Scriptaculous default of 25 is adequate; setting it higher rarely achieves better results. Setting it lower, on the other hand, can make the animation appear choppy. If this is desirable, by all means use it to your advantage.

Use the Effects Lab to observe the changes in behavior of the effects as you modify this value.

Controlling the transition of an effect

The transition option specifies a transform function that defines how the values between the from and to values are applied to the effect. This is a deep enough subject to warrant its own section; we'll deal with this particular option in section 5.6.

Synchronizing parallel effects

The sync option is a Boolean value that defines how frames should be rendered (manually or automatically). When combining effects (such as with Effect.Parallel) you should set sync to true. Otherwise, leave it at its default value of false.

We'll look a bit more closely at Effect.Parallel in section 5.9.

Queuing effects

The `queue` option is used when queuing up multiple effects. Again, this is a deeper subject than we want to deal with here. We'll discuss how to apply multiple effects, including the concept of queuing, in section 5.9.

5.4.3 *Exploring the core effects*

The core effects are basic animation effects that can be used directly, but they are also the foundation upon which all the combination effects are based. Though they are fairly simple, they can still be useful in your pages when the combination effects either don't suit your needs or exhibit behaviors that you might wish to avoid.

The Opacity effect

We've already seen the Opacity effect in action with the Quick Win example in listing 5.1, as well as on the Effects Lab page. Essentially, the Opacity effect adjusts the opacity level of the target element over the specified `duration` from the `from` option value to the `to` option value, where 0.0 is fully invisible and 1.0 is fully opaque. Opacity is the only effect that performs no operation without at least one explicit `from` or `to` option value.

Try setting the `duration` to 3.0, and `to` and `from` to 0.0 and 1.0, and apply. The target element disappears, and then over three seconds gradually becomes fully opaque.

Now change the `to` and `from` values to 0.25 and 0.75 and apply. The effect now starts at one-fourth opacity and increases to only three-quarters opacity when done. Also note that the element is left at the ending opacity and does not revert to full opacity when the effect completes.

This is the general form of the Opacity effect:

```
new Effect.Opacity( element, options );
```

As noted earlier, at least one of the `from` or `to` options must be explicitly set for this effect to do anything.

For this effect, as well as for all the others, the `element` parameter can be a string containing the DOM ID of the target element, or it can be a reference to the DOM element itself. If you've wrapped your head around the Prototype `$()` function, you can readily understand why Scriptaculous makes this feature available at no cost to itself.

A typical usage of the Opacity option could be as follows:

```
new Effect.Opacity( 'elementName',
                    {
                        from: 1.0,
                        to: 0.0,
                        duration: 2.0
                    }
                  );
```

This will cause the target element to fade from view over the course of two seconds.

Next, let's see another effect that changes the appearance of the target element.

The Highlight effect

The Highlight effect is used to call attention to the target element by changing its background color. Without any options, the background color of the element will change to yellow, and then, throughout the course of the effect duration, morph back into the original background color.

The colors used at both ends of the effect's spectrum can be designated with effect-specific options as described in Table 5.3.

Table 5.3   The effect-specific options for the Highlight effect

Option	Description
startcolor	Sets the starting color of the element's background. If omitted, a light yellow color is used.
endcolor	Sets the ending color of the element's background. If omitted, the original background color of the element is used if it can be determined. The default is white.
restorecolor	Sets the final color of the background after the effect has completed.

Here is an example of the Highlight effect:

```
new Effect.Highlight(element,
                    {
                        startcolor: #ff0000,
                        endcolor: #0000ff,
                        restorecolor: #00ff00,
                        duration: 8
                    }
                  );
```

This rather jarring use of Highlight changes the background color of the element to red, then morphs that background color to blue over the course of eight seconds, displaying some interesting shades of purple along the way. After the color morph has completed, the background color of the element is set to green.

The Scale effect

The Scale effect, as you might surmise by its name, changes the size of its target element. It is one of the few effects that require extra parameters to its constructor in addition to the element and options object.

The general form of this effect is as follows:

```
new Effect.Scale( element, scaleToPercent, options );
```

The `scaleToPercent` parameter specifies a numeric value that indicates the percentage of the starting size to which the target element is to be scaled. So a value of 200 would scale the target to twice its starting size, while a value of 50 would scale it to half of its starting size.

Go ahead and give the Scale effect a bit of a workout in the Effects Lab if you haven't already done so. Leave all the other options at their defaults for the moment, and just play around with the `scaleToPercent` value until you understand how it controls the behavior of the Scale effect.

How the `to` and `from` options affect this effect is interesting as well as important. The Scale effect is frequently a component of many of the combination effects, so the way these options are interpreted by this effect carries over into many of the combination effects. You might think that `to` and `from` would control the starting and ending sizes, but as we have seen, the default starting size is the actual size of the target element before the effect is applied, and the ending size is computed by applying the `scaleToPercent` value.

So what exactly do the `to` and `from` values control? Essentially, these values clip the range of the effect.

To illustrate this, reload the Effects Lab page (to make sure you are at known starting conditions) and enter 200 for the `scaleToPercent` value, and 0 and 1 for the `from` and `to` values respectively. (These are their default values, but we're making them explicit at this point to see what the effect of changing them will be.) Also, you might want to set the `duration` option to 3 or so, to slow down the effect a bit, making it easier to see what's going on. When you click the Apply Effect button, the target elements will grow from their starting size (100 percent) to twice that (200 percent) in a smooth fashion (or at least as smooth a fashion as the browser is capable of).

Now reload the page (to reset the size of the targets), change the `from` and `to` values to 0.25 and 0.75 respectively, and apply the effect again. Whoa! Is that what you expected? Can you figure out what the difference is?

By specifying values of 0.25 and 0.75, we have clipped the range of the effect. So rather than growing from 100 percent to 200 percent, these values caused the effect to be clipped to 125 percent through 175 percent of the starting size. The result is that when the effect starts we see a "jump" as the target is immediately resized to 125 percent of its starting size. Then the effect causes the target to grow over the three-second duration to 175 percent of the target size, where it stops.

Now reload and reverse the from and to values to 0.75 and 0.25 respectively. We've now caused the effect to run from 175 percent to 125 percent. The not-so-great result is that the target "jumps" to 175 percent of its size, then shrinks to 125 percent of the starting size over the course of the effect. Not something that might seem all that useful at first glance, but this feature is put to use in some of the combination effects.

The Scale effect also features a handful of effect-specific options, which are outlined in table 5.4. Using the Effects Lab page, play around with various settings of the supported options to see how their values affect the effect, and how they interact with each other.

Table 5.4 The effect-specific options for the Scale effect

Option	Description
scaleX	Specifies whether scaling in the horizontal direction should occur. Defaults to true. If false, only vertical scaling takes place.
scaleY	Specifies whether scaling in the vertical direction should occur. Defaults to true. If false, only horizontal scaling takes place.
scaleFrom	Specifies the starting percentage for the effect; defaults to 100. When from and scaleFrom are both specified, the clipping applied by the from value is applied after the scaleFrom value has been accounted for.
scaleContent	Specifies whether the em value of the contents is scaled along with the container. Defaults to true. If false, the contents are not scaled. Content scaling occurs by modifying the base size of the em measurement. For best cross-browser compatibility, it's best to specify font sizes in em units rather than points or pixels. Images contained in the target element will not be scaled unless they too have had their dimensions assigned using em units. This is rather an odd and painful way to size an image, but if you want it to scale, you'll have to deal with it. Note that if the target itself is an image, it is scaled as you would expect. The "em restriction" only applies to target content, not the target itself.

Table 5.4   The effect-specific options for the Scale effect *(continued)*

Option	Description
scaleFromCenter	When `true`, specifies that the target element's center is to remain in its fixed position and that the element is to grow (or shrink, as the case may be) around that point. Defaults to `true`.
scaleMode	Allows you to indicate the size of the element that should be used as "box" (the default) for the visible size of the element on the page or "content" to take the full size of the element into consideration including any scrollable content that may not be actually visible. Assigning a hash object containing `originalHeight` and `originalWidth` properties can specify a precise size.

One particularly interesting experiment to run is setting the percent value to 0 and seeing how the borders and margin of the second and third targets are handled by the effect.

Now that we can change the size of the element, shouldn't we think of changing its position next?

The MoveBy effect

You might surmise that an effect named MoveBy would be used to change the position of an element within the page, and you'd be correct. But it isn't a free lunch.

In order for this effect to work correctly across all browsers, the element to be moved must be a positioned element. That is, it must have a CSS `position` rule applied, and the value of the position may be either `absolute` or `relative`. The use of `relative` is more conventional, as it does not remove the element from the normal flow of the page layout.

Like the Scale effect, the constructor of the MoveBy effect expects required parameters other than the element and options object. This is the general form of the effect:

```
new Effect.MoveBy( element, y, x, options );
```

In this syntax, y specifies the change in vertical position, and x specifies the delta horizontal position. For the y parameter, a negative value moves the element up the page. A negative x value moves the element to the left.

The MoveBy effect accepts no effect-specific options. The behavior of the `from` and `to` options on the MoveBy effect is similar to how those options affect the Scale effect; that is, they clip the movement by the percentages that they specify. Display the Effects Lab page in your browser and experiment with the values of x and y, and then with the `from` and `to` options until you are familiar and comfortable with their operation.

Consider this simple MoveBy example:

```
new Effect.MoveBy(element,10,10,{duration:10});
```

This will slowly move the target element down and to the right by 10 pixels each.

The effects that we've discussed so far compose the core effects. More elaborate effects that use or extend the core effects are called the combination effects, and they are the next focus of our attention.

5.4.4 *Exploring the combination effects*

The combination effects are so named because they are created by combining core effects to achieve new effects.

Each combination effect is described in the subsections that follow. For some effects, there isn't much to say except to describe its operation. Others have nuances that are worth digging in to. A few of the combination effects are natural pairs with each other, where one effect undoes the action of the other: the Appear and Fade effects, for example. In the following sections, these effects are discussed as a unit.

The Fade and Appear effects

The Fade and Appear effects cause an element to fade from view and to appear in view by adjusting its opacity.

At first, you might wonder how these differ from the Opacity effect, whose job is to similarly adjust opacity. For example, if we were to set the `from` option to 1.0 and the `to` option to 0.0 for the Opacity effect, how would that differ from the Fade effect? Are these effects just a repackaging of the Opacity effect with default sets of options? The answer is no—there's a subtle difference.

To see this difference, first use the Effects Lab page to observe the behavior of the end-of-page bar when operating the Opacity effect as described in the previous section. Now reload the page (to be sure all settings are reset), and apply the Fade effect with no options specified. Did you notice the difference in the way the end-of-page bar behaved when the effect was applied? Using the Opacity effect, the bar stayed in place once the test subject element disappeared from view. But in the case of the Fade effect, the horizontal rule moved up to fill the space left by the now-invisible test subject.

This is because after the Fade effect is through adjusting the opacity, it removes the element from the document flow. Any elements following the target element cinch up to take the space left vacant. Similarly, the Appear effect will ensure that the element is part of the document flow before it adjusts the opacity.

So, if you want the element to remain part of the document display while its opacity is changed, use the Opacity effect. To remove and replace the element from the document as part of a fade-out/fade-in sequence, use Fade and Appear.

Note that if you explicitly specify a to option for the Fade effect, any value other than 0 will cause the effect to not remove the element from the document flow.

Adjustments in opacity aren't the only way to hide or reveal elements. Let's take a look at another set of effects for making elements come in and out of view.

The BlindUp and BlindDown effects

BlindUp and BlindDown are another effects pair for hiding and revealing an element. Rather than fading in or out, these effects adjust the vertical size of the element, shrinking it from the bottom up, or growing it from the top down, so that it appears that a blind is being drawn up or down to reveal or hide the element's contents.

Like the Fade effect, the BlindUp effect removes the element from the document flow once the "blind" has finished "raising." The BlindDown effect ensures that the element is restored into the document flow prior to "lowering" the blind.

Because these combination effects are built upon the Scale effect, the options available for the Scale effect will also affect BlindUp and BlindDown. Usually, you would leave these options at their default values, but some funky things can be made to happen by adjusting them.

The SlideUp and SlideDown effects

Another pair of effects for hiding and revealing elements, SlideUp and Slide-Down are similar to the blind effects in that the size of the element is adjusted vertically to either show or hide the element. However, where the contents of the element in the blind effects remain stationary, in the slide effects the contents move up or down as the element is resized. This creates the illusion that the contents are part of the blind that is moving up or down, rather than the blind being a shutter that shows or hides the element.

Another difference between these effects and the blind effects is that the slide effects place a bit of a restriction on the element to which they are applied. The target element for the slide effects must have an inner block element, usually a <div>, which contains the content that is to slide within its parent. For example, the following snippet is correctly formed:

```
<div id="testSubject">
  <div>Content that is to "slide"</div>
</div>
```

Without the inner `<div>`, the effect would be unable to create the slide illusion.

Any attempt to apply this effect to an element without this inner block element results in a rather unhelpful error message from the JavaScript interpreter (the exact nature of the message is browser-dependent).

Because of this restriction, the Effects Lab only applies the SlideUp and Slide-Down effects to the third test subject element (the only one that follows the required pattern) in order to avoid this error.

The Shrink and Grow effects

The Shrink and Grow effects are the last pair we will examine that are used to hide and show elements.

Like the other hide and reveal effects, the element is removed and replaced in the document flow as appropriate. With Shrink and Grow, the elements appear to grow from, or to shrink into, their centers.

Given your familiarity with how the Scale effect operates, it's easy to guess how this pair of effects was implemented. Again, use the Effects Lab page to become familiar with the operation of these effects.

The Puff effect

Not all combination effects come in show/hide pairs. The Puff effect is a combination of the Opacity and Scale effects that causes the element to be removed from the relative document flow, and then to grow from its center while fading away into invisibility. The net effect is that the element appears to get blown off the page in a puff of smoke.

The DropOut effect

Like the Puff effect, the DropOut effect combines core effects to remove an element from the document flow in an animated fashion. In this case, the Opacity and MoveBy core effects are combined to make it look as if the element drops off the page toward the floor.

The SwitchOff effect

Those who remember watching television before the advent of LCD and plasma flat-panel displays will recognize the inspiration for this effect. When older CRT television sets were turned off, the picture appeared to shrink from the top and bottom of the tube toward a single bright horizontal line in the center of the screen before going completely dark.

The SwitchOff effect similarly resizes the target element vertically from the top and bottom toward its center line, and then removes it from the document layout. A bit of opacity flickering is added to help mimic its real-world inspiration.

The Squish effect

The Squish effect animates the removal of the target element from the document display by scaling its size down to nothing in the vertical and horizontal directions, while holding its upper-left corner stationary. The net visual effect is that the element is squished into its upper-left point until it vanishes.

The Fold effect

The Fold effect is similar to the Squish effect, except that the scaling is performed serially, first in the vertical direction, then horizontally, giving the illusion that the element is being folded up, then over. The target element is then removed from the document display.

The Shake effect

Up to this point, all of the combination effects are used to remove elements from the page, or to make them appear or reappear after removal. The remaining two combination effects do not remove or replace elements, but instead call attention to them in some way.

The Shake effect causes the target element to move back and forth horizontally three times, simulating the shake of a head. This effect ignores any setting of the `duration` option.

The Pulsate effect

The Pulsate effect fades the target element to invisibility and back to full opacity five times, giving the effect of pulsating in and out of existence.

That completes our tour of the effects. We've noted that some of the combination effects are effect pairs that hide and reveal the target element. In the next section, we'll take a look at a facility that makes using those paired effects a snap.

5.5 *Easy toggling of Show and Hide effects*

Now you see it, now you don't! As you now know, a good number of the combination effects are devoted to hiding and revealing their target elements.

Some of these effects are arranged in pairs, where one effect uses a particular visual metaphor to hide the element, and the partner effect reveals the element using the same visual metaphor. For example, Fade is paired with Appear, each adjusting the opacity of the element to animate the process of hiding and reveal-ing the target element. Making an element disappear and reappear on a page is almost always achieved using these complementary pairs. There's nothing to stop us from using Fade to hide an object and then BlindDown to reveal it, but that would seem a bit odd and possibly rather jarring to the user.

With this in mind, Scriptaculous provides a utility function named `toggle()` that can be used to hide or show an element. Which procedure gets employed (hiding or revealing) depends upon the current state of the element; hidden objects will be revealed, and visible objects will be hidden.

This utility function is most useful in scripts where the current state of the ele-ment is unknown or moot, and toggling the element to the opposite state is all that matters. This saves us from having to determine the state of the object in order to know whether a hiding or revealing effect should be invoked.

When the hide and reveal actions will be invoked in different handlers, this utility function is not all that useful. For example, a menu system might have a handler for the main menu entries that trigger revealing a submenu, while click handlers on the submenu items cause the submenu to be hidden. In each of these separate handlers, the action to be taken is known and fixed: either reveal or hide. A toggle utility isn't helpful in this case.

So where would this type of function be useful? First we'll discuss the use of the toggle utility function, then we'll design a widget that employs it to good effect.

5.5.1 The Effect.toggle() utility function

The general form of the toggle utility function is as follows:

```
Effect.toggle( element, effectType, options );
```

The `effectType` is one of these strings: `'appear'`, `'slide'`, or `'blind'`, and `options` is the usual options hash.

If the `effectType` is `'appear'`, the Fade and Appear effects are used to toggle the element in and out of visibility. If `'slide'` is specified, the SlideUp and Slide-Down effects are used. And if `'blind'` is provided, the BlindUp and BlindDown effects are employed. If the `effectType` is omitted, the default is `'appear'`.

For some reason, the Grow and Shrink effects are not supported by this func-tion. We can only guess at what transgression they performed to become the black sheep of the effects family.

A typical usage might be something like this:

```
Effect.toggle('testSubject','appear',{duration:1.5});
```

How about an example?

5.5.2 *The Toggle Pane widget*

Often, especially on complicated pages, employing a "now you see it, now you don't" technique proves useful. Think, perhaps, of a complicated entry form where some sections are required and some are optional. In order to keep from overwhelming the user, we'd like to hide the optional parts until the user wishes to view them, if at all. We obviously want to make it clear that the optional portions exist (even when hidden), and to make it ridiculously simple for the user to control the visibility of the optional sections.

The Toggle Pane widget achieves these goals by taking a simple (but seemingly little-known) HTML element, the fieldset, and animating it using Scriptaculous effects. The HTML `<fieldset>` element, in conjunction with a child `<legend>` element, creates a nifty little container that doesn't require a whole lot of HTML markup and CSS.

In its unstyled form, this HTML snippet,

```
<fieldset>
  <legend>This is the legend</legend>
  This is the content of the fieldset.
</fieldset>
```

would render as shown in figure 5.4.

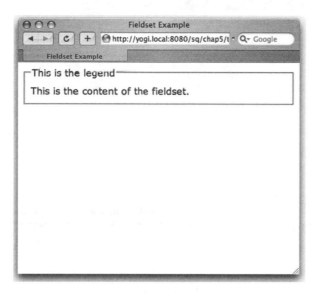

Figure 5.4
"Vanilla" fieldset element with no styling

This is a good starting point for our widget, which we'll modify such that the legend becomes the control for the toggling behavior. Clicking the legend will cause the content of the fieldset to be hidden if it is visible, and visible if it is hidden. This will be the perfect use for the toggle utility function, but first we need to make a few changes.

If you look at figure 5.4, it's immediately clear that there are no visual clues to the user indicating that the legend is an active element. How would he or she know that clicking on it would do something wonderful?

Users are conditioned to recognize button-like things as active elements, so one thing we'll do as part of the widget setup is apply styling to the legend to make it clear that it's an active element. Figure 5.5 shows the result.

By applying some simple CSS styling to the legend element of the fieldset, we have given it the familiar appearance of an active button. Notice that we also applied a cursor style that changes the mouse pointer to the familiar hand when it hovers over the legend button.

A number of different approaches can be taken when creating JavaScript widgets, also sometimes termed controls. A common approach is to have the JavaScript code for the widget generate all the DOM elements for the control as part

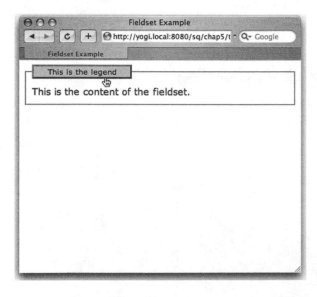

Figure 5.5
Enhanced legend element that looks like a clickable element

of widget initialization. A container element (frequently a div element) is usually passed to the constructor for the widget, and the constructor code places any generated elements within this container.

Although this is frequently a good approach to widget creation, it has the drawback in our case of how to specify the contents of the fieldset. We could get pretty fancy about it and use some advanced DOM manipulation, but to keep things simple we will have the JavaScript code for the Toggle Pane expect a reference to an existing fieldset (complete with its contents) to be passed to the constructor. Rather than generating widget elements within the passed element, the constructor code will transform the fieldset into a Toggle Pane widget by manipulating its properties, as well as the properties of its legend. This is a tactic that we will see employed again when we examine Scriptaculous controls in the next chapter.

Let's take a look at the code for the constructor of our Toggle Pane widget in listing 5.2. This code can be found in the togglepane/TogglePane.js file.

Listing 5.2   The Toggle Pane constructor

```
function TogglePane( fieldset, useDefaultStyling ) {   ❶
  //
  // Get references to the fieldset and its legend
  //
  this.fieldset = $(fieldset);   ❷
  if (!this.fieldset)
    throw new Error('cannot locate fieldset ' + fieldset);
  if (this.fieldset.tagName != 'FIELDSET')
    throw new Error('passed element must be a fieldset');
  this.legend = this.fieldset.getElementsByTagName('legend')[0];
  if (!this.legend)
    throw new Error('cannot locate fieldset\'s legend');
  //
  // Add the togglePane class to the fieldset
  //
  Element.addClassName(this.fieldset,'togglePane');   ❸
  //
  // Set up the onclick handler for the legend
  //
  var fieldsetElement= this.fieldset;   ❹
  this.legend.onclick = function() {
    $A(fieldsetElement.childNodes).each(
      function(child) {
        if (child.nodeType == Node.ELEMENT_NODE &&
            child.tagName != 'LEGEND') {
          Effect.toggle(child);
        }
      }
    );
```

```
    }
    //
    // Apply default styling to the legend if enabled
    //
    if (useDefaultStyling == true) this.applyDefaultStyling();    ❺
}
```

The constructor of the Toggle Pane ❶ accepts a fieldset reference and an optional Boolean value that specifies whether the caller wants us to set up the styling of the legend element (if `true`) or if they are expecting to handle it themselves (if `false`).

The first thing that we want to do is to establish instance references to the fieldset element as well as its legend ❷. We set up an instance variable, `this.fieldset`, and assign it the fieldset value passed through the Prototype `$()` function. This allows the user to pass either an element ID for the fieldset or a reference to the fieldset element itself to the constructor. In either case, the instance variable will have an element reference after the assignment.

We then perform two checks on this reference: the first makes sure that a null reference or unknown ID was not passed, and the second checks that the reference we ended up with is indeed to a fieldset element. Failing either check results in a JavaScript error.

After we know we have a good reference to a fieldset, we locate the legend element within the fieldset. If one cannot be found, again a JavaScript error is thrown.

Once this first section has completed, we know that we have references to the fieldset and its legend at our disposal, and we can begin to manipulate them.

As a convenience to the caller, we add a class name to the fieldset element ❸; in this case `togglePane`. This gives the user of our widget a handle upon which to hang CSS styling. For example, if the calling page wanted to apply styling to the legend element within the fieldset, the CSS selector

```
.togglePane legend
```

would match only legends within the fieldset that have been converted into Toggle Pane widgets.

Now we need to transform the legend into an active element that will perform the toggling operation ❹. We're going to do this by assigning an `onclick` handler to the legend. For our own convenience, this handler will be a closure so that we can easily reference the fieldset associated with the click. We have a reference to the fieldset as an instance variable, but that's not going to help us, since we know that the this reference doesn't propagate to closures. But local variables do, so we copy the this.fieldset reference into a local variable named fieldsetElement, which we can reference within our closure handler.

In the onclick handler for the legend, we want to find all the children of the fieldset, and either hide or reveal them. All except for the legend, of course; we always want to keep that visible so the user has something to click on!

Let's take another look at that handler:

```
this.legend.onclick = function() {
  $A(fieldsetElement.childNodes).each(
    function(child) {
      if (child.nodeType == Node.ELEMENT_NODE &&
          child.tagName != 'LEGEND') {
        Effect.toggle(child);
      }
    }
  );
}
```

We obtain the child nodes of the fieldset (using the fieldsetElement local variable that we set up to be available to the closure), and iterate over them by transforming the childNodes node list to an array (via Prototype's helpful $A() function) and then applying yet another closure to each child element using the each() mechanism.

For each child node, we check that the node is a DOM element (we'll also get things like text nodes and comment nodes in this list, and we want to ignore those), and unless the child element is the legend element, we apply the Scriptaculous toggle function to the child. Note that because the toggle function just does the right thing (reveals if hidden; hides if revealed) we are spared the task of keeping track of which state the Toggle Pane is in. The toggle utility function handles that for us.

One problem. This code doesn't work in Internet Explorer. Most modern browsers define the Node object, which declares useful constants for the node types, like ELEMENT_NODE, but Internet Explorer does not. Boo! Hiss! To fix this problem, we could substitute the Node.ELEMENT_NODE reference with its value of 1, but don't you hate it when magic numbers appear in the code without explanation?

Instead, we'll leave the code as is, and place the following line at the top of the TogglePane.js file:

```
if (document.all) Node = { ELEMENT_NODE: 1 };
```

This line defines the value for us in Internet Explorer. Note that we're still hard-coding the value in this case, but the code remains readable, and we're only doing this for the one browser that doesn't define the value for us.

Note that it's usually better to use object detection rather than browser detection when making browser-specific decisions, but IE throws a JavaScript error on any attempt to detect the presence of the Node object.

Finally, in the Toggle Pane constructor, we test whether the user specified `true` for the `useDefaultStyling` parameter ❺, and if so, call the `applyDefaultStyling()` function. This function sets style values for the legend element to give it a generic gray-button appearance as shown in listing 5.3. If a page author wishes a different rendition, the `useDefaultStyling` parameter can be omitted, or specified as `false`, and appropriate CSS styling can be added.

> **Listing 5.3 The applyDefaultStyling() function**

```
TogglePane.prototype.applyDefaultStyling = function() {
  this.legend.style.borderWidth = '3px';
  this.legend.style.borderStyle = 'outset';
  this.legend.style.borderColor = '#888888';
  this.legend.style.backgroundColor = '#bbbbbb';
  this.legend.style.cursor = 'pointer';
  this.legend.style.paddingTop = '1px';
  this.legend.style.paddingBottom = '1px';
  this.legend.style.paddingLeft = '18px';
  this.legend.style.paddingRight = '18px';
  this.legend.style.fontSize = '0.8em';
}
```

The TogglePane widget can be put through its paces by opening the togglepane/toggle-pane.html file in the source code for this chapter, or by clicking the appropriate link in the chapter's control panel page. When initially displayed, the TogglePane widget in the middle of the page is closed. Upon clicking the legend button, the TogglePane opens (using the Appear effect), revealing its contents. Figure 5.6 shows the two states of this page.

Having the toggle facility around proved pretty handy in this case.

All of the samples that we've played around with to this point have left the `transition` option at its default value. Let's learn exactly what "transitions" are, and how we can use them.

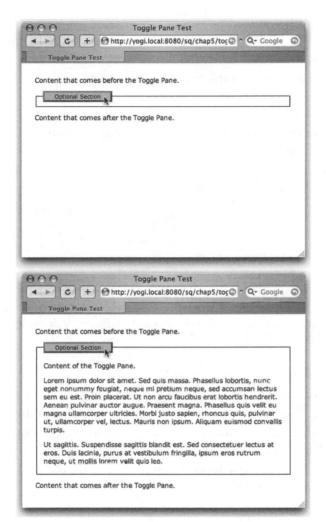

**Figure 5.6
The two states of the
Toggle Pane test page**

5.6 *Working with transitions*

Each effect runs through a range of values that control its animation. Playing around with the Effects Lab page demonstrated that the `from` and `to` common options specify the range of these values. Unless otherwise specified, these values run from 0.0 to 1.0 inclusive, and which values are actually applied to a particular "frame" of the animation depends upon the settings of the other options, such as `duration` and `fps`. It also depends upon the selected transition.

A transition, as it applies to Scriptaculous effects, is a function that transforms an input value to another value and returns it. As Scriptaculous is applying an effect, it needs to calculate the "magnitude" to apply to each frame of the transition, starting with the `from` value and ranging to the `to` value. Rather than just using a linear progression from start to end, Scriptaculous applies the transition function to each frame value, and uses the transformed result.

By using transition functions, we can achieve interesting variations on any Scriptaculous effect that we choose to employ. Scriptaculous has seven built-in transitions that you can specify using the `transition` common option.

Here is an example of applying a built-in transition:

```
new Effect.Opacity(
  testSubject,
  {
    duration: 2,
    from: 0,
    to: 1,
    transition: Effect.Transitions.pulse
  }
);
```

In the next few sections, we'll look at each of the built-in transitions, investigate a means to chart exactly how the transitions transform the frame values, and even learn how to write our own transitions.

5.6.1 *Using the built-in transitions*

The built-in transitions are listed in table 5.5, along with a description of the qualitative visual effect of each. You'll find a more thorough explanation of the quantitative nature of the transitions in section 5.6.2. As you read the descriptions of the built-in effects, use the Effects Lab to see how they affect the progression of the effect animation from start to finish. This is best seen by setting the `from` and `to` option values to 0.0 and 1.0 respectively.

Table 5.5   The Scriptaculous built-in transitions

Option	Description
`Effect.Transitions.sinoidal`	Apparently a misspelling of *sinusoidal*, this transition applies a transform that maps the input values onto a trigonometric curve. This is the default value, as it provides a more visually pleasing progression of the effect from start to finish than if the values were mapped linearly.
`Effect.Transitions.linear`	The linear transition passes the input value directly as its result. Thus the effect progresses in a completely linear fashion from the start value to its end.

Table 5.5   The Scriptaculous built-in transitions *(continued)*

Option	Description
`Effect.Transitions.flicker`	As its name implies, this transition applies a transform to its input values that presents a "flickery" (for want of a better word) progression from start to finish.
`Effect.Transitions.pulse`	This transition applies a transform that causes the applied effect to pulsate as it is being applied.
`Effect.Transitions.wobble`	This transition is a variation on the pulse transition; in this case, the pulsating takes place more rapidly toward the end of the effect.
`Effect.Transitions.reverse`	This transition applies a transform that inverts its input value so that the effect is applied linearly in the reverse of the specified `from` and `to` option values.
`Effect.Transitions.full`	This transition ignores its input value and always returns the value 1.0. This has the result of causing the effect to be applied as if both the `from` and `to` values were specified as 1.0.

After playing around with these transitions in the Effects Lab a bit, move on to the next section for an analysis of how these transitions map their input values to their result values.

5.6.2   *Introducing the Transition Mapper*

In order to wrap our heads around how the built-in transitions work, as well as provide a tool to analyze our own transitions, an HTML page named `general/ transition-mapper.html` is provided in the source code for this chapter. Open that file in your browser, and you will see the page shown in figure 5.7.

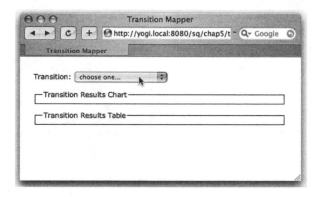

**Figure 5.7
Initial state of the Transition
Mapper before charting an effect**

Upon choosing a transition from the drop-down list (ignore the undo transition for now), the values 0.0 through 1.0 in 0.01 increments are applied to the transition function, and the results are tallied. A chart of the results is shown in the section labeled Transition Results Chart, while the actual numeric result values are shown in the Transition Results Table section, as shown in figure 5.8 (cropped to save space). Some builds of Internet Explorer seem to have a bit of trouble rendering the chart cleanly. But even so, the nature of the transition is clear.

Looking at the charts for the various built-in functions, each of which is shown in figure 5.9, it's much easier to get a handle on how the functions map their input values (x-axis, ranging from 0.0 to 1.0, left-to-right) to output values (y-axis, ranging from 0.0 to the maximum result value, bottom-to-top).

The Transition Mapper is not only a useful tool for quantitatively analyzing the built-in transitions, but it will also serve us well when writing our own transitions. Let's write a few now!

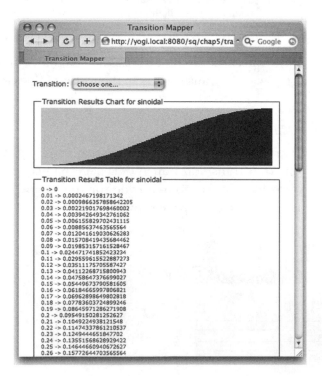

Figure 5.8
Transition Mapper after
charting the sinoidal transition

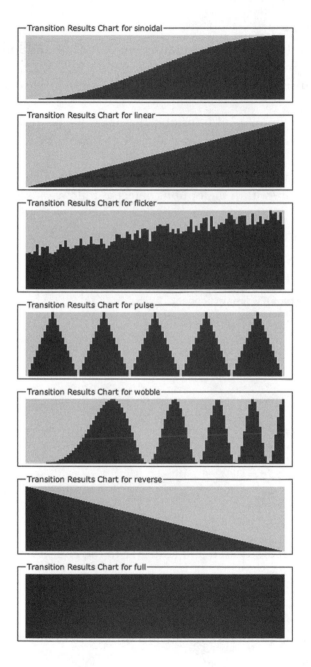

**Figure 5.9
Charts of the Scriptaculous
built-in transitions**

5.6.3 *Writing your own transitions*

Writing your own transition functions is ridiculously simple. All a transition function needs to do is accept a numeric value in the range 0.0 through 1.0, transform it in some manner, and return the transformed value (usually also in the 0.0 to 1.0 range).

Let's create a completely brain-dead transition that we will call "half." It will map whatever input value comes in to half its value, thus muting or shortening the range of the effect.

There are a number of ways we can apply such a transition. One way would be to specify it directly as a closure within the options object as follows:

```
new Effect.Opacity(
  testSubject,
  {
    duration: 2,
    from: 0,
    to: 1,
    transition: function(pos) { return pos/2.0; }
  }
);
```

We could also create it as a standalone function:

```
function halfTransition(pos) { return pos/2.0; }
```

This could then be used in the effect:

```
new Effect.Opacity(
  testSubject,
  {
    duration: 2,
    from: 0,
    to: 1,
    transition: halfTransition
  }
);
```

We could even extend Scriptaculous itself and add `half` to the collection of built-in functions:

```
Effect.Transitions.half = function(pos) { return pos/2.0; }
```

We could then apply it to any effect, just as we would any built-in transition.

Now let's define a slightly more interesting, but no more complicated, transition:

```
Effect.Transitions.undo = function(pos) {
  return 2 * ((pos < 0.5) ? pos : (1 - pos));
}
```

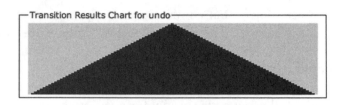

Figure 5.10
Transition Mapper chart for the undo transition, showing its ramping behavior

This transition maps its input value to the same value when less than 0.5, and inverts the value if it is 0.5 or greater. This result is multiplied by two in order to scale the value to full "height" prior to return. The result is that the effect is applied to its full range during the first half of the effect, and then reversed during the second half, effectively undoing the effect. The Transition Mapper chart for this transition is shown in figure 5.10.

If you'd like, modify the Effects Lab page to add the Undo Effect, and put it through its paces! What other transitions you dream up and apply to the effects is limited only by your imagination (and perhaps math skills).

Whether or not you apply transitions, you may want to receive notifications during the course of an effect. In the next section, we'll take a look at the callback options available to us.

5.7 *Gaining control during effects*

There may be times when you'd like to trigger your own code during an effect. All effects allow you to specify callback routines that will be triggered at specific points during an effect. These callbacks can be specified as part of the options object by using the options shown in table 5.6.

Table 5.6 The Scriptaculous effect-control callback options

Option	Description
beforeStart	This routine will be called before the effect starts.
beforeUpdate	This routine will be called on each iteration of the effect loop before the redraw for that iteration takes place.
afterUpdate	This routine will be called on each iteration of the effect loop after the redraw for that iteration takes place.
afterFinish	This routine will be called at the end of the effect.

Each callback is passed a hash object that contains a number of properties that might be of use to the callback routine. The more interesting of these are listed in table 5.7.

In the folder containing the examples for this chapter, open the general/callbacks.html page in your browser. This page shows a rudimentary use of callbacks for an effect. You will see the following code snippet for creating the effect:

Table 5.7 The Scriptaculous effect-control callback object properties

Option	Description
currentFrame	The ordinal of the current effects frame
startOn	The timestamp (in milliseconds) for when the effect starts
finishOn	The timestamp (in milliseconds) for when the effect will finish
element	The element to which the effect is being applied
Options	The options that were passed to the effect

```
new Effect.Opacity( 'testSubject', {
  duration: 5,
  from: 0,
  to: 1,
  beforeStart: function(o) { report('beforeStart',o); },
  beforeUpdate: function(o) { report('beforeUpdate',o); },
  afterUpdate: function(o) { report('afterUpdate',o); },
  afterFinish: function(o) { report('afterFinish',o); }
});
```

Note that we have specified a call to a function named report() for each callback, passing the name of the callback and the effect object to each activation. The report() function simply updates a display <div> with the callback type and the value of the currentFrame property of the effect object. When you click on the Apply button on this page, the effect is started and the callbacks are invoked, allowing you to see the progress (by frame number) through the effect.

Besides using this for diagnostic purposes (very important when developing your own effect or determining why an effect isn't working as expected), you might want to employ such callbacks when you want to trigger other effects or DHTML events at certain points during the execution of an effect. For example, imagine a series of objects whose effects start when the previous object in the series effect is halfway through, yielding a cascading series of overlapping effects.

Another thing you may wish to do within a callback is cancel the effect that is in progress. Let's see how.

5.8 Canceling effects

Generally effects are applied with such a short duration that the idea of canceling an effect may seem silly. But there could be times when stopping an effect in its tracks would be desirable. Perhaps you have a fairly long and drawn-out effect for emphasis that you might want to halt based on user input or other changing conditions, or perhaps you want to prevent multiple effects from triggering at the same time if all that activity on a page could be confusing to the user.

The latter condition is easy to envision for a menu system that uses effects like Grow and Shrink or BlindUp and BlindDown to reveal submenus as a result of mouse-over events. If multiple menus are constantly in the process of opening or closing while the user moves the cursor over your page, it would be difficult to tell which submenu is the "current" menu. In such a system, you'd want to cancel the opening or closing of one submenu before starting another effect on a new submenu.

In the folder containing the examples for this chapter, you'll find a page named cancel.html. Bring up that page in your browser. This page is a copy of the page discussed in section 5.7 (the one showing the effect callbacks) with the addition of a Cancel button. The code creating the effect has been modified to store the effect instance—something we've never seen a need to do in all of our prior discussion—in a window global variable:

```
window.effect = new Effect.Opacity( 'testSubject', {
  duration: 15,
  from: 0,
  to: 1,
  beforeStart: function(o) { report('beforeStart',o); },
  beforeUpdate: function(o) { report('beforeUpdate',o); },
  afterUpdate: function(o) { report('afterUpdate',o); },
  afterFinish: function(o) { report('afterFinish',o); }
});
```

The Cancel button is coded as follows:

```
<div>
  <button type="button" onclick="window.effect.cancel()">Cancel</button>
</div>
```

This simply calls the `cancel()` function for the stored effect. (Global variables aren't the best way to store references, but we've kept this example simple to focus on the `cancel()` function.)

Click on the Apply button to start the effect, and click the Cancel button before the effect completes. Note how the effect is stopped in its tracks. Also note how no restoration or fast-forwarding to the end of the effect is performed. The effect is just stopped wherever it happened to be when the `cancel()` function was called. If you want the target element to be completely visible or hidden after the effect is canceled, you'll need to add code to adjust the CSS properties accordingly.

In this section, we referred to situations in which multiple, simultaneous effects were an undesirable circumstance. But what if we want to start up multiple effects? Let's take a look at several ways the effects library gives us this control.

5.9 *Controlling multiple effects*

With all these effects at our fingertips, it's natural that we'd want to combine them in various ways. The Scriptaculous Effects library has facilities that give us two ways of executing multiple effects: running them simultaneously in parallel, or serializing them into a queue. Let's start by looking at running parallel effects.

5.9.1 *Running simultaneous effects*

Even though the online documentation calls this facility the Parallel effect, it isn't really an effect at all, but rather a container for a combination of other effects.

Let's say, for example, that we want to move an element on the page while simultaneously changing its size. We could just start a MoveBy effect and then start a Scale effect, like this:

```
new Effect.MoveBy(targetElement, 100, 200);
new Effect.Scale(targetElement, 200);
```

Sometimes this seems to do the job just fine, but the vagaries of different browsers and the ways they interpret JavaScript can sometimes cause irregular pacing of the effects. In order to ensure that the effects proceed smoothly in parallel, the Parallel "effect" can be used, in conjunction with the `sync` option, to ensure a fluid progression of the individual effects.

When using the Parallel effect, rather than providing a target element as the first parameter to the constructor, an array of the individual effects to be coordinated is passed. For example, to ensure that the previous example would run smoothly, it could be written as follows:

```
new Effect.Parallel(
  [
    new Effect.MoveBy(targetElement, 100, 200, { sync: true }),
    new Effect.Scale(targetElement, 200, { sync: true })
  ],
  {}
);
```

For your learning convenience, we have set up a lab page that you can use to explore the Parallel effect; it uses the MoveBy and Scale effects as examples, and it is available within the example code for this chapter. Use the chapter's control panel page to launch it, or find it within the chapter 5 folder (labs/lab-parallel.html).

The common `duration`, `from`, and `to` options can be specified within the options hash of the Parallel effect, and they will be applied equally to all effects being managed by the Parallel effect container.

OK, that covers the running of multiple simultaneous effects. But what about running effects serially?

5.9.2 *Running serial effects*

If we want to run multiple effects serially, say to make an element move to a new location, then grow to a new size, and finally fade from view, we'd have to have some means of coordinating the individual effects.

If we just coded the effects one after the other, like this,

```
new Effect.MoveBy( ... );
new Effect.Scale( ... );
new Effect.Opacity( ... );
```

the separate effects would all try to execute simultaneously, and outside of an Effect.Parallel container they might not interact all that gracefully.

In order to keep one effect from starting until the previous effect is finished, we could use the `afterFinish` callback of one effect to trigger the start of another. It would work, but it would involve a bit of coding and could make for some code-maintenance headaches.

The Effects library makes it easier to run effects serially by providing the `queue` option, which we've taken great pains to avoid talking about up to this point. When the `queue` option is specified on an effect, it creates a queue that controls the order in which the effects placed into it are executed.

We're probably all too familiar with the concept of a queue in our day-to-day lives, be it waiting in line at the pump to gas up a vehicle, at the bank to deposit or withdraw money, or at the store to pay for our groceries. In all these cases, the client of a service must wait his or her turn before engaging in the desired activity. For effects, Scriptaculous creates a global queue that we can use, or we can create our own named queues in order to run effects in the order we'd like. To queue up effects in the global queue, the value assigned to the `queue` option should be either `front` or `end`, specifying which end of the queue the effect is to be placed in. If named queues are to be used, the value of the queue option should be a hash object with two properties: position, which specifies either front or end, and scope, which assigns the name of the queue to be created and used.

Let's look at examples of using each of these.

Using the global queue

Let's initially tackle the simpler technique of using the global queue and rework our three-effect example, adding queue options as follows:

```
new Effect.MoveBy( ... , { ... , queue: 'front'});
new Effect.Scale( ... , { ... , queue: 'front'});
new Effect.Opacity( ... , { ... , queue: 'front'});
```

When we execute these effects, we note that, because we specified a queue, the effects execute serially, one after the other. That's exactly what we would expect. But we also observe that the Opacity effect is applied first, followed by the Scale effect, followed by the MoveBy effect. What's up with that?

Look at the order in which we specified the effects, and where we placed them according to the values of the queue option. First, we added the MoveBy effect to the front of the queue. Then we added the Scale effect to the front of the queue, which placed it before the MoveBy effect. Finally we placed the Opacity effect, again at the front of the queue, which placed it before the Scale effect. The result is that they execute in the reverse order that the effects were added. By placing the effects at the front of the queue, we effectively created a stack of the effects.

If we wanted the effects to execute in the same order that we created them, we'd place all the effects at the end of the queue so that their creation order would be reflected in the queue order.

But what if we wanted to combine some serial behavior with some parallel behavior?

Using named queues

Any effects that we place in a queue will execute serially with respect to each other. If we want multiple threads of effects to execute simultaneously, we can't use a single queue like the global queue.

For that reason, the Effects library allows us to declare multiple queues. Each queue executes in parallel with the other queues, but any effects within a particular queue execute serially with respect to the effects in that same queue. You can look at the effects in a queue as defining some uber-effect that is the serial union of the effects in that queue, and this uber-effect can be run in concert with other uber-effects defined by other queues.

To define our multiple queues, we can use the hash object notation for the value of the `queue` option. Within this object, the `position` entry defines `front` or `end`, controlling the end of the queue that an effect gets placed onto, just as with the global queue. The `scope` entry defines which queue the effect is to be placed in.

Here is an example of creating four effects and placing them into two queues:

```
new Effect.MoveBy( ... , { ... ,
  queue: {position:'end',scope:'queue1'});
new Effect.Scale( ... , { ... ,
  queue: {position:'end',scope:'queue1'});
new Effect.Opacity( ... , { ... ,
  queue: {position:'end',scope:'queue2'});
new Effect.MoveBy( ... , { ... ,
  queue: {position:'end',scope:'queue2'});
```

One queue contains a MoveBy and a Scale effect, and the other an Opacity and a MoveBy effect. The MoveBy and Scale effects in `queue1` will execute one after the other, and the Opacity and MoveBy effects in `queue2` will also execute one after the other. The two queues, however, will execute in parallel. How the various effects within these queues overlap greatly depends on the other options specified, particularly the `duration` option.

Not surprisingly, we have set up a Queues Lab page to help you grasp the outcome of applying the queue option. Let's see how that page can help us figure out how all this works.

Exploring the Queues Lab page

The Queues Lab page, available from the chapter's code control panel or by opening the labs/lab-queues.html file in your browser, allows you to set up queuing options for four different effects. Bring this page up in your browser, and you will see it laid out as in figure 5.11.

When you click the Apply button on this page, the four effects are created in the order shown (from left to right). Using the controls on this page, you can specify that the effect is to be unqueued (no queue option specified), placed at the front or end of a queue, and optionally placed on a named queue. Leaving the Scope field blank for an effect places that effect in the global queue. The `duration`, `from`, and `to` options of all effects are set to the values 3.0 (to make sure you have time to see the effects in action), 0, and 1 respectively.

Start by making sure that all effects are set to Unqueued and click the Apply button. You will see that all effects are applied simultaneously (and depending upon your browser and the power of your machine, they may be choppy or smooth).

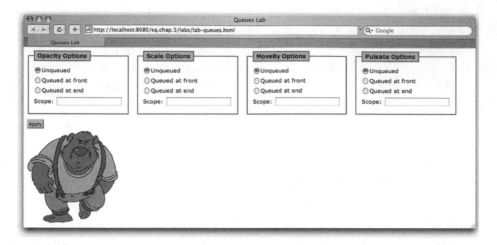

Figure 5.11   The Queues Lab page allows you to queue four effects

Now, refresh the page to restore the test subject to its original size and position, and set all the effects to Queue at front. Click Apply. All of the effects are applied, one at a time, in the reverse order in which they were created. Reread the previous section on queuing if this was not what you expected.

Refresh the page, and set all effects to Queued at end. Click Apply. Again, all of the effects are applied, one at a time, but this time in the same order in which they were created.

Now play around with the settings of the various effects, changing them among unqueued, front, and end, and see the effect the settings have on the order in which the effects are applied. Be sure to refresh after each experiment to reset the test subject to its original conditions.

For the next exercise, refresh the page and set all effects to Queue at end. For the Opacity and Scale effects, enter `queue1` for the scope, and for the MoveBy and Pulsate effects, specify a scope of `queue2`. Click Apply. With these settings, we have created two queues that will execute simultaneously, while serially executing the effects within each queue. In this case, the Opacity and MoveBy effects are applied simultaneously, followed by the simultaneous execution of the Scale and Pulsate effects. Because all effects are 3 seconds in duration, their beginnings and endings coincide.

Make up your own experiments on this page by mixing the settings of the queue options in interesting ways and observe the behavior. It should give you a good handle on how effect queues operate.

As a further exercise, you could enhance the lab page to allow the specification of disparate durations for the various effects. That should lead to some interesting outcomes!

5.10 *Summary*

This chapter introduced the Scriptaculous Effects library. We looked at the core and combination effects, how they affect their target elements, how you can create them, and how their various options affect their operation.

These effects give you a powerful tool to use in adding not only pizzazz, but in emphasizing the interface and interaction paradigms that your page is presenting to users. But like all powerful tools, they can turn on their wielder if not used properly.

Remember when desktop publishing programs first became available? For the first time, the general population was introduced to the ability to use multiple fonts. A lot of people went completely off the deep end with this newfound ability, and felt that they needed to use every fancy font that they could find on every page. The resulting "ransom notes" were rarely pleasing.

Similar restraint with Scriptaculous effects is required. Use the effects to good purpose. Use them sparingly. And use them wisely.

Scriptaculous Controls

This chapter covers

- Using the Scriptaculous in-place editor controls
- Using the Scriptaculous autocompleter controls
- Using the Scriptaculous slider control

In the previous chapter, we saw how Scriptaculous effects could be used to help reinforce the semantics of user interface interaction, or just to add some dazzle. Scriptaculous also provides extended controls beyond the set that is usually available to web developers. In this and the following chapter, we'll take a look at some of the controls Scriptaculous provides that extend the traditional HTML control set.

Web applications—applications that exist not on the local system but at a remote location and that are accessed through a web browser—have made hefty inroads into spaces where their "desktop" counterparts once ruled supreme. There are many advantages, both to the application service provider and to the client, to delivering applications and services in this manner. But web applications have always suffered from restrictions placed upon them by the limitations of the browsers used to present them. In particular, the set of user interface controls made available to web application authors by the browsers, and as defined by the HTML standards, is very limited compared to the controls generally available to programmers of traditional desktop applications.

However, with advances in browser capabilities, particularly in the areas of Java-Script and CSS, and with the addition of technologies such as Ajax, web application developers have been cleverly bypassing these limitations, using DHTML to create their own controls or to extend the capabilities of the existing controls.

In this chapter, we'll take a look at three control types that Scriptaculous makes available: in-place editors, autocompleters, and sliders.

6.1 Using the sample programs for this chapter

Most of the sample programs used to illustrate the material covered in this chapter require the facilities of back-end resources. For this chapter, these resources take the form of JavaServer Pages (JSP) and Java servlets. As such, you will need to set up an application server capable of serving resources conforming to the Java Servlet 2.4 and JSP 2.0 specifications.

While that may sound daunting if you're not familiar with these types of servers, there's really no need for trepidation. Setting up the freely available Tomcat 5.5 application server is not at all difficult, and details for installing this server, as well as the minimal configuration needed to run the samples in this chapter, are provided in appendix C. If you set up the Tomcat server exactly as outlined in that section, you can view the control panel for this chapter's example at this URL: http://localhost:8080/sq.chap.6/. Using localhost as the server domain in this URL causes the browser to connect to a server running on your local computer rather than heading out onto the Web to find it. The :8080 suffix is the port that

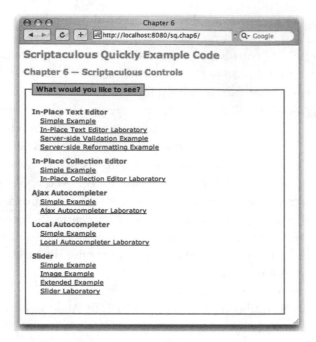

Figure 6.1
The chapter 6 control panel page

Tomcat will be listening on and must be specified (by default, a browser will send HTTP requests to port 80).

As you can see in figure 6.1, this control panel page displays links to the various examples discussed in this chapter. When working through this chapter and its sample programs, you can use this control panel to launch the samples, or you can poke around in the folders directly if you prefer.

Now let's dig in and see what Scriptaculous has to offer for extended controls. We'll start with the in-place text editor.

6.2 · *The in-place text editor*

We'll start our journey into extended controls with "in-place editors." Let's look at what is meant by an in-place editor and how it will be useful on our pages.

In many traditional web applications, some read-only data is displayed to the user with an Edit button that redisplays the data for editing (whether in a dialog box, a pop-up window, a floating <div> masquerading as a modal dialog box, or even a new page). While this model may be fine in most circumstances, there are times when such heavy-handed interaction is disruptive to the application workflow.

Consider, for example, a situation where a single word needs to be changed (perhaps as part of a spellcheck operation), or a single field needs a badly formatted value changed. In such circumstances, in-place editing might come in handy. This concept allows an element that normally appears as a simple read-only value to be transformed into a read-write control for editing and to then revert to the read-only format.

Standard HTML provides no such capabilities, but by using DHTML, we can fake it by using the JavaScript and CSS tools at our disposal. Scriptaculous has done a lot of this work for us in the guise of its in-place editor control. Let's see how to use it.

6.2.1 *Creating an in-place text editor*

Creating a Scriptaculous in-place text editor is relatively simple. We'll follow a paradigm that should be familiar to you by now: an instance of an Ajax.InPlaceEditor is created, and some parameters are passed to its constructor, including an anonymous object consisting of a hash (associative array) containing the control's options. A simple example is shown in listing 6.1.

Listing 6.1   Creating an InPlaceEditor

```
new Ajax.InPlaceEditor(        ❶ The target
    'theElement',          ◁─────┘  element
    'transform.jsp',    ◁──┐
    {                      ❷ The server-
                             side resource
       formId: 'whatever',   ◁──┐
       okText: 'Upper me!',     ❸ The options
       cancelText: 'Never mind'
    }
);
```

In this code snippet, an Ajax.InPlaceEditor object is created and associated with a target element that is provided as the first of the parameters ❶. In the usual Prototype fashion, this can either be a reference to the element itself or the ID of the target element. As the "Ajax" namespace of the Ajax.InPlaceEditor class might lead you to believe, this control connects back to the server using Ajax technology. This connection can be established for two purposes, but the primary purpose is to submit the edited value back to the server for whatever reason the application's author might deem appropriate.

The second parameter to the Ajax.InPlaceEditor specifies the URL ❷ to the server-side resource that is contacted when an edited value is completed.

The third parameter specifies a hash of the options to be applied to this instance of the InPlaceEditor ❸. We'll be taking a look at the various options in detail shortly.

Now that you know how they're created, let's look at how an InPlaceEditor is used in a complete page, as shown in listing 6.2 (inplace-text/simple-example.html in the sample code).

Listing 6.2   A simple InPlaceEditor example

```html
<html>
  <head>
    <title>Simple InPlaceEditor Example</title>
    <script type="text/javascript"
            src="../scripts/prototype.js"></script>
    <script type="text/javascript"
            src="../scripts/scriptaculous.js"></script>
    <script type="text/javascript">
      window.onload = function() {
        new Ajax.InPlaceEditor(          ◁──── ❶ Create the
          'theElement',                          control
          'transform.jsp',
          {
            formId: 'whatever',
            okText: 'Upper me!',
            cancelText: 'Never mind'
          }
        );
      }
    </script>
  </head>

  <body>
    <div id="theElement">Click me!</div>   ◁──── ❷ Define the element
  </body>                                          to be controlled

</html>
```

In this page, we have initialized our simple InPlaceEditor in the onload function of the page ❶, and targeted it to a `<div>` element in the body ❷. You can launch this sample from the sample-code control panel for this chapter (see section 6.1). When initially displayed, this rather simple page looks like the one shown in figure 6.2.

Figure 6.2 Simple InPlaceEditor before we do anything

When you follow the compelling advice and click the text on the page, the display is much more interesting, as shown in figure 6.3. Note that the `<div>` element has been replaced (at least visually) with a text entry control, a button, and an active link. The text of the button and active link match those that we specified via the options hash.

Figure 6.3 Simple InPlaceEditor in its active editable state

If we don't type anything new into the text box and click the Upper me! button, we find that the text reverts to a read-only element, as show, in figure 6.4. But the text has been uppercased! How did that happen?

Recall that when we constructed the InPlaceEditor, we specified the trans-form.jsp URL as the second parameter to

Figure 6.4 Simple InPlaceEditor with the changes that were made

the constructor. This JSP page is activated with the value of the text control when the button is clicked, and its response value is taken as the new value of the control.

The transform.jsp source is shown in listing 6.3.

Listing 6.3   Code for the transform.jsp page

```
<%@ taglib uri="http://java.sun.com/jsp/jstl/functions"
           prefix-"fn" %>
<% Thread.sleep(3000); %>
${fn:toUpperCase(param.value)}
```

This rather trivial JSP page converts the value of the query parameter with the key "value" to its uppercase equivalent, and writes the result back to the response. The body of the response becomes the new value for the control. (The call to the `sleep()` method creates an artificial 3-second delay to simulate the lag that might occur if this interaction occurred over a network connection rather than on a local server).

You cannot create an InPlaceEditor that is disconnected from the server. Specifying a null, empty string, or anything other than a valid server-side resource for the second parameter to the constructor will not create an InPlaceEditor that does not contact the server when the button is clicked (or the Enter key is pressed).

If you want an InPlaceEditor that has no apparent server-side effects, you can create a simple "reflector" resource that simply returns whatever value is fed to it. In JSP 2.0, something as simple as the following single-line JSP page would do the job:

```
${param.value}
```

Now that we can create an InPlaceEditor, let's look at how we can control it.

Script control of the InPlaceEditor

Once we've got an editor on our page, we will want to exert some control over it with our code. If you store a reference to the editor instance, like this,

```
var inPlaceEditor = new Ajax.InPlaceEditor( ...
```

you will be able to use scripts to control the activity of the editor.

For example, if you need to force the editor into active mode, you can do so with the editor's enterEditMode() function, as shown in the following code snippet:

```
function onSomeEvent(event) {
  //do something
  inPlaceEditor.enterEditMode();
}
```

This function takes an optional parameter that accepts the current event and cancels that event. If, for example, the preceding function were triggered by the user clicking a link, passing the click event to the enterEditMode() function would cancel loading the link.

You can also disconnect the InPlaceEditor functionality from its associated element if, for whatever reason, your page needs to prevent the target element from entering active mode. You would do so by invoking the dispose() function on the editor instance as follows:

```
inPlaceEditor.dispose();
```

Now that you've seen a simple example, let's take a look at how we can use the option hash to further tailor the control to our needs.

6.2.2 The InPlaceEditor options

There is a long list of options that can be applied to an InPlaceEditor in order to assert control over its appearance and operation, as shown in table 6.1. Each of these options will be discussed in more detail in the following subsections.

Table 6.1 The Ajax.InPlaceEditor options

	Option	Description
Appearance options	okButton	A Boolean value indicating whether or not an OK button is to be shown. Defaults to `true`.
	okText	The text to be placed on the OK button. Defaults to "OK".
	cancelLink	A Boolean value indicating whether a cancel link should be displayed. Defaults to `true`.
	cancelText	The text of the cancel link. Defaults to "cancel".
	savingText	A text string displayed as the value of the control while the save operation (the request initiated by clicking the OK button) is processing. Defaults to "Saving...".
	clickToEditText	The text string that appears as the control's tooltip upon mouse-over.
	rows	The number of rows that will be displayed when the edit control is active. Any number greater than 1 causes a text area element to be used rather than a text field element. Defaults to 1.
	cols	The number of columns displayed when in active mode. If omitted, no column limit is imposed.
	size	Same as `cols` but only applies when `rows` is 1.
	highlightcolor	The color to apply to the background of the text element upon mouse-over. Defaults to a pale yellow.
	highlightendcolor	The color that the highlight color fades to as an effect. Note that some browsers don't entirely support this option.
	loadingText	The text to appear within the control during a load operation. (We'll be looking at that option shortly.) The default is "Loading...".
CSS styling and DOM ID options	savingClassName	The CSS class name applied to the element while the save operation is in progress. This class is applied when the request to the saving URL is made, and it is removed when the response is returned. The default value is "inplaceeditor-saving".
	formClassName	The CSS class name applied to the form created to contain the editor element. Defaults to "inplaceeditor-form".
	formId	The ID applied to the form created to contain the editor element.

Table 6.1   The Ajax.InPlaceEditor options *(continued)*

	Option	Description
Callback options	callback	A JavaScript function that is called just prior to submitting the save request in order to obtain the query string to be sent to the request. The default function returns a query string equating the query parameter `value` to the value in the text control
	onComplete	A JavaScript function that is called upon successful completion of the save request. The default applies a highlight effect to the editor.
	onFailure	A JavaScript function that is called upon the failure of the save request. The default issues an alert showing the failure message.
Other options	loadTextURL	The URL of a server-side resource to be contacted in order to load the initial value of the editor when it enters active mode. By default, no back-end load operation takes place, and the initial value is the text of the target element.
	externalControl	An element that is to serve as an external control that triggers the editor into active mode. This is useful if you want another button or other element to trigger editing the control.
	ajaxOptions	A hash object that will be passed to the underlying Prototype Ajax object to use as its options hash.

While exploring these options in greater depth, it will be handy to have some code that will let us see the options in action. So, with great fanfare, we introduce the InPlaceEditor Lab page.

The InPlaceEditor Lab

In order to demonstrate the options available for the InPlaceEditor control, the InPlaceEditor Lab page has been included in the source code for this chapter. You can launch this lab page via the control panel for this chapter's example programs. When you initially display the lab page, it will appear as shown in figure 6.5.

The InPlaceEditor Options section allows you to play around with some of the more commonly used options for this control. Once you have entered the options that you'd like, click the Create Editor button to create the editor control, which will appear below the InPlaceEditor Options section.

The Applied Options section will display the options that you have selected, and the Status area uses an `onComplete` callback function to display the value of the control element's `innerHTML` property.

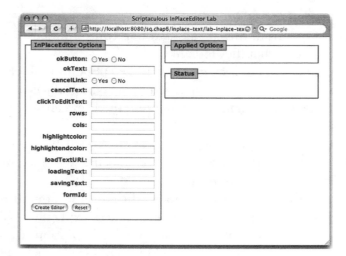

**Figure 6.5
Initial state of the
Scriptaculous InPlace-
Editor Lab page**

A typical usage scenario is shown in figure 6.6.

As you read through the following sections on the options, please experiment with them in the lab page until you are familiar with their actions. You are welcome to make a copy of the lab, or of the simple example pages, and edit to your heart's content, such as to add options that are not currently included in the lab page.

Now let's dig in and get to know the various options.

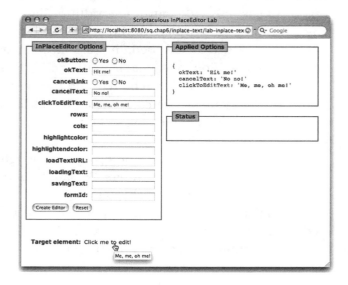

**Figure 6.6
The Scriptaculous
InPlaceEditor Lab in action**

Controlling the appearance of the editor

The set of InPlaceEditor Options in the lab allows you to control which elements of the editor are displayed, and what they look like.

The okButton option allows you to include or omit the OK button, which saves the editor value to the server-side resource, specified as the editor object's second constructor parameter. When the OK button is omitted, the user can still initiate the save action by pressing the Enter key.

When an OK button is displayed, its text value is controlled by the okText option. By default, the OK button is displayed and contains the text "ok". We saw an example of supplying alternate text in listing 6.2.

The cancelLink option controls a link that cancels the editor without invoking a save operation. The text of the link, which appears unless explicitly disabled, defaults to "cancel" and can be controlled with the cancelText option. Unfortunately, there is no option to make the cancel link a button rather than a text link.

While the editor is invoking the save operation, the text "Saving..." is displayed within the editor control. You can override this value with the savingText option.

Normally, when the editor is placed into edit mode, an HTML input element of text type is used as the active control. When an explicit value greater than 1 is supplied for the rows options, however, an HTML <textarea> element with the specified number of rows is used instead.

Regardless of how many rows are specified (or whether rows is left to the default of 1), the cols option can be used to control the width of the control. When a single row is being used, the size attribute of the text area is set to the value of the cols option. If a multirow text area is used, the cols attribute of the text area is set to the value of the cols option. Note that in neither case does this setting affect the number of characters that can be entered into the control. It merely sets the display width of the element (which arguably would be more appropriately set using CSS rules, as outlined in the next section).

You can affect how the Scriptaculous Highlight effect is applied to the InPlace-Editor with the highlightcolor and highlightendcolor options, although the results seem to vary rather broadly across different browsers. We saw the Scriptaculous Highlight effect in section 5.5.3 of the previous chapter.

The loadingText option is similar to the savingText option in that it specifies the text to be displayed while a back-end operation is taking place. This text is displayed only if the loadTextUrl option is also set, as discussed a little later in this section.

Specifying CSS and DOM ID options

The Scriptaculous InPlaceEditor control also gives you a small degree of control over some of the DOM IDs used, as well as CSS-style class names.

Unless you specify otherwise, the name of the form generated to hold the control (when in active mode) is formed by suffixing the text "-inplaceeditor" to the end of the ID of the target element. So if the target element has an ID of `targetElement`, the name assigned to the form would be `targetElement-inplaceeditor`. If that doesn't suit your fancy for whatever reason, the `formId` option can be used to assign another name to the form.

One reason you might want to replace the default form name is if you are planning to access the form or its elements via JavaScript. The hyphen in the default name makes referencing the form within JavaScript expressions rather problematic. A reference such as this,

```
var form = document.targetElement-inplaceeditor;
```

will result in an error, since the hyphen will be construed as a subtraction operator.

We could solve this problem by using the general referencing notation:

```
var form = document['targetElement-inplaceeditor'];
```

Or we could simply use the `formID` option to give the form a name we like better.

There may be times when you want the element's appearance to change while the save operation is taking place (above and beyond merely changing the text to "Saving..." or whatever else you specified with the `savingText` option). To make this possible, the InPlaceEditor's code adds a class name to the element while a save operation is under way, and then removes it when the save operation completes. By default, the name of this class is `inplaceeditor-saving`. Should that prove undesirable or unwieldy, or if you already have an existing CSS class name that you'd rather use, you can override this name with the `savingClassName` option.

It is important to note that this class name is added to the list of class names for the element. You can rest assured that any class names that you have assigned to the element for other purposes will not be replaced by the class name that Scriptaculous adds to the element during a save operation.

To help you style the contents of the form created while the control is in active mode, Scriptaculous assigns a class name of `inplaceeditor-form` to the form. The `formClassName` option can be used to specify a different class name for the form.

Now let's see what our controls are doing, so that we can react appropriately to the various state changes that the controls will go through as they are used on the page.

Using the callback options

When a save operation is initiated (either by clicking the Save button or pressing the Enter key while the editor's text field has focus), a JavaScript function is called to generate the query string that will be applied to the server-side post operation. Unless you specify otherwise with the `callback` option, an internal method that serializes the generated form is called. This method uses the `Form.serialize()` method from the Prototype library.

If you'd like to replace the callback function with one of your own (so that you can perform some custom activity before initiating the save operation) you must similarly return a suitable query string as the result of the callback, in order for the save operation to proceed normally. If you specify a custom callback function, it will be passed a handle to the generated form, so producing an appropriate querystring is rather simple, as shown in listing 6.4.

Listing 6.4   A custom callback function for the InPlaceEditor

```
function myVeryOwnCallback( form ) {
  //
  // custom actions performed here...
  //
  return Form.serialize(form);
}
```

This custom callback function also permits you to change the name of the query parameter used to pass the entered data to the server-side resource. The InPlace-Editor always creates its text input control with a name of `value`, and there is no analogous option to `formId` to reassign this name. But you can use the `callback` option to force the query parameter name to be anything you choose.

Let's say that you'd rather that the query parameter passed to your server-side resource be named `steve` rather than `value`. You could replace the default callback with your own function, as shown in the following fragment from the options hash:

```
callback: function(form) {
  return 'steve=' + form.value.value;
}
```

You can also register callback functions to be invoked after the save operation has completed. The `onComplete` option specifies a callback that will be invoked if the save operation returns successfully, and the `onFailure` option registers a callback to be invoked in the event of a failure.

The `onComplete` callback is called with two parameters: a reference to the XMLHttpRequest instance used to make the save post, and a reference to the target element. If no value is specified for the `OnComplete` option, the InPlaceEditor uses an internal function that applies a Scriptaculous Highlight effect to the target element using the value specified in the `highlightcolor` option.

The `onFailure` option is invoked if the response to the save post returns an error code; the default function issues an alert with the failure code provided in the XMLHttpRequest instance. This callback function is passed a single parameter consisting of the reference to the XMLHttpRequest instance.

You can use either of these callback options to customize what happens upon success or failure. For example, alerts can be a rather annoying means of issuing messages. If we had a `<div>` element on a page designed to contain such messages, let's say with an ID of `messageArea`, we could replace the default `onFailure` callback function with one of our own:

```
onFailure: function(xmlReq) {
  $('messageArea').innerHTML = xmlReq.responseText.stripTags();
}
```

Note the use of the handy `stripTags()` method from the String extensions of the Prototype library—they will remove any pesky HTML markup in the error message.

Now that we know how to keep track of what's going on with our editors, it's time to see how we can exert further control over them. For example, we can control how they initially get loaded.

Loading text from the server

Unless you specify otherwise by using the `loadTextURL` option, the initial value of the text field when the control becomes active will be the content of the target element.

You can specify the URL of a server resource to provide a text value for the `loadTextURL` option, but this post is not passed any data from the client, such as the content of the target element. How can the server-side resource know what text to load, if it doesn't have any client-side contextual information?

Fortunately, the `ajaxOptions` option comes to our aid here. This option specifies another hash object that is passed to the underlying Prototype Ajax.Request object that is used to make the server-side post. By specifying the `parameters` option to this hash, we can cause the value of the text field to be passed to the back-end resource:

```
ajaxOptions: {
 parameters: 'initialValue='+$('targetElement').innerHTML
},
```

This will cause the content of the target element (in this case, assume it's named `targetElement`) to be passed as a query parameter named `initialValue`. Bear in mind that this query parameter will be passed to all Ajax operations, including the save operation. Be sure that the query parameter name you choose for controlling the load operation will not interfere with any required for the save operation.

Note that the `ajaxOptions` option also allows you to pass the value back as any query parameter name you want, without forcing you to override the `callback` option.

Now that you've learned about the options to the InPlaceEditor, let's see how it all works in a few common scenarios.

6.2.3 *Some usage examples*

One of the major features of the Scriptaculous InPlaceEditor is its connection to a back-end resource. The examples we'll explore in this section will exploit that capability to perform server-side operations on the data that is entered.

First, we'll couple an InPlaceEditor with a server-side resource that will validate the value typed into the control. Then we'll enhance that example by adding a data-reformatting operation, demonstrating the level of server-side control that we can exert upon the control's data.

If you haven't already set up Tomcat 5.5 (or an equivalent application server) as outlined in appendix C, now is the time to catch up.

Server-side setup for the examples

So far in this chapter we have employed only simple JSP files as server-side resources. This was quick and easy—we just dropped the JSP files into the same folder as the page we were testing, and used page-relative referencing to address them. However, using JSP files for anything other than presentation is a rather egregious violation of currently accepted best practices. In a properly structured MVC (Model-View-Controller) web application, JSP pages should be relegated to presentation duty only; servlets are the more appropriate mechanism for any heavy-duty server-side operations. So in this section, we will set up and employ a few servlets to do our back-end operations.

Because servlets aren't simple files like HTML and JSP pages, the type of page-relative addressing we have been using up to this point just won't cut it anymore. We need to employ server-relative addressing which begins with the context path of the web application. (See section C.3 in appendix C for an explanation of the context path concept.) It is rightly considered a poor practice to hard-code context paths into pages. Rather, the context path should be rendered programmatically in the pages so that the web application will work as expected, regardless of what context path was chosen for the application.

To that end, our examples are JSP pages rather than static HTML pages, as most of our other examples have been. If you are operating in an environment where servlets are being employed as back-end resources, you are likely to be familiar with JSP pages being used for presentation.

Within the JSP pages discussed in this section, only a single JSP-ism is utilized: a JSP Expression Language snippet that automatically resolves to the context path for the application. That snippet looks like this:

```
${pageContext.request.contextPath}
```

The details of how and why this expression resolves to the context path of the web application are beyond the scope of this book, but any modern JSP book (or the JSP specification itself) will explain this concept in great detail.

Because this is the only JSP mechanism employed on the pages, you can turn them into simple HTML pages by replacing the expression (including the ${ and } delimiters) with the hard-coded context path of the application.

The Java code for the servlets themselves can be found in the WEB-INF/src folder of the chapter 6 web application. The source code for a web application would not normally be included with the structure of the web application like this—we've just included it here so you can review the servlet source code if you wish.

Within the WEB-INF folder, you will also find a file named web.xml. This is the deployment descriptor for the application, and within it you will find declarations that define the servlets to the Tomcat container, and that specify the URLs used to access them.

Performing server-side validation with an InPlaceEditor

Now that we're all set up to run our examples, let's use an InPlaceEditor to perform validation. In our first example, we'll use an InPlaceEditor to accept an email address, then send it back to the server for validation.

The JSP file for this example is named validation-example.jsp, and you'll find it with the web application code for this chapter, in the inplace-editor folder. Open this page in your browser. Be sure that the page is being served by your local Tomcat instance—just opening the file in the browser by dragging the file into it will not cause the active resources to be interpreted.

The page you will see is quite simple, consisting of a label, "Email address:", and a `<span>` element, which is the target element for the InPlaceEditor. Figure 6.7 shows this page when the editor is active.

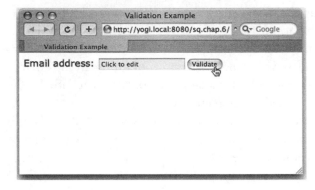

**Figure 6.7
The InPlaceEditor validation
page before any editing**

In this example, the text typed into the text box will be validated by a server-side resource. If the entry passes validation, the editor will revert to display mode as expected. However, if the entry fails validation, the server will indicate that, and our code will place a new style class on the text, showing the user that the entry is not valid. Sounds simple enough! The code for the page is shown in listing 6.5.

Listing 6.5   Source for the InPlaceEditor validation example

```html
<html>
  <head>
    <title>Validation Example</title>
    <script type="text/javascript"
            src="../scripts/prototype.js"></script>
    <script type="text/javascript"
            src="../scripts/scriptaculous.js"></script>
    <script type="text/javascript">
      window.onload = function() {              ❶ Create
        new Ajax.InPlaceEditor(        ←─          InPlaceEditor
          'emailField',
          '${pageContext.request.contextPath}/checkEmailAddress',  ←─
          {
            okText: 'Validate',          Define completion ❸   Specify the
            cancelLink: false,                     handler        server-side
            onComplete: function(req,element) {  ←─               resource ❷
              if (req.getResponseHeader('x-valid')=='false') {
                $('emailField').addClassName('fieldInError');
              }
            },
            callback: function(form,entry) {  ←─ ❹ Define callback
              $('emailField').removeClassName('fieldInError');   handler
              return 'value=' + entry;
            }
          }
        );
```

```
        }
      </script>
      <style type="text/css">      ⑤ Apply error
        .fieldInError {        ◁──┘   styling
          border: 1px solid maroon;
          color: maroon;
        }                          ⑥ Apply inline styling
        .inplaceeditor-form {  ◁─┘   to the form
          display: inline;
        }
      </style>
    </head>

    <body>

      <p>
        <label>Email address:</label>
        <span id="emailField">Click to edit</span>  ◁──┘ Declare target
      </p>                                                 element

    </body>

  </html>
```

By now, most of the code on this page should be at least somewhat familiar. The page imports the Prototype and Scriptaculous libraries as usual, and, as in prior examples, we set up the InPlaceEditor within the onload handler for the page. The creation of the editor itself ❶ specifies the <span> element with the ID of emailField as its target element.

The parameter for the server-side resource ❷ specifies this odd-looking URL:

```
'${pageContext.request.contextPath}/checkEmailAddress',
```

The construct within the ${} delimiters was explained in section 6.2.3 and will resolve to the context path for the application (to /sq.chap.6 if you set up the web application exactly as recommended).

The remaining portion of the URL, /checkEmailAddress, is the servlet path. This path was set up in the web.xml deployment descriptor as the mapping for the servlet named CheckEmailAddressServlet. Note that this mapping does not correspond to physical file on the file system (as would be expected with HTML and JSP files), but to the named servlet class on the Java classpath. (In this class, the class file can be found in the folder hierarchy rooted at WEB-INF/classes). We'll take a brief look at that servlet later in this section.

One of the more interesting aspects of this example is the onComplete callback specified for the editor ❸. Remember that this function is called upon successful completion of the save operation performed by the servlet. The XMLHttpRequest instance and target element are passed to the callback function as parameters, and the first thing our handler does is check the XMLHttpRequest object for a special response header named "x-valid". This header indicates whether or not the text passed back to the servlet has passed validation.

Wait a minute! If the validation fails, shouldn't the servlet simply return an error response that would trigger an onFailure handler? Well yes, it could have been written that way. But there are a number of issues that can be avoided by not doing so. By not returning an error code, it's easy for our code to distinguish between actual server errors (servlet not found, forbidden access, and the like) and validation failures. Even though we are calling them validation failures, they are not really errors in the request/response cycle—they are one of the expected, successful results, and as such shouldn't use a response error code.

We also don't want to use the body of the response to somehow indicate a validation failure. The body of the response is the value that will be placed into the editor control, and we don't want to mess around with that. If the user typed in a long string that contained one wrong character, he or she would be mighty annoyed if we didn't reload that string back into the editor, requiring it to be completely retyped.

This is why we set up a response header to return the validation status—we didn't want to use a response error code, and we didn't want to use the response body. We named the header "x-valid", using the prefix "x-" to avoid accidentally stepping on a response header name defined by the HTTP protocol (none of which begin with "x-"), and we can use the getResponseHeader() method of XMLHttpRequest to get its value.

If the value is the string "false", as set by the servlet in the case of validation failure, the Prototype addClassName() method is called to add the CSS fieldInError class name to the target element. This CSS class ❺ places a maroon border around the element and changes the color of the text to indicate that the entry is in error. More elaborate error indications are possible, of course (such as adding flyouts that describe the error, issuing alerts, adding error icons, and so on).

After the user makes a correction to the entry and resubmits the value, the default callback handler is replaced with one of our own ❹ that removes the fieldInError class just before the save operation is carried out.

One last point before we take a quick gander at the servlet: <form> elements are by default block elements. Left to its own devices, our InPlaceEditor would jump to the next "line" under the label when placed into active mode due to the dynamic creation of the form that encloses the text field. To prevent that, we specify a CSS rule that changes the form from a block element to an inline element ❻. This keeps the InPlaceEditor, well, in place when it makes the transition to active mode.

On the server side, a servlet that performs the validation makes use of Java regular-expression processing to validate an email address. Since the subject of regular expressions is clearly beyond the scope of this discussion, the servlet uses a very simple expression that would never be used in an actual production system.

The servlet code is shown in listing 6.6.

Listing 6.6   The CheckEmailAddressServlet source code

```
package org.bibeault.sq.chap6;

import javax.servlet.http.HttpServlet;
import javax.servlet.http.HttpServletRequest;
import javax.servlet.http.HttpServletResponse;
import java.util.regex.Pattern;
import java.io.IOException;

public class CheckEmailAddressServlet extends HttpServlet {

    private static final String KEY_VALUE = "value";
    private static final String REGEX_EMAIL =
        "(\\w)+@(\\w)+\\.(\\w)+";
    private static final String HEADER_VALID = "x-valid";

    public void doGet( HttpServletRequest request,
                       HttpServletResponse response )
        throws IOException {
        String value = request.getParameter( KEY_VALUE );
        boolean ok = Pattern.compile( REGEX_EMAIL )
            .matcher( value ).matches();
        response.setHeader( HEADER_VALID, String.valueOf( ok ) );
        response.getWriter().write( value );
    }

    public void doPost( HttpServletRequest request,
                        HttpServletResponse response )
        throws IOException {
        doGet( request, response );
    }

}
```

Without belaboring how this servlet functions, we can see that the doGet() method obtains the value of the request parameter named value, and matches it against a simple (borderline brain-dead) pattern. The "x-valid" response header is set to true or false depending upon the outcome of the match, and the original value is written as the response body. The doPost() method is written in terms of the doGet() method so that the servlet will respond to GET and POST requests in the same manner.

While this is a simple example, there are two important ideas that it introduces: a servlet can be used as a server-side resource for an InPlaceEditor (or for any Scriptaculous control that initiates server-side requests), and custom response headers can be used to pass ancillary data back to the client without usurping either response error codes or the response body.

This is impressive stuff! We can use the power of the server to perform validations that would be difficult or impossible if we were limited to merely validating on the client. Now let's take a look at how the server can play a more active role in extending the capabilities of our controls by actively reformatting the data.

Performing server-side reformatting with an InPlaceEditor

In the previous example, we used a server-side resource (implemented as a servlet) to perform a validation check. Regardless of whether the user typed in a valid entry, the entry was returned (and restored to the InPlaceEditor) exactly as the user entered it. In this example, we'll enhance our server-side check to go beyond mere validations and reformat valid entries for display.

Rather than an email address, this page will accept a 10-digit North American phone number whose standardized format is (999)555–1212, where 999 is the area code, and the remaining digits are the phone number within that area. It's mighty unfriendly to force users to type in all that punctuation, so we'll allow them to enter the digits in any way they want. By ignoring anything but digits in the input, we can allow them to enter 9995551212, 999–555–1212, 999.555.1212, or any other variation, as long as there are exactly 10 digits in the input. Upon receiving a valid entry, the page will redisplay the entry in the standard format, regardless of which format the user entered. That's nice. And users like nice.

The JSP page for this example is named reformat-example.jsp, and it is found in the inplace-editor folder of the web application. This page is almost identical to one in the validation example, except for simple name and text changes reflecting the different data to be entered. The server-side servlet, this time mapped to the servlet path /checkPhoneNumber, is implemented as a class named CheckPhoneNumberServlet, and is shown in listing 6.7.

Listing 6.7   The CheckPhoneNumberServlet source code

```java
package org.bibeault.sq.chap6;

import javax.servlet.http.HttpServlet;
import javax.servlet.http.HttpServletRequest;
import javax.servlet.http.HttpServletResponse;
import java.io.IOException;

public class CheckPhoneNumberServlet extends HttpServlet {

    private static final String KEY_VALUE = "value";
    private static final String HEADER_VALID = "x-valid";

    public void doGet( HttpServletRequest request,
                       HttpServletResponse response )
        throws IOException {
        String value = request.getParameter( KEY_VALUE );
        StringBuilder digits = new StringBuilder();
        for (int n = 0; n < value.length(); n++) {
          if (Character.isDigit( value.charAt( n ) )) {
            digits.append( value.charAt( n ) );
          }
        }
        if (digits.length() == 10) {
          value = new StringBuilder()
              .append( '(' )
              .append( digits.substring( 0, 3 ) )
              .append( ')' )
              .append( digits.substring( 3, 6 ) )
              .append( '-' )
              .append( digits.substring( 6 ) )
              .toString();
          response.setHeader( HEADER_VALID, Boolean.TRUE.toString() );
        }
        else {
          response.setHeader( HEADER_VALID, Boolean.FALSE.toString() );
        }
        response.getWriter().write( value );
    }

    public void doPost( HttpServletRequest request,
                        HttpServletResponse response )
        throws IOException {
        doGet( request, response );
    }

}
```

In this servlet, the `doGet()` method obtains the value of the passed request parameter and iterates through it, collecting any digits that it finds in a StringBuilder instance named `digits`. If exactly 10 digits are found, a new string is constructed (using another instance of StringBuilder) placing the digits into the standard format, and returning them as the response body after setting the "x-valid" response head to `true`. If more or fewer than 10 digits are found, the header is set to `false` and the original value is returned unchanged. Again, `doPost()` is defined to perform the same action as `doGet()`.

This example shows us that the server-side save action resource can manipulate the value that will be placed in the InPlaceEditor in any way—presumably to make life easier for your users.

Now that you know how to use the InPlaceEditor for presenting and editing text, let's look at another editor that Scriptaculous offers for when accepting a more restricted set of inputs from the user: the InPlaceCollectionEditor.

6.3 *The InPlaceCollectionEditor*

The InPlaceEditor allows us to place a seemingly display-only text element into an active edit mode so that the user is free to change the element's value to anything he or she desires. But sometimes you may want to restrict the values that can be entered to a particular set of valid values. We could utilize a server-side validation resource, like the one we discussed in the previous section, to make sure that the user enters a valid value, but this essentially makes the user guess at what the valid values are, and it is a less-than-friendly way to approach the issue.

If we were using normal HTML form elements to present such a control, we'd probably employ either a set of radio buttons or a select element to let the user choose a single value from among a set of valid choices. The Scriptaculous set of controls doesn't provide an in-place editor that displays radio-button style choices. However, it does offer a control that uses a select element while in active mode, in place of the text-input element that the InPlaceEditor uses.

This control is the InPlaceCollectionEditor. Our first step is creating one—we will find it to be similar in nature to its free-form-entry counterpart.

6.3.1 *Creating an InPlaceCollectionEditor*

In many respects, the InPlaceCollectionEditor is very similar to its text-based counterpart: a display-only target element is transformed into an active element that accepts user input. But rather than displaying a text box, a `<select>` element (configured for single selection) is employed to present a predefined list of values to the user.

Unlike the InPlaceEditor, which had no set of predefined elements, the values for the InPlaceCollectionEditor's select options are specified via a client-side list of values. A typical creation snippet for an instance of an InPlaceCollectionEditor might look like this:

```
new Ajax.InPlaceCollectionEditor(
  'targetElement',
  'doSomething.jsp',
  {
    okText: 'OK',
    collection: [value1,value2,value3]
  }
);
```

This looks strikingly familiar to the creation of an InPlaceEditor, except for the new option named collection, which accepts an array whose elements serve as the options to the select element when the editor is placed into active mode. Omitting the collection option will not result in an error, but you'll get a less-than-useful select element with no options.

A simple example page, similar to the example in listing 6.2 for the InPlace-Editor, is shown in listing 6.8.

Listing 6.8   A simple InPlaceCollectionEditor example

```
<html>
  <head>
    <title>Simple InPlaceCollectionEditor Example</title>
    <script type="text/javascript"
            src="../scripts/prototype.js"></script>
    <script type="text/javascript"
            src="../scripts/scriptaculous.js"></script>
    <script type="text/javascript">
      window.onload = function() {
        new Ajax.InPlaceCollectionEditor(
          'theElement',
          'transform.jsp',
          {
            okText: 'Upper me!',
            cancelText: 'Never mind',
            collection: ['one','two','three','four','five']
          }
        );
      }
    </script>
  </head>
```

```
<body>
  <div id="theElement">Click me!</div>
</body>

</html>
```

This code is almost identical to the code of listing 6.2, except that we invoked the constructor for an Ajax.InPlaceCollectionEditor object and supplied a `collection` option providing five text strings as the collection choices. When this page is displayed and the editor is placed into active mode, we see a slightly different result than when we used an InPlaceEditor, as we can see in figure 6.8.

Figure 6.8
Simple InPlaceCollectionEditor in active mode

Rather than the free-entry text box that was created when we used the InPlaceEditor, the InPlaceCollectionEditor creates an HTML `<select>` element. Expanding the element, as in figure 6.9, reveals that the choices we specified in the `collection` option have been used as the options for the select element.

As with the InPlaceEditor control, we have options! Let's take a look at them.

Figure 6.9
The InPlaceCollection-Editor with the select element opened

6.3.2 *The InPlaceCollectionEditor Options*

Aside from the addition of the `collection` option, the list of options for the InPlaceCollectionEditor is a subset of the options inherited from the InPlaceEditor. The options are listed in table 6.2.

Table 6.2   The Ajax.InPlaceCollectionEditor options

	Option	Description
Appearance options	`okButton`	A Boolean value indicating whether or not an OK button is to be displayed. Defaults to `true`.
	`okText`	The text to be placed on the OK button. Defaults to "ok".
	`cancelLink`	A Boolean value indicating whether a cancel link should be displayed. Defaults to `true`.
	`cancelText`	The text of the cancel link. Defaults to "cancel".
	`savingText`	A text string displayed as the value of the control while the save operation (the request initiated by clicking the OK button) is processing. Defaults to "Saving...".
	`clickToEditText`	The text string that appears as the control's tooltip upon mouse-over.
	`highlightcolor`	The color to be applied to the background of the text element upon mouse-over. Defaults to a pale yellow.
	`highlightendcolor`	The color to which the highlight color fades as an effect. Support for this option seems to be spotty in some browsers.
	`collection`	An array of items that are used to populate the select element.
CSS styling and DOM ID options	`savingClassName`	The CSS class name applied to the element while the save operation is in progress. This class is applied when the request to the saving URL is made, and it is removed when the response is returned. The default value is "inplaceeditor-saving".
	`formClassName`	The CSS class name applied to the form created to contain the editor element. Defaults to "inplaceeditor-form".
	`formId`	The ID applied to the form created to contain the editor element.
Callback options	`onComplete`	A JavaScript function that is called upon successful completion of the save request. The default function applies a highlight effect to the editor.
	`onFailure`	A JavaScript function that is called upon failure of the save request. The default function issues an alert showing the failure message.

Table 6.2 The Ajax.InPlaceCollectionEditor options *(continued)*

	Option	Description
Other options	loadTextUrl	The URL of a server-side resource to be contacted in order to load the initial value of the editor when it enters active mode. By default, no back-end load operation takes place and the initial value is the text of the target element. In order for this option to be meaningful, it must return one of the items provided in the collection option to be set as the initial value of the select element.
	externalControl	An element that is to serve as an external control that triggers placing the editor into active mode. This is useful if you want another button or element to trigger editing the control.
	ajaxOptions	A hash object that will be passed to the underlying Prototype Ajax object to use as its options hash.

If you compare table 6.2 with table 6.1 (which listed the options for the InPlace-Editor), you will see that the following options are missing here: rows, cols, size, loadingText, and callback. Seeing as the active element is a select element rather than a text field or text area, the omission of rows, cols, and size should not be surprising. Also, since there is no longer a text field in which to show any loading text, the loadingText option unnecessary, even though the loadTextURL option is still available to fetch a server-side value for the initial value of the select element. The omission of the callback option is a bit puzzling. The internal code for the InPlaceCollectionEditor overwrites any callback you specify with a function of its own (one that creates the query string for the save operation). This may be intentional, or it may be a bug in the version of Scriptaculous available when this chapter was written.

Use the InPlaceCollectionEditor Lab page (available from the chapter's control panel, or at chap6/inplace-collection/lab-inplace-collection.html) to test the effect these options have on the creation and operation of an instance of an Ajax.InPlaceCollectionEditor.

Next, we'll explore another class of control for helping users enter values into our applications.

6.4 *The Ajax autocompleter control*

The in-place editors gave us the ability to create controls that transformed display-only text into editable text, and those controls could tap into the power of the server. Another class of controls, the autocompleters, will help us make life easier for our users when they are faced with the dreaded situation of too much information!

Yes, it really is possible to have too much information—having the amount of information on the Web available at our fingertips is very useful, but it's easy to be overwhelmed with a deluge of data. When designing user interfaces, particularly those for web applications, which have the ability to access huge amounts of data, it is important to avoid flooding a user with too much data or too many choices. In this section and the next, we will explore Scriptaculous controls that help page authors present large lists of choices to users in a friendly and manageable fashion.

When presenting large data sets, such as report data, good user interfaces give the user tools they can employ to gather data in ways that are useful and helpful. For example, filters can be employed to weed out data that is not relevant to the user, and large sets of data can be paged so that they are presented in digestible chunks.

As an example, let's consider a data set that we'll be using throughout this chapter: a list of science fiction movies compiled from Internet sources. This data set consists of 1,460 titles. It's a large set of data, but still a small slice of larger sets of data (such as the list of all movies ever made, for example).

Suppose we wish to present this list to users so that they could pick their favorite sci-fi flick. We could set up an HTML <select> element that they could use to choose one title, but that would hardly be the friendliest thing to do. Most usability guidelines recommend presenting no more than a dozen or so choices to a user at a time, let alone many hundreds! And usability concerns aside, how practical is it to send such a large data set to the page each time it is accessed by potentially hundreds, thousands, or even millions of users on the web? Web application authors are often faced with such dilemmas.

In this section, we will explore the Ajax autocompleter control, and in the next, the local autocompleter control. The Ajax autocompleter (the Ajax.Autocompleter class) implements a control that utilizes Ajax mechanisms to present the user with a filtered list of choices from the server based upon a partial entry of the data. The Scriptaculous local autocompleter (the Autocompleter.Local class) performs a similar function, except that it uses data uploaded to the client rather than data stored on the server, and it may be more appropriate in situations involving a smaller data set that can be efficiently uploaded.

Let's get right to it.

6.4.1 *Creating an Ajax autocompleter*

The process of creating an Ajax Autocompleter instance with a class constructor specifying a few parameters and an options hash is a simple operation. However, there are some rather stringent requirements that must be met regarding the nature of the HTML elements that the Autocompleter manipulates, the response that the server returns, and even the CSS rules that must be defined in order for the control to operate reasonably.

The easiest part of the whole process is constructing the instance of the Ajax.Autocompleter class:

```
new Ajax.Autocompleter(
  'autoCompleteTextField',
  'autoCompleteMenu',
  'fixed-list.html',
  {
    minChars: 1
  }
);
```

The constructor accepts four parameters: the element name of (or a reference to) a text field that is to be populated with a data choice, the element name of (or a reference to) a `<div>` element to be used as a menu of choices by the control, the URL of the server-side resource that will supply the choices, and the usual options hash.

Listing 6.9 shows a simple example in a complete HTML page. You can launch this page from the control panel for this chapter's code examples, or open it directly at autocomleter-ajax/simple-example.html.

Listing 6.9 A simple example page for the Ajax.Autocompleter control

```
<html>
  <head>
    <title>Simple Ajax Autocompleter Example</title>
    <script type="text/javascript"
            src="../scripts/prototype.js"></script>
    <script type="text/javascript"
            src="../scripts/scriptaculous.js"> </script>
    <script type="text/javascript">
      window.onload = function() {
        new Ajax.Autocompleter(          ◁──┐  Create the
          'autoCompleteTextField',        ❶ Autocompleter
          'autoCompleteMenu',
          'fixed-list.html',
          {}
```

```
        );
    }
  </script>
</head>

<body>
  <div>
    <label>Text field:</label>        ❷  Declare the
    <input type="text"      ◁――――         text field
            id="autoCompleteTextField"/>
    <div id="autoCompleteMenu"></div>   ◁――┐  Declare the
  </div>                              ❸    menu container
</body>

</html>
```

This page creates an Ajax Autocompleter instance ❶ in the `onload` function of the page. The parameters to the constructor reference a text field ❷ and an empty `<div>` element ❸. It specifies a URL of "fixed-list.html" as its server-side resource, and specifies an empty options hash. When displayed, the page is rather less than exciting, as shown in figure 6.10.

But upon typing a character in the text box, we get some action going, as shown in figure 6.11. But what does the displayed list mean? And what does it have to do with the x character that was typed?

If you click on one of the listed choices, "Four" for example, you will note that the list that appeared when you typed a character into the text field goes away, and that the clicked text becomes the value of the text field. This list is the menu of autocompletion choices that the server-side resource returned when it was contacted by the control. The presented choices actually have nothing to do with

**Figure 6.10
Initial state of the simple
example page for the Ajax
Autocompleter**

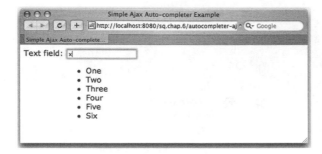

Figure 6.11
The simple example page for the Ajax Autocompleter showing choices

the x character—the fixed-list.html server resource returns (as its name implies) a fixed list, no matter what information it is fed, as shown in listing 6.10.

Listing 6.10   Brain-dead fixed-list server resource

```
<ul>
  <li>One</li>
  <li>Two</li>
  <li>Three</li>
  <li>Four</li>
  <li>Five</li>
  <li>Six</li>
</ul>
```

This server resource doesn't seem very useful, and it isn't. But it does depict the format of the response the server-side resource is expected to return: an unordered list element populated with list item elements representing the choices the user can pick from to populate the text field. In order to be truly useful, the server-side resource needs to respond to the text already entered in the text field, using it to present a list of meaningful choices to the user. We will create just such a resource in section 6.4.3.

Another problem with this simple example is that when the menu of choices pops up, it just doesn't look, or even act, like a menu. It looks like, well, the unordered list that it is. Additionally, there is no feedback of any type indicating that clicking on one of the list items will do anything at all. These are grave usability problems that we will need to solve with CSS. More on that subject will be covered in section 6.4.4.

So far we've seen how we can construct the Autocompleter instance, and how we need to structure the HTML element that it will manipulate. Now let's take a look at the options.

6.4.2 Ajax.Autocompleter options

As was done for the in-place editor controls, a lab page has been set up for the Ajax.Autocompleter control, where you can play around with setting various options for the control. You can call up the page via the chapter's control panel, or find the page at autocompleter-ajax/lab-autocompleter-ajax.jsp.

The set of options available for the Ajax.Autocompleter control is shown in table 6.3.

Table 6.3   The Ajax.Autocompleter options

Option	Description
paramName	The name of the query parameter containing the content of the text field posted to the server-side resource. Defaults to the name of the text field.
minChars	The number of characters that must be entered before a server-side request for choices can be fired off. Defaults to 1.
frequency	The interval, in seconds, between internal checks to see whether a request to the server-side resource should be posted. Defaults to 0.4.
indicator	The ID or reference to an element to be displayed while a server-side request for choices is under way. If omitted, no element is revealed.
parameters	A text string containing extra query parameters to be passed to the server-side resource.
updateElement	A callback function to be triggered when the user selects one of the choices returned from the server. This function replaces the internal function that updates the text field with the chosen value.
afterUpdateElement	A callback function to be triggered after the updateElement function has been executed. By default, no function is triggered.
tokens	A single text string, or array of text strings, that indicate tokens to be used as delimiters to allow multiple elements to be entered into the text field, each of which can be autocompleted individually.

Let's look at how these options are used to tailor the Autocompleter control to our needs.

Specifying server-side parameters

The paramName option allows you to specify the name of the query parameter used to relay the contents of the text field when the Ajax request is sent to the server. The server resource uses the value of this parameter to filter the list of choices that it will return to the client.

Usually, the server resource will use whatever string is passed to it as a prefix filter to determine which choices to return (hence the "autocompleter" name for the control), but you can write the server resource to use the value in any way you deem fit. You can even ignore the input value completely, as our previous simple did, but that's generally of little use. In the lab page for this control, the value of this parameter is hard-coded to "value", as that is the parameter name expected by the server-side resource that provides the autocompletion list. (This resource is discussed in section 6.4.3.)

The `parameters` option can be used to pass extra query parameters to the server resource when a request for choices takes place. This string should be sets of name/value pairs, separated by ampersands, that follow the rules of querystrings. Be sure that any values containing non-alphanumeric characters are properly encoded using the `encodeURIComponent()` function. For example, if you wanted to pass three extra query parameters, the parameters option string could look like this:

```
one=1&two=2&three=3
```

The Ajax Autocompleter Lab page uses this option to pass any server delay setting that you might specify. (The purpose of this value is to artificially delay the server response to simulate a longer network latency than you get with a local server.)

Speaking of server-side latency, we want to have some control over how often and when the server gets hit by our control. Let's see what options we have to help us with this.

Controlling when the autocompleter triggers

The `minChars` option allows you to specify the minimum number of characters that need to be entered into the text field before a server-side request can be made. Let's say, for example, that we know that all or most of the choices begin with the word "The." In such a case, you might wish to set the `minChars` options to 5, because until the fifth character is entered, all entries in the list would match and be returned as choices.

Internally, the control's code checks at regular intervals to see whether a server request for more choices is appropriate. The `frequency` option allows you to override the default interval of 0.4 seconds. You might want to specify a smaller value if your server and connection are fast and can support a more frequent request load, or a larger value to slow it down if the default value hammers your server too quickly for it to keep up.

Now that we know how to keep the server happy, what about our users?

Keeping the user informed

The `indicator` option allows you to specify an HTML element on your page that is revealed while a server request for choices is being made, and that is hidden again when the request completes. This is most often used to display a message stating that a server operation has taken place, or to reveal an animation that indicates an active operation. This lets the user know that something is still happening when network latency delays the display of the choices.

The lab page for this control references a GIF animation that is revealed if you select the "Yes" radio button for the indicator option. You can set the server delay value to something like 3000 (3 seconds) to make sure that the request takes long enough for you to see the effect of this option.

Now let's see how we can keep ourselves as well informed as the users of our pages.

Keeping your code informed

There are two options you can use as callbacks into your own code: `updateElement` and `afterUpdateElement`.

The `updateElement` option allows you to replace the function that will gain control when a choice is made from the available list presented to the user. That selection is passed as the single parameter to this callback function. Since this function replaces the internal function that updates the text field, that responsibility will fall on your callback function. This option is most useful when you want your page to do something other than update the text field.

If you want to let the control's code update the text fields as normal, but also to be informed, you could register a callback with the `afterUpdateElement` option. This callback is invoked after the function identified by the `updateElement` option (be it yours or the internal function) has been executed. It is passed a reference to the text field as its first parameter, and the selected choice from the completion list is the second.

That's all good stuff. Now let's see what other capabilities the options can add to our control. For example, what if we would like the user to be able to enter multiple elements?

Allowing multiple completion items in the text field

You can enable the entry of multiple autocompleted items in the single text field attached to the Ajax.Autocompleter control by supplying the character (or characters) that you want to use to separate the entries as the value of the `tokens` option. This option should be either a string consisting of the single character you want to use as a token (the comma is a popular choice), or a string array of single-character strings containing the characters to be used as delimiters.

For example, either of the following lines could be used:

```
tokens: ',',
tokens: [',',';'],
```

The latter example makes both the comma and the semicolon token characters. When a token character or characters are specified, entering the token character(s) at the end of the text field starts another, completely new autocompletion entry.

To demonstrate this capability, display the Ajax.Autocompleter Lab page, leaving all other options empty, but entering a single comma into the tokens field. Type "The" into the Movie Title text field. The autocompleter will list many movies starting with "The". Pick a short one, and enter a comma at the end of the text field (which should now be populated with the short movie title that you picked) and type "The" again. The autocompletion menu reappears. Choose another short title and repeat. You can see that each entry separated by the token character (in this case, the comma) is treated as a separate choice.

That completes our tour of the Autocompleter options. Now let's take a look at how we powered the back-end for the lab page we used to examine these options.

6.4.3 *The sci-fi movie autocompleter servlet*

If you've toyed around with the Ajax.Autocompleter Lab page at all, you will have noticed that when the autocompleter activates, it displays choices from a list of science fiction and horror movie titles. In this section, we will explore the server-side resources that provides this list. The pattern employed by this resource is suitable for most back-end elements that can power an autocompleter.

So far in this chapter, the active server-side resources we have employed have been fairly simple snippets of code suitable for small JSP pages. The autocompleter resource, on the other hand, is a bit more complex. Generally, autocompletion choices may come from text files on the server, or even from a database. Such complex operations are unsuitable for coding into a JSP page, so we will be utilizing the services of a Java servlet to perform the heavy lifting.

In fact, following modern web application best practices, the servlet will perform the processing necessary to create the list of items that match the autocompletion string passed to it, and will then forward the request on to a JSP page which will use those values to create the unordered HTML list. This pattern of performing processing in a servlet and using a JSP page to render the view is known as the Model 2 Pattern. It follows the accepted practice of structuring web applications according to the MVC Pattern, at least to the extent that the limitations of the HTTP protocol allow.

Let's start by taking a peek at the servlet class.

The MoviesAutocompleterServlet class

The controller portion of our autocompletion server-side resource is a servlet named MoviesAutocompleterServlet. In the source code provided for this chapter, you will find the source of this servlet under the WEB-INF/src folder in the package hierarchy. Note that it is not customary to place the source code for web applications in the WEB-INF folder, or anywhere in the web application structure, for that matter; we have done so here as a convenience for you.

Data such as a list of movie titles would be kept in a database or in files on the filesystem. However, in order to keep these examples focused on the current subject matter, the servlet will obtain the list of possible choices from a string hardcoded into the program itself. Do not take this as an endorsement of this approach; it is used here only for demonstration purposes.

The source for the servlet is shown in listing 6.11.

Listing 6.11   The MoviesAutocompleterServlet class

```
package org.bibeault.sq.chap6;

import javax.servlet.http.HttpServlet;
import javax.servlet.http.HttpServletRequest;
import javax.servlet.http.HttpServletResponse;
import javax.servlet.ServletException;
import java.io.IOException;
import java.util.ArrayList;
import java.util.List;

public class MoviesAutocompleterServlet extends HttpServlet {

    public static final String KEY_VALUE = "value";        ◁──┐  ❶ Declare
    public static final String KEY_DELAY = "delay";            │      constant
                                                               ●      string

    public static final String VAR_LIST = "list";

    public static final String VIEW_RESOURCE =                 ❷ Define
            "/autocompleter-ajax/unordered-list.jsp";          ●   POST in
                                                                   terms of
    public void doPost( HttpServletRequest request,     ◁──┘      GET
                        HttpServletResponse response )
            throws IOException, ServletException {
```

```
        doGet( request, response );
}
                                                    ← ③ Declare the
public void doGet( HttpServletRequest request,          GET handler
                   HttpServletResponse response )
        throws IOException, ServletException {
    //
    // If a delay was requested, cause the delay to occur
    //
    if (request.getParameter( KEY_DELAY ) != null) {    ←
        delay(request.getParameter( KEY_DELAY ));         ④ Obtain delay
    }                                                       value
    //
    // Get the passed prefix and obtain the list of matches
    //
    String prefix = request.getParameter( KEY_VALUE );  ←
    List<String> matches = findMatches( prefix );        Obtain ⑤
    //                                                   prefix value
    // Set the matches as a scoped variable on the request
    // and shuffle off to the JSP            Set list as a request- ⑥
    //                                         scoped variable
    request.setAttribute( VAR_LIST, matches );  ←
    request.getRequestDispatcher( VIEW_RESOURCE   )
        .forward( request, response );          Forward to
}                                               the JSP page ⑦
                              Effect the delay ⑧
private void delay( String delayValue ) {  ←
    try {
        Thread.sleep( Integer.parseInt( delayValue ) );
    }
    catch (Exception e) {
        //On failure, perform no delay
    }                                    Declare method to ⑨
}                                          find matches

private List<String> findMatches( String prefix ) {  ←
    List<String> matches = new ArrayList<String>();
    for (String choice : MoviesList.getMovies()) {
        if (choice.startsWith( prefix )) {
            matches.add( choice );
        }
    }
    return matches;
}

}
```

This servlet, extended as usual from HttpServlet, is fairly simple in structure and operation. As it is generally considered poor practice to embed strings in code where they are difficult to find or reuse, the servlet first declares a number of constant strings ❶ for use in the code.

As we have no foreknowledge of whether the page author who will be using this servlet is going to specify a GET or POST operation, we support both by coding the doPost() method ❷ to simply call the doGet() method ❸.

Within the doGet() method, we first check to see if a delay parameter was passed ❹ as a query parameter (known in servlet parlance as a request parameter). If so, we pass that value to a private function ❽ that causes the thread running this code to go to sleep for the specified number of milliseconds. This delay is not a normal function that one would put into such a servlet. Rather, it exists only to help users of the Ajax.Autocompleter Lab page simulate longer network latencies than are normally experienced when serving data from a local server. Most readers of this chapter are probably serving their data locally, so this option is useful when checking how options like indicator act when network delays occur.

After causing any artificial delay, the servlet gets down to the real business at hand: building the list of movie titles that match the data passed as the value request parameter. The value of that parameter is obtained and is passed ❺ to a private method ❾ that creates a List of strings matching the prefix. It is this private method (the findMatches() method) that you would refactor in order to obtain the list from a more realistic data store, such as a database.

After the List is obtained, it is placed onto the request as a scoped variable named list ❻, and the request is forwarded to the JSP resource ❼ whose job is to render the list in an appropriate fashion before it is returned as the response. This JSP page is discussed in the next section.

The findMatches() method ❾ simply obtains the full list of movies from an abstract class named MoviesList (which we won't bother to show here, as it is simply a wrapper around a string array of movie titles—the source is included in the same folder as the servlet if you are curious). It then constructs the matching list from all titles that begin with the passed prefix.

As you can see, no knowledge of how the data is to be rendered as HTML is included in this servlet. It simply creates a List of the results and forwards it along to another component (a JSP page in this case) whose job it is to format the HTML. This is a good application of the principle of Separation of Concerns, and would allow this servlet to be reused to render the list in any format if we were to parameterize to which JSP the matching list were forwarded.

So how about that JSP page? How does it do its job?

The unordered-list-builder JSP page

When the autocompleter servlet we looked at in the previous section finished building its list of matching movie titles, it placed the list in a request-scoped variable named `list` and forwarded to a JSP page. That JSP page, unordered-list.jsp, is shown in listing 6.12.

Listing 6.12   The unordered-list-builder JSP page

```
<%@ taglib uri="http://java.sun.com/jsp/jstl/core" prefix="c" %>
<ul>
  <c:forEach items="${list}" var="item">
    <li>${item}</li>
  </c:forEach>
</ul>
```

The purpose of this JSP page is to take a list of items and render an HTML `<ul>` element with the list items as the `<li>` elements. To do this, it employs the services of the JSTL (JavaServer Pages Standard Tag Library) `<c:forEach>` action. The tag library for the JSTL core actions is declared, and the HTML construct for the unordered list is emitted by iterating over all elements in the scoped variable named `list`.

Note that this resource also exhibits the principle of Separation of Concerns. This JSP page could be used by any other server-side resource wishing to create an unordered HTML list out of a collection of elements. As long as the forwarding resource places the collection as a scoped variable named `list` (this requirement would be known as the page contract for this JSP page), this page will dutifully convert that collection into a `<ul>` construct.

Moreover, because we employed the JSTL `<c:forEach>` action, the exact nature of that scoped variable can be of many supported formats. We used a List implementation in our servlet, but other resources could have used a Set, a Map, or any other iterable member of the Java collection classes. It could even be a Java array. By keeping our controller and view resources decoupled in this fashion, each is more versatile, as well as easier to create, understand, and maintain. Ah, the joys of following best practices!

6.4.4 *Styling the choices menu*

You probably remember that when we ran the simple-example.html page for this control, the autocompletion menu looked pretty lousy. (Refer back to figure 6.11 if you need reminding.) If you subsequently ran the lab page for this control, you would have seen that the menu looked (and acted) much better (assuming you like burnt orange). The menu in the former page was unstyled, while the latter employed some CSS magic to make the menu look and act a lot better. In this section, we will take a look at some of the CSS rules we employed to achieve that. These rules can be found in the styles.css file in the same folder as the lab page.

One of the first elements we want to style is the unordered list itself, in order to make it look like a menu container. Since the `<ul>` element is contained within a `<div>` element with an ID of `autocompleteMenu`, the CSS selector `#autocomplete-Menu ul` will cause the style rules to be applied to our unordered list while ignoring any other `<ul>` elements that might be on the page.

The rule is as follows:

```
#autocompleteMenu ul {
   border: 2px outset #cc9933;
   background-color: #cc9933;
   margin-left: 12px;
   padding: 4px 6px;
   width: 288px;
   height: 360px;
   overflow: auto;
}
```

We apply a border and background color to the element in order to make it look like a container. Its left margin is offset slightly from where it would normally appear, because we felt that made it look a bit better in relation to the autocompletion text field. Padding was added to keep the internal elements from looking too crowded. And finally, a fixed width and height were applied to constrain the size of the menu, along with an overflow rule that causes a scroll bar to be added to the menu if its contents exceed the constraining dimensions.

Now, on to styling the list items themselves. For that we used the following rule:

```
#autocompleteMenu li {
   color: white;
   list-style-type: none;
   padding: 0px;
   margin: 0px;
   border-bottom: 1px solid black;
   cursor: pointer;
}
```

We made the text color white and removed any bullets that might be shown on the items by setting the list style to none. All padding and margins were removed from the items so that they pack together tightly in the menu. In order to help visually separate the items from one another, a bottom border of a single pixel line was added. And finally, in order to clue the user in to the fact that the items are clickable elements, the cursor is set so that it changes to the little-hand pointer when the mouse pointer is over an item.

To add even more user feedback to the menu, we also added a selected rule, so that the item over which the cursor is positioned highlights itself:

```
#autocompleteMenu li.selected {
  color: #ffcc66;
  font-weight: bold;
}
```

This lightens the color of the item and makes it bold when the cursor passes over it.

The difference between the unstyled and styled versions of the menu can be seen in figure 6.12.

The Scriptaculous Ajax Autocompleter gives us a powerful server-assisted control. But what about cases where the server doesn't really need to be involved?

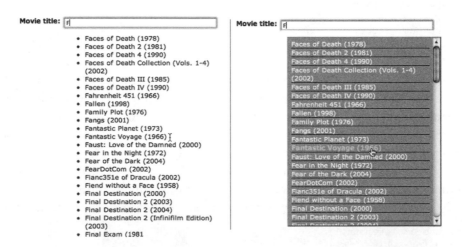

Figure 6.12 Lousy-looking menu vs. styled menu

6.5 *The Scriptaculous local autocompleter control*

One of the great features of the Ajax autocompleter control is that it allows you to access a large amount of data stored on the server in a fashion that is fairly seamless to a user of your application. The price paid for this access is, of course, network latency. Depending upon the nature of the data set, and the corresponding nature of the prefix entered by the user, a small or a large amount of data may need to be transferred. And that, of course, takes time.

There are times when you want to use a control similar in functionality to the Ajax autocompleter but with a backing data set that is small enough to upload to the client as part of the page load. For just such occasions, Scriptaculous makes available the local autocompleter control. As we will see, the local autocompleter shares a lot of characteristics with the Ajax autocompleter (and behind the scenes, a lot of code as well). But before just assuming that a local autocompleter will be faster than a remote one, be sure to test that supposition!

The local autocompleter must perform frequent calculations over what may still be a large data set, and in an environment that is usually not quite as swift as its server-side counterpart. You may find that there are occasions when any network delay experienced when using a remotely fed autocompleter may actually be faster than sorting through a large set of data on the client machine. So don't assume—test!

Once you have convinced yourself that a local control is the way to go for a particular situation, you'll need to create one. Let's see how.

6.5.1 *Creating a local autocompleter*

Creating a local autocompleter is almost identical to creating an Ajax autocompleter, which we did in section 6.4.1. The same type of constructor is used with almost the same parameters, and the HTML elements that the created autocompleter will manipulate must follow the same stringent rules. The major difference lies in how the backing data set used for autocompletion is identified to the control.

With an Ajax autocompleter, we supplied the URL of a server-side resource that would perform the necessary filtering, given the user input, and that would return only the data elements that matched. With a local autocompleter, we instead supply the full list of data elements as a JavaScript String array, and the control itself performs the filtering operation within its own client code. No server interaction whatsoever takes place (except for the initial loading of the page, of course).

A typical construction sequence might look like this:

```
new Autocompleter.Local(
  'autoCompleteTextField',
  'autoCompleteMenu',
  ['abcdef','abcdeg','abcdfg','abcefg','abdefg','acdefg'],
  {}
);
```

We can see that, except for the third parameter, the parameters to the constructor are the same: the ID of the text field element, followed by the ID of the menu element, and with the options hash as the fourth parameter. For the third parameter, instead of the URL we used for the server-assisted autocompleter, we supply a small String array that contains all of the possible values. Generally, rather than typing in a large data set, such pages are generated with server-side templates (such as PHP or JSP) so that the array can be easily built into the page from server-side data.

The name of the object may seem a little odd: Autocompleter.Local. After seeing the Ajax.Autocompleter, I suppose one would expect the object to be named Local.Autocompleter, but for whatever reason, that's not the case.

An example of using the local autocompleter is shown in listing 6.13, and it can be found using the control panel for this chapter's code or by visiting the page at autocompleter-local/simple-example.html.

Listing 6.13 A simple example of a local autocompleter

```html
<html>
  <head>
    <title>Simple Local Autocompleter Example</title>
    <script type="text/javascript"
            src="../scripts/prototype.js"></script>
    <script type="text/javascript"
            src="../scripts/scriptaculous.js"></script>
    <script type="text/javascript">
      window.onload = function() {
        new Autocompleter.Local(
          'autoCompleteTextField',
          'autoCompleteMenu',
          ['abcdef','abcdeg','abcdfg','abcefg','abdefg','acdefg'],
          {}
        );
      }
    </script>
  </head>
```

```
<body>
  <div>
    <label>Text field:</label>
    <input type="text" id="autoCompleteTextField"/>
    <div id="autoCompleteMenu"></div>
  </div>
</body>

</html>
```

When the page is displayed and the character a is typed into the text box, the page shown in figure 6.13 will be displayed.

As you type successive letters in the alphabet, b, then c, then d, and so on, note how the available matching data is pared down to show only the items that match what you have typed into the text box, until you type the f, which uniquely identifies the item.

Also note the rather unsightly styling of the menu. We dealt with that for the Ajax autocompleter in section 6.4.4, and the exact same styling tips presented there also work for the local autocompleter. After all, the HTML elements are identical to those used for its Ajax counterpart.

You might expect that like all the other controls we've seen, the local autocompleter sports a number of options to adjust its behavior, and you'd be right. Let's take a look at them.

6.5.2 *Autocompleter.Local options*

The local autocompleter shares a great deal of code with the Ajax autocompleter and inherits all of the options that class supports. Please refer to table 6.3 in section 6.4.2 for details on those options, which work exactly the same way for a local autocompleter as they do for an Ajax autocompleter.

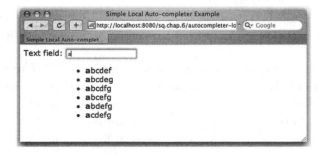

Figure 6.13
A simple example page for the local autocompleter

However, even though all the options may be inherited in code, it doesn't mean that they all make sense. The `paramName` and `parameters` options can be set, but because they make no sense in the context of a control that makes no server-side request, they are ignored. From the user point of view, the local autocompleter effectively does not support these two options.

The `indicator` option is another special case. This option is supported in code, and the element identified by the indicator is set to be displayed while the computations to determine the list are taking place. But because of the manner in which the browser and script engine interact, the element is hidden again before the browser ever gets a chance to actually show it. So while this option causes the appropriate code to execute, its effects are never seen, meaning that it is effectively not supported by the local control.

The local autocompleter does, however, sport a number of options that are not available for the Ajax autocompleter, and they are listed in table 6.4.

Table 6.4 Options for the Autocompleter.Local class

Option	Description
choices	The number of choices to display. Defaults to 10.
partialSearch	A Boolean option that enables or disables matching at the beginning of words embedded within the completion strings. Defaults to true (enabled).
fullSearch	A Boolean option that enables or disables matching anywhere within the completion strings. Defaults to false (disabled).
partialChars	The number of characters that must be typed before any partial matching is attempted. Defaults to 2.
ignoreCase	A Boolean option that specifies whether case is ignored when matching. Defaults to true.

In order to help you wrap your head around all these options, we created a lab page for the local autocompleter. You can access this page via this chapter code's control panel, or simply open the autocompleter-local/lab-autocompleter-local.jsp page.

This page allows you to manipulate the most common options for the local autocompleter and to specify the data set to be used for completion matching. You can either type your own data into the text area control, one entry per line, or you can click the Preload button. Clicking this button initiates an Ajax request that copies the movie titles you saw in the previous section into the text area.

When you click the Create Autocompleter button, an instance of Autocompleter.Local is created using the specified options and taking the contents of the text area (converted to a String array) as the completion data set.

Let's explore the options and customize how this control operates. You can follow along with the lab page loaded into your browser.

Controlling how many choices are shown

The `choices` option is a fairly straightforward setting. It limits the number of choices that are displayed in the menu. The default for this option seems a bit low at 10, so it is frequently overridden with a higher value. Specify a larger value (up to the size of the entire candidate set) if you want more choices to be shown.

To see this option in action, launch the lab page and populate the Choices List with the list of movie titles (by clicking the Preload button). Leave the Choices option field blank, and create the autocompleter by clicking the Create Autocompleter button. Type "The" into the autocompleter field and note that only 10 choices are shown, even though many more choices are available in the list.

Now set the Choices field to 100 and create a new autocompleter. Clear the autocompleter field and type "The" into the field again. Many more choices will be displayed.

Now let's see how we can control how the control performs matching.

Matching more than the beginnings of strings

The local autocompleter has four options that control how the matching algorithm is applied to the candidate data: `partialSearch`, `minChars`, `partialChars`, and `fullSearch`.

The `partialSearch` option tells the code to use the text in the autocompleter field to match the beginning of any word in the candidate strings. The `partialChars` option specifies the number of characters that must be typed before partial matching is attempted (not to be confused with `minChars`, which specifies the number of characters necessary before performing any matching at all).

Bring up the Local Autocompleter Lab page and leave all options blank except Choices. Enter a fairly high number for this option, such as 100, so that we can better see the results of the matching options. Preload the choices list with movie titles, and create the autocompleter. Type "day" (without the quotes, of course) into the autocompleter field. Note that because `partialSearch` is enabled by default, not only did we get matches such as "Day of the Triffids," which begins with the text we typed, candidates that include the word "day" or words that start with "day" are also included: "The Day the Earth Stood Still" and "Seven Days to Live."

Since `partialChars` defaults to 2, this partial matching was applied after we typed the two characters d and a. Change `partialChars` to 4, create a new auto-completer, clear the field, and type in "day" again. Notice that because we have not reached the threshold for partial matching to take place, only choices with "day" at the beginning of the candidate string are displayed.

When the `fullSearch` option is enabled the typed text is matched anywhere within the candidate string—not only at the beginning of the strings, and not only at the beginnings of words within the strings.

Set `partialChars` back to 2 (or clear its field), enable the `fullSearch` option, and create a new autocompleter. Clear the autocomplete field and type in "day" once again. Not only do we now get the set of choices we saw before (those that begin with "day" or contain words beginning with "day"), but we also get choices with "day" anywhere within the string, such as "Friday the 13th."

Note that in order for `fullSearch` to take effect, `partialSearch` must also be enabled. If you specifically disable `partialSearch` (it is enabled by default), the `fullSearch` option is ignored.

What other options do we have for controlling matching? Let's take a look.

Controlling the case sensitivity of matching

The matching that we've seen so far has all been case-sensitive. The `ignoreCase` option, when enabled (as it is by default), allows case-insensitive matching to take place.

Let's see it in action. In the lab page, enable partial and full searching, and be sure that `ignoreCase` is enabled. Create an autocompleter and type "DAY" (all caps) into the text field. Note that matches are made regardless of the fact that the entry text was all uppercase.

Now, disable `ignoreCase`, create a new autocompleter, and type "day" into the text field. Note that the matching is now case-sensitive, and that only titles with the text "day" in all lowercase are displayed.

We now have two flavors of in-place editors and two flavors of autocompleters under our belts; we've broadened the scope of control types that we can add to our web application pages. Next, let's take a look at yet another Scriptaculous control for our toolbox.

6.6 *The slider control*

So far we have seen two types of Scriptaculous controls that close the gap between desktop applications and web applications: the in-place editor and the autocompleter. The in-place editor is useful for switching between display-only and editable versions of data, and the autocompleter is great for presenting users with filtered lists of choices that match text they are typing into a text field. But another powerful desktop control that is not available to web developers as a native control is the slider, which allows users to choose a single value from a range.

A slider control is usually presented as a track that represents the range of values available, and a handle that represents the selected value within that range. Figure 6.14 shows some representative slider controls from various desktop programs:

- (a)   The volume control from Apple's iTunes
- (b)   The screen resolution control from the Windows XP
         Display Options Control Panel
- (c)   The Mac OS X System Preferences dock size control
- (d)   The volume control from the Windows XP Sound Panel

Note that sliders can be displayed in either a horizontal or vertical orientation. When horizontal, the left end of the track usually represents the lowest value, while in a vertical orientation, the bottom of the slide is usually the lowest value. The slider is controlled by "grabbing" the handle with the mouse and dragging it to the desired position within the track. It can also be manipulated by clicking in the track itself, which moves the handle toward or exactly to the location of the click.

The slider is a powerful control in that it allows users to select from a range of values without needing to type values into a text field, and without the possibility

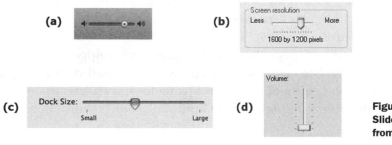

**Figure 6.14
Sliders of various types
from desktop applications**

of a validation error. Because HTML provides no slider control for the Web, Scriptaculous provides one for you to use on your pages.

6.6.1 *Creating a slider control*

A slider control is created by constructing an object and providing parameters and an options hash, as usual. In the case of the slider control, the object class is Control.Slider, and a typical construction statement might look like this:

```
new Control.Slider(
  'sliderHandle',
  'sliderTrack',
  {}
);
```

The first parameter must be the ID of (or element reference to) the block element serving as the handle of the slider, and the second parameter is the ID of (or element reference to) the track. The third parameter is the ubiquitous options hash.

As with the other controls, the HTML elements to which the slider will be attached must follow certain rules. In the case of the slider there are two elements: the track element, which must be a block element (most often a `<div>` element, but we'll see the use of another element type in just a little while), and the handle element, which should be contained within that track element. A typical HTML structure for the slider control is as follows:

```
<div id="sliderTrack">
  <div id="sliderHandle"></div>
</div>
```

Placed on a page with no styling, you wouldn't see much, as the `<div>` elements have nothing to display, and the Control.Slider doesn't do anything about that. It is the responsibility of the page author to apply styling to the `<div>` elements to achieve the desired look for the control. When `<div>` elements are used, as in the previous example, width and height CSS attributes, along with borders, background colors, and similar rendition attributes, are applied to achieve the visual aspects of the control.

Let's take a look at a page that uses the preceding snippets to create a functional slider control. The code for this page can be accessed via the Simple Example link in the Slider section of the control panel for this chapter's code examples, or within the file slider/simple-example.html. The code is shown in listing 6.14.

Listing 6.14 A simple Slider control example

```html
<html>
  <head>
    <title>Simple Slider Example</title>
    <script type="text/javascript"
            src="../scripts/prototype.js"></script>
    <script type="text/javascript"
            src="../scripts/scriptaculous.js"></script>
    <script type="text/javascript">
      window.onload = function() {
          new Control.Slider(
            'sliderHandle',
            'sliderTrack',
            {}
          );
      }
    </script>
    <style type="text/css">
      #sliderTrack {
        width: 175px;
        height: 12px;
        background-color: white;
        border: 1px blue solid;
        cursor: pointer;
      }
      #sliderHandle {
        width: 4px;
        height: 12px;
        background-color: green;
        cursor: pointer;
      }
    </style>
  </head>

  <body>
    <div id="sliderTrack">
      <div id="sliderHandle"></div>
    </div>
  </body>

</html>
```

Note that the CSS styles we applied in this example create simple box elements. The track is a hollow blue-outlined box completely containing the handle, while the handle is a solid green box. We also added the pointer cursor to these elements, so that the user can see that these are active elements.

Figure 6.15
A simple Slider control
example

When displayed, this page appears as shown in figure 6.15. It's not all that exciting, but it is a working slider control, if not a particularly useful one.

With the page displayed, click anywhere within the track element. Note how the handle jumps to the clicked location, as shown in figure 6.16. This change in location also changes the value represented by the control. Just what that value is, we have no way of knowing at this point, but we'll rectify that in a later example.

Display the page again (if you closed it) and, this time, click and drag on the handle. Note how the handle follows the movement of the cursor until you let go of the mouse button.

Even though we used some very simple styling in this example, you have a lot of leeway in how you style sliders. By simply changing the CSS rule for the track a bit, as follows, we can change the visual appearance of the slider to what is shown in figure 6.17.

```
#sliderTrack {
  width: 175px;
  height: 4px;
  background-color: pink;
  cursor: pointer;
}
```

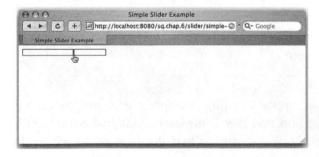

Figure 6.16
Slider handle moves to
a clicked location on the track

Figure 6.17
A Slider control with a
narrow track

This is usable, but perhaps a trifle austere. In the next section, we'll see if we can spiff it up a bit by employing images.

6.6.2 *Using images with a slider*

The desktop examples of slider controls that were presented in figure 6.14 looked a bit nicer than the sliders we created in the previous section using simple blocks of color. To spruce up the control, we'll use some images for the track and the handle.

Using the control panel for this chapter's code, click on the Image Example link in the Slider section. The page shown in figure 6.18 will be displayed. Now that's more like it!

Implementing this change to the slider (which is obviously modeled after slider *c* in figure 6.14) is surprisingly simple. The code for this page, available in slider/image-example.html, is almost a carbon copy of the simple example page we examined in listing 6.14. The new page is shown in listing 6.15, with the differences from the simple example page highlighted in bold.

Figure 6.18
A Slider control constructed
using images

Listing 6.15 The Image Slider Example page

```html
<html>
  <head>
    <title>Image Slider Example</title>
    <script type="text/javascript"
            src="../scripts/prototype.js"></script>
    <script type="text/javascript"
            src="../scripts/scriptaculous.js"></script>
    <script type="text/javascript">
      window.onload = function() {
          new Control.Slider(
            'sliderHandle',
            'sliderTrack',
            {}
          );
      }
    </script>
    <style type="text/css">
      #sliderTrack {
        width: 175px;
        height: 10px;
        background-image: url(track.gif);
        background-repeat: no-repeat;
        cursor: pointer;
      }
      #sliderHandle {
        margin-top: -4px;
        cursor: pointer;
      }
    </style>
  </head>

  <body>
    <div id="sliderTrack">
        <img id="sliderHandle"
            src="handle-green.gif"/>
    </div>
  </body>

</html>
```

1 Adjust the appearance of the track

2 Shift the location of the handle

3 SUse an image for the handle

The first change (other than the page title) rearranges the track styling **1** to have a slightly different size (the height of the track image), and to have a nonrepeating background image that resembles a grooved track. Even though we've made the <div> element the same size as the background image, the no-repeat attribute is necessary, as some browsers (such as Internet Explorer) will expand the size of the <div> to accommodate its contents, and we'd see the track image tiled across its background. We can't make the track an <img> element, since it needs to contain the handle element, and image elements aren't containers. So the background image trick will work just as well.

The next change was to the CSS rule for the handle **❷**. We removed the dimension attributes (as the handle is no longer a <div>, as we'll see next) and used a negative margin value to nudge the top of the handle up a bit in relation to the track. The handle element itself was changed from a <div> to an image element **❸** that references the image for the pentagonal handle.

The green version of the handle was used for this example. Within the slider folder you will find handle images in numerous colors, as well as a gray one useful for indicating when the control is disabled.

This isn't the only construct that would work. If you'd rather use two images instead of using the background image trick, you could place the images within a relatively positioned parent, and use absolute positioning to place the image elements in the correct locations with respect to the parent and each other. Which construct (or any possible others) you choose depends upon the context in which the control will appear, as well as your own whims.

That is all very nice, but we still don't have a control that's all that useful. In section 6.6.4, we will explore a more in-depth example that shows the slider in a more useful light, but first we'll take a look at some of the options available to a Slider control.

6.6.3 *The Control.Slider options*

As we write this, the documentation for the Slider control on the Scriptaculous site is rather seriously out of sync with what is actually implemented and working in the code. In this section, we discuss only the options that are known to be supported and that work correctly with the version of the Slider control upon which this book is based. The options for the Control.Slider control are shown in table 6.5.

Table 6.5   The Control.Slider options

Option	Description
axis	The orientation of the control, which can be set to horizontal or vertical. The default orientation is horizontal.
range	The range of the slider values, defined as an instance of a Prototype ObjectRange instance. Defaults to 0 through 1.

Table 6.5 The Control.Slider options *(continued)*

Option	Description
values	The discrete set of values that the slider can acquire. If omitted, all values within the range can be set.
sliderValue	The initial value of the slider. If omitted, the value represented by the left-most (or top-most) edge of the slider is the initial value.
disabled	A Boolean value that specifies whether the slide is initially disabled. Defaults to false (not disabled).
onChange	Callback invoked when the slider value changes.
onSlide	Callback invoked when the handle is being dragged.

As with the other controls, a lab page has been set up where you can play around with various settings for the most common Slider options. You can open the page from the control panel for this chapter's code, or simply open the slider/lab-slider.html file.

This lab is a bit different in some ways from those of the other controls. In most of the other lab pages, values that you enter into the lab page become direct properties of the options hash for the control. In the Slider Lab page, a bit of interpretation or extra processing is needed (for example, the minimum and maximum values you specify need to be converted to an ObjectRange object rather than being directly placed into the options hash). The Applied Options section of the lab page is much more important here, as it will show you what options were actually created and passed to the control's constructor.

With that said, let's dig in.

Setting the orientation

The axis option can be used to specify a horizontal or vertical orientation for the Slider control. As we have seen in our examples so far, the control defaults to a horizontal orientation.

In a horizontal control, it's usually natural to have the lowest value at the left end of the control, and the highest value at the right end. But in a vertical control, depending upon the context, it can make sense either way, with the highest values at the top of the control, or at the bottom. The manner in which the values are assigned is covered in the next section.

Note that the orientation of the axis does not in any way affect the appearance or dimensions of the control. When placing a Slider control in a vertical orientation, just be sure to specify your CSS dimensions (or images) to create a tall narrow control rather than a long, low control, as would be natural for the horizontal orientation.

When you select a vertical orientation in the Control.Slider Lab page, not only is the axis option added to the options hash, but the CSS rules that apply to the control element are also changed to use alternate styling and images to create a tall control. It is your responsibility as a page author to ensure that the appearance of the HTML elements attached to the control match its orientation.

When creating a slider control in either orientation, we'll obviously want to indicate the value range it represents. Let's see the options that allow us to do just that.

Setting the range of values

Two options, `range` and `values`, set the range of values that the slider can acquire.

The `range` option specifies a pair of values that represent the extreme ends of the control. When in horizontal orientation, the first value is assigned to the left-most edge of the slider, and the second value to the right-most edge. In vertical orientation, the first value is assigned to the top of the control, and the second value to the bottom.

This option is expressed as an instance of a Prototype ObjectRange class. You can either create such an instance the "normal" way, like this,

```
new ObjectRange(value1,value2)
```

or you can employ the handy `$R()` Prototype helper function to create a range using this shortened notation:

```
$R(value1,value2)
```

If we wanted to set up a slider such that the range of values spans from 1 at the left end of the control to 100 at the right end, we would specify the `range` option as follows:

```
range: $R(1,100)
```

If we could see the values that the slider was acquiring (patience, that's coming up next), we'd notice that the slider acquires not only integer values, but also all real values within the range. If we move the handle to about what we think is the middle of a control with a range of 1 through 100, we might expect the value to be 50, but instead we may find that the value is 48.7573572347. If we want to specify the discrete values within the range that the slider should acquire, we can do that with the `values` option.

The `values` option specifies an array of the values that the slider can be set to. Interesting (but not always pleasing) behavior can be achieved by making the `values` and `range` options not match each other, but usually you want to make sure that they are in sync. For example, if we set the range to 1 through 100, as shown in the previous code examples, and specified the `values` option as follows,

```
values: [1,25,50,75,100]
```

the slider can only be set to the discrete values listed as the handle is moved.

If we wanted to allow the slider to achieve all integer values within the range, we'd construct an array containing all those values to pass as the values option. The Control.Slider Lab page demonstrates this when you choose to enable the Discrete option. When Discrete is true, all integer values within the specified range are added to an array used as the value of the `values` option.

At any time, the value of the slider can be set programmatically by calling the `setValue()` method of the Slider instance:

```
sliderInstance.setValue(47);
```

If a `values` list was provided, and the value specified in the `setValue()` method is not one of the discrete values in the list, the value will be rounded to the nearest permissible value.

If, for some reason, we wanted to reverse the direction and have the control span from 100 down to 1, we would simply use a range option like this,

```
range: $R(100,1)
```

and specify a `values` option with valid decreasing values. Omitting the `values` option when using a reversed range seems to put the control in an odd state, so be sure to use the `values` option when using a reversed range.

Next, we'll look at toggling between an enabled and a disabled state. Many of the HTML form controls exhibit such an ability, and the slider is no exception.

Enabling and disabling the control

By default, a Slider instance is created in the enabled state. However, you can start the slider in a disabled state by specifying this option:

```
disabled: true
```

You can also affect the state of the option programmatically with the `setDisabled()` and `setEnabled()` methods of the Slider instance. Note that these methods will have no effect on the appearance of the control. If you want a visual difference between states, you will need to modify the CSS attributes of the Slider elements accordingly. The Control.Slider Lab page shows an example of such machinations.

It's all well and good to be able to configure the slider with the options we've seen so far. But we also need to know what's going on once the slider is put into operation. Let's see how.

Receiving notification of value changes

A slider whose value is unknown is a poor control indeed. Two callback options allow you to be notified when the value of the slider changes, and to obtain the specific value that the slider has acquired. These callbacks are most often used to cause the current value of the slider to be displayed to the user. The lab page uses these callbacks for this purpose, and the extended example of section 6.6.4 will show how this can be achieved.

The `onChange` callback is invoked whenever the value of the slider changes, and its single parameter contains the current value of the slider. It is even invoked when the value is changed by the control's `setValue()` method.

The `onSlide` callback is invoked, also with the current value as its parameter, whenever the handle is being dragged along the track.

Either or both of these callbacks are most often used to keep a display of the slider's value in sync with the internal value of the control, but they can be used for any other purpose related to the current value of the control (such as adjusting the size of chart elements).

Now that we know the range of options available to us, let's use that knowledge in a more in-depth example.

6.6.4 A more absorbing example

The simple example in listing 6.14 showed us a working slider, but without a display of the slider's value, it wasn't a very useful control. In this section, we will examine a page with a slider control that not only displays its current value, but also can visually change its appearance when toggled between enabled and disabled states. This page builds upon the pages we saw in listings 6.14 and 6.15, and it can be found in the slider/extended-example.html file, or you can display it from the chapter code's control panel.

When initially displayed, the page will appear as shown in figure 6.19.

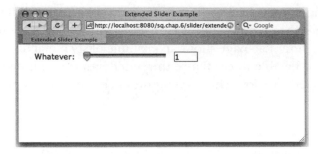

**Figure 6.19
Initial state of
the Extended Slider
Example page**

This page presents a slide constructed using images that are labeled, and it shows its current value to its right. If you modify the value of the slider by dragging the handle or clicking in the track, the numerical display changes to reflect the new value, as shown in figure 6.20.

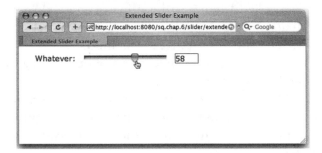

**Figure 6.20
The extended example with a
new value**

The complete listing for this page is shown in listing 6.16, and its important aspects will be discussed in the following subsections:

Listing 6.16 Code for the Extended Slider Example page

```html
<html>
  <head>
    <title>Extended Slider Example</title>
    <script type="text/javascript"
            src="../scripts/prototype.js"></script>
    <script type="text/javascript"
            src="../scripts/scriptaculous.js"></script>
    <script type="text/javascript">
      window.onload = function() {
        createSlider(1,100);
      }

      function createSlider(minValue,maxValue) {
        var values = [];
```

❶ Create slider in onload

❷ Generate discrete values array

```
      for (var n = minValue; n <= maxValue; n++) values.push(n);
      new Control.Slider(        ←┐    Construct
        'sliderHandle',          ❸    slider control
        'sliderTrack',
        {
          range: $R(minValue,maxValue),
          values: values,
          sliderValue: minValue,          ❹    Define callback
          onChange: function(value) {  ←┐       closures
            $('sliderValue').innerHTML = value;
          },
          onSlide: function(value) {
            $('sliderValue').innerHTML = value;
          }
        }
      );                                    ❺    Initialize value
      $('sliderValue').innerHTML = minValue;  ←┘    display
    }
  </script>
  <style type="text/css">
    body {
      margin: 16px;                  ❻    Apply track
    }                                     styles
    #sliderTrack {              ←─────
      background-image: url(track.gif);
      background-repeat: no-repeat;
      background-position: 0px 4px;
      width: 175px;
      height: 10px;
      cursor: pointer;
    }                        ❼    Apply handle
    #sliderHandle {    ←┘         styles
      cursor: pointer;
    }                  ❽    Line up
    #controlContainer label,  ←┘    elements
    #controlContainer #sliderTrack,
    #controlContainer #sliderValue {
      float: left;
      margin-left: 18px;
    }
    #sliderValue {
      border: 1px solid maroon;
      width: 26px;
      font-size: 88%;
      padding: 3px 6px;
    }
  </style>
</head>

<body>
```

```
                                            ❾ Declare HTML
    <div id="controlContainer">     ⟵┘      elements
      <label>Whatever:</label>
      <span id="sliderElements">
        <div id="sliderTrack">
          <img id="sliderHandle" src="handle-red.gif"/>
        </div>
      </span>
      <span id="sliderValue"></span>
    </div>
  </body>

</html>
```

The following sections examine the important aspects of this example, referring back to the code as necessary.

Creating and styling the HTML elements

In our previous examples, we've seen the simple HTML elements that can be used to represent the track and the handle of the slider control. In this example, we've used a construct similar to the image example (shown earlier in listing 6.15) in that the track is a <div> element with a background image, and the handle is an image element.

We've also defined a sort of uber-control in this example, where the label and the value display are both considered elements of the slider, along with the track and handle. To this end, the HTML elements that define the uber-control are a bit more complicated than what we have seen so far, but not by much.

In order to contain the elements that make up the control, we created a <div> element named controlContainer ❾. Obviously, if we're going to be creating more than one of these on a page, we're going to have to be a lot smarter in our naming. But this is just a simple example. Once we get a handle on how to get our uber-slider working on this test page, we would want to create a JavaScript object out of it that would handle all the details and ensure that generated IDs are unique.

Within controlContainer we placed the control elements: the <label> element, a <span> to contain the track <div> and handle image named sliderElements, and a <span> to serve as the value display named sliderValue.

That's all pretty straightforward, but if we were to display that in a browser without any styling, we wouldn't be thrilled with the result. The styling applied to the track ❻ and handle ❼ should seem familiar by now. The track is given a background image and a pointer cursor, and the handle, already an image, is given only the active cursor.

However, unstyled, the various elements of the uber-control will not lay out in a line. In order to make the elements line up as we expect, we applied a style **8** to them that forces them to float left rather than to wrap to another line in the browser. We also gave them a little margin to prevent any bunching up.

With the elements created, we're ready to create the Control.Slider instance.

Setting up the slider's range

The instance of Control.Slider, which we'll hook up to the track and handle we created in the previous section, is created in the createSlider() function, which we invoke from the page's onload handler **1**. The createSlider() function accepts two parameters that specify the minimum (left-most) and maximum (right-most) values for the slider. No checks are made to ensure that minValue is less than maxValue, but that's a check we'd want to add (or to add code to account for) in a real-world implementation.

The minimum and maximum values are used to create the ObjectRange instance that will be used as the slider's range option, and they are also used to populate an array **2** of integer values that will be used as the slider's values option.

The slide is constructed **3** using these values and specifying the slider's initial value as minValue. That's actually the default, but since it's an assumption made by other elements on the page, we felt it was best to be explicit about it.

Now that the slider's range and value are set up, we want to make sure that the slider's current value will always be displayed in the <span> element with the ID of sliderValue.

Displaying the slider's value

Recall that we set up a <span> named sliderValue that will display the current value of the slider. In order to cause the value to be displayed in this element whenever the slider's handle is moved or its track is clicked (or even if some code calls the slider's setValue() method), we set up two callback closures in the options hash of the Control.Slider constructor **4**. The onChange and onSlide options are set up to perform the same task of placing the passed value into the sliderValue element.

Since these closures perform the same function, it might have been wiser to implement a named function that could be referenced by both options. Certainly if the code were any more complex than that shown here, repeating it twice would be a poor thing to do.

These closures will display the value of the slider once its value has been changed. In order to show the value when the page is initially displayed, the initial value is set into the `sliderValue` element right after the constructor completes ❺.

And that's it! You should now have enough knowledge at your fingertips to go about creating a JavaScript object class for the uber-slider. Once you have finished this book, particularly the Prototype sections on extending and creating object classes, actually implementing such an uber-slider control would be a great exercise to ensure that you've thoroughly understood the material.

6.7 Summary

In this chapter, we've examined some controls that Scriptaculous makes available to us as page authors. These controls help give web application developers some of the power that is enjoyed by their desktop application counterparts.

We saw a set of two in-place editor controls that transformed static display values into active elements for editing. The InPlaceEditor utilizes text fields and text areas in order to give the user the ability to enter free-form text, and the InPlace-CollectionEditor utilizes a single-selection select element to give the user a list of finite choices. Both of these controls employ Ajax technology to allow for assistance from server-side resources, be it for validation, reformatting, model updates, or whatever other server-side activity is appropriate.

We also discussed two autocompleter controls that present the user with a list of filtered choices based upon the text that they have already entered into a text box. Though differing in some key aspects, these controls are reminiscent of the combo box control available for desktop applications; they present a drop-down list where users can either choose from the list or type their own nonlisted value. The two autocompleter controls differ in that one obtains its filtered list from the server (the Ajax autocompleter) and the other filters a list of all candidate values on the client (the Scriptaculous local autocompleter).

And lastly, we examined a slider control that mimics its desktop counterpart, allowing users to select one value from within a predefined range. These controls not only give you some prepackaged extended controls to use within your web application's pages, they can serve as inspirations to create your own controls that perform functions that might be difficult or awkward using the predefined set of HTML form controls. Just as Scriptaculous uses the power of Prototype to easily create such controls in an object-oriented fashion and with a minimum of fuss and bother, so can we.

In the next chapter, we'll take a look at another feature that Scriptaculous brings to the party in order to help close the gap between desktop and web applications: drag and drop.

Scriptaculous
Drag and Drop

7

In the previous two chapters, we've seen ways that Scriptaculous effects and extended controls can extend the capabilities of our web applications beyond the capabilities provided by native HTML form elements. In this chapter we'll explore yet another capability that Scriptaculous gives us to create spectacular user interfaces.

Few usability experts would argue that among the most ubiquitous and useful user interface interactions is the technique of drag and drop. Sometimes also termed click and drag, drag and drop is an easily adopted metaphor for moving items around an application, performing various activities, or creating associations between items. It has been a part of the graphical user interface for just about as long as that interaction paradigm has been in existence (introduced commercially with the first Macintosh systems in 1984). Unless you've spent your entire programming life staring at a command line, the concept of drag and drop is bound to be a natural and customary part of your everyday computer life.

Even so, you probably don't actually think too much about the steps involved in dragging and dropping, so we'll go over a typical drag-and-drop interaction, introducing terms that Scriptaculous uses and that we will utilize within this chapter. The particular interaction we will examine is deleting a file by dragging it to the desktop Trash (or Recycle Bin, or whatever your desktop calls it). This interaction, seemingly universally used as a demonstration of drag and drop, emphasizes the desktop metaphor, as little is more natural to a user than picking up a piece of paper and throwing it in the trash bin next to the desk (though usually there's no drag-and-drop metaphor for crumpling up the paper beforehand).

The various steps of this procedure are shown in figure 7.1 with screenshots taken from a Mac OS X system.

(a)

(b)

(c)

(d)

(e)

Figure 7.1 A drag-and-drop sequence: deleting a file by "dragging" it to the "trash"

In part a, the mouse pointer is approaching the file to be deleted. The icon representing the trash can resides on the lower part of the positionable Mac OS X Dock, which is shown at the right of the screen. The Dock can be moved elsewhere in OS X, and the trash icon itself may appear directly on the desktop of other operating systems.

Part b shows that the user has moved the mouse pointer over the file's icon and has pressed down on the mouse button without letting it back up, which distinguishes this action from a simple click operation (where the mouse button is depressed and immediately released). Note how the system has given the user feedback by altering the visual rendition of the icon.

In part c, the user has begun moving the file icon toward the trash can icon by moving the mouse with the button still pressed down. This is the drag part of the operation. (An icon or other user interface element that is capable of being dragged in this fashion is termed draggable.) Consistent with many other drag-and-drop systems, while the icon is being dragged around, the original icon stays in place and a visually distinct rendition of the icon (usually somewhat transparent) is shown to move with the mouse pointer. This is known as ghosting.

Part d shows that the user has moved the draggable icon until it is hovering over the trash can icon. The icon acknowledges that a recognized draggable element is about to be dropped upon it by changing its own rendition (in this case, highlighting itself and displaying the caption "Trash"). This serves as a cue to the user that dropping the draggable icon at this point will cause something to happen. That something is, of course, dependent upon the types of the draggable and target items.

In part e, with the operation completed, we see that the ghost has disappeared and that, because the interaction represents a delete operation, the original icon has been removed from the screen and the Trash target has returned to its normal rendition.

The interface elements that can accept draggable items are generally known as drop targets. Scriptaculous uses the somewhat ambiguous term droppable—it could be argued that "droppable" should mean something able to be dropped (in other words, a synonym for a draggable), rather than something upon which things can be dropped. But since this chapter will focus on the Scriptaculous drag-and-drop system, we'll use the term "droppable" to mean an interface element that will accept draggable items.

Drag and drop is a powerful interface technique on the desktop, but it is regrettably missing from the repertoire of web application developers, at least as far as native HTML capabilities are concerned. The Scriptaculous Drag and Drop

Library brings this compelling technique into the toolbox of page authors, allowing them to make another incursion into territory previously held by their desktop counterparts.

7.1 *The sample code for this chapter*

The sample code for this chapter is key to understanding the concepts that we're going to explore. If you have not downloaded the sample code up to this point, we strongly urge you to do so. Interacting with the sample pages while you work through this chapter will be an enormous help in grasping the material.

The sample code can be found in the subfolder named chap7. Since no server-side resources are required for any of the sample code for this chapter, you can choose to set up a web server to serve the pages, or you can simply open the HTML files in your browser.

A control panel page has been set up to help guide you through the example code; just open the index.html file in the chap7 folder. This page, shown in figure 7.2, contains links to the various example pages that we'll be referring to throughout this chapter. Or, if you prefer, you can simply find the sample page files and open them directly in your browser.

Enough of the preliminaries! Let's get on to dragging and dropping. But before we can drag and drop, we first need to learn how to drag.

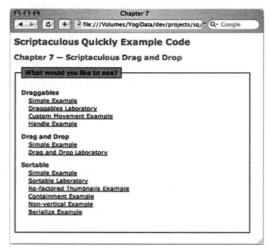

Figure 7.2   The chapter 7 control panel page

7.2 *Dragging things around*

As we have already discussed, there are two major elements to consider when talking about drag and drop: the items to be dragged (the draggable), and the item onto which the draggable will be dropped (the droppable). Without outside intervention, once a user interface element on a web page is displayed, it is pretty much fixed in place within the flow of the page document. There are things that might cause it to change position within the window (hiding something that appears before it, for example), but there are no native facilities for inducing what we have dubbed "draggable" behavior.

The Scriptaculous Draggable class uses the powers of JavaScript, CSS, and HTML to provide us with an easy way to add this behavior to a user interface element.

7.2.1 *Making an element draggable*

Converting an element from a "normal" element into a draggable one is as simple as creating an instance of the Draggable class, and identifying the element to be made draggable. Here's how it works:

```
new Draggable( element, options );
```

The first parameter to the constructor identifies the element to be made draggable (either as the ID of the element, or a reference to the element). The second parameter is the now-familiar options hash that specifies optional information on how the draggable element is to behave.

The element can be any block element, and even some nonblock elements like `<span>` seem to work just fine. But beware of table subelements (such as `<tr>` and `<td>`) which behave inconsistently across browsers, or just don't work with the Draggable class.

To see draggable elements in action in the sample code for this chapter, use the control panel to view the Simple Example in the Draggables section, or use your browser to view the draggables/simple-example.html file. You will see the page shown in figure 7.3, which contains five distinct elements: three `<div>` elements, an `<img>` element, and a paragraph element containing an embedded `<span>`.

Click on any of the visible elements (note that the clickable `<span>` of the bottom-most element is highlighted in blue) and (holding the mouse button down, of course) drag the element around the screen.

Let's take a look at how we enabled those elements to be whizzed around the window like that. The source for this simple example page is shown in listing 7.1.

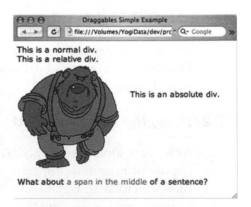

Figure 7.3   Initial display of the Draggables Simple Example page

Listing 7.1   Source for the Draggables Simple Example page

```html
<html>
  <head>
    <title>Draggables Simple Example</title>
    <script type="text/javascript"
            src="../scripts/prototype.js"></script>
    <script type="text/javascript"
            src="../scripts/scriptaculous.js"></script>
    <script type="text/javascript">
      var elements = [          Define the elements to
        'normalDiv',          ❶ become draggable
        'relativeDiv',
        'absoluteDiv',
        'anImage',
        'aSpan'
      ];

      window.onload = function() {  ❷ Make them
        elements.each(                draggable
          function(item) {
            new Draggable(item, {});
          }
        );
      }
    </script>
    <style type="text/css">   ❸ Apply various styles
      #relativeDiv {              to the elements
        position: relative;
      }
      #absoluteDiv {
        position: absolute;
        left: 240px;
        top: 100px;
      }
      #aSpan {
        color: blue;
      }
    </style>
  </head>
                       ❹ Declare the
  <body>                   elements

    <div id="normalDiv">
      This is a normal div.
    </div>

    <div id="relativeDiv">
      This is a relative div.
    </div>
```

```
    <div id="absoluteDiv">
      This is an absolute div.
    </div>

    <img id="anImage" src="../images/bear.gif"/>

    <p>
      What about <span id="aSpan">a span in the middle</span> of
      a sentence?
    </p>

  </body>

</html>
```

In this example, we defined five elements that are made draggable: three <div> elements, an <img> element, and a <span> element. The purpose of the three different <div> elements is to demonstrate that regardless of whether an element starts off with a positioning rule of static (the default), relative, or absolute, the drag behavior is unaffected.

Following all the necessary header declarations to include the JavaScript libraries for Prototype and Scriptaculous, we defined an array of the element IDs for the elements that are to become draggable ❶.

Then, this array is traversed over in the onload handler for the page ❷, making each named element draggable by creating an instance of a Draggable, using the ID of the element as the first parameter to the constructor. Note that we supplied no options to the Draggable instances. The available options will be explained in the next section.

A <style> element ❸ is used to apply the various positioning rules to the <div> elements, as well as to highlight the portion of the bottom paragraph that is made draggable. And finally, the elements themselves are declared in the body of the page ❹.

Not too hard to do! But we can get fancier with the options to the Draggable class.

7.2.2 *Draggable options*

There are any number of interaction types for which we will want to apply dragging behavior (including, but not limited to, dragging and dropping), and the behavior we want the draggable elements to exhibit may differ depending upon exactly what we are trying to convey. The options available to the Draggable class give us the means to control the behavior of a drag operation. They are listed in table 7.1.

Table 7.1 Draggable options

Option	Description
revert	A Boolean value that specifies whether the `reverteffect` callback will be invoked when the drag operation stops. Defaults to `false`.
snap	A dimension (in pixels) used to specify whether movement during a drag operation "snaps" to a grid of that size. Defaults to no snapping.
zindex	A value that specifies the CSS z-index to be applied to the element during a drag operation. By default the element's z-index is set to 1000 while dragging.
ghosting	A Boolean value specifying whether ghosting is enabled during a drag operation. Defaults to `false` (no ghosting).
constraint	A setting that constrains movement to the horizontal or vertical axis. By default, no constraint is applied.
handle	An element to be used as the handle to start the drag operation. Omitting this option specifies that an element is its own handle.
change	A callback function invoked during a drag operation whenever the position of the element changes.
starteffect	A callback function invoked at the beginning of a drag operation to apply an effect to the element. By default, an Opacity effect is applied.
reverteffect	A callback function invoked at the end of a drag operation to perform whatever operation is appropriate to implement `revert`. It is only called if `revert` is `true`. When enabled, the default behavior is to move the element back to its original position.
endeffect	A callback function invoked at the end of a drag operation to apply an effect to the element. By default, the element is returned to normal Opacity.

As for the previous Scriptaculous libraries we've discussed, a lab page has been set up to allow you to see the effects of applying various options to a Draggable element. Use the chapter code control panel to access the Draggables Lab page, or open the draggables/lab-draggables.html file in your browser.

The sections that follow describe how the options in table 7.1 allow us to tailor the behavior of the draggable elements to our needs.

Reverting the element to its original position

Sometimes you want a dragged object to stay where you dragged it to, but what about situations where the represented interaction would make more sense if the dragged object moved back to its original position when the drag was completed?

When `revert` is set to `true`, the element will move back to its original position when the drag operation completes (when the mouse button is released). At least that's the default behavior. In actuality, this option calls the function identified by the `reverteffect` callback. If you don't supply a `reverteffect` callback of your own, the default function moves the element back to its original position. (See the upcoming "Changing effects" section for more details about changing effects and replacing the `reverteffect` callback with your own function.)

To see how this works, open the Draggables Lab page, and either leave the `revert` option be, or specify it as `false`. Click the Apply to Items button and move the draggable elements around. Note that when the drag operation is complete, the elements stay where you moved them. Next, set `revert` to `true` and click the Apply to Items button again. Now when you drag the elements around, note how they move back to their original positions when you release the mouse button.

Constraining movement to a grid

The `revert` option gives us a level of control over the behavior of the dragged object after the drag operation, but what about during the drag? The `snap` option creates a virtual grid whose vertices constrain the movement of the element during a drag operation.

In our simple example of listing 7.1, as well as when testing the `revert` option, you may have noted that you could move any of the draggable elements to any pixel position on the page. With the `snap` option, you can constrain the movement to specific grid positions, with a grid of any size.

To create a square grid—one in which the vertical and horizontal vertices are the same dimensions—you would provide a single dimension as the value of the `snap` option, like this:

```
snap: 100
```

This will constrain the movement of the dragged element to a grid with horizontal and vertical vertices spaced 100 pixels apart. Note that the grid created by this option has its origin at the original location of the element, not at the origin of the page.

To see this in action, in the lab page specify a `snap` value of `100` and apply the changes. Move one of the elements around the page and notice the new behavior. Rather than allowing you to move the image freely to any pixel position, you are now constrained to positions separated by 100 pixels in either direction.

If you want a grid that isn't square, you can specify separate horizontal and vertical dimensions for the grid by supplying an array of two elements. The first element specifies the horizontal dimension of the grid, and the second specifies the vertical dimension. Here's an example:

```
snap: [100,200]
```

This would create a grid with horizontal vertices 100 pixels apart and with vertical vertices 200 pixels apart.

You could also use this option to provide a custom movement function that maps the movement of the mouse to whatever position you deem appropriate. Any such function will be passed the horizontal and vertical position of the mouse, and is expected to return a two-element array containing the mapped horizontal and vertical positions to which the element is to be moved.

Just such a function is demonstrated in the Custom Movement Example. You can open this page from the chapter control panel or by opening draggables/custom-movement.html. In this example, the snap option is specified as follows:

```
snap: function(x,y) {
   return [x*2,y*2];
}
```

This function multiplies the incoming coordinates by two, and returns the result. The effect, which you can clearly see if you click on the image on the page and drag it downward and to the right, is to move the dragged element out ahead of the position of the mouse cursor by a factor of two.

If you're good at trigonometry, you could conceivably write a mapping function that causes the element to make a sine wave around the path of the mouse, or perhaps perform loops around the mouse position. Such bizarre movement mappings may not have a place in business applications, but sometimes you're writing a web page in which you just want to have some fun!

If you were at all distressed that the grid created when using numeric values for this option didn't meet your requirements (perhaps you want the grid origin at the upper-left corner of the page?), a custom mapping function is an excellent way to institute your own rules!

Constraining movement to an axis

We've seen that we can constrain the movement of the dragged element by creating a custom mapping function for the snap option, but constraining the movement of a dragged element to either of the horizontal or vertical axes is such a common need that another option, constraint, is available to easily specify such behavior.

This option can be set to either horizontal or vertical, which will constrain the movement to along the *x*-axis or *y*-axis respectively:

```
constraint: 'vertical',
```

By default, or if the option is specified as false, no constraints are placed on the element's movement (except as specified by other options).

Affecting the stacking order

Now that we can exercise control over the behavior of the drag operation, let's look at an option that might come in handy when things aren't acting exactly as we'd like. When you are moving elements around on a page, sooner or later some of them are going to overlap.

In order to make sure that the item being dragged is visible among overlapping items, its z-index CSS attribute is changed to 1000 during the drag. This will cause the item to appear "above" all other items on the page, unless you've set the z-index of other items to values higher than 1000. For situations where the default value of 1000 is inadequate, or where you might want to exercise some control over the stacking order during a drag operation, you can specifically set the z-index that is assigned to the dragged item while a drag operation is under way by using the `zindex` option:

```
zindex: 1001
```

In all cases, the original z-index of the dragged element is restored after the drag operation completes.

Enabling ghosting

At the beginning of this chapter, we examined the sequence of a typical desktop drag operation and noted that often the dragged item is *ghosted*. That is, the original item remains in place, and a "ghost" copy of the item is what is dragged around. The actual item is moved only when the drag operation concludes with a successful drop.

In our example drag operations thus far, no ghosting was evident; the original element was moved during the operation. In order to enable ghosting, you need to set the `ghosting` option to `true`:

```
ghosting: true
```

When `ghosting` is set to `true`, a drag operation appears to leave the original target element in place, while a semi-transparent version of the element is dragged about.

To see ghosting in action, display the Draggables Lab page, enable ghosting, and click the Apply to Items button. Now when you drag one of the elements, you will see the classical ghosting behavior, as depicted in figure 7.4.

Figure 7.4 The original image (left) and its moving ghost

We've now seen a number of options that give us control over the movement of the dragged object, but what about gaining some control over how a drag operation starts?

Using a drag handle

In all the examples we have seen so far, the drag operation was initiated by clicking on the element to be dragged. In this respect, the element acts as its own handle for drag operations, where the handle is the item you click on to initiate the drag operation.

Most often, draggable items serve as their own handles, but there may be times when you might want an alternative element to initiate a drag—a caption, or list bullet, perhaps. Frequently this might be an element contained with a larger element—a small image embedded in a draggable <div>, for example—or it could be an entirely separate element.

The handle option specifies an alternative element to be used as the handle for the draggable element:

```
handle: 'dragHandle'
```

Here, dragHandle is the ID of the desired handle element.

This option is demonstrated in the Handle Example page, displayed via the control panel for this chapter, or by viewing the draggables/handle-example.html file. When displayed, this page shows an image and a small red block. Clicking on and dragging the image produces no response, but clicking on the red square and dragging it initiates a drag operation on the larger image.

Viewing the code for this example, we see that the ID of the red square, dragHandle, is used as the value for the handle option:

```
new Draggable(
  'targetElement'
  {
    handle: 'dragHandle'
  }
);
```

Note that when a drag operation takes place, it is still the element that was specified as draggable that is moved, not the handle element.

Getting notified of movement

If you'd like to keep track of where a dragged item is moving, or perform some other type of bookkeeping, or if you want to initiate other operations on a page in response to a drag operation, the change option allows you to specify a callback that is invoked at intervals while a drag operation is under way. If provided, this callback is passed a reference to the Draggable instance itself. The element property of the Draggable instance can be used to access the target element of the operation.

The Draggable Lab page uses this callback option to show the position of the element during a drag operation in the message area of that page. Note that while you drag an element around the screen, the display in this pane is updated with the current position of the element as the callback is repeatedly called during the operation.

In the code of the lab page, we see that the change option is specified as follows:

```
options.change = function(draggable){showInfo(draggable.element);}
```

The showInfo() function is defined like this:

```
function showInfo(element) {
  $('messagesDisplay').innerHTML =
    'element position: (' + element.offsetLeft + ',' +
    element.offsetTop + ')';
}
```

Note that because we have a reference to the Draggable instance in this callback, we can reference any of its properties. We could also conceivably modify them; however, while doing so might prove useful in some circumstances (I personally haven't found any yet), it could also lead to bizarre and destructive side effects. If you elect to do so, be sure you understand the ramifications of changing any properties of the Draggable on the fly.

You may have noted some animated effects that are applied to the draggable element during the drag operation. Let's take a look at how we can gain control over those effects.

Changing effects

A drag operation performs at least two effects on the draggable target when a drag operation takes place: one at the beginning of the operation and one at the end. A third, optional effect is applied at the end of the drag operation (but prior to the end effect) if, and only if, the revert option is set to true. You can override any of these effects by supplying functions of your own choosing for the starteffect, endeffect, and reverteffect options.

By default, the effect applied upon the start of a drag operation is a Scriptaculous Opacity effect that changes the opacity of the draggable element from its initial value to a value of 0.7 over a duration of 2/10 of a second. When the drag operation completes, the default end effect is to use the Opacity effect once again to change the draggable element's opacity from 0.7 back to its original value, over the same duration of 2/10 of a second. If you supply your own start or end effect functions, they will be passed a reference to the draggable element.

Since the change callback option isn't all that useful for getting notifications regarding when a drag operation commences or terminates, these callbacks could be used for that purpose. Bear in mind, however, that usurping the default functions for start and stop notification means that you'll need to apply any start and end effects yourself, in addition to whatever intended activity you want to perform. Unfortunately, the default functions are defined as closures within the Scriptaculous drag and drop code, so they are not directly callable by your own functions. The code for applying the Opacity effect is fairly simple, however, and can be easily copied into your own functions.

The reverteffect option specifies the function to be called just prior to the endeffect function when the revert option is set to true. The default version of this function moves the target element back to its original starting position. You would only replace the default function with one of your own choosing if you wanted to redefine the semantics of the revert option.

You now know everything you need to know about making objects draggable. You've seen how you can enable elements to be moved around the page, with or without ghosting, with or without reverting to their original positions, and with various constraints on their movement.

On its own, dragging elements around the page is fun for a few minutes, but it's ultimately not all that useful. Such capabilities could be used on pages with many discrete elements in order to allow a user to rearrange the page elements to their own liking (and if you wanted to be really nice, you could remember the arrangement in cookies to retain the new layout next time the page is visited). But things really get interesting when there are items to which we can drag the draggable elements, and that do interesting things when we drop those dragged items onto them. Let's see how we can do that.

7.3 Dropping dragged things

Now that we can drag things around, we need something interesting to drop them onto! In the file deletion scenario at the beginning of this chapter, a trash can icon served as the droppable element in the drag-and-drop interaction. In our web apps, drag and drop could be used for any number of user interface activities: placing items into a specific order, grouping them into separate buckets, mapping items to actions to be performed upon them, or myriad other possibilities including, yes, dragging something to a trash can for deletion.

In this section, we'll look at how Scriptaculous allows us to create drop targets for the things that we learned how to drag in the previous section.

7.3.1 *Defining drop targets*

Many of the Scriptaculous controls we have seen for attaching control code to existing page elements require us to construct an instance of a class. Contrary to that pattern, this is not how you create drop targets. One might naturally expect that a drop target might be created by constructing an instance of a class named Droppable, passing the ID of an element to be made into a drop target. But a different mechanism is used.

An element is converted into a drop target via a call to the add() method within a namespace called Droppables. The Droppables namespace has two important methods: add(), which creates a drop target, and remove(), which removes a drop target.

The syntax of the add() method is simple:

```
Droppables.add(element,options)
```

The syntax for remove() is even simpler:

```
Droppables.remove(element);
```

The add() method creates a drop target out of the element passed as its first parameter, using the options in the hash passed as the second. The remove() method removes the drop target behavior from the passed element.

Here is an example of a call to add() to create a drop target:

```
Droppables.add('dropZone',{});
```

This will create a drop target out of the page element with an ID of dropZone, with defaulted options.

As it turns out, however, a drop target created with default options is pretty much useless. It functions perfectly fine as a drop target, but it does absolutely nothing of interest. Since it makes no sense to examine sample code that doesn't do anything, we're going to break with the tradition we've established so far and delay looking at any examples until after we've discussed the options available for drop targets.

7.3.2 *Drop target options*

There are surprisingly (perhaps frustratingly) few options that can be applied to drop targets. The available options are shown in table 7.2.

Table 7.2 Droppables.add() options

Option	Description
hoverclass	A class name that will be applied to the drop target when a draggable hovers over it. There is no default.
accept	A class name, or array of class names, that a draggable item must possess in order to be accepted by the drop target. By default, no class name constraints are applied.
containment	An element, or array of elements, that must be a parent of a draggable item in order for it to be accepted by the drop target. By default, no containment constraints are applied.
onHover	A callback function that is activated when a suitable draggable item hovers over the drop target.
overlap	A value specifying that extra positioning information is to be supplied to the onHover callback. The value may be set to horizontal or vertical. The droppable will only react to a draggable if it is overlapping the droppable by more than 50 percent in the specified direction.
onDrop	A callback function that is called when a suitable draggable element is dropped onto the drop target.

As with other controls, a lab page has been included in the sample code for this chapter. You can display it via the control panel for this chapter's code or by opening the dragndrop/lab-dragndrop.html file. With the help of the lab page, let's look at these options in detail.

Providing visual cues

It is almost always a good idea to give the user a visual cue when a drop target recognizes a dragged item that is hovering over it. This gives the user positive feedback that something will happen when the item is dropped onto the target.

The hoverclass option lets us supply a class name to be applied to the drop target when an item that will be accepted if dropped hovers over the target. Usually this style class will apply some sort of highlight to the droppable element that conveys "Hey! You can drop that on me, and I'll do something wonderful" to the user. It's important to note that the active point of the hover is the mouse cursor itself, and not the entire region of the draggable item.

In the Drag and Drop Lab page, select "use dropActive class" for the hoverclass option, and click the Apply to Items button. This applies a CSS class (named dropActive) as the hoverclass option.

Now "grab" the bear by his right wrist (to your left) and drag him toward the drop target. Note that even as his left arm and the bulk of his body enters the

Figure 7.5 Drop target before and after the mouse cursor passes over its boundary

drop area, nothing appears to happen, as shown in the first part of figure 7.5. Keep dragging the bear into the drop target, and you will see that only when the mouse cursor itself enters the drop area does it react by highlighting the area, as shown in the second part of figure 7.5. The item is not considered to be "over" the drop target until the mouse cursor enters the target.

Try this exercise again, except this time grab the bear by his left elbow. Note how the target area is highlighted when much less of the bear has intersected the drop area, again emphasizing that it's the transition of the mouse cursor into and out of the drop zone that triggers it. Now move the bear over the page, into and out of the target area, noting how it highlights when, and only when, the dragged item is in a position to be accepted by the drop zone.

Generally, you'd want to use a subtler highlight than the rather bold statement we're making here; but in this lab page, we're trying to make a point!

Constraining recognized draggables

Just because a dragged item is placed over a drop area doesn't mean that the drop target must recognize it. You can make your drop targets as selective as you'd like regarding which draggables they will let into their private little clubs. There are two options you can use to add a touch of snobbery to your drop targets: one that excludes or accepts draggables by class name, and one that excludes or accepts by parentage. (Maybe the analogy of a snobby private club isn't all that much of a stretch.)

The accept option lets you specify a list of CSS class names, and only draggables that possess one of those class names are recognized. The value of the option can be a single string to specify a single class name, or a string array of multiple class names.

To see this exclusionary activity in action, bring up the Drag and Drop Lab page and, being sure that the hoverclass option is set to "use dropActive class," try the three different settings for the `accept` option. Be sure to click the Apply to Items button whenever you make a change to an option.

When you choose "default," no `accept` option is added to the drop target, and the default behavior of accepting all draggables regardless of class name takes precedence. This can be demonstrated by dragging the bear into and out of the drop zone and seeing that it reacts to the draggable item (which is why it's important to set the `hoverclass` option as instructed).

Choosing "class includesDraggables" causes an `accept` option to be added with the value of `includesDraggables`. Since the bear image does possess this class name, the drop zone continues to recognize the bear when it is dragged over the target area.

Finally, choosing "class excludesDraggables" causes an `accept` option with a value of `excludesDraggables` to be added to the drop target. Since the bear draggable does not have this class name, the drop zone no longer reacts when the bear is moved over it. In this instance, the bear is apparently not "classy" enough for the drop zone's tastes.

You can also specify exclusionary behavior with the `containment` option. This option specifies an element (via an ID string or element reference), or array of elements, one of which must be in the parental hierarchy of the draggable item for it to be recognized by the drop zone.

Visit the lab page again, making sure that that the `hoverclass` option is set to "use dropActive class," and that the `accept` option is set to "default." Try the three different settings for the `containment` option, being sure to click the Apply to Items button whenever you make a change to an option.

The bear image is contained in a `<div>` element with an ID of `includesDraggables`, and it does not have any parent with an ID of `excludesDraggables`. So as you might expect, the bear will be accepted if the setting of the `containment` option is "default" or "includesDraggables," but not if the setting is "excludesDraggables."

You will note that when a draggable item is rejected by the target area, due to one of these constraint options, the `hoverclass` option is not applied to the target area. We will find that the same is true of the notification callback functions: they will not be triggered unless the drop target will accept the draggable element.

Getting notified of a pending drop

We've let the user know when a drop operation is pending by providing a `hoverclass` option that applies visual cues to the target area when a drop is possible. But how are we (our code) to know when such a state is entered? The `onHover` option allows us to specify a callback function that is called whenever a recognized draggable item is over the target area. This callback will be invoked repeatedly as the draggable element is moved over the drop zone. If a draggable element is rejected by a drop target, due to a setting of one of the constraint options (accept or containment), this callback is not invoked for that draggable element.

When called, the callback function is passed three parameters: a reference to the draggable element, a reference to the droppable element, and a numeric position value. This latter argument is always the value 0 unless the overlap option (discussed next) is explicitly set.

In the lab page, make sure the constraint options are set to not exclude our bear (click the Reset button to easily do this), and set the value of the onHover option to "none" (or leave it unset). This will ensure that no onHover callback is specified. Drag the bear over the drop target and watch the message area. No messages appear.

Change the setting of onHover to "activate hover function." This will add an onHover callback that will write a message to the message area whenever it is invoked. Apply the change and drag the bear over the drop zone again, and you will see a message. A timestamp is embedded in the message so that you can clearly see that the callback is being invoked repeatedly as the draggable element moves over the drop area.

The overlap option can be set to either horizontal or vertical. When set to one of these values, it causes the third parameter to the onHover callback to be set to a value between 0 and 1, depending upon the position of the mouse cursor within the drop area. If the value of overlap is horizontal, the third parameter will range from 1.0 down to 0.0 spanning from the left side of the drop target to the right side. If the value is vertical, the third parameter value will range from 1.0 to 0.0 from the top of the target area to the bottom.

Whether this information is useful to your onHover function is questionable; this option and positioning value is primarily intended to be used by the Sortable library that we will be examining in section 7.4.

We've now seen that we can be notified of an impending drop with the onHover callback, but all of that is just a precursor to the final climatic event: the drop!

Getting notified of a drop

To be notified when the actual drop occurs, you need to register a callback function with the onDrop option. This callback is invoked in the event of a drop; the draggable element is the first argument, and the drop target is the second.

In the lab page, an onDrop callback is unconditionally added to the options for the drop target. The callback sends a message to the message area whenever the draggable element is dropped within the drop zone. Like the onHover callback, a draggable element rejected due to the setting of one of the constraint options will not trigger this callback when it is dropped on the target area.

Now that we've wrapped our heads around the available options, let's look at an actual example that employs them!

7.3.3 *Drag and drop example*

Now we can understand why an optionless drop target is less than useful. Without at least one of the `hoverclass`, `onHover`, or `onDrop` options, there'd be no way to tell that anything at all had occurred! But now that we've seen the various options in action, we're ready to take a look at a sample page that uses drag-and-drop operations to accomplish its task.

In our example page, we have two side-by-side columns: one initially filled with thumbnail photo images, and one initially empty (except for instructional text). We want to allow the photo thumbnails to be moved from one column to the other via drag and drop.

Open the page by choosing the Simple Example link from the Drag and Drop section of the control panel for this chapter, or display the dragn-drop/simple-example.html file in your browser. The initial display will look like the window in figure 7.6.

One by one, and in any order, drag the photo images from the left column to the right column and drop them. Note that upon a drop, the image moves from one column to the other and retains the order in which it is dropped. Figure 7.7 shows the page with two photo thumbnails already moved and a third drag operation in progress.

The code for this page is shown in listing 7.2.

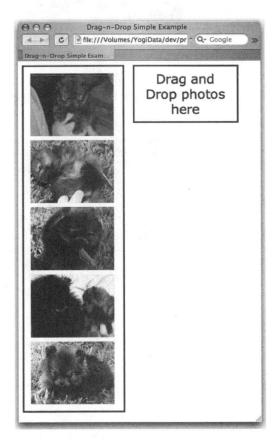

Figure 7.6 Initial state of the Drag-n-Drop Simple Example page

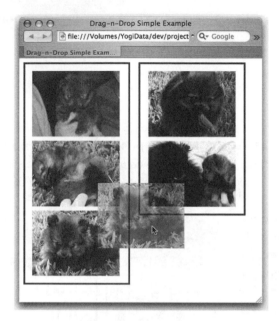

Figure 7.7
Example page after a few moves

Listing 7.2   Code for the Drag-n-Drop Simple Example page

```html
<html>
  <head>
    <title>Drag-n-Drop Simple Example</title>
    <script type="text/javascript"
            src="../scripts/prototype.js"></script>
    <script type="text/javascript"
            src="../scripts/scriptaculous.js"></script>
    <script type="text/javascript">
      window.onload = function() {
        $A($('draggables').getElementsByTagName('img')).each(
          function(item) {
            new Draggable(
              item,
              {
                revert: true,
                ghosting: true
              }
            );
          }
        );
        Droppables.add(
          'dropZone',
          {
```

Initiate activity upon page load ❶

❷ Make all the images draggable

❸ Make the drop zone droppable

```
            hoverclass: 'hoverActive',
            onDrop: movePhoto
          }
        );
        $('dropZone').cleared = false;
      }

    function movePhoto(draggable,dropZone) {
      if (!dropZone.cleared) {
        dropZone.innerHTML = '';
        dropZone.cleared = true;
      }
      draggable.parentNode.removeChild(draggable);
      dropZone.appendChild(draggable);
    }
  </script>
  <style type="text/css">
    #draggables {
      width: 172px;
      border: 3px ridge blue;
      float: left;
      padding: 9px;
    }
    #dropZone {
      float: left;
      margin-left: 16px;
      width: 172px;
      border: 3px ridge maroon;
      text-align: center;
      font-size: 24px;
      padding: 9px;
      float: left;
    }
    .hoverActive {
      background-color: #ffffcc;
    }
    #draggables img, #dropZone img {
      margin: 4px;
    }
  </style>
</head>

<body>
  <div id="draggables">
    <img src="../images/photo-1.jpg"/>
    <img src="../images/photo-2.jpg"/>
    <img src="../images/photo-3.jpg"/>
    <img src="../images/photo-4.jpg"/>
    <img src="../images/photo-5.jpg"/>
  </div>
```

④ Move image upon a drop

⑤ Define styles for page elements

⑥ Apply style on hover

⑦ Create container of draggable images

**⑧ Create drop
zone**

```
<div id="dropZone">     ←┘
  Drag and Drop photos here
</div>

</body>

</html>
```

Let's begin at the end, so to speak, by looking at the HTML elements for the page. Two <div> elements are created: one initially holding the photo thumbnail images ⑦, and the other a simple snippet of instructional text ⑧. Style rules applied to these elements ⑤ give them their shape and position upon the page.

In order to give these elements the behavior we have described, we created Draggable instances attached to the photo thumbnails ② and added the drop target element to the list of Droppables ③. In the window's onload handler ①, you can see the following code:

```
$A($('draggables').getElementsByTagName('img')).each(
  function(item) {
    new Draggable(
      item,
      {
        revert: true,
        ghosting: true
      }
    );
  }
);
```

This code uses Prototype's handy $A() function to convert a node list of all the <img> elements in the element with the ID of draggables to an array. It then operates upon each element of that array, creating an instance of Draggable that attaches to each one. The revert and ghosting options are enabled, since we want the dragged items to revert to their natural positions, and we don't want to appear to yank them out of their original columns until we are sure that we're going to move them.

When adding the dropZone element to the list of Droppables ③, we specified a hoverclass of hoverActive ⑥, which applies a light yellow background to the drop target when it is ready to accept one of the dragged thumbnails.

We also specified an onDrop callback that registers the movePhoto() function as the callback to be invoked when a thumbnail is dropped onto the target element.

The movePhoto() function ❹ performs the action of relocating the dropped thumbnail image from its location in the first column to its new home in the second:

```
function movePhoto(draggable,dropZone) {
  if (!dropZone.cleared) {
    dropZone.innerHTML = '';
    dropZone.cleared = true;
  }
  draggable.parentNode.removeChild(draggable);
  dropZone.appendChild(draggable);
}
```

As you may recall, the target drop area contains a snippet of instructional text that should be removed when the first thumbnail is dropped onto it. We could examine the contents of the drop zone to see if any thumbnails exist, and if so, clear out the element. But in this example, we elected to mark the state with a simple property named cleared that we attached to the drop zone itself in the onload handler. The property is initially set to false, and when the movePhoto() function detects this condition, it clears the contents of the element and sets the property to true so that we won't execute the clear operation again. The function then removes the draggable from its current parent, and appends it to the drop zone element.

There are a few interesting behaviors, or missing behaviors, to note in this example. First, we made no provisions for moving the thumbnails back to the original column. This is not the most user-friendly thing to do (or to not have done) because the user is unable to back out of a decision. Once a thumbnail is moved to the second column, there's no turning back.

We also did not alter the draggability of the thumbnails once they were moved. Because of this, we can click on a thumbnail that has already been moved into the second column, and move it out of the second column and back into that second column. When this occurs, the image is moved to the bottom of the column. This is an interesting example of how sometimes one bug can cancel or mitigate another. We can't move thumbnails back into the first column, but we can reorder the second column by dragging thumbnails out of the second column and back into it in a certain order. This isn't the most intuitive interaction we could provide, so it would be better to actually fix the bugs in our page rather than deciding that what we have is good enough.

As an exercise, change the code of this page as follows:

- Allow the thumbnails to be moved freely back and forth between the two columns.

- Do not allow a thumbnail to be dragged and dropped into the column it is already in.

Whether you've left the page as it was or made the suggested changes, reordering the thumbnails is still a bit of a chore for the user. There are many user interface interactions that the drag-and-drop technique is suitable for, and one of those is affecting the order of elements in a list; in other words, sorting. This is such a common interaction that Scriptaculous provides a library, built on top of the drag-and-drop code, to make the sorting of elements easy to implement on our pages.

7.4 Sorting by drag and drop

In the previous section, we used drag and drop for one possible interaction type: to reorder, or sort, some thumbnail images. Because of an oversight (completely intentional, of course) in the code of that page, we observed an interesting side effect. If we dragged a thumbnail out of and back into the same droppable target, it was removed from that parent and reattached as a child at the end of the children list for that element. This gave us a sort of "poor man's sort" capability. Not ideal from a usability standpoint, but it worked after a fashion.

But this ability to shift the position of elements around leads us to a broader question: why not just implement a sort by moving elements around (via drag and drop) within the parent element rather than dragging them to a separate drop target? Apparently, the authors of Scriptaculous asked the same question, and the result was the Sortable library.

7.4.1 Creating a sortable element

For many control types, an object instance is created, specifying the element or elements to be attached. For others, such as droppables, no object instances are created, but rather, the element information is passed to a library method.

The Sortable library follows the lead of the Droppables library in that no object instances are created; the element to become sortable is passed to the `create()` method in the `Sortable` namespace:

```
Sortable.create(element,options);
```

Let's dive right in and take a look at a simple example of creating sortable controls. From the control panel for the chapter's code, click the Simple Example link under the Sortable heading, or open the sortable/simple-example.html page in your browser. You will see the page shown in figure 7.8.

Two lists are displayed in the page: one made up from the usual `<ul>` and embedded `<li>` elements, and the other composed of an outer `<div>` with inner `<div>` children as elements.

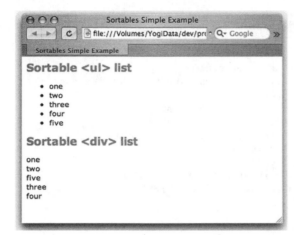

Figure 7.8
Sortables Simple Example page

Move your mouse pointer over the "three" list item in the top list (the one with the bullets), and use the drag-and-drop technique to move the item up and down the list. Note how the other items in the list move out of the way to make room for the item you are dragging. This is shown in figure 7.9.

You can drop the dragged item into any of the vacancies opened for it, effectively reordering the list. Try again with other items and with the lower list as well. Note how each list can be individually reordered, but that items from one list cannot be moved to the other list; at least not in this example. (If that's not a blatant example of foreshadowing, I don't know what is!)

Let's take a look at the page code used to set up these lists, shown in listing 7.3.

Figure 7.9
Making room for the dragged element

Listing 7.3   Code for the Sortables Simple Example page

```
<html>
  <head>
    <title>Sortable Simple Example</title>
    <link rel="stylesheet" type="text/css" href="../styles.css"/>
    <script type="text/javascript"
            src="../scripts/prototype.js"></script>
    <script type="text/javascript"
            src="../scripts/scriptaculous.js"></script>
    <script type="text/javascript">
      window.onload = function() {
        Sortable.create('sortableList',{});
        Sortable.create('sortableDiv',{tag:'div'});
      }
    </script>
  </head>

  <body>

    <div>
      <h1>Sortable &lt;ul&gt; list</h1>
      <ul id="sortableList">
        <li>one</li>
        <li>two</li>
        <li>three</li>
        <li>four</li>
        <li>five</li>
      </ul>
    </div>

    <div>
      <h1>Sortable &lt;div&gt; list</h1>
      <div id="sortableDiv">
        <div>one</div>
        <div>two</div>
        <div>three</div>
        <div>four</div>
        <div>five</div>
      </div>
    </div>

  </body>

</html>
```

Not much to it, is there? The really interesting part of the page is the two lines that compose the `onload` handler:

```
Sortable.create('sortableList',{});
Sortable.create('sortableDiv',{tag:'div'});
```

Each of these lines calls the `Sortable.create()` function, first for the top list (`sortableList`) and then for the bottom list (`sortableDiv`). The first call lets all options default, while the second gives you a sneak peek at an option named `tag` that we will discuss without further ado.

7.4.2 *Sortable element options*

There are a fair number of options available for sortable elements, none of which are required as long as your sortable element is a list element containing list item (`<li>`) elements. We saw an example of that in our simple example, where the second list, composed of `<div>` elements, required at least one option to function correctly.

The options available for the `Sortable.create()` method are shown in table 7.3 and are detailed in the subsections that follow.

Table 7.3 Sortable.create() options

Option	Description
tag	The type of the elements within the sortable container that are to be sortable via drag and drop. The default if none is specified, is `li`.
hoverclass	A CSS class name to be applied to nondragged sortable elements as a dragged element passes over them. By default, no CSS class name is applied.
ghosting	Similar to the Draggable option of the same name, this option, when set to `true`, causes the original element of a drag operation to stay in place while a semitransparent copy of the element is moved along with the mouse pointer. Defaults to `false`.
only	A CSS class name, or array of class names, that a draggable item must possess in order to be accepted by the drop target. This is similar to the `accept` option of Draggable. By default, no class name constraints are applied.
containment	An element, or set of elements, whose sortable subelements can be dragged into this Sortable, allowing for sortable elements to be moved between lists. By default, only elements in the current Sortable can be dropped.
dropOnEmpty	This option, if `true`, allows sortable elements to be dropped onto an empty list. Defaults to `false`.

Table 7.3 Sortable.create() options *(continued)*

Option	Description
`handle`	Same as the Draggable option of the same name, specifying an element to be used to initiate drag operations. By default, each element is its own handle.
`constraint`	This option can be set to `false`, `horizontal`, or `vertical` to constrain the movement of dragged sortable elements. The default is `vertical`.
`overlap`	This can be set to `false`, `horizontal`, or `vertical` to control the point at which a reordering is triggered. Defaults to `vertical`.
`tree`	This option, if `true`, enables sorting with subelements within the sortable element. The default is `false`.
`treeTag`	If the `tree` option is enabled, `treeTag` specifies the container element type of the subelement whose children take part in the sortable behavior. Defaults to `ul`.
`scroll`	If the sortable container possesses a scroll bar due to the setting of the CSS `overflow` attribute, this option enables autoscrolling of the list beyond the visible elements. Defaults to `false`.
`scrollSpeed`	When scrolling is enabled, this option adjusts the scroll speed. Defaults to `15`.
`scrollSensitivity`	When scrolling is enabled, this option adjusts the point at which scrolling is triggered. Defaults to `20`.
`onChange`	A function that will be called upon at intervals during a drag operation.
`onUpdate`	A function that will be called upon the termination of a drag operation that results in a change in element order.
`format`	A regular expression that specifies the format of ID values for sortable elements that are to take part in a serialization operation. The default is `/^[^_]*_(.*)$/`.

As usual, a lab page has been set up so you can experiment with the options. Launch it from the Sortable section of this chapter's control panel, or open the sortable/lab-sortable.html file.

Armed with the lab page, on to the options!

Specifying what is to be sorted

In our simple example of listing 7.3, we saw that in order to enable sorting of child `<div>` elements, we needed to specify an option to trigger the appropriate behavior. That option was `tag`, and it is used to specify which types of elements within the sortable container are to be made sortable. If unspecified, the Sortable code assumes that `<li>` children are to be sortable. If the child elements of the sortable container are of any other type, that type must be explicitly provided with a `tag` option.

Only one element type can be specified, and the elements that work well across browsers are rather limited. First, all form element types are specifically excluded by the library code. Some other types, even if not barred by the code, are problematic; image elements as sortable children, for example, do not work within Internet Explorer.

List item elements and `<div>` elements work well across all tested browsers, so if you want to sort something other than these elements, it's best to contain the other element type within a `<div>` or `<li>` element.

As an example, let's rework our thumbnail drag-and-drop page (from listing 7.2) to use the Sortable library. The markedly shorter, refactored code can be opened from the chapter's control panel or from the sortable/thumbnails-example.html file. The code is shown in listing 7.4.

Listing 7.4 Refactored thumbnails example code

```
<html>
  <head>
    <title>Sortable Thumbnails Example</title>
    <script type="text/javascript"
            src="../scripts/prototype.js"></script>
    <script type="text/javascript"
            src="../scripts/scriptaculous.js"></script>
    <script type="text/javascript">
      window.onload = function() {  |#1
        Sortable.create('thumbnails',{tag:'div'});
      }
    </script>
    <style type="text/css">
      #thumbnails {
        width: 172px;
        border: 3px ridge blue;
        padding: 9px;
      }
      #thumbnails img {
        margin: 4px;
      }
    </style>
  </head>

  <body>

    <div id="thumbnails">
```

❶ Make elements sortable upon page load

❷ Create container of elements to be sortable

```
      <div><img src="../images/photo-1.jpg"/></div>
      <div><img src="../images/photo-2.jpg"/></div>
      <div><img src="../images/photo-3.jpg"/></div>
      <div><img src="../images/photo-4.jpg"/></div>
      <div><img src="../images/photo-5.jpg"/></div>
   </div>

 </body>

</html>
```

We've made quite a few changes to the original code. Most obviously, we've eliminated the second column drop area completely, leaving only a single column of images ❷. We've also enclosed the image elements in <div> elements to keep Internet Explorer happy.

The page's onload handler ❶ has been replaced with a single line that turns the thumbnails element into a sortable container:

```
Sortable.create('thumbnails',{tag:'div'});
```

Note the use of the tag option to tell the Sortable library that the <div> element children of the container are to be made sortable. Without this option, no sorting behavior would be enabled, as the code would be looking for the default child <li> elements rather than the <div> elements.

It's also important to note that the tag option's value of div has nothing to do with the fact that the container element is a <div>, but rather specifies that the child elements that are to be sorted are <div> elements.

Display the page and move the thumbnails around. All the behavior that you see is provided by the defaults to the remaining options.

You can explore these options further in the lab page for Sortable. The three list containers at the bottom of the page use <li>, <div>, and <li> elements respectively as their sortable children. Using the setting for the tag option, you can control which of these element types are enabled. This means that for any run of the applied options, either the first and third, or the second, target containers will be actively sortable.

Because the tag option cannot accept more than one element type, and because the same set of options is always applied to all three targets on the lab page, it's not possible for all of the targets to be actively sortable at the same time. This is not a restriction on your own pages. You can have multiple sortable containers, each with their own child types, as long as you apply the appropriate tag option to each container. What you cannot do is have a single container that mixes multiple child element types. If you do need to mix and match sortable elements—images and text, for example—be sure to enclose them in a single element type, such as `<div>` or `<li>` as we did in the refactored thumbnails example.

Now let's take a look at exercising control over the behavior of the sort.

Controlling the behavior of the drag

As you most certainly have realized by this point, the Sortable library code makes heavy use of the drag-and-drop capabilities we explored earlier in this chapter. A few of the options from those areas are exposed for use when creating a sortable container.

The `hoverclass` option allows you to specify a CSS class name that is applied to a sortable element over which another sortable element is being dragged. This can be used to give the user strong feedback regarding the location of the dragged element, and to indicate that some overt activity will take place in the event of a drop.

To see this option in action, bring up the Sortable lab page, and with the `hoverclass` option set to "default," sort some list elements and observe the appearance of the elements over which you are dragging. Now, set the option to "user hoverActive class" (which assigns a predefined CSS class to the option) and repeat. You will see that when the style class is applied, the sortable elements over which the dragged element is hovering change their appearance according to the rules of the CSS class.

The `ghosting` option determines whether the dragged element appears to be removed from the container while it is being dragged (the default), or whether it appears to stay in place while a ghost image (a semitransparent clone) is dragged.

In the Sortable lab page, set the `ghosting` option to its various settings, and observe the original item when you perform a drag operation. Note that Internet Explorer has some issues with the appearance of the ghost image when `ghosting` is enabled. This problem seems to be purely visual and does not affect the actual sort operation.

Sometimes, however, you might not want everything in a container to be sortable. Let's look at the options we have for controlling which elements are to be sortable.

Constraining what is to be sorted

Another option that made its way from the Droppables library into Sortable is the `only` option. This option is a renaming of the Droppables `accept` option, and it allows us to specify a CSS class name, or array of class names, that limit what is and is not to be sortable. When specified, only eligible child elements (as determined by the tag option) that possess one of the specified class names become sortable.

In the Sortable lab page, every sortable child in the target containers has been assigned a class of "odd" or "even," depending upon its original position within its parent. Making sure that the only option is either unset, or set to "default," click the Apply to Items button and note that you can freely move all the elements (except for the indented subelements—ignore those for now) within whatever sortable containers are active.

Now change the only option to "class even," and see which elements can be moved, and which cannot. Change the setting to "class odd" and try again. You will see that when the only option is applied, only elements with the specified class name are active. For example, when an only option of "even" is applied, the "A", "C", "E", and other "odd" entries are unsortable.

Now that we know how to constrain sortable elements, let's turn that around and unfetter elements from the confinement of their parent elements.

Moving items between sortables

As you might recall from our exploration of Droppables, its containment option can be used to limit which dragged items are recognized by specifying an ID that must be a parent container of the dragged item. Similarly in the Sortable library, the containment option can be used to specify from where sortable elements can be dragged.

Without any provision for a containment value, a sortable container will accept only dragged sortable items that come from within itself. By specifying the ID of another sortable container, or an array of sortable containers, you can enable the dragging of items between containers.

A Containment Example sample page demonstrates this functionality. It is available from the chapter's control panel in the Sortable section, or you can open the sortable/containment-example.html file. The page is shown in figure 7.10.

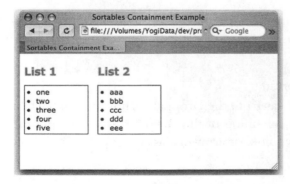

Figure 7.10
Initial state of the Sortables
Containment Example page

Here is the code that sets up these two sortable containers (in the `onload` handler, as usual):

```
Sortable.create(
  'sortableList1',
  {
    containment: ['sortableList1','sortableList2'],
    dropOnEmpty: true
  }
);
Sortable.create(
  'sortableList2',
  {
    containment: ['sortableList1','sortableList2']
  }
);
```

Note that the `containment` option for each container lists both containers as containment elements. By doing so, we have enabled the child elements to be sorted not only within the context of their parent, but also to be moved between the two containers.

When the `containment` option is used, the innate ability for child elements to be sorted within their parents is no longer automatic. If, in the example, we were to curtail the `containment` options to only refer to the other container element, we would no longer be able to sort the child elements within their own parent.

Play around with this example for a while, seeing how you can freely sort the elements within the original container as well as move them between containers. You could end up with a mixed up set of lists as shown in figure 7.11.

Next, move all the elements from List 2 to List 1, so that List 2 is completely empty. Now, try to move an element back to the empty container. Oops. We can't do it. Why not?

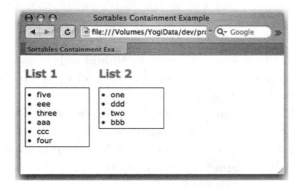

Figure 7.11
Crazy mixed up lists!

The Sortable library works by making the sortable child elements not only draggable, but droppable as well. This is how the movement of dragged elements is detected. You might have guessed this was what was going on when you saw the hoverclass option in action. Once List 2 is emptied of child elements, there are no longer any droppable elements to detect a drag and drop.

Enter the dropOnEmpty option. When set to true, this option makes the container, itself, a droppable, so that a container without sortable elements can detect when a sortable element is dropped upon it. By default, this option is false, in order to eliminate overhead and allow you to specify the container as a droppable for other uses.

In our example, we set dropOnEmpty to true for List 1. To see the effect this option has on that list, move all the elements from List 1 into List 2 so that List 1 is empty (refreshing the page will get you halfway there). Once List 1 is empty, try to move one of the elements in List 2 back into List 1. Success!

But not to sit on our laurels, what about sortables with other orientations?

Creating nonvertical sortables

All of the sortable containers we've explored thus far have had children that were oriented vertically. This is quite common, as it's a natural orientation for many lists, especially those composed of text. But the Sortable library also makes provisions for sorting elements horizontally, or even in a grid.

Placing the elements in the desired orientation is the responsibility of the page author, and it's done using the appropriate HTML markup and CSS rules. It is also the responsibility of the page author, using options to the Sortable.create() method, to tell the Sortable library (which always assumes a vertical orientation) about the orientation.

The principle option that you should always use when creating a nonvertical container is the constraint option. This option specifies how the movement of dragged elements should be constrained. As you may recall, this option is available for all draggable elements.

A value of vertical specifies that dragged elements should only move up and down. A value of horizontal constrains movement to left and right. A value of false applies no constraints to the movement.

As usual, a page has been set up to help demonstrate this behavior. Open the Non-Vertical Example link from the chapter's control panel, or open the sortable/nonvertical-example.html file in your browser. You will see four sortable containers containing thumbnail images in nonvertical orientations: three horizontal, and one in a 3-by-2 grid, as shown in figure 7.12.

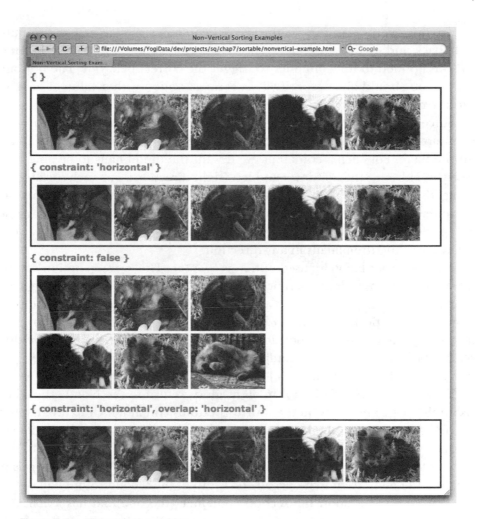

Figure 7.12 Nonvertical sortables

The first list has had no constraint option applied to it, allowing the default of vertical to be applied. Attempt to sort the elements in this first container, and you'll note that it works, sort of, but acts rather oddly. As the elements are constrained to move up and down only, moving the mouse left and right causes the thumbnail to quiver in place, instead of following the mouse pointer, and then to jump into a new position once the mouse has reached a certain threshold. Not all that pleasing an interaction, is it? And hardly what one would consider user friendly!

Try this exercise again with the second container. Notice how the thumbnails slide back and forth as expected. The `constraint` option with a value of `horizontal` was applied to this container to trigger the correct behavior. The bottom line is that you should always specify a `constraint` option with a value of `horizontal` for horizontally oriented containers unless you really like quivering images.

Since the default value for `constraint` is `vertical`, we need a way to explicitly turn movement constraints off for grid-oriented containers, such as the third one on the page. For such a container, we'd want the thumbnails to be able to move freely in either of the up/down and left/right directions. For such sortables, specifying the value `false` (the Boolean literal) will disable any constraints on the movement of the dragged items. The third container, with `constraint` set to `false`, demonstrates this behavior. Within that container, notice how you can freely move the thumbnails in any direction.

Another orientation-focused option is `overlap`. The `overlap` option controls at what point during a drag operation the "swap" behavior between a draggable and its droppable is triggered. When enabled in the direction appropriate to the container's orientation, this option causes the dragged item and the item over which it is being dragged to swap positions when the 50 percent mark over the droppable has been reached. The default value is `vertical`, so we've actually been seeing it in action all along, but it's subtle, so you may not have really noticed.

To see the `overlap` behavior in all its glory, return to the Non-Vertical Sorting Examples page and focus on the fourth (bottom) container. Grab the first thumbnail in its center (roughly, the puppy's nose), and slowly drag it to the right over the second thumbnail until that second thumbnail jumps to the first position. You will have noticed that the swap occurred when the mouse pointer (the puppy's nose) reached the 50 percent mark across the width of the second thumbnail.

Now, let's focus upon the second container (the one that has a `containment` option of `horizontal`), and repeat the exercise. (You might want to refresh the page to get all the images back in their original positions.) Grab the puppy's nose, and move it to the right until the swap is triggered. Notice anything different? The second image jumped into the first position as soon as the mouse cursor moved into it, rather than waiting until the 50 percent mark had been reached. Because the `overlap` default is `vertical`, and no `overlap` option was specified for this container, the overlap behavior was effectively disabled. To disable `overlap` for vertically oriented containers, you can specify `false` for its value.

You might consider the orientation of a sortable to be a type of "shape" that the element can attain. Another "shape" that we may want to consider is that of sortable elements that contain other sortable elements.

Enabling nested sortables

We've seen that even though the Sortable library can be used with other element types, it is primarily focused (via the option defaults) on vertically oriented lists using `<ul>` elements as the container, with `<li>` element children as the sortables. When encountering or using such lists, it is not uncommon to have nested sublists within lists.

Just such a structure has been implemented in the first two sortable containers on the Sortable lab page. The first list, implemented as a `<ul>` element, contains another embedded `<ul>` element (at the "H" element). The second target, composed of `<div>` elements within a `<div>` element, contains a `<div>` element that contains grandchild `<div>` elements (at the "M" element).

Reset the options and click the Apply to Items button. In the first list, grab the "A" item and slowly move it down the list, noting the behavior that is exhibited around the sublist (at the "H" item). You will notice that the whole subelement acts as a unit. You can place the dragged element before the sublist, or you can place it after the sublist, but if you wanted to place the dragged element between the "HAL" and "Host" items, you're out of luck. But not for long.

There are two options that we can use to instruct the Sortable code to allow sublists to join in on the sortable behavior. The first of these is the `tree` option. When `tree` is set to `true` (it defaults to `false`), the Sortable library enables subelements in the container to join the sorting party. The second option, `treeTag`, tells the library what element type to expect to contain the subelements. By default, `<ul>` elements are expected.

On the Sortable Lab page, reset the options and set the `tree` option to `true`. Apply the options and repeat the earlier exercise. Notice that now when you drag an item over the sublist, its elements participate in the sort behavior.

To try this out on the second list, reset the options, set `tag` to `div`, `tree` to `true`, and `treeTag` to `div`. Apply the options and repeat the exercise on the second list. In this case, `treeTag` is required because the sublist is contained in a `<div>` element that the default of `<ul>` would cause to be ignored.

Nested or not, lists can sometimes be long—sometimes longer than the window height allows, or just longer than good old user interface design would deem prudent. Let's take a look at options that will help us take control of lengthy lists.

Controlling scrolling

When we run into the issue of lists so long that they become unwieldy, CSS comes to our rescue with the `overflow` attribute. Set to `auto` or `scroll` on a container with a fixed height, this attribute will cause a scroll bar to be placed on the container element. This allows a long list (or other elements) to be placed within it, and the user can scroll though it as desired.

Just such a list is set up on the Sortable Lab page as the third sortable container. This container is set to a fixed height that is shorter than its contained list requires, and it has an `overflow` attribute of `auto`, which applies a scroll bar to the container. This works wonderfully for users—the scroll bar gives them complete control over what portion of the longer list they will view.

However, this is not so useful when attempting a sort operation. Reset and apply the options. Grab the "A" item in the third (right-most) list, and drag it down toward the bottom of the list. Once you hit the lower border of the scrollable container, all bets are off. In actuality, the sort is still occurring. Continue to drag the item down an inch or so below the bottom of the container, and release. Scroll the container and you will notice that the item has been placed in the appropriate location. But because we couldn't see what was going on, it was impossible to precisely place the dragged element where we wanted it.

What we need is for the container to automatically scroll when we reach the bottom (or the top, as appropriate), and that is precisely the purpose of the `scroll` option. To enable such autoscrolling, the `scroll` option is set to the element reference or ID of the container.

On the Sortable Lab page, reset the options and set `scroll` to `yes`. Apply the option. This will set the value of `scroll` to the element ID for the third list. Now repeat the exercise, and note how the container automatically scrolls when you reach the bottom of the container and drag near or beyond it. The same happens in the upward direction when necessary.

The proximity of the mouse cursor to the border triggers the scrolling, and this can be controlled with the `scrollSensitivity` option. This option, which has a default value of `20`, determines at what distance from the border the scroll behavior is triggered.

On the lab page, set the `scrollSensitivity` to `1` and apply. Approach the border slowly, and note that you have to get very, very close to the border before the scrolling begins. Now set it to `60`, apply, and repeat the exercise. You will see that the distance from the border at which scrolling begins has increased.

The speed at which the scrolling occurs is controlled by the `scrollSpeed` option, which has a default value of `15`. Lower values will slow the scrolling down, while higher values will speed it up.

Now let's take a look at the notification options that will let us know when things are going on with our sortable elements.

Getting notified

Two options to `Sortable.create()` give you the opportunity to be notified whenever something interesting happens to your sortable element: `onChange` and `onUpdate`.

The more commonly used is the `onChange` option. It allows you to specify a function or closure to be repeatedly called whenever a drag operation on a child of the container is under way. This function is also called if a child of another container is dragged into the current container (if enabled by the `containment` option). A single argument with a reference to the dragged child is passed to this function.

You may have noticed that whenever you moved an item in the Sortable Lab page, that a message showing the position of the item appeared in the message area. This message is the result of an `onChange` callback added to the options hash of each sortable container.

The other notification option, `onUpdate`, allows you to specify a callback that is activated when a dragged item is dropped that results in a change in the order of the list. But there's a big "but" regarding this callback. The way that the library determines whether the order of the child items has changed is by using the `Sortable.serialize()` function that we'll look at in section 7.4.3. The Sortable library code stores successive values of the results of calling the `serialize()` function for the container, and it uses these values to detect whether the sort order of the child elements has changed.

`Sortable.serialize()` places some rather stringent demands on the child elements, and if these demands are not met, your `onUpdate` callback will never be called. See section 7.4.3 for more information on how to make sure your container and its elements are properly set up for the serialization function to return meaningful results.

When the `onUpdate` callback is invoked, it is passed a reference to the sortable container whose elements have been changed.

7.4.3 Serializing the sortable elements

Once the user is done with all that sorting, you'll usually want to do something with the results. After all, `Sortable.create()` creates a control that's analogous to the built-in HTML form controls.

We could write our own JavaScript code to examine the elements within the sortable container and perform whatever processing we like upon them, but if we wanted to simply submit the resulting order of elements to an Ajax call, the Sortable library has a handy, if rather limited, function that will generate a querystring from the sortable container's elements. This querystring is suitable for submission as the body of a POST operation, or as the querystring of a GET.

The function is named `Sortable.serialize()`, and it accepts two familiar parameters:

```
Sortable.serialize(element,options);
```

The first parameter is a reference to (or the ID of) the sortable container whose sortable elements are to be serialized, and the second is the ubiquitous options hash. The first of these options is name, and it sets the query parameter name to be used in the querystring. If not provided, the ID of the sortable container is used.

Whatever name is used is suffixed with square brackets when the querystring is constructed. So if the name were "xyz" (either because we supplied that name as the name option, or it defaulted from the ID of the sortable container), the querystring could look like this:

```
xyz[]=value1&xyz[]=value2&xyz[]=value3
```

The values in this string are derived from the IDs of the child elements in the order that they appear within the container.

The algorithm for determining the value for each sortable child of the container is straightforward but not without its nuances. We'll discuss those nuances in the next section, but first let's examine the default behavior.

The ID of each child in the sortable element is matched against a pattern consisting of a prefix, followed by an underscore, followed by the rest of the identifier. If the ID does not match that pattern, the child is ignored. If the ID matches the pattern, the prefix is stripped (including the underscore), and the remainder of the ID serves as the query parameter value for that child.

The reason for this default behavior is so that you can use different prefixes to create unique IDs for all your child elements. After all, remember that each ID that appears on a page must be unique. The discardable prefix lets you make sure that each and every ID is unique within the page.

Once more, an example is worth a thousand words, so let's take a look at a simple one. Using the chapter's control panel, click on the Serialize Example link, or open the sortable/serialize-example.html file in your browser.

The page shows two lists, each with a Serialize button. Leaving the lists in their original order, click each of the buttons to see the serialization of the lists. Now, reorder some elements and click the buttons again. Note how the order of the values changes to reflect the order of the elements in the sortable containers.

The first list creates a querystring with keys named `sortableList1[]`, while the second uses keys with the name of `fred[]`. We'll see why when we examine the code for the page, which is shown in listing 7.5.

Listing 7.5   Code for the Sortables Serialize Example page

```html
<html>
  <head>
    <link rel="stylesheet" type="text/css" href="../styles.css"/>
    <title>Sortables Serialize Example</title>
    <script type="text/javascript"
            src="../scripts/prototype.js"></script>
    <script type="text/javascript"
            src="../scripts/scriptaculous.js"></script>
    <script type="text/javascript">
      window.onload = function() {                 ◄——      ❶ Set up sortables
        Sortable.create('sortableList1');                     on page load
        Sortable.create('sortableList2');
      }
                                                   ❷ Display result of
      function serialize(container,name) {   ◄—┘     serialization
        $('display').innerHTML =
            'Serialization of ' + $(container).id +
            ' is:<br/><pre>' +
            Sortable.serialize(container,{name:name}) + '</pre>';
      }
    </script>
    <style type="text/css">
      ul {
        width: 88px;
        border: 1px solid blue;
        padding: 3px 3px 3px 20px;
      }
    </style>
  </head>

  <body>

    <div style="float:left">                ❸ Create first
      <h1>List 1</h1>                           list
      <ul id="sortableList1">   ◄—┘
        <li id="list1_one">one</li>
        <li id="list1_two">two</li>
        <li id="list1_three">three</li>
        <li id="list1_four">four</li>
        <li id="list1_five">five</li>      ❹ Create button to
      </ul>                                    serialize first list
      <button type="button"   ◄—┘
              onclick="serialize('sortableList1')">
        Serialize
```

```
        </button>
    </div>

    <div style="float:left;margin-left:32px">
      <h1>List 2</h1>
      <ul id="sortableList2">          ◁
        <li id="list2_one">one</li>        ❺  Create
        <li id="list2_two">two</li>            second list
        <li id="list2_three">three</li>
        <li id="list2_four">four</li>
        <li id="list2_five">five</li>   ❻  Create button to
      </ul>                                serialize second list
      <button type="button"            ◁
              onclick="serialize('sortableList2','fred')">
        Serialize
      </button>
    </div>

    <div id="display" style="clear:both;padding-top:32px"></div>

  </body>

</html>
```

In the onload handler of this page ❶, two sortable containers are created from list elements defined later in the page. No fancy options are applied.

The lists, themselves, are simple structures composed of <ul> parents with <li> children (❸ and ❺). The twist that we have added in this example is that each <li> element possesses an ID value that will be used when we attempt to serialize the sortable container.

Note that because the contents of the two lists are the same, it's quite conceivable that we'd want the serialized values for the elements to be the same as well. But since we know that each ID in a page must be unique, we use a different prefix for each list (list1_ for the first list, and list2_ for the second) to make each ID unique. This prefix will not become part of the serialized querystring—its purpose is to allow us to create unique ID values.

The buttons for the two lists (❹ and ❻) call a function that will perform the serialization and display the result on the page ❷. This function accepts the container element to be serialized and a name to be used as the query parameter keys. If the name is omitted, the Sortable.serialize() function defaults to using the container's ID.

The button for the first list omits the name argument, so the parameter key used is the name of the sortable container: sortableList1. The second button provides the name `fred`, so it produces a serialization with parameter keys named `fred[]`.

The use of the square brackets as a suffix to the supplied name is simply a convention used to indicate that the parameter key will be submitted to the form with multiple values (mimicking the square bracket notation used for arrays in numerous programming languages).

The `Sortable.serialize()` function accepts a second option, `tag`, which determines the tag type of the children to be serialized. By default, the same tag type that was specified for the container (either explicitly or implicitly) is used. Because that's the type of the sorted children, the usefulness of this option to specify an alternative element type is rather questionable. However, it does exist should you wish to serialize values from an element type other than the sorted children.

The querystring produced by `Sortable.serialize()` will automatically encode the values of the query parameters appropriately for use within a URL.

Customizing the ID matching pattern

Now for that nuance we mentioned prior to discussing the example code. We saw that, by default, the `serialize()` method matches ID values that consist of a prefix followed by an underscore followed by more identifier characters. That default pattern can be overridden by supplying a regular expression defining the overriding matching pattern as the `format` option to the `Sortable.create()` method.

If no `format` option is specified, the default regular expression is as follows:

```
/^[^_]*_(.*)$/
```

Without delving too deeply into regular expressions (which are definitely beyond the scope of this chapter), this is what the default value specifies:

- the beginning of a string
- any number of characters (including none) that are not an underscore
- an underscore
- any number of characters (including none)
- the end of a string

Note also that the subexpression indicating the trailing characters is designated as a submatch by enclosing it in parentheses. The characters that match the first parenthesized portion (submatch) of the regular expression are the characters that will end up serving as the value for the element.

By supplying your own value for the format option, you can customize the pattern that your sortable child element IDs can be matched against. Let's say that rather than an underscore, we wanted to separate the prefix from the value with a colon. And, for whatever reason, we also wanted all the IDs to begin with the letter "p". We would supply the following regular expression as the format option:

```
/^p[^_]*:(.*)$/
```

Unless you are very comfortable with regular expressions, and have a really good reason for wanting to use an alternate pattern, it's probably best to just use the default value.

And that wraps up our discussion of sorting using the Scriptaculous library.

7.5 *Summary*

In this chapter, we've explored another powerful tool for page authors: drag and drop.

We first learned how to enable items to be moved around the page via dragging. On its own, this isn't a tremendously useful ability, but coupled with the ability to drop the dragged item onto a target element in order to indicate an action, or to create an association, or to trigger any number of other user interaction activities, this is a powerful addition to our on-page toolbox.

We saw one built-in example of such an interaction with the Sortable library, which allows us to add in-place reordering of elements, or even to move elements between containers. But that's only the tip of the iceberg of possible uses for drag and drop. The types of controls you can add to your pages using this ability are virtually unlimited.

You can use the knowledge you've gained regarding Prototype and Scriptaculous to create your own controls; ones that do exactly what you need them to do to delight the users of your applications.

This completes our survey of the extensions Scriptaculous adds to our web developer toolboxes. As we looked at the various elements, it became quite clear that the Scriptaculous libraries depend heavily upon the capabilities provided by the Prototype library. In the next part of this book, we'll delve deeper into the facilities that Prototype makes available to us as web developers.

Part 3

Prototype in Depth

Part 2 of this book provided a detailed tour of the Scriptaculous library, and part 3 performs a similar function for Prototype. Prototype is a much lower-level library than Scriptaculous, and is concerned primarily with improving the experience of writing JavaScript. Hence, three of the four chapters in this part of the book are concerned with JavaScript as a language. Only the final chapter looks at Prototype's features for working specifically with web browsers.

Throughout the language chapters, we begin by discussing the features of unadorned JavaScript, and then relate these to the improvements provided by Prototype. This part of the book can be read, then, as a primer on the JavaScript language, as well as a discussion of Prototype. While it's possible to get by as a JavaScript coder without knowing all the details of the language, the topics that we cover in this part of the book will improve your coding, whether or not you end up using Prototype and Scriptaculous.

Chapter 8 deals with JavaScript objects and the mechanisms that Prototype provides to enable you to develop simple object hierarchies. Chapter 9 looks at JavaScript Function objects, and in particular at Prototype's support for closures, one of the darkest and most mysterious corners of JavaScript, and one of the more powerful! Chapter 10 discusses JavaScript Arrays, and shows you how Prototype provides an entirely new way of working with Arrays.

Chapter 11 returns to the world of the web browser, and tours the capabilities that Prototype provides for working with the Document Object Model, and with HTML forms.

Throughout this part of the book, we're dealing with small, focused topics, and often ones with no visible user interface. In order to demonstrate our points, we've developed an interactive Scratchpad application that we use to run over 100 snippets of code, and to visualize their results. The Scratchpad has proven its worth as a teaching tool for the purposes of this book, and it can also serve as an interactive console during your day-to-day development.

All About Objects

8

This chapter covers

- Declaring JavaScript objects
- Defining reusable object types
- Writing object-oriented JavaScript using Prototype

In part 2, we looked at how we can use Prototype and Scriptaculous to achieve a number of quick wins for our application development. Using the libraries in this way requires relatively little understanding of the internal functioning of the libraries themselves. Indeed, it requires little understanding of the language features that the libraries make use of. That's one of the strengths of these libraries— for the casual user, the learning curve is not at all steep, and the payback is considerable. You may not need to take your use of the libraries beyond this level, in which case you've already got a very good return on your investment.

On the other hand, the libraries also provide a great deal of power and elegance for the more advanced user. Much of the advanced, low-level capability is provided by Prototype.js, and in the next few chapters, we will explore these capabilities more thoroughly. In part 4, we will take a second look at Scriptaculous, in light of what we have learned. That extra knowledge will make it easier to understand how Scriptaculous does what it does, but it will also help you to extend the Scriptaculous code base yourself.

Prototype provides a lot of its power by extending the core JavaScript classes. We'll begin our tour of these by looking at the most fundamental of all classes, the Object.

8.1 *Introducing the Scratchpad application*

Throughout this and the next two chapters, we're going to look at a number of low-level language features. As such, most of the code examples in this section will be short. Rather than providing a standalone web page to host each example, we've created a simple interactive JavaScript interpreter web application, into which the example code, called "snippets," can be loaded and edited. The URL of the Scratchpad application is http://localhost:8080/scratchpad/ps-sandbox.html. A screenshot of the Scratchpad application is shown in figure 8.1.

The simplest way to use the Scratchpad is to type some JavaScript into the script editor, and click the "run the code" button to evaluate it. Any code you have entered will be evaluated instantly.

To make things slightly easier to use, we've provided two additional features. The first is a set of predefined scripts, corresponding to the examples in this book, which can be loaded into the script editor (using Prototype's Ajax.Request, of course), and can subsequently be modified. The second is an output region, to the right of the editor, which simply serves as a holding place for any graphical elements that the script might generate.

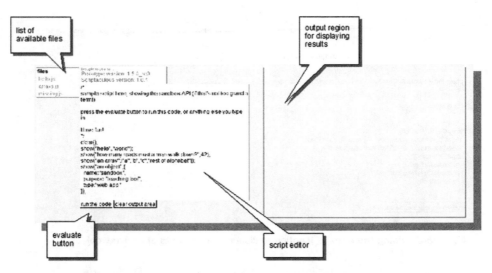

Figure 8.1   User interface of the Scratchpad application, used to evaluate small snippets of JavaScript on the fly

Here in part 3 of the book, we'll be manipulating and generating lots of values, objects, and arrays. We've therefore written a simple helper method that displays a value graphically in the output area. The function signature is as follows:

```
show(title,obj)
```

The `title` is the heading to be shown above the elements, and `obj` is the object to be displayed. The `show()` function supports simple objects such as strings and numbers, and also JavaScript Objects and Arrays, for which it will list all members or elements. It won't recurse into complex members or elements, though.

Figure 8.2 shows a simple invocation of this function, using the example script that is present when the Scratchpad first loads. We've called `show()` four times here, passing in a string, a number, an Array, and an Object respectively. (The Array and Object are defined inline using the compact JSON syntax—if you're not familiar with it, we'll explain it fully later in this chapter.) The string and number are displayed as is. The Array is listed alongside numerical indices, and the Object is displayed as a set of name-value pairs, corresponding to its properties.

We'll make use of the Scratchpad application throughout this part of the book (chapters 8–11) to run the code snippets and demonstrate their results. For now, let's get back to our discussion of JavaScript objects.

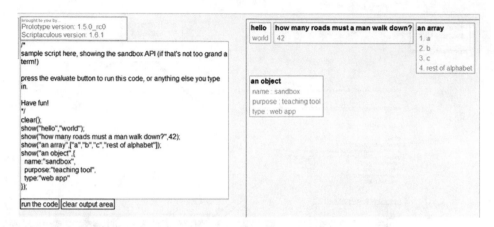

Figure 8.2   **Using the `show()` function to display the contents of an Array object**

8.2 *The Object type*

The most fundamental core object types are those that define how the language itself works. The Object type defines all JavaScript objects, and all other core object types, native objects, and JavaScript-defined objects inherit the behavior of this object. The main behavior of the Object type is the ability to contain members, that is, other objects.

In most object-oriented programming languages, such as C++, Java, and C#, an Object will have a predefined set of members corresponding to its properties and methods. This set is defined by the class definition for the object, and it will remain constant throughout the lifetime of the object. In JavaScript, however, there are no class definitions as such, and an object can accept new members at any point in its life. In many ways, the JavaScript Object type is best thought of as an associative array or hash table.

The most obvious expression of this is the fact that the dot notation usually associated with objects and the square-bracket notation associated with arrays are interchangeable in JavaScript. To define a value for an object's property in Java, C#, etc., we would normally write something like this:

```
myObject.something = "hello world";
```

In JavaScript, that notation works, but it can also be written as follows:

```
myObject['something'] = "hello world";
```

The net effect of the two statements is exactly the same—the value of a property called something is set to the string hello world. In Java or C#, the object would need to be defined as an instance of a class containing a property called something, of course, but in JavaScript, it isn't so; if the property something was previously unset for our object, it will simply add it in.

Extending a JavaScript object with new properties extends the state that it contains. More excitingly, extending it with new methods extends the behavior that it is capable of. JavaScript objects that we create ourselves can be extended in this way, and so can native objects. An object can be extended on a case-by-case basis, but the base definition for an entire type of object can also be extended. Prototype provides support for all of these capabilities, as we'll see in the following sections.

8.2.1 Creating an Object

In simple JavaScript code, we can get by without using objects, but in any moderately complex project, using objects can help to structure our code considerably. In the first section of this book, we presented a web-based image gallery application. At the end of chapter 4, the JavaScript code was responsible for parsing the results of Ajax requests, and it generated user interface markup directly from the server response data. When we add new features to the gallery, we might want to decouple the user interface generation from the Ajax response parsing, and model the gallery on the client tier as a set of objects. The images in the gallery are organized into folders, so we already have two types of objects in our application: one representing the image, and another representing the folder to which the image belongs.

JavaScript is a flexible language, and there's more than one way to do most things. We'll look at two different ways of creating objects in the following sections.

Verbose Object declaration

Let's assume that we've decided to use an object-based approach to structuring our app, and we'll go ahead and make some objects. The easiest way to create an Object in JavaScript is to simply declare one:

```
var picture=new Object();
```

We can then add new properties to it as we wish:

```
picture.id=3;
picture.title="middle way";
picture.date=new Date("01/01/1970");
```

We aren't limited to simple properties. An Object property can be a complex object itself:

```
picture.details=new Object();
picture.details.type="photograph";
picture.details.keywords=new
   Array("landscape","tranquil","green","vegetation");
```

We can also attach methods to our object:

```
picture.getAge=function(){ return new Date()-this.date; }
```

Let's put this together into the Scratchpad application—take a look at snippet 8.1

Snippet 8.1

```
var picture=new Object();
picture.id=3;
picture.title="middle way";
picture.date=new Date("01/07/2005");
picture.details=new Object();
picture.details.type="photograph";
picture.details.keywords=new
   Array("landscape","tranquil","green","vegetation");
picture.getAge=function(){ return new Date()-this.date; }

show("picture",picture);
show("details",picture.details);
show("age (years)",picture.getAge()/(1000*60*60*24*365)); .
```

From the output of the Scratchpad, it's evident that we've created a moderately complex object successfully. However, we had to write a lot of code to do so. There is a more concise way of accomplishing the same thing, as we'll see in the next section.

Terse object declaration using JSON

Creating anything but the simplest object in this way will be tedious and long-winded. Fortunately, JavaScript provides another notation for creating objects that reveals the associative array nature of the object more clearly. We can define our entire object in a single statement, as shown in snippet 8.2.

Snippet 8.2

```
var picture={
  id: 3,
  title: "middle way",
  date: new Date("01/07/2005"),
  details: {
    type:"photograph",
    keywords:"landscape, tranquil, green, vegetation"
  },
  getAge: function(){ return new Date()-this.date; }
};

show("picture",picture);
show("details",picture.details);
show("age (years)",picture.getAge()/(1000*60*60*24*365));
```

picture	**details**
id : 3	type : photograph
title : middle way	keywords : landscape, tranquil, green, vegetation
date : Thu Jan 1 00:00:00 PST 1970	
details : [object Object]	**age (years)**
getAge : function(){ return new Date()-this.date; }	36.99025146965373

We've indented the statement for readability here, but the whitespace is entirely optional. This style of notation is commonly known as JSON (short for JavaScript Object Notation), and we'll refer to it as such in this book. We've already encountered it in section 3.1.2, and throughout chapters 5 through 7, where we saw the complex options arguments being passed to various Prototype and Scriptaculous helper objects, such as the Ajax request and the Effects objects. Now the time has come to take a closer look at JSON and see how it works.

JSON has only two rules.

First, objects are represented as key-value pairs, with each pair being separated by a comma, and the key and value within each pair being separated by a colon. The object itself is bounded by curly braces. Note that we can attach functions as well as data values to the object in this way, effectively adding methods to our objects. We'll examine functions more thoroughly in the next chapter.

Second, arrays are represented as comma-delimited lists, bounded by square braces. The keywords property is an array.

Objects and arrays can be nested within each other to any depth, to create arbitrarily complex objects.

JSON is a core feature of the JavaScript language and requires no external libraries or helper code. Defining objects using JSON has been possible since the early days of JavaScript, but it has only recently become common practice. Prototype's coding style makes considerable use of JSON. There is also a lot of coverage of JSON within the Ajax press as a lightweight, friendlier alternative to XML for encoding Ajax responses. We already encountered JSON briefly in this capacity in chapter 3.

JSON is easy to write and satisfyingly simple, but it is still limited to creating unique instances of objects. In the next section, we'll see how to define reusable object types.

8.2.2 *Defining object types using prototypes*

The ways in which we've created objects so far has been suitable for defining one-off objects, but often we will want to define a type of object with standard properties and behavior that we can then create several instances of. In our image gallery application, for example, we'll want to create tens, if not hundreds, of objects to represent pictures. In an object-oriented language, we would accomplish this by defining a class definition, but, as we noted, we have no class definitions in JavaScript.

We do, however, have access to object prototypes. A prototype is a collection of properties and methods that can be automatically attached to an object when it is created. To define a custom object type, we simply need to define a function that will serve as a constructor, and attach other properties and methods to the prototype of that function. This may sound complex, but in practice, it is reasonably straightforward.

Let's look at how to define a reusable object type for our picture class. First, we define a constructor function:

```
function Picture(id, title, date, details){
  this.id=id;
  this.title=title;
  this.date=date;
  this.details=details;
}
```

Our picture object also had a getAge() method, which we would like to make available to the Picture type. We could define the method inside the constructor:

```
function Picture(id, title, date, details){
  this.id=id;
  this.title=title;
  this.date=date;
  this.details=details;
  this.getAge=function(){ return new Date()-this.date; }
}
```

Doing this, however, is not recommended, as we create a new, albeit identical, function for each instance of the object. A more efficient approach is to add the function to the prototype, outside of the constructor function:

```
Picture.prototype.getAge=function(){ return new Date()-this.date; }
```

If we're adding several methods to the object type at once, the simplest approach (and one used widely in the Prototype code base) is to use JSON, like this:

```
Picture.prototype={
  getAge: function(){ return new Date()-this.date; },
  fetchThumbnail:function(){ ... },
  showDetails: function(div){ ... }
};
```

We've omitted the method bodies here, for now. While we're exploring the way JavaScript objects work, we don't want to get bogged down in the details of our gallery application.

Once our object type is defined, we can then create instances of it simply by calling the constructor:

```
var picture=new Picture(
  3,
  "middle way",
  new Date("01/07/2005"),
  {
    type:"photograph",
    keywords: [
      "landscape", "tranquil", "green", "vegetation"
    ]
  }
);
```

We can then call the methods of the object, like so:

```
var age=picture.getAge();
```

Let's put this together before we move on. Snippet 8.3 illustrates the complete code required to define our Picture type, create an instance, and display its details in the Scratchpad.

Snippet 8.3

```
function Picture(id, title, date, details){
  this.id=id;
  this.title=title;
  this.date=date;
  this.details=details;
  this.getAge=function(){ return new Date()-this.date; }
}
```

```
Picture.prototype={
  getAge: function(){ return new Date()-this.date; },
  fetchThumbnail:function(){ /*...*/ },
  showDetails: function(div){ /*...*/ }
};
var picture=new Picture(
  3,
  "middle way",
  new Date("01/07/2005"),
  {
    type:"photograph",
    keywords: [
      "landscape", "tranquil", "green", "vegetation"
    ]
  }
);
show("picture",picture);
show("details",picture.details);
show("age (years)",picture.getAge()/(1000*60*60*24*365));
```

In addition to extending our own defined object types, we can extend the prototypes of the core JavaScript language types too. Snippet 8.4 illustrates how to add a utility method to the Array class to clear out the contents of the array.

Snippet 8.4

```
var keywords = [
    "landscape", "tranquil", "green", "vegetation"
  ] ;
show("keywords : before",keywords);
Array.prototype.clear=function(){ this.length=0; }
keywords.clear();
show("keywords : after",keywords);
```

The native Array class has no `clear()` method, but by adding to the prototype of that class, we've extended the core functionality of all instances of the class—even those defined before the prototype was extended. The Prototype library makes extensive use of this facility to enhance the core JavaScript language, and we'll look at these extensions in this and the following two chapters. Before moving on to Prototype, though, we'll take a quick look at how JavaScript handles object reflection.

keywords : before	keywords : after
1. landscape	
2. tranquil	
3. green	
4. vegetation	

8.2.3 *Reflecting on objects*

Most modern programming languages that support objects support *reflection*. Reflection is the process of examining an object to find out what properties and methods it contains. In strictly typed object-oriented languages, such as Java and C#, one usually knows what types of objects one is dealing with, and reflection is a relatively esoteric business. In loosely typed languages, such as JavaScript, the need for reflection is perhaps more common. We present the mechanism here for two reasons. First, to illustrate how simple it is in JavaScript. And second, to set the scene for some of the design decisions that Prototype has taken in the way it handles objects.

There are generally two stages to reflecting on an object: iterating over the members of the object—all of its properties and methods—and then querying the individual properties and methods to find out what type they are.

The first step is easy. Because JavaScript objects are like associative arrays, we can iterate through them using a simple `for...in` loop:

```
for (name in obj){
  var value=obj[name];
  /* now do something with it... */
}
```

Note the use of the array-like syntax to reference properties of the object.

The good news is that the second step is easy too. JavaScript provides an `instanceof` operator that can tell us the type of an object—whether it is an Array, a String, an Object, or a user-defined type.

Our Scratchpad application uses simple JavaScript reflection to work out what to do with objects passed to the `show()` function. First, it determines what type of object it is dealing with, limiting the categories to Array, Object, or anything else:

```
function show(title,obj){
  if (obj instanceof Array){
    showList(title,obj);
  }else if (obj instanceof Object){
    showObj(title,obj);
  }else{
    showVal(title,obj);
  }
}
```

Note that we test for Arrays before Objects. Arrays are a subclass of Object, so instanceof Object will return true for any JavaScript object.

When rendering an object using the showObj() function, we make use of the for...in loop to iterate through the members and list them all out:

```
function showObj(title,obj){
  var html="<div class='list'>"
    +"<div class='listHdr'>"+title+"</div>";
  for (i in obj){
    var item=obj[i];
    var itemValue=displayVal(item);
    html+="<div class='listItem'>"+i+" : "+itemValue+"</div>";
  }
  html+="</div>";
  new Insertion.Bottom($('output'),html);
}
```

The Scratchpad application is bundled with the code downloads for this book, so feel free to examine the source code if you want to understand this in more detail.

The second reason for raising this topic now is to note that there is a side effect to extending the prototype of an object—every new function or property that we add to the prototype will appear when iterated over by the for...in loop. Normally, this is what we want in the case of properties, but functions are included too.

As an example, let's suppose that we want to be able to timestamp our image objects with the current time. We write a function called timeStamp() to add a timestamp property to the object. Then we realize that this might be useful for our Folder objects too, so we decide to add it to the base Object class instead, allowing us to timestamp any object in our system. Snippet 8.5 shows us doing this for an object describing the details of an image.

Snippet 8.5

```
Object.prototype.timeStamp=function(){
  this.timestamp=new Date();
}
var details={
  type: "photograph",
  keywords: [
    "landscape", "tranquil", "green", "vegetation"
```

```
    ]
  };
  details.timeStamp();
  show("details",details);
```

```
details
type : photograph
keywords : landscape,tranquil,green,vegetation
timestamp : Thu Jun 22 2006 22:15:54 GMT+0100 (GMT Standard Time)
timeStamp : function () { this.timestamp = new Date(); }
```

As expected, the `timestamp` property showing the current time is there, but so is the function definition. In fact, the function definition will now pop up when we iterate through the members of any object.

For this reason, it's generally considered bad manners to extend the Object prototype, and Prototype.js doesn't do that. It does extend String, Array, and Function, and we'll look at some of these features too in this part of the book. First, though, we're going to look at how Prototype makes it easier to work with objects without extending the Object prototype.

8.3 *Objects and Prototype*

Prototype provides two main features for working with objects. The first, the Class object, is a simple syntactic helper that makes the declaration of object types more compact. The second, the `Object.extend()` method, is a more generic feature that can be used with objects in a variety of ways. We'll kick off this section with a look at the Class object.

8.3.1 *Simplifying constructors with Class.create()*

In snippet 8.3, we saw how to define a reusable object type by defining first the constructor function, and then the prototype using JSON syntax. While this syntax works, it requires us to define the constructor outside of the rest of the class definition.

Prototype's Class object contains a single useful helper method, `create()`, that allows us to move the body of the constructor into the prototype definition. The `create()` method does this for us by defining a constructor automatically that delegates to an `initialize()` method, which we then define manually. Snippet 8.6 shows what this looks like.

Snippet 8.6

```
var Picture=Class.create();

Picture.prototype={
  initialize:function(id, title, date, details){
    this.id=id;
    this.title=title;
    this.date=date;
    this.details=details;
    this.getAge=function(){ return new Date()-this.date; }
  },
  getAge: function(){ return new Date()-this.date; },
  fetchThumbnail:function(){ /*...*/ },
  showDetails: function(div){ /*...*/ }
};
var picture=new Picture(
  3,
  "middle way",
  new Date("01/07/2005"),
  {
    type:"photograph",
    keywords: [
      "landscape", "tranquil", "green", "vegetation"
    ]
  }
);
show("picture",picture);
show("details",picture.details);
show("age (years)",picture.getAge()/(1000*60*60*24*365));
```

---

picture

showDetails : function(div){ /*...*/ }
fetchThumbnail : function(){ /*...*/ }
timeStamp : function(){ this.timestamp=new Date(); }
initialize : function(id, title, date, details){ this.id=id; this.title=title;
this.date=date; this.details=details; this.getAge=function(){ return new Date()-
this.date; } }
id : 3
title : middle way
date : Fri Jan 7 00:00:00 PST 2005
details : [object Object]
getAge : function(){ return new Date()-this.date; }

details

timeStamp : function(){ this.timestamp=new Date(); }
type : photograph
keywords : landscape,tranquil,green,vegetation

age (years)

1.9491821836314053

The initialize() method of the prototype is an exact copy of the old constructor function. The new constructor function that Class.create() generates for us simply calls the initialize() method, passing in the arguments verbatim.

Class.create() doesn't buy us anything other than cleaner-looking code. There is no need to use it to benefit from Prototype's other object-based features, and the decision as to whether to use it is largely a matter of taste. You'll find it within the Prototype and Scriptaculous code base quite a lot, so we present it here for reference. We'll also defer to Prototype house style and use it ourselves in the rest of this chapter.

The second Prototype feature that we'll address in this section offers a lot more power and functionality, so let's look at it now.

8.3.2 Declaring object hierarchies with Object.extend()

We've already moved from declaring one-off structured objects to defining object types in our review of JavaScript objects. In many cases, we've gone far enough—after all, we don't need to remodel the entire hierarchy of business objects inside the browser, and we'd be making a lot of extra work for ourselves if we did. Nonetheless, there are frequently times when it's useful to define an object hierarchy of some sort, with shared base functionality defined in one place, and specialist behavior overlaid on top of it. Defining the base behavior in one place prevents us from repeating ourselves and generally keeps the code tidy.

We've already seen this sort of hierarchy at work in the Prototype and Scriptaculous libraries themselves. Prototype's Ajax helper classes that we looked at in chapters 3 and 4 followed a clear hierarchy, from Base through Request to the Updaters. The Scriptaculous library's Autocompleter component, which we looked at in chapter 6, also bundles all the shared housekeeping of updating the GUI and responding to user events into a base class, on top of which it builds two concrete implementations, for client-side and server-side supply of data.

Sadly, JavaScript doesn't offer any mechanisms for class inheritance out of the box. So how do Prototype and Scriptaculous do it? And how can we utilize the same capabilities in our own code? There are actually several mechanisms at work. Let's start with the simplest and work our way through them.

8.3.3 Simple object merging

The simplest mechanism that Prototype offers for extending one object with the capabilities of another is the Object.extend() method. Note that we said earlier that it was bad manners to extend the Object prototype. This is not bad-mannered code, as extend() is attached directly to Object, not to its prototype. In object-oriented terms, it's a static method.

Object.extend() takes two objects as arguments, and it iterates through the members of the second object, attaching the members to the first object using the same identifying name. In snippet 8.7, we create two simple objects using JSON syntax, and extend the first with the second, in order to extend the metadata for a picture in our gallery.

Snippet 8.7

```
var picture={
  id: 3,
  title: "middle way",
  date: new Date("07/01/2005"),
  details: {
    type:"photograph",
    keywords:"landscape, tranquil, green, vegetation"
  },
  getAge: function(){ return new Date()-this.date; }
};

show("details",picture.details);

Object.extend(
  picture.details,
  {
    camera: "Nikon Coolpix 300",
    location: "Batsford, Gloucestershire",
    photographer: "Dave"
  }
);

show("extended details",picture.details);
```

We could have extended the details object from the second, anonymous object one member at a time, but Object.extend() gives us a very concise way of doing so as a single operation. We defined the second object using JSON here, just to keep the example simple, but extend() will work equally well on any JavaScript object, however it has been created.

details
type : photograph
keywords : landscape, tranquil, green, vegetation

extended details
type : photo
keywords : landscape, tranquil, green, vegetation
camera : Nikon Coolpix 300
location : Batsford, Gloucestershire
photographer : Dave

In this case, the two objects didn't share any attributes with a common name. Let's see what happens when we do have a clash in namespaces. Snippet 8.8 tells the story.

Snippet 8.8

```
var picture={
  id: 3,
  title: "middle way",
  date: new Date("07/01/2005"),
  details: {
    type:"photograph",
    keywords:"landscape, tranquil, green, vegetation"
  },
  getAge: function(){ return new Date()-this.date; }
};

show("details",picture.details);

Object.extend(
  picture.details,
  {
    type:"photo",
    camera: "Nikon Coolpix 300",
    location: "Batsford, Gloucestershire",
    photographer: "Dave"
  }
);

show("extended details",picture.details);
```

The two details objects now share the `type` property in common. When the second extends the original, it simply overwrites any existing values. The hybrid object, then, has properties originating from three sources. `Type` is present in both objects, but has been overwritten by the second object. `Camera`, `location`, and `photographer` are present only in the second object, and have been added to the first as new properties. Finally, `keywords` was present only in the first object, and has survived unchanged.

details
type : photograph
keywords : landscape, tranquil, green, vegetation

extended details
type : photograph
keywords : landscape, tranquil, green, vegetation
camera : Nikon Coolpix 300
location : Batsford, Gloucestershire
photographer : Dave

So far, our details objects are simply data structures. Real objects encapsulate both data and behavior, and as we noted earlier, object methods in JavaScript are simply functions attached as properties. As such, `Object.extend()` will treat them just as it does any other properties. In snippet 8.9, we'll define a few methods for our details, to see what the implications of this are.

Snippet 8.9

```
var picture={
  id: 3,
  title: "middle way",
  date: new Date("01/01/1970"),
  details: {
    type:"photograph",
    keywords:"landscape, tranquil, green, vegetation",
    about: function(){ return "This is a "+this.type; }
  },
  getAge: function(){ return new Date()-this.date; }
};

show("about",picture.details.about());

Object.extend(
  picture.details,
  {
    type:"photo",
    camera: "Nikon Coolpix 300",
    location: "Batsford, Gloucestershire",
    photographer: "Dave",
    summarize:function(){
      return "This "+this.type
        +" was taken by "+this.photographer
        +" at "+this.location
        +" while thinking of "+this.keywords;
    }
  }
);

show("about",picture.details.about());

show("about",picture.details.summarize());
```

about	about
This is a photograph	This is a photo

about
This photo was taken by Dave at Batsford, Gloucestershire while thinking of landscape, tranquil, green, vegetation

After we've extended the details object with the extra details, we can still call the about() method, but it will refer to overridden properties from the second object, specifically the type. It will also gain access to any methods defined only in the second object, such as summarize().

On its own, `Object.extend()` provides us with a useful way to merge functionality from one object into another. When it comes to working with predefined types of objects, though, it can be used to form the basis of a full inheritance system. By operating on the prototype rather than the object itself, we can make object types extend from one another, as we'll see in the next section. It can also be used, however, to provide multiple inheritance in JavaScript, through a mechanism known as *mixins*. We'll look at mixins in more detail in the next section.

8.3.4 *Modeling Object hierarchies*

In section 8.2.1, we saw how to define a simple one-off object, and in section 8.2.2 we moved on to defining reusable types by employing the `prototype` property. In this section, we'll make the same leap for inheritance, taking the `Object.extend()` mechanism that we discussed in the previous section, and applying it to object types rather than standalone objects. There are two ways in which we can do this, which can be characterized in object-oriented terms as single and multiple inheritance. Many modern object-oriented languages, notably Java and C#, don't support multiple inheritance, so it will be less familiar to many readers. We'll look at single inheritance first, and return to look at multiple inheritance later.

Single inheritance

Let's suppose that we've decided that we want to model our image gallery to contain two item types in each folder—images and subfolders. That is, rather than displaying subfolders separately down the left side of the page, we'll show them as icons, so as to resemble a file-explorer program more closely. Both types of objects will share some common functionality, such as having a name, date, and keywords (allowing us to tag individual photos and entire collections). Both will also have functionality not possessed by the other. For example, the items representing images will have a method to show the close-up and members defining file size and dimensions. The items representing subfolders might list the number of images in the folder and provide a method for opening them as the current folder. It's a perfect fit for an object-oriented approach.

Defining the base class is straightforward, following the approach that we outlined in the previous section. First we define a constructor function:

```
var Item=Class.create();
```

Here, we're using `Class.create()` to define the constructor for us, as per snippet 8.6. The technique we're demonstrating here would also work for manually written constructors, such as the one in snippet 8.3.

We then define the base class's prototype, which contains all the functionality of that class. Because we've used `Class.create()`, we'll include an `initialize()` method:

```
var Item=Class.create();
Item.prototype={
  initialize:function(){
    this._init.call(arguments);
  },
  _init:function(name,date,keywords){
    this.name=name;
    this.date=date;
    this.keywords=keywords || [];
  },
  addKeyword:function(word){
    if (!this.keywords.include(word)){
      this.keywords.push(word);
    }
  }
};
```

The `initialize()` method here provides the real implementation of the constructor. We've delegated the setting of the shared properties to a second function, `_init()`. We did this because when we create the subclasses, we will have to override `initialize()`, and we want to still have access to the `_init()` method. The underscore at the beginning of the function name indicates that this is an internal method of the class that shouldn't be called from outside. JavaScript has no hard support for public and private members, but the convention signals our intent to other programmers who might read or modify the code.

To make the example sufficiently interesting, we ought to include methods as well as properties in the base class. We've provided a simple `addKeyword()` method here to help manage the tagging process. `Array.include()` is provided by Prototype rather than by the core JavaScript engine, but we'll worry about that when we get to chapter 10.

So, the next thing we need to do is create the subclasses. Let's start with the one to represent subfolders. We'll use `Class.create()` to declare a constructor and define the prototype, as before:

```
var Folder=Class.create();
Folder.prototype=Object.extend(
  new Item(),
  {
    initialize:function(name,date,count,keywords){
      this._init(name,date,keywords);
      this.addKeyword("folder");
```

```
      this.count=count;
    },
    open:function(){ alert("opening "+this.name); }
  }
);
```

There's a twist here. Rather than declaring the prototype as a new JSON object, we've extended an instance of the parent class using `Object.extend()`. Properties and methods defined in the base class then become accessible to the subclass. For example, the `_init()` method from the base class is used in the constructor for Folder. We've also added the keyword `folder` to every folder (more to illustrate the ability to call methods of the base class than to provide a useful classification system).

We've now defined a parent and a child class. Let's put our code to the test. Snippet 8.10 defines the base class and subclasses, and creates an instance of the Folder class.

Snippet 8.10

```
var Item=Class.create();
Item.prototype={
  initialize:function(){
    this._init.call(arguments);
  },
  _init:function(name,date,keywords){
    this.name=name;
    this.date=date;
    this.keywords=keywords || [];
  },
  addKeyword:function(word){
    if (!this.keywords.include(word)){
      this.keywords.push(word);
    }
  }
};

var Folder=Class.create();
Folder.prototype=Object.extend(
  new Item(),
  {
    initialize:function(name,date,count,keywords){
      this._init(name,date,keywords);
      this.addKeyword("folder");
      this.count=count;
    },
    open:function(){ alert("opening "+this.name); }
  }
);
```

```
var folder=new Folder(
  "New Year '05",
  new Date("01/01/2005"),
  7
);
```

```
show("folder name",folder.name);
show("folder count",folder.count);
show("keywords",folder.keywords);
folder.addKeyword("interesting");
folder.addKeyword("amusing");
show("keywords",folder.keywords);
```

folder name	folder count	keywords	keywords
New Year '05	7	1. folder	1. folder
			2. interesting
			3. amusing

We can now successfully retrieve properties set by the parent and the base class, and invoke the addKeyword() method defined in the base class.

Defining the second subclass, to represent pictures, is done in exactly the same way as defining the Folder subclass:

```
var Picture=Class.create();
Picture.prototype=Object.extend(
  new Item(),
  {
    initialize:function(name,date,url,dimensions,weight,keywords){
      this._init(name,date,keywords);
      this.addKeyword("picture");
      this.url=url;
      this.dimensions=dimensions;
      this.weight=weight;
    },
    show:function(){ alert("showing "+this.name); }
  }
);
```

Again, we've omitted many of the implementation details here, but we've demonstrated the principles of creating a simple object hierarchy by applying Object.extend() to the prototypes of objects. Prototype and Scriptaculous both make use of these mechanisms internally, and they provide a way of defining common functionality that will be familiar to programmers used to working with object-oriented languages. However, Object.extend() can be used in another way, to mimic multiple inheritance. We'll look at that in the next section.

Multiple inheritance using mixins

In a single-inheritance-based language, such as Java, a child class can have only one direct parent, with a chain of grandparents and ancestors stretching back to the base Object class. If we want to attach functionality to an object outside of this linear chain, we can use a virtual class or interface. Alternatively, we can use object composition, wrapping up the extra functionality into a separate class that then becomes a member of our class. Single inheritance is simple, easy to understand, and doesn't leave a lot of room for making mistakes.

In languages that support multiple inheritance, a class may extend directly from more than one parent, directly inheriting the properties and methods of both. Multiple inheritance provides a lot of extra flexibility, but it also introduces the danger of namespace clashes between the two parents. Imagine that we define a class that inherits from both a Volcano class and a Balloon class. Both might provide a method called `blowUp()`, but the consequences of each would be radically different!

So far, we've mimicked inheritance in JavaScript using `Object.extend()` on the prototypes. There's nothing to stop us from implementing multiple inheritance using `Object.extend()` if we simply extend one parent by the other before extending by the base class. In fact, the Prototype libraries themselves do just that when extending the JavaScript Array, as we'll see in chapter 10.

Prototype takes a lot of its inspiration from Ruby, and Ruby supports multiple inheritance of sorts through a type of object called a mixin. A mixin provides implementations of behavior but is typically incomplete in some way. For example, the Enumerable mixin in Ruby provides a lot of higher-level functionality for working with array-like objects, but lacks the lower-level capability of iterating over the elements of the array. Any array-like structure, including Arrays, Hashes, and user-defined objects, can be enhanced by the Enumerable interface, provided they can offer a way of iterating over their members (which they do).

The same could be accomplished using single inheritance, but it would require all classes enhanced by Enumerable to have Enumerable as their base class. This would not always be appropriate, though, as the class being extended may already have a parent class that is more directly related to its purpose. Directories in a file-system, or the rows returned by a database query are good examples. In a single inheritance world, we could solve this issue using composition or an interface, but being able to mix in the additional functionality is an intriguing alternative, particularly where the functionality is of a secondary nature.

Let's return to JavaScript, then, and to the modeling of the items in our picture gallery. We have two quite distinct item types that might be resident inside a folder, namely folders and pictures, and both require some common functionality, such as being able to provide a name and a date, and to manage the keywords required to tag the items. In the previous section, we modeled all of the common functionality inside a base class. Now, let's look at how we might do things differently, using mixins.

The first step is to define an object that contains the common functionality we want to abstract. The tagging is an ideal candidate for abstracting out this way, so let's define an object that contains all the functionality needed to manage keywords.

```
var Taggable={
  addKeyword:function(word){
    if (!this.keywords.include(word)){
      this.keywords.push(word);
    }
  },
  removeKeyword:function(word){
    this.keywords=this.keywords.reject(
      function(value){ return value==word; }
    );
  },
  clear:function(){
    this.keywords=[];
  }
};
```

We've added a bit more functionality here, to allow keywords to be removed as well as added. Again, we're using Prototype's Array extensions here, which we will explain in detail in chapter 10. Looking at the structure, though, there are two things to note about our mixin object. First, it is simply a standalone object, not an object type. Second, it is incomplete—every method makes a reference to this.keywords, and yet we haven't provided a keywords property. However, any object that does provide a keywords array can be extended by Taggable and instantly get access to its functionality.

Let's apply this to our object hierarchy, then. We want all types of items to be taggable, so we'll extend the base class Item.

```
var Item=Class.create();
Item.prototype={
  initialize:function(){
    this._init.call(arguments);
  },
  _init:function(name,date,keywords){
    this.name=name;
```

```
      this.date=date;
      this.keywords=keywords || [];
      Object.extend(this,Taggable);
    }
  };
```

The Item class has changed in two ways. First, we've used `Object.extend()` to mix in the functionality of Taggable within the constructor. Note that we extend the class with Taggable, not the other way around. That way, Taggable remains unchanged, and our class is modified. Second, we've removed the methods from the base class that dealt with tagging, as Taggable now provides them.

Our Folder and Picture classes can inherit from Item as before. Because they will call the `_init()` method, they too will be mixed in with Taggable. Snippet 8.11 puts it to the test.

Snippet 8.11

```
var Taggable={
  addKeyword:function(word){
    if (!this.keywords.include(word)){
      this.keywords.push(word);
    }
  },
  removeKeyword:function(word){
    this.keywords=this.keywords.reject(
      function(value){ return value==word; }
    );
  },
  clear:function(){
    this.keywords=[];
  }
};

var Item=Class.create();
Item.prototype={
  initialize:function(){
    this._init.call(arguments);
  },
  _init:function(name,date,keywords){
    this.name=name;
    this.date=date;
    this.keywords=keywords || [];
    Object.extend(this,Taggable);
  }
};

var Folder=Class.create();
Folder.prototype=Object.extend(
  new Item(),
  {
    initialize:function(name,date,count,keywords){
```

```
        this._init(name,date,keywords);
        this.addKeyword("folder");
        this.count=count;
      },
      open:function(){ alert("opening "+this.name); }
    }
);

var folder=new Folder(
  "New Year '05",
  new Date("01/01/2005"),
  7
);

show("folder name",folder.name);
show("keywords",folder.keywords);
folder.addKeyword("interesting");
folder.addKeyword("amusing");
show("keywords",folder.keywords);
folder.removeKeyword("interesting");
show("keywords",folder.keywords);
```

folder name	keywords	keywords	keywords
New Year '05	1. folder	1. folder	1. folder
		2. interesting	2. amusing
		3. amusing	

As you can see, once the folder is created, we have ready access to the addKeyword() and removeKeyword() methods provided by the Taggable mixin. In this case, we applied the mixin to a base class and used it alongside a standard single-inheritance approach, but it would also be possible to apply mixins individually to child classes.

Object.extend(), then, provides a powerful addition to our programming arsenal. On its own, we can use it to combine objects in an elegant way. It really comes into its own, though, when applied to object modeling, in which capacity it can provide us with mechanisms for both single and multiple inheritance.

8.4 Summary

This concludes our review of the JavaScript Object type, and the ways in which Prototype enhances it. We began this chapter by looking at the JavaScript Object, and discovered that it was quite far removed from the objects that we encounter in strongly typed object-oriented languages, resembling an associative array in many ways.

Fun with Functions

This chapter covers

- Understanding JavaScript functions
- Function context and closures in JavaScript
- Working with closures using Prototype

In chapter 8, we looked at the JavaScript Object type in some detail. Coming to it with the expectations of object-oriented programmers, we were surprised to see how little resemblance it bore to the objects of mainstream OO programming. In this chapter, we're going to look at the JavaScript Function from a similar perspective.

Functions look a bit like class methods, but they are really quite different. As with the Object, Prototype extends the capabilities of the Function in quite elegant ways. The crown jewel of Prototype's support for functions is its ability to make closures easier to work with. Closures are a somewhat obscure, but very powerful, feature of the JavaScript language. Understanding closures can be useful when writing any JavaScript code, but the event-driven style of programming used to handle mouse and keyboard events in JavaScript, and used by the XHR object (see chapters 3 and 4), require the use of closures. We'll begin with a review of the Function object and closures as defined by the JavaScript language itself, and then move on to look at Prototype's enhanced capabilities.

In keeping with the previous chapter, we'll be dealing with a lot of low-level coding details, so we'll work with the Scratchpad application that we introduced in chapter 8 to help us visualize the results.

9.1 *JavaScript functions*

JavaScript is a widely used language, but not a deeply used one. The majority of JavaScript is written by people whose primary role is to do something else, whether that be graphics and design, or server-side programming. As a result, JavaScript is often approached without a full understanding of how the language works. When developing Ajax apps, we generally make greater demands on JavaScript than with a traditional web app, so a deeper understanding of the language is important.

Just as we began the previous chapter by dissecting the Object, in this chapter we'll begin with a ground-up review of JavaScript functions, and then move on to see how Prototype makes it simpler to work with them.

The bottom line is that JavaScript Functions don't really resemble the methods of an object defined in a proper object-oriented language such as Java or C#. In JavaScript, a Function is a first-class object that exists in its own right, unlike the method of an object in an object-oriented language. Once we dig deep into functions, we'll discover some very interesting differences, but let's begin at the beginning by seeing how to create a function.

9.1.1 Declaring functions

When working with functions, there are generally two steps. First, we declare the function, which involves defining the code that it executes. Second, we invoke the function (or some other object invokes it for us). For example, if we provide a callback to the Ajax.Request object (see chapter 3), defining the code to be executed when an HTTP response is returned to the browser, we declare the function when we create the request. The response will arrive some time later, depending on server load, network congestion, and other factors, and it is only then that the function will be executed.

Let's start by looking at the declaration stage. On the surface, there are two ways to declare a function. We can declare a named function as a top-level object, or we can define the function inline. Let's look at each in turn.

If we declare a function as a top-level object, the syntax looks similar to other scripting languages, such as PHP. Snippet 9.1 shows a very simple example.

Snippet 9.1

```
function hello(){
  return "hello world!";
}

show("result",hello());
```

The first statement declares the function, with a name `hello`. We can subsequently invoke the function by name, as we've done here. There's nothing very surprising about this syntax.

> **result**
> hello world!

As an alternative, we can define the function inline, as in snippet 9.2.

Snippet 9.2

```
var hello=function(){
  return "hello world!";
}

show("result",hello());
```

Here, we've declared a top-level variable called `hello`, to which we have assigned a value. The value is, in this case, an anonymous function defined using the `function()` keyword. The effect of this code is identical to snippet 9.1, but it points the way toward more interesting uses of inline or anonymous functions.

> **result**
> hello world!

In snippet 9.3, we've assigned anonymous functions as the values to object properties, rather than as top-level variables.

Snippet 9.3

```
var greeter={
  traditional:function(){
    return "hello world!";
  },
  unusual:function(){
    return "howdy globe!";
  }
};

show("result",greeter.traditional());
```

Greeter is an object, declared using the JSON syntax that we saw in chapter 8. The object has two properties, both of which are anonymous functions declared using the same sort of syntax that we saw in snippet 9.2. We don't have global references to these function objects afterwards, but we do have a reference to the greeter object, so we can invoke the functions as properties of that object. To an object-oriented programmer, this should look reassuringly familiar. We've effectively created an object with methods.

```
result
hello world!
```

Under the hood, snippets 9.1 through 9.3 have all done the same thing, namely create JavaScript Function objects. Remember, in JavaScript, a Function is a first-class object that exists in its own right. The only difference between the top-level functions we created in snippets 9.1 and 9.2, and the "object method" that we created in snippet 9.3 is the way we referenced the function after it had been declared.

Interestingly, the Function object has properties and methods of its own. In the previous chapter, we looked at the prototype property of functions, and how this allows any Function to act as an object constructor by invoking it using the new keyword. Function objects also have a property that references the arguments passed into them. Interestingly, there is no property defining the function's name. Under the covers, all functions are anonymous. Any name that we assign to a function is simply a reference to the Function object.

As well as properties, Function objects have methods. In the next section, we'll look at two methods of the Function object that allow us to invoke functions with greater flexibility.

9.1.2 Calling functions

Declaring functions is all very well, but in order for it to be worth our while, we'll want to run the code that they contain. We generally refer to this as calling or invoking the function. In snippets 9.1 through 9.3, we invoked functions simply by adding a set of parentheses to the end of the function name. Let's revisit the syntax for doing this.

Taking snippet 9.3 as an example,

```
greeter.traditional
```

provides a reference to the Function object, whereas

```
greeter.traditional()
```

invokes the Function object. We haven't passed in any arguments to the function here, but if we had wanted to, we could place them between the parentheses, like so:

```
greeter.traditional("hello",123,myObject)
```

Snippet 9.4 provides an example function that accepts arguments, and shows us how to call it.

Snippet 9.4

```
var f=function(name,age){
  return { name:name, age:age };
}

show("too few",f("mummy bear"));
show("too many",f("daddy bear",42,"porridge"));
show("just right",f("baby bear",2));
```

too few	too many	just right
name : mummy bear	name : daddy bear	name : baby bear
age : null	age : 42	age : 2

According to the declaration of the function f, it accepts two arguments, called name and age, which it returns as a simple JSON-style object. Function f is obviously designed to be called with two arguments, but in JavaScript (and unlike Java or C#), this is nothing more than a guideline. We invoke f() three times in our code snippet. In our invocations, we call it first with only one argument. The second argument, age, is simply set to null. In the second case, we pass in an extra argument, which is simply ignored. We don't see any exceptions when we do this; the function just accommodates the missing or extra arguments.

If we have a reference to a Function object, we can also invoke it using the call() or apply() Function object methods. (Yes, Functions can have Functions attached to them too!) Snippet 9.5 shows us how these work.

Snippet 9.5

```
var f=function(name,age){
  return { name:name, age:age };
}

show("just right",
  f.call(null,"baby bear",2)
);
show("just right",
  f.apply(null,["baby bear",2])
);
```

The `call()` method takes an arbitrary number of arguments. The first is reserved for the function context object, which we'll look at in the next section. Subsequent arguments are passed in to the

just right	just right
name : baby bear	name : baby bear
age : 2	age : 2

function as arguments. So, the second argument to `f.call()` is passed as the first argument—that is, `name`—to the invocation of `f`, and so on.

The `apply()` method operates similarly, except that it expects all arguments to the function invocation to be bundled as an array that is passed in as the second argument to `apply()`. Subsequent arguments are ignored.

Both `call()` and `apply()` make it easy to invoke functions indirectly in cases where we want to construct the list of arguments programmatically, but their main benefit lies in their ability to assign the context object. We'll look at what that means in the next section.

9.1.3 *Function context*

We've already seen that Functions in JavaScript are first-class citizens, and that this allows us to treat them a little differently than methods in an OO object. This has implications for the way we write the code inside functions, as well as how we pass references to them. We'll explore this issue in this section.

In JavaScript, as in Java and C#, `this` is a reserved keyword that refers to the object whose method is being invoked. Let's say we define an object representing a household item:

```
var c={ item: "chair" };
```

We've assigned a property called `item` to the object. If we want to provide a method that reads that property, we can refer to it as `this.item`, like so:

```
var c={
  item: "chair",
  describe: function(){ "I am a "+this.item; }
};
```

Again, it looks as if we've defined an object with a method, but we haven't. The function hasn't been bound to the object; it will simply be passed the object as an extra hidden argument when it is invoked. this is a keyword for defining that hidden argument, which we refer to as the context object.

Many object-oriented languages operate in the same way under the hood, so surely this is just splitting straws? It might well be, were it not for the fact that we can reassign the context object when we use Function.call() or Function.apply(). Snippet 9.6 shows how this is done.

Snippet 9.6

```
var p={ item:"porridge", act: "eating" };
var c={
  item: "chair",
  act: "sitting in",
  ask: function(){
    return "who's been "+this.act+" my "+this.item;
  }
};

show("simple",c.ask());
show("not so simple",
  c.ask.call(p)
);
```

simple	not so simple
who's been sitting in my chair	who's been eating my porridge

Here, we've defined two objects describing household items: p refers to a bowl of porridge, and c refers to a chair. Each contains an item property and an act property; act describes how the householder might interact with the item. This information allows us to construct simple sentences about the items.

We've defined an ask() function that creates just such a simple sentence. Unfortunately, we've attached it to the chair, c, but not to the bowl of porridge, p. We can therefore call the method on the chair simply as c.ask(), but to call it on the bowl of porridge, we need to use call(). In this case, we refer to the function as c.ask, but then pass p in as the first (and in this case, the only) argument to call(). When ask is invoked in this way, this magically refers to p, not to c, and we get a different result.

If we wanted a function that could be applied to different objects, we'd normally define an object type with a constructor and a prototype, as we discussed in chapter 8. However, this example serves to illustrate that it is possible to switch function contexts. It's useful to know that it is possible, as we'll see shortly, but first we'll look at the final surprise that JavaScript functions have up their sleeves, namely the closure.

9.1.4 *Function closures*

We've seen that Functions are first-class objects, and how this fact allows us to modify the context of a function. In this section, we'll look at another unusual feature of Functions, namely the closure. We've got by so far in describing most language features of JavaScript as being similar to something in proper object-oriented languages such as Java and C#. Object prototypes are kind of like classes, but with subtle and significant differences. Function objects are kind of like class methods, with similar caveats. This strategy won't get us very far in describing closures, as there is no close analogy in the object-oriented world.

For the language aficionados out there, we can point to some analogies. Python's lambdas, Ruby's blocks, and Smalltalk's compiled blocks are all similar to closures in JavaScript. So what is closure, then? Put simply, a closure is a Function object, plus any necessary information required to execute it at a later date. When writing Ajax apps, we're frequently required to pass callback functions that will be executed at some point in the future, so being able to reference locally scoped variables when the function is invoked can be very useful.

That kind of makes sense, but let's flesh it out with an example. Snippet 9.7 shows us a closure at work.

Snippet 9.7

```
var story={};

function breakAndEnter(){
  var thief={
    name: "goldilocks",
    species: "human"
  };
  story.discovery=function(){
    show("who's been eating my porridge?",thief.name);
  }
}

breakAndEnter();

story.discovery();

show("the thief", thief.name);
```

Snippet 9.7 is doing some rather strange things. Again, this isn't an exercise in good coding practice, but a deliberate attempt to create a closure. Let's pick through what's going on, line by line, and we'll look at the bigger picture later.

Following on from the subject matter of snippet 9.6, we've now reached the point in the story of the three bears where Goldilocks enters the scene and commits various petty felonies. First, just to keep track of things, we've defined the story as a global object, to which we can attach scenes. Next, we've defined a top-level function, `breakAndEnter()`, which will define the Goldilocks character, and then we've attached a scene to the story. The scene is defined as a Function object that will refer to the Goldilocks character. After defining `breakAndEnter()`, we invoke it, so our `story` object is no longer empty. We can then invoke the `discover()` method of the `story` object, and find out who has been eating the bears' porridge. It was, of course, Goldilocks.

Let's stop there for now and have a look at the code in more detail. The `thief` object, representing the Goldilocks character, was defined within the `breakAndEnter()` function. As such, the scope of that variable was limited to the inside of that function. Outside of the invocation to `breakAndEnter()`, we should have no reference to the `thief` object. And yet, we called `story.discover()` after `breakAndEnter()` had been invoked, and it was still able to provide us with a name. Were we wrong about the scope rules in JavaScript? Is the `thief` object still in scope? In the final line of snippet 9.7, we checked this out by trying to reference the `thief` object directly. As you can see, it doesn't work—the `thief` object is indeed out of scope. So, what's going on?

We declared `story.discover` inline as an anonymous function. Within that function, we referenced the `thief` object. At this point, the JavaScript interpreter created a closure for us, making a note that the `thief` object be preserved in memory for later use by the function. Outside of the `discover` function, we can no longer access the `thief` object, because we have no references to it, but it's still there, waiting to be used.

The key point to note about closures in JavaScript is that they are created implicitly. Unlike Ruby, for example, there is no special syntax for creating closures. This might be considered convenient in some situations, but it raises two problems. First, it can be hard, when reading someone else's code, to spot that a closure has been created. Second, it is easy to create closures accidentally.

The code in snippet 9.7 is a strange sort of parlor trick, and we don't hold it up as an example of good coding style. Are there situations, then, in which it's a good idea to create closures? There are, in fact, and we'll look at the practical use of closures and function context in the next section.

9.1.5 *When to use context and closures*

When writing JavaScript in a web browser, a lot of the code that we write takes the form of callback functions. That is, we define functions that will be called by the browser later on our behalf, in response to a mouseclick or keypress, for example. Looking beyond the user interface, we can define our own event-driven systems with callbacks of their own. Prototype's Ajax helper classes, which we looked at in chapters 3 and 4, provided callback functions such as onSuccess and onComplete. The Scriptaculous Effects framework, which we covered in chapter 5, came with callbacks too, such as beforeStart and afterFinish.

If we're working with a moderately complex set of code, we may well be defining callback handler functions that talk to any of these APIs within our own objects. When we do so, we'll run into an interesting problem, to which closures provide the solution. In snippet 9.8, we'll create a clickable element on the screen and also show the nature of this problem. We'll then go on to solve the problem in snippet 9.9.

Snippet 9.8 (broken)

```
var Button=Class.create();
Button.prototype={
  initialize:function(message){
    this.message=message;
    this.el=square();
    this.el.onclick=this.showMsg;
  },
  showMsg:function(){
    show("click!",this.message);
  }
}

new Button("hello!");
```

We want to create a clickable button on the screen that will present a message when clicked. We've wrapped up the user interface, the message, and the response to the click event inside a little object, which we defined using Prototype's Class.cre-

ate() mechanism. In the constructor (the initialize function), we took a reference to the message to be assigned to this button. We then created the user interface using a square() method provided by our sandbox environment. square() will return a DOM element, to which we can assign an onclick event handler. Rather than defining the event handler inline, we simply referred to a second function of our object, showMsg.

So far, so good, but now we're going to run into the problem that we alluded to earlier. We then created an instance of the Button object, and clicked on the red square that it creates. Although we've passed in a message String to the constructor, the message that comes back is null. What has gone wrong?

The fact is that when the browser invokes the callback handler for us, it switches the context of the function call to the DOM element receiving the event. Inside showMsg(), we refer to this.message. Our Button object has a property called message, but the DOM element doesn't, and this now refers to the DOM element. It's important to understand function contexts, because the browser uses them behind our backs for common event-handling routines.

We need the onclick callback to know about our Button object, or about the message property at least. The most common way to get around the problem is to use a closure, as illustrated in snippet 9.9. We've highlighted the changes that we made from snippet 9.8.

Snippet 9.9

```
var Button=Class.create();
Button.prototype={
  initialize:function(message){
    this.message=message;
    this.el=square();
    var btn=this;
    this.el.onclick=function(){
      btn.showMsg();
    }
  },
  showMsg:function(){
    show("click!",this.message);
  }
}

new Button("hello!");
```

To get around the problem that we saw in snippet 9.8, we've modified the initialize() function to create a closure within it. Let's walk through the steps needed to do that.

In order to create the closure, we first needed to make a reference to the current object. We declared a local variable called btn, with a value of this. We then defined an anonymous function that refers to the function btn.showMsg. The context of the anonymous function will be switched to the DOM element, but in this simple case we don't need to refer to the DOM element, so we can ignore it. We can refer to the Button object within the function as `btn`, and this time the code works. A reference to the `Button` object is preserved within the closure, and we can use that to call `showMsg()` without switching contexts.

Function contexts and closures go together, then. When working with event-driven code that makes heavy use of callbacks, we will often find that a callback function is invoked with a different context from the one we had in mind when we wrote the callback (or with no context at all). This is particularly true when we're writing functions as methods of JavaScript objects, as in snippets 9.8 and 9.9. Closures provide us with a way of taking back control of the function context, and of passing in any necessary references for use when the callback is invoked.

That wraps up our survey of the JavaScript Function object. In the next section, we'll look at how Prototype takes things a step further to simplify our coding.

9.2 Extending functions with Prototype.js

Prototype provides a few simple extensions to the Function object. They're not quite as complex as the object inheritance mechanisms that we looked at in chapter 8, but the enhancements that Prototype does offer make for markedly simpler coding. In this section, we're going to cover Prototype's extensions to the Function object.

The enhancements to Function that Prototype provides are designed to solve a particular problem, and we've already encountered that problem in the previous section. Let's review it briefly here. Snippet 9.9 presented a way of working with the JavaScript event model. The solution made effective use of closures, but it was somewhat ungainly. We needed to create a temporary variable, `btn`, and, within the anonymous event handler, refer to our Button object by this name rather than as `this`.

We got around the problems of the browser switching context for us, but mentally we were required to switch context ourselves! Implementing the solution required two disconnected steps, namely creating the local reference to the object and using that reference within the callback. We're far away from a callback function in Ajax coding, and we might be writing a lot of code of this nature. It would be nice to be able to create the closure in a simpler way. Fortunately, Prototype provides a couple of useful methods that make it easier to do just that, and we'll look at them in this section.

9.2.1 The bind() method

Prototype extends the prototype of the Function object with two useful methods. This may sound odd, but remember that Function is just a type of object, and that any object can have methods. We can invoke these methods on any function that we write.

The first method of the Function object that Prototype provides is `bind()`. `Function.bind()` returns a second function that wraps the function doing the calling. The function that is returned internally switches contexts using a closure and then invokes the first function.

This sounds complex—we won't often come across functions that return a Function object when invoked, but in practice it's quite easy to use. Snippet 9.10 applies it to our example Button object.

Snippet 9.10

```
var Button=Class.create();
Button.prototype={
  initialize:function(message){
    this.message=message;
    this.el=square();
    this.el.onclick=this.showMsg.bind(this);
  },
  showMsg:function(){
    show("click!",this.message);
  }
}

new Button("hello!");
```

In snippet 9.9, we had to manually create a temporary `btn` variable and write an anonymous function. Using `bind()`, we can simply specify which context object we'd like our `showMsg()` function to be invoked with, and do the same thing as a single line of code. The anonymous function is created for us by `bind()`, and we don't need to worry about the details.

The `bind()` method serves the purpose here, because our requirements are simple. When the event is processed, we don't need to know anything about the event, such as the key pressed or the mouse coordinates. Let's suppose now that we want to report the mouse coordinates along with our message in response to a mouseclick. We can get this information from the JavaScript Event object, but in order to reference it, we'll need to look at Prototype's second extension to the function object.

9.2.2 *The bindAsEventListener() method*

The `bind()` method makes it easy to create closures, which are especially useful when writing callback functions. One of the most common uses of callback functions in Ajax is to provide interactivity in the user interface in response to mouse movement, clicks, and keypresses. Typically, the callbacks to these operations will expect an Event object to be available in the callback, in order to provide valuable information on where the mouse was clicked, which key was pressed, and so on. Prototype has anticipated this situation and provides us with another useful method on the Function object, bindAsEventListener().

Designed specifically to work with user-interface event handlers, bind-AsEventListener() is simply a special version of bind() that takes care of retrieving the event object in a cross-platform fashion and passes it to the function in question as an extra argument. Snippet 9.11 illustrates its use in our Button class example.

Snippet 9.11

```
var Button=Class.create();
Button.prototype={
  initialize:function(message){
    this.message=message;
    this.el=square();
    this.el.onclick=this.showMsg.bindAsEventListener(this);
  },
  showMsg:function(event){
    show(
      "click!",
      this.message
        +" ["+event.clientX+" x "
        +event.clientY+"]"
    );
  }
}

new Button("hello!");
```

As you can see, bindAsEventListener() slots in as a direct replacement to bind(), with no additional parameters needed. In order to take advantage of it, though, we need to modify our showMsg() function, adding the event object as an argument. We can then refer to the event's properties, in this case clientX and clientY, which report the mouse coordinates offset from the top-left corner of the browser client area. Clicking on the button several times displays the coordinates of each click.

Although relatively little has been added to the Function object, the `bind()` function in particular makes it extremely easy to write callback functions, which is a great boon indeed in an event-driven programming environment.

9.3 *Summary*

This concludes our review of the JavaScript Function object. We saw that, in JavaScript, functions are first-class objects. When writing JavaScript objects, we can attach functions so that they behave like methods of the object, but there are a few crucial differences. Specifically, functions can be invoked with any object as their context (that is, the object that is resolved by the special variable `this`), and they also operate as closures, allowing locally scoped variables to be preserved. Both of these special features can be confusing, but they also play an important role in event-driven programming.

Having identified the main issues that will come up in working with functions, we went on to examine how Prototype simplifies these operations using the `bind()` and `bindAsEventListener()` methods. These greatly simplify the way in which we can work with callback functions.

We'll conclude our review of the language features in the next chapter, where we'll look at the rather larger extensions that Prototype provides to the Array object.

Arrays Made Easy

This chapter covers

- Working with JavaScript arrays
- Understanding Prototype's functional approach to arrays
- Extending arrays and hashes using the Enumerable mixin

We've covered the most common language features now, namely the Object and the Function. Using these, we can easily organize our data and invoke operations on it. In the previous two chapters, we've already seen how Prototype makes it easier to work with these features in a meaningful way.

There is a third element that is almost as fundamental to most programming languages, and that is the array. Arrays can be used to organize data into lists, and recursively into more complex structures. JavaScript supports arrays through the Array object in a powerful and flexible way. Prototype extends the standard Array in quite remarkable ways, adding over thirty new methods. Along the way, it adds some more array-like power to other objects too.

We'll begin this chapter by reviewing the capabilities provided for Arrays by the JavaScript language. We'll then look at the way Prototype handles Arrays, and see how this can streamline our code when working with complex data structures. We'll finish off with a short look at the way in which Prototype makes some of its Array capabilities available to other objects.

10.1 *Introducing Arrays*

Arrays are a feature of most programming languages, and JavaScript is no exception. Arrays allow us to organize variables into groups and build up complex data structures. Given that most computer programs are concerned with organizing information in one form or another, arrays are one of the most fundamental features of a programming language.

Arrays commonly come in two types. Numerical arrays are arranged in sequence, and elements of the array are retrieved by their numerical index. Associative arrays, on the other hand, store elements using non-numerical keys and are sometimes referred to as maps, dictionaries, or hashes in other languages.

In JavaScript, the built-in Array type provides the functionality of a numerical array. The Array is unbounded; that is, its length is not predetermined, but can be extended or truncated at runtime. In this sense, the Array is more like a linked list than the fixed-length arrays of C-like languages.

JavaScript does not support a native associative array class, because, as we saw in chapter 8, every object in JavaScript can have arbitrary properties assigned to it by name at runtime, and can therefore be used as an associative array. So if we want to store key-value pairs, we can just use an ordinary object. We'll revisit the Object later in this chapter, in section 10.5, but first we'll concentrate on the Array class and the way in which it supports numerical arrays.

10.2 *The native JavaScript Array*

Before we look at what Prototype does for Array objects, let's take a look at what it has to build upon. The Array object as provided by the core language has a number of properties and methods for operating upon its members. Let's quickly look at each in turn, using the Scratchpad application that we introduced in chapter 8.

10.2.1 *Iterating over Arrays using length*

The length property of the Array object should be familiar to programmers of C-style languages. Used in the conventional way, it allows us to iterate through the members of an Array. Snippet 10.1 illustrates this for a simple array of Strings (each of which describes the name of a type of cloud—unlikely to be something you'd encounter in your own web application, but the words have a nice sound to them!).

Snippet 10.1

```
var clouds=[ "cumulus", "nimbus", "cirrus" ];
for (var i=0;i<clouds.length;i++){
  clouds[i]="I wandered lonely as a "+clouds[i];
}
show("some clouds",clouds);
```

Iterating over Arrays in this fashion is common practice in JavaScript coding. Prototype, however, provides a more elegant way, as we'll see in the next section.

It's also worth noting that the length property is read/write and can be used to increase the length of an Array, truncate it, or even empty it completely, as shown in Snippet 10.2

> **some clouds**
> 1. I wandered lonely as a cumulus
> 2. I wandered lonely as a nimbus
> 3. I wandered lonely as a cirrus

Snippet 10.2

```
var clouds=[ "cumulus", "nimbus", "cirrus" ];
clouds.length=7;
show("more clouds",clouds);

clouds.length=2;
show("fewer clouds",clouds);

clouds.length=0;
show("what clouds?",clouds);
```

As you can see in this snippet, the length of an Array can be modified on the fly, making Arrays more like a linked list than an array in a C-style language. They also behave like other common data structures, as we'll see in the next section.

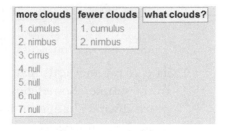

10.2.2 Treating Arrays like stacks : pop() and push(), shift() and unshift()

In addition to behaving like ordinary arrays, JavaScript Arrays act like *stacks*. A stack is a collection of items in which elements can only be added to or removed from the end. In many card games, the deck of cards is treated as a stack. Snippet 10.3 shows how JavaScript Arrays exhibit stack-like behavior.

Snippet 10.3

```
var clouds=[ "cumulus", "nimbus", "cirrus" ];
show("some clouds: 1",clouds);

var c1=clouds.pop();
show("some clouds: 2",clouds);

var c2=clouds.pop();
show("some clouds: 3",clouds);

clouds.push("cumulonimbus");
show("some clouds: 4",clouds);

show("missing", [c1,c2]);
```

In this example, push() adds an element to the end of the Array, increasing its length by 1. The pop() method removes the end-most element from the array, and returns that element. The shift() and unshift() methods do the same, but remove and add at the front of the Array rather than the end. Snippet 10.4 shows shift() and unshift() at work.

Snippet 10.4

```
var clouds=[ "cumulus", "nimbus", "cirrus" ];
show("some clouds: 1",clouds);

var c1=clouds.shift();
```

```
show("some clouds: 2",clouds);

clouds.unshift("cumulonimbus");
show("some clouds: 3",clouds);
```

The Array methods that we've seen so far are relatively simple. Sometimes we will want to perform more drastic changes to an Array, such as removing or adding entire sections from the middle. While we could rearrange an Array completely using stack-like methods, it would be very cumbersome. The next set of methods that we'll look at makes these sorts of operations much simpler to perform.

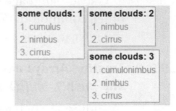

10.2.3 Chopping and changing with slice(), splice(), and concat()

For more complex Array manipulations, the Array object provides a few more utility methods. The slice() method returns a subsection of an Array as a separate Array object, as shown in snippet 10.5.

Snippet 10.5
```
var clouds=[ "cumulus", "nimbus", "cirrus", "cumulonimbus"  ];
show("some clouds",clouds);

show("a subset",clouds.slice(1));

show("another subset",clouds.slice(1,3));
```

The first argument to slice() is the offset index of the first element to be included in the result Array. (Remember that JavaScript Arrays are indexed from zero upward, so 1 indicates the second element, and so on.) The first subset that we've created is a slice of the original Array containing everything from the second element onward.

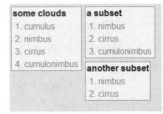

We can also call slice() with two arguments. The optional second element gives the end index of the slice—that is, the index of the first element not to be included in the result. The second subset that we've created contains the second through to the third element of the original array.

The slice() method takes Arrays apart; the concat() and splice() methods are both used to join arrays together. concat() simply concatenates two Arrays, returning a single Array as a result. Snippet 10.6 shows how to join two arrays into a larger whole with a single call.

Snippet 10.6

```
var clouds1=[ "cumulus", "nimbus" ]
var clouds2=[ "cirrus", "cumulonimbus"  ];
var clouds=clouds2.concat(clouds1);
show("some clouds",clouds);
```

The `splice()` method is a bit more complex, as it modifies the argument Array, in addition to returning a second Array containing the removed items. A simple invocation of `splice()` removes elements from an Array, as snippet 10.7 illustrates.

some clouds
1. cirrus
2. cumulonimbus
3. cumulus
4. nimbus

Snippet 10.7

```
var clouds=[ "cumulus", "nimbus", "cirrus", "cumulonimbus"  ];
var removed=clouds.splice(2,2);
show("removed",removed);
show("remaining",clouds);
```

The first argument to `splice()` is the starting index for the operation (the same as for `slice()`). The second argument is the number of elements to delete (unlike `slice()`, in which the second argument is the end index).

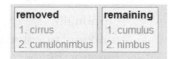

removed
1. cirrus
2. cumulonimbus

remaining
1. cumulus
2. nimbus

`splice()` also allows elements to be added to the Array, in place of those deleted. Any arguments beyond the second will be inserted into the Array at the deletion point, as illustrated in snippet 10.8.

Snippet 10.8

```
var clouds=[ "cumulus", "nimbus", "cirrus", "cumulonimbus"  ];
show("original",clouds);
var removed=clouds.splice(1,2,"snow","rain","hail");
show("removed",removed);
show("modified",clouds);
```

We provided three extra arguments after the indices indicating position, and these have been inserted into the Array in place of the removed elements. Note that the number of inserted arguments need not be the same as the number of removed ones. The array will simply resize itself to fit.

original
1. cumulus
2. nimbus
3. cirrus
4. cumulonimbus

removed
1. nimbus
2. cirrus

modified
1. cumulus
2. snow
3. rain
4. hail
5. cumulonimbus

Together, `slice()`, `concat()`, and `splice()` are a powerful set of tools for modifying Arrays. There is still more to come though. In the next section, we'll see how to alter the order of Array elements.

10.2.4 *Reordering Arrays with reverse() and sort()*

The Array object provides a couple of useful methods to reorder the Array object. The reverse() method simply reverses the order of the Array elements, and sort() will sort the array elements, using standard numerical or alphabetical criteria for simple objects. Snippet 10.9 shows reverse() and sort() at work. Note that both modify the original Array rather than returning a copy.

Snippet 10.9

```
var clouds=[ "cumulus", "nimbus", "cirrus", "cumulonimbus"  ];
show("original",clouds);

clouds.sort();
show("sorted",clouds);

clouds.reverse();
show("reversed",clouds);
```

Optionally, sort() will accept a user-defined function to compare the Array elements. The function ought to return a negative value if the second value should be sorted above the first, a positive value if it should be sorted later, or 0 if the two elements are equivalent for purposes of the sorting. (Internally, sort() uses a bubble sort algorithm, and these values are the convention for comparator functions.) Snippet 10.10 illustrates use of a custom sort function that sorts elements by length.

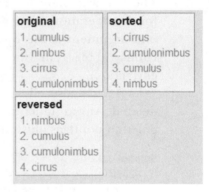

Snippet 10.10

```
var clouds=[ "cumulus", "nimbus", "cirrus", "cumulonimbus"  ];
show("original",clouds);

clouds.sort(
  function(a,b){ return b.length-a.length; }
);
show("sorted by length",clouds);
```

The comparator function that we've provided compares the length of two elements in the Array. When we use this as the basis of sorting the Array, the resulting Array is ordered by the length of the Strings, in descending order. The

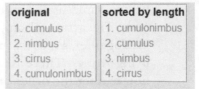

comparator function can perform any logic that we like, and can compare Strings, numbers, or complex objects, providing a great degree of flexibility when sorting objects.

We've now covered all the Array methods that modify the contents of Arrays. In the next section, we'll look at how Arrays relate to Strings in JavaScript, and then move on to see how Prototype extends these already formidable capabilities.

10.2.5 *Arrays and Strings: join() and split()*

The final native capability of JavaScript Arrays is their facility for converting between Arrays and Strings using `join()` and `split()`. `join()` is a method of the Array object, and it returns a String; `split()` is a method of the String object, and it returns an Array. Snippet 10.11 shows a simple example.

Snippet 10.11

```
var clouds=[ "cumulus", "nimbus", "cirrus", "cumulonimbus" ];
show("original",clouds);

var joined=clouds.join(" and ");
show("joined", [ joined ] );

var split=joined.split(" ");
show("split",split);
```

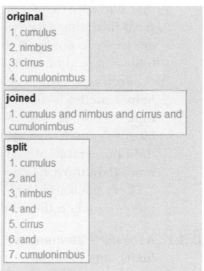

In this example, we first joined the Array into a single String using `join()`, adding the word "and" to glue the elements together. Then we split this string on whitespace, returning all the original elements and the "and"s as a new Array.

We've now covered all the methods of the Array object. Before we look at Prototype's Array capabilities, we'll look at another native JavaScript class of object that has some similarities to Arrays and some important differences.

10.2.6 *Other Array-like objects*

When working with the Document Object Model (DOM), one frequently encounters objects that look like Arrays, but aren't. For example, the object returned by `document.forms`, or the `childNodes` property and `getElementsByTagName()` method of DOM nodes, bear a superficial resemblance to Arrays. In particular, they expose a `length` property that allows one to enumerate over them using the

C-style `for` loop approach shown in section 10.2.1. However, because they aren't Array objects, they don't support operations such as `slice()`, `splice()`, or `sort()`. Prototype.js has an elegant way of dealing with these pseudo-Array objects, which we'll return to shortly.

So, JavaScript Arrays are reasonably powerful on their own. However, the Prototype library adds a lot of extra power to working with Arrays, and with other Array-like objects. In the next section, we'll see how more complex operations on Arrays can be made really easy by using Prototype.

10.3 *Prototype.js and Arrays*

In most Ajax apps, we need to work with collections of data, and Arrays are an indispensable feature. The methods that we presented in section 10.2 provide a powerful foundation for working with Arrays, but we would still find ourselves iterating through Arrays by hand, as we did in snippet 10.1, to perform complex operations. Prototype provides an alternative mechanism for working with Arrays that allows us to define complicated transforms on Arrays concisely, and with great flexibility. Once you get used to working with Arrays in this way, you'll wonder how you got by on the manual iteration technique for so long. In this and the following section, we'll present the details of these new methods.

Prototype enhances Array objects in two ways. First, it provides a few simple helper methods directly to the `Array.prototype`, which we'll look at in this section. Second, it provides a collection of methods within an object called Enumerable, designed to operate on Array-like objects. The Array prototype is extended by the Enumerable object, giving Arrays even greater power and flexibility. Overall, more than thirty new methods are added to the Array type by Prototype.js.

Let's get started by looking at a set of simple methods for accessing Array elements based on their index in the array.

10.3.1 *Accessing elements by position using first(), last(), and indexOf()*

The new Array methods, `first()` and `last()`, do exactly what it says on the tin, returning the first and last element of the Array respectively. Snippet 10.12 shows how it's done.

Snippet 10.12

```
var clouds=[ "cumulus", "nimbus", "cirrus", "cumulonimbus"  ];
show("first",clouds.first());
show("last",clouds.last());
```

The indexOf() method accepts an object as an argument and returns the numerical index of the first occurrence of that object in the Array. If the Array doesn't

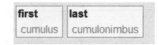

contain the object, it returns -1. (The return codes are borrowed from the JavaScript String, which has a built-in indexOf() method. In snippet 10.13, we interrogate our list of clouds using indexOf().

Snippet 10.13

```
var clouds=[ "cumulus", "nimbus", "cirrus", "cumulonimbus"  ];
show("index of cumulus",clouds.indexOf("cumulus"));
show("index of tumulus",clouds.indexOf("tumulus"));
```

Our Array doesn't contain the word "tumulus" (in fact, it's an ancient burial mound, not a kind of cloud). Hence, indexOf() returns -1 for that argument.

The indexOf() method provides an easy way to perform simple searches on Arrays. Without it—and without Prototype—we'd need to manually iterate through the array, and we'd end up writing a lot more code.

10.3.2 Modifying Arrays using clear(), compact(), without(), and flatten()

The functions that we'll look at in this section are used to return modified versions of Array objects. The clear() method is the simplest, removing all elements from the Array. compact() returns a copy of the Array from which all null or undefined elements have been removed. without() accepts an arbitrary number of arguments and returns a copy of the Array omitting all of the arguments.

Snippet 10.14 presents our list of clouds padded with some additional values, and it uses compact() and without() to get things back into shape.

Snippet 10.14

```
var clouds=[
  "cumulus", "nimbus",
  "pit bull terrier", null,
  "cirrus", null, null,
  "teapot", "Thursday",
  "cumulonimbus"
];
```

```
show("original",clouds);
clouds=clouds.compact();
show("compacted",clouds);
clouds=clouds.without(
  "pit bull terrier","teapot","Thursday"
);
show("filtered",clouds);
```

original	compacted
1. cumulus	1. cumulus
2. nimbus	2. nimbus
3. pit bull terrier	3. pit bull terrier
4. null	4. cirrus
5. cirrus	5. teapot
6. null	6. Thursday
7. null	7. cumulonimbus
8. teapot	**filtered**
9. Thursday	1. cumulus
10. cumulonimbus	2. nimbus
	3. cirrus
	4. cumulonimbus

Note that `Array.without(null)` is equivalent to `Array.compact()`, and that `null` can be included alongside other arguments to `without()`.

These methods make it very easy to tidy up Arrays, removing stray elements. Again, without them, we'd need to manually iterate through the Array ourselves, and write a lot more code.

The final Array method that we'll look at in this section is `flatten()`, which converts Arrays of Arrays into a single linear Array. Snippet 10.15 demonstrates how it works.

Snippet 10.15

```
var stuff=[
  "cumulus",
  "nimbus",
  ["pit bull terrier", "teapot", "Thursday" ],
  "cirrus",
  { species:"dog", name: "Fido" },
  "cumulonimbus"
];
show("original",stuff);
show("flattened",stuff.flatten());
```

original
1. cumulus
2. nimbus
3. pit bull terrier,teapot,Thursday
4. cirrus
5. [object Object]
6. cumulonimbus

flattened
1. cumulus
2. nimbus
3. pit bull terrier
4. teapot
5. Thursday
6. cirrus
7. [object Object]
8. cumulonimbus

The original Array is a mixture of simple and complex elements. Most are Strings, but the third element is an Array, and the fifth, an Object. `flatten()`, flattens the Array, but leaves the object alone, as we see in the results. Once more, Prototype adds brevity to our coding of a relatively common operation.

That concludes our review of the simple Array helpers provided by Prototype. The methods that we've presented in this section are undoubtedly useful, but they are only the beginning of what Prototype can do for us regarding Arrays. Most of the heavy lifting is done by the Enumerable object, and we'll look at that in the next section.

10.4 *Methods of the Enumerable object*

Most of the real power-user capabilities that Prototype provides for Array objects are defined within an object called Enumerable. The methods of this object are mapped onto the Array prototype. Because it is defined separately, it can also be mapped onto other array-like objects, notably the Hash and the ObjectRange, which we'll look at later in this chapter. Purely as a point of interest, the inspiration for defining the Enumerable as a standalone object in this way comes from the Ruby language, in which Enumerable is defined as an abstract class that can be mixed into other classes such as Arrays and Hashes. We'll demonstrate the Enumerable methods using Array objects in this section, and return to them again when we look at other Enumerable types.

Prototype's Enumerable object exploits a key feature of the JavaScript language, namely that functions are first-class objects (see chapter 9). Because of this, they can be passed as arguments to other functions. The style of programming that this allows looks downright odd to a Java or C programmer at first, but it provides a very powerful and fluid way of working.

The key to the Enumerable's capabilities is the each() method, which executes a given function for every element. each() takes a single argument, the function to be executed, as illustrated in snippet 10.16.

Snippet 10.16

```
var clouds=[ "cumulus", "nimbus", "cirrus"  ];
var iterator=  function(value,index){
  show("result","element "+index+" is "+value);
}
clouds.each(iterator);
```

As this snippet shows, we first define the iterator function—that is, the function that will be applied to each element of the Array. (Iterator is the standard term used within the Prototype code base for this function. Again, Java developers may need to

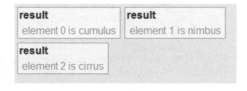

make a mental adjustment here. A Java Collections Iterator object traverses the Collection, whereas a Prototype Iterator is applied as a consequence of traversing the Array. In general algorithmic terms, Prototype is providing an internal iterator, and

Java Collections an external iterator.) The iterator function should accept two arguments, which will be populated with the value of the element and the element's numerical index respectively.

Second, we pass the iterator function as an argument to the each() method. In snippet 10.16, we defined the iterator first, for clarity. It's more common, however, to define iterators as anonymous functions inline, like so:

```
clouds.each(
  function(value,index){
    show("result","element "+index+" is "+value);
  }
);
```

In itself, each() provides a concise and powerful way of iterating through Arrays. More importantly, though, it is the foundation for a wide range of additional methods provided by Prototype. We'll run through each of these briefly now.

10.4.1 Searching through arrays: all(), any(), and include()

It is common practice in programming to test whether variables meet specific conditions, typically using if() or while() statements. When working with arrays, it can be useful to apply conditional logic to each element of the array in turn.

Prototype provides a couple of helpers to the Array object that allow one to test whether elements conform to a given test. Both require a function to be passed in as an argument and return a Boolean. The all() method will return true only if all the Array elements satisfy the condition. The any() method will return true if at least one element does.

Snippet 10.17 shows a simple example of these methods. Because we will reuse the test function to demonstrate all() and any(), we've defined it in advance. The function returns true if the first letter of the argument is *c*, either uppercase or lowercase.

Snippet 10.17

```
var clouds=[ "cumulus", "nimbus", "cirrus" ];

function beginsWithC(str){
  var first=str.substring(0,1).toLowerCase();
  return first=="c";
}

var allDo=clouds.all(beginsWithC);
show("all clouds begin with c? ",allDo);

var anyDo=clouds.any(beginsWithC);
show("any clouds begin with c? ",anyDo);
```

Under the hood, the function is used in an iterator passed to `Array.each()`. As such, it will accept two arguments: the value of the element, and the numerical index. Our `beginsWithC()` function omits the numerical argument, simply because it doesn't make use of it.

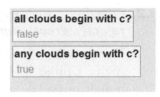

To illustrate the use of the numerical argument, we could test whether each element in an array has the same number of characters as its numerical index. Snippet 10.18 implements this as a single-line statement.

Snippet 10.18

```
show("index always matches value length?",
  [""," a","be","sea"].all(
    function(value,index){
      return value.length==index;
    }
  )
);
```

A third method, `include()`, also provides a capability for testing Arrays. It takes a single argument and returns `true` if the array returns that element. Snippet 10.19 shows `include()` at work, detecting whether a list of ingredients includes salt.

> **index always matches value length?**
> true

Snippet 10.19

```
var potatoCrisps=["potato","sunflower oil","salt","flavourings"];
var verdict=(potatoCrisps.include("salt")) ?
  "yuck! too salty" : "yuck! too bland!";

show("my verdict on these crisps",verdict);
```

The `include()` method looks only for exact matches. If our ingredients list had contained "Salt" (note the capital *S*), or "sea salt", `include()` would have returned `false`.

> **my verdict on these crisps**
> yuck! too salty

The functions that we've looked at so far are designed to test whether an Array meets certain criteria, and return a Boolean value indicating whether the test passed or failed. This is fine if we're just looking, but in some cases we may want to collect the results of such a test, rather than just a yes/no verdict, so that we can perform some further operation on them. Prototype also provides a raft of functionality to support this, as we'll see next.

10.4.2 *Filtering arrays with detect(), findAll(), reject(), grep(), and partition()*

The functions that we'll look at in this section allow us to test the contents of an Array. Unlike `all()`, `any()`, and `include()`, though, they return the results of the match rather than a Boolean. This is useful if we want to manipulate the results further. For example, `any()` will tell us whether a list of clouds contains a name beginning with the letter *c*, but it won't help us if we want to look up the names in a dictionary.

The simplest of the functions in this section is `detect()`, which returns the first element of an Array to pass the test function. Snippet 10.20 shows `detect()` at work.

Snippet 10.20

```
var clouds=[ "cumulus", "nimbus", "cirrus"  ];

function beginsWith(str,letter){
  var first=str.substring(0,1).toLowerCase();
  return first==letter;
}

show("a cloud that begins with c",clouds.detect(
  function(str){ return beginsWith(str,"c"); }
));

show("a cloud that begins with p",clouds.detect(
  function(str){ return beginsWith(str,"p"); }
));
```

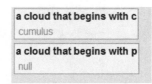

We've reused the `beginsWithC()` function from snippet 10.14, making it more generic. Passing it to `detect()` rather than `any()`, returns the first matching value. In cases where no elements match, (such as cloud names that begin with the letter p), the result is the undefined value.

It's worth noting here that Prototype supports aliases for some of its methods. That is, the same method is attached to the Enumerable interface under more than one name. For example, `detect()` is also known as `find()`, and `Array.find()` will have identical results to `Array.detect()`.

If several elements match, we might like to collect all of them. `Array.find-All()`—also known by the alias `select()`—handles that task for us, returning an Array of all matching elements. `Array.reject()` performs a very similar job, returning an Array of all values that don't match the test function. Snippet 10.21 illustrates how these work.

Snippet 10.21

```
var clouds=[ "cumulus", "nimbus", "cirrus", "stratus"  ];

function beginsWith(str,letter){
  var first=str.substring(0,1).toLowerCase();
  return first==letter;
}

show("clouds that begin with c",
  clouds.findAll(
    function(str){ return beginsWith(str,"c"); }
  )
);

show("clouds that don't begin with c",
  clouds.reject(
    function(str){ return beginsWith(str,"c"); }
  )
);
```

Now that the methods are returning Array objects, we're able to make use of our show() function to display the results of our method calls. The findAll() and reject() methods are fairly straightforward to use, each returning a single Array as a result.

If we're interested in both the pass and fail results of our test, we can take a shortcut and use Array.partition(). This returns all elements of an Array, divided into those that pass and those that fail, as shown in snippet 10.22.

clouds that begin with c
1. cumulus
2. cirrus

clouds that don't begin with c
1. nimbus
2. stratus

Snippet 10.22

```
var clouds=[ "cumulus", "nimbus", "cirrus", "stratus"  ];

function beginsWith(str,letter){
  var first=str.substring(0,1).toLowerCase();
  return first==letter;
}

var results=clouds.partition(
  function(str){ return beginsWith(str,"c"); }
);

show("clouds that begin with c",results[0]);
show("clouds that don't begin with c",results[1]);
```

The partition() method returns an Array containing two elements, each of which is an Array. The first Array contains all those elements that have passed the test, and the second contains those that haven't.

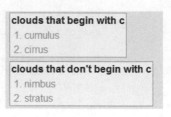

The final method in this category is really a specialist case of findAll(), making use of JavaScript's support for regular expressions. Array.grep() is named after the Unix command-line tool for searching for regular expressions inside streams of text. Using regular expressions, we can quickly perform more complex searches on String objects, as snip- pet 10.23 shows.

Snippet 10.23

```
var clouds=[ "cumulus", "nimbus", "cirrus", "stratus" ];

show(
  "clouds that begin with c",
  clouds.grep("^[C|c]")
);
show(
  "clouds that contain m and u",
  clouds.grep(".*[m]+.*[u]+")
);
```

The sole required argument to grep() is a regular expression pattern. (Regular expression syntax is beyond the scope of this book. A good primer on Java-Script regular expressions can be found at http://developer.mozilla.org/en/docs/Core_JavaScript_1.5 _Guide:Regular_ Expressions.)

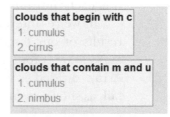

Optionally, grep() can accept a second argument, which is an iterator function. If this function is present, the results Array will contain the output of the iterator function, not the element value. Snippet 10.24 illustrates this capability.

Snippet 10.24

```
var clouds=[ "cumulus", "nimbus", "cirrus", "stratus" ];

show(
  "details about clouds that contain m and u",
  clouds.grep(
    ".*[m]+.*[u]+",
    function(value,index){
      return value+" [length="+value.length+", index="+index+"]";
    }
  )
);
```

The iterator function that we've used here simply calculates some basic information about the result string and formats it for us, but more powerful transformations are also possible.

> **details about clouds that contain m and u**
> 1. cumulus [length=7, index=0]
> 2. nimbus [length=6, index=1]

So far, we've restricted our examples to Arrays of Strings, for simplicity's sake as much as anything. But what if we want to work with more complex Array elements? So far, grep() is the only function we've shown that requires the elements to be Strings. In the next section, we'll look at a set of methods that provide support for working with more complex Array elements.

10.4.3 *Handling complex array elements with pluck(), invoke(), and collect()*

So far, we've mostly been exercising Prototype on Arrays containing simple elements such as numbers and Strings. In an application, we'll often want to store collections of complex objects too, and we can use Arrays for this purpose. In this section, we're going to look at ways of working with arrays of more complex objects using Prototype.

Using JSON, we can easily define arrays of more complex types and use the array methods that we've already covered. Let's take findAll(), from the previous section, as an example. In snippet 10.21, we used findAll() to retrieve a list of the cloud names that begin with letter *c*.

In a complex application, however, we're unlikely to have an isolated list of cloud names that are disconnected to any real data. Let's suppose, for the sake of example, that our information on clouds comes from a database, and each cloud has been assigned an ID, a name, and an optional description. We might represent this data as JavaScript objects, either by declaring a Cloud constructor, or simply by creating ad hoc objects using JSON. For simplicity, we'll adopt the latter approach right now. Snippet 10.25 puts findAll() through its paces with some more complex objects.

Snippet 10.25

```
var clouds=[
  { id:0, name: "cumulus", description: "fluffy" },
  { id:1, name: "nimbus", description: "flat" },
  { id:2, name: "cirrus" },
  { id:3, name: "stratus", description: "wispy" }
];

function beginsWith(obj,prop,letter){
```

```
    var first=(obj[prop])
      ? obj[prop].substring(0,1).toLowerCase()
      : null;
    return letter==first;
  }

  show("clouds that begin with c",
    clouds.findAll(
      function(str){ return beginsWith(str,"name","c"); }
    )
  );
```

We've defined the JSON objects to hold the data on our clouds, complete with a mock database ID. We then modi- fied the beginsWith() test function that we used earlier to work with objects rather than Strings. An extra argument

clouds that begin with c
1. [object Object]
2. [object Object]

allows us to specify which property of the object we want to examine. In the anon- ymous test function that we passed to findAll(),we asked it to find all elements whose name property begins with the letter c.

The result is correct, but it's rather hard to determine that from the output we receive, as the JavaScript Object simply renders itself as [object Object]. Ideally, we'd like to pull out the name or description property of each object, and display that instead. Prototype has an Array method called pluck(), suitable for just this purpose, as illustrated in snippet 10.26.

Snippet 10.26

```
  var clouds=[
    { id:0, name: "cumulus", description: "fluffy" },
    { id:1, name: "nimbus", description: "flat" },
    { id:2, name: "cirrus" },
    { id:3, name: "stratus", description: "wispy" }
  ];

  function beginsWith(obj,prop,letter){
    var first=(obj[prop])
      ? obj[prop].substring(0,1).toLowerCase()
      : null;
    return letter==first;
  }

  var cloudObjects=clouds.findAll(
    function(str){ return beginsWith(str,"name","c"); }
  )
  var cloudNames=cloudObjects.pluck("name");

  show("clouds that begin with c",cloudNames);
```

The `pluck()` method will visit each element in an array and read the property corresponding to the argument passed in to it. These property values will then be returned as an Array. So we filter our list of clouds using `findAll()`, and subsequently pluck out the values we need to display.

clouds that begin with c
1. cumulus
2. cirrus

We've broken the Array manipulation into several lines of code here, for clarity. If we don't want to use the Array of objects returned by `findAll()` for any other purpose, we could write the entire operation in one line, like so:

```
show("clouds that begin with c",
  clouds.findAll(
    function(str){ return beginsWith(str,"name","c"); }
  ).pluck("name");
);
```

Written this way, the code is more compact, arguably much cleaner and more satisfying, and arguably more obscure. It is also more in keeping with the Prototype and Scriptaculous house style, so whether or not you like to write your code this way, you'll probably end up reading code like this.

With `pluck()` it is easy to extract a property that already exists in each element, but we might want to return a list of composite values that we calculate on the fly. For example, if we have a list of rectangular plots of land as objects that give a width and length, we might want to list out the areas. Prototype provides the `collect()` method for this purpose. The iterator function provided to `collect()` can return any arbitrary value, which will be added to the result Array. Snippet 10.27 shows how we can gather a list of plot areas using the `collect()` method.

Snippet 10.27

```
var plots=[
  { length: 300, width: 200 },
  { length: 50, width: 250 },
  { length: 90, width: 20 }
];

show("plot areas",
  plots.collect(
    function(value,index){
      return value.length*value.width;
    }
  )
);
```

plot areas
1. 60000
2. 12500
3. 1800

The `collect()` method—also known as `map()`—allows us to define the logic that operates on our methods separately from the objects themselves. In simple examples such as these, that's OK, but if we're dealing with more formally defined objects, the logic that we want to run might be defined as a method of the object.

In the case of our plots of land example, we could easily define a constructor and prototype, and then instantiate instances of a Plot object type. In this case, we could still use `collect()`, simply modifying the iterator function to use the object methods, as follows:

```
function(value,index){
    return value.area();
}
```

Prototype also provides an `invoke()` method on Array, which accepts a method name as an argument. Snippet 10.28 shows `invoke()` at work calculating our plot areas for us.

Snippet 10.28

```
function Plot(l,w){
    this.length=l; this.width=w;
}
Plot.prototype.area=function(){ return this.length*this.width; }
var plots=[
    new Plot(200,300),
    new Plot(50,250),
    new Plot(90,20)
];

show("plot areas",
    plots.invoke("area")
);
```

plot areas
1. 60000
2. 12500
3. 1800

We've defined a simple constructor, added an `area()` method to the Plot prototype, and declared our data Array elements as Plot objects. `invoke()` then makes it simple to call the `area()` method for each element.

The `area()` method is simple because it takes no arguments, but `invoke()` can also work with methods that require arguments. Let's add a second function to the Plot prototype that calculates the cost of a plot of land at a given price and currency.

```
Plot.prototype.cost=function(price,currency){
    currency=currency || "US$";
    return currency+(this.area()*price);
}
```

Note that the second argument is optional, defaulting to US dollars. We can invoke this function with or without the optional argument, as shown in snippet 10.29.

Snippet 10.29

```
function Plot(l,w){
  this.length=l; this.width=w;
}
Plot.prototype.cost=function(price,currency){
  currency=currency || "US$";
  return currency+(this.area()*price);
}
Plot.prototype.area=function(){ return this.length*this.width; }
var plots=[
  new Plot(200,300),
  new Plot(50,250),
  new Plot(90,20)
];

show("plot costs at $5/m2",
  plots.invoke("cost",2)
);
show("plot costs at 500Kr/m2",
  plots.invoke("cost",500,"Kr")
);
```

plot costs at $5/m2	plot costs at 500Kr/m2
1. US$120000	1. Kr30000000
2. US$25000	2. Kr6250000
3. US$3600	3. Kr900000

10.4.4 *Constructing complex array elements with inject() and zip()*

We've seen how to extract simple values from complex array elements in the previous section. Prototype also provides some Array helpers that allow us to construct complex elements from Arrays.

The first method that we'll look at in this section is inject(), a specialized method that operates similarly to collect(). As illustrated in snippet 10.27, collect() allows us to perform arbitrary operations on objects, but it always returns the results as an ordered list. In some cases, we may prefer to return results as a lookup, for example, or simply to collect an aggregate value, such as a String or number. The inject() method gives us the power to specify an arbitrary type of result object, which is built up by visiting each element of the Array. Snippet 10.30

shows how we can operate on our list of cloud objects to return a JavaScript object that indexes each description by the name of the cloud.

Snippet 10.30

```
var clouds=[
  { id:0, name: "cumulus", description: "fluffy" },
  { id:1, name: "nimbus", description: "flat" },
  { id:2, name: "cirrus" },
  { id:3, name: "stratus", description: "wispy" }
];

var result=clouds.inject({},
  function(lookup,value,index){
    lookup[value.name]=(value.description) ? value.description : "no
  description";
    return lookup;
  }
);

showObj("descriptions", result);
```

The inject() method takes two arguments. The first object (commonly referred to as the memo) is going to store the results and will eventually be returned to us. Think of it as a notepad being passed around a room of people at the end of an informal meeting. Everyone who wants to stay in touch writes down their contact details and hands the pad on.

descriptions
cumulus : fluffy
nimbus : flat
cirrus : no description
stratus : wispy

Eventually, the organizer receives back the same notepad, but everyone in the room has modified it in some way. In our case, the "memo" is an empty JavaScript object declared using object literal syntax.

The second argument is the iterator function. Note that the iterator takes three arguments. The first is a reference to the memo object; the name that we give to this argument is arbitrary and will be used only within the iterator function. We've called it lookup because we're constructing a lookup of descriptions by name. The second and third arguments are the familiar value and index of the element being visited.

The iterator function checks that the element being visited has a description field, and it fills in a helpful "no description" message if none exists. It then adds the element to the lookup and returns it. Alternatively, we could choose not to add an entry for elements that don't have a description field, and simply return the memo unchanged. We leave that as an exercise for the reader.

It's important that the iterator function returns the memo object, as the result of the iterator is what is passed on to the next element. There may be unusual cases where we don't want to pass the same memo all the way around, but generally it isn't helpful. In the example of passing the notepad around for the contacts list, substituting the original notepad for an empty replica, or for one containing a different set of names, would be less than helpful.

When all elements in the Array have been visited, the result is returned from the inject() method. As we can see, we have a lookup object indexing each description field by name.

The second method we'll look at in this section is zip(). This method is named after the teeth of a clothing zipper, rather than the software compression format. When open, the teeth of a zipper form two separate linear groups. When the zipper is closed, the elements are brought together into a single line, in strict alternation. Array.zip() does the same thing to JavaScript Arrays, as illustrated in snippet 10.31.

Snippet 10.31

```
var lengths=[300,50,90];
var widths=[200,250,20];
var plots=lengths.zip(widths);

show("plots",plots);
show("first plot",plots[0]);
show("second plot",plots[1]);
```

We start with two areas of three elements each. Then zip() brings them together into a single array of three elements, with each element being an array of two elements. We've shown the first two elements in the output, as well as the entire result, to show that these are indeed Arrays.

plots	first plot	second plot
1. 300,200	1. 300	1. 50
2. 50,250	2. 200	2. 250
3. 90,20		

The teeth of a real zipper are limited to being on one of two sides. The zip() method, however, takes an arbitrary number of arguments, and will happily zip several strands together into a single thread. It supports an additional feature too—if the last argument is a function, it is used to transform each element of the result Array. The function accepts the Array of elements for that step of the result as input, and whatever it returns will be inserted into the result Array instead. In snippet 10.32, we've used it to create a simple object, similar to those that we defined in snippet 10.27 using JSON.

Snippet 10.32

```
var lengths=[300,50,90];
var widths=[200,250,20];
var locations=["downtown","out west","middle of nowhere"];
var plots=lengths.zip(widths,locations,
  function(value){
    return { length: value[0], width: value[1], location: value[2] };
  }
);

show("plots",plots);
show("first plot",plots[0]);
show("second plot",plots[1]);
```

We've added an extra input strand to the zip operation here, listing the location of each plot of land. `zip()` will collate these three strands into little Arrays for us, collecting the first elements as `[300,200,"downtown"]`. The final argument that we pass to `zip()` will convert this array into an object for us. As you can see, the results are populated with objects of that type.

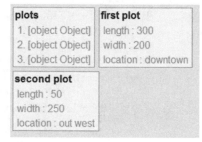

We've now covered all the Array methods that help us work with complex objects. In the following section, we'll look at some methods that will help us work with arrays containing numbers.

10.4.5 *Numerical ordering with max(), min(), and sortBy()*

We've already seen how the JavaScript Array object's `sort()` and `reverse()` functions can add a degree of order to numerical arrays. Prototype builds on that capability with a few helper methods. The simplest of these are `max()` and `min()`, which return the largest and smallest elements of an Array respectively. Snippet 10.33 illustrates these functions at their simplest.

Snippet 10.33

```
var data=[1492,1817,1604,1066];
show("max",data.max());
show("min",data.min());
```

The data that we are working with here is numerical, so a maximum or minimum can easily be determined. If we want to work with more complex objects, such as the plots of land that we introduced in snippet 10.27, we can provide our own comparison functions, as illustrated in snippet 10.34.

Snippet 10.34

```
var plots=[
  { length: 300, width: 200 },
  { length: 50, width: 250 },
  { length: 90, width: 20 }
];

show("longest",
  plots.max(
    function(value,index){ return value.length; }
  )
);
```

The comparison function takes the now-familiar `value` and `index` as arguments, and returns the value to be compared. Note that `max()` and `min()` will return the value returned by the comparator function, not the Array element itself, so we're only told the greatest length, not the plot that it belongs to.

> **longest**
> 300

The `sortBy()` method allows us to sort complex objects as if they were simple numerics. It accepts an iterator function as an argument, which should return a ranking for that object. Once a rank for each object has been established, the native `sort()` method is used to order the Array by ranking. Snippet 10.35 illustrates how `sortBy()` can be used to order our plots of land by length.

Snippet 10.35

```
var plots=[
  { length: 300, width: 200 },
  { length: 50, width: 250 },
  { length: 90, width: 20 }
];

var sorted=plots.sortBy(
  function(value,index){
    return value.length;
  }
);

show("sorted by length",sorted);
show("sorted by length",
  sorted.collect(
    function(value,index){
      return value.length+" x "+value.width
    }
  )
);
```

The iterator passed in to `sortBy()` simply returns the `length` property of each plot. In displaying the results, we've used `collect()` to provide a readable summary of each plot, and to illustrate that they have indeed been sorted.

sorted by length	sorted by length
1. [object Object]	1. 50 x 250
2. [object Object]	2. 90 x 20
3. [object Object]	3. 300 x 200

Back in section 10.2.6, we noted that, when working with the DOM, we'd encounter objects that behaved like Arrays, but weren't. In sections 10.3 and 10.4, we've seen a radical change in how we can deal with Arrays, and it's unfortunate to note that none of these methods will be available to the collections of DOM nodes that we'll encounter. All is not lost, however, as we'll discover in the next section.

10.4.6 *Working with DOM collections*

As we noted in section 10.2.6, the DOM exposes objects that look at first sight to be Arrays, but in fact support little more than the `length` property and the square bracket syntax. Now that Prototype has supercharged our Arrays with all the extra power that we've been discussing in the last two sections, this is even more of a problem. Fortunately, Prototype also has the solution.

A top-level `$A()` method is provided, the importance of which can be clearly seen by the length of its name! `$A()` converts objects that are sort of like Arrays into the real thing. Any object that supports the square bracket syntax and `length` property can be rescued by `$A()`.

Let's put `$A()` through its paces quickly. Say, for example, that we have a list of elements visible on the screen, representing entries in a diary. We've attached a Date object to each DOM element indicating when that entry will expire, and we want to quickly remove all expired entries, to ensure that the diary is up to date. All the DOM elements are housed in a single DIV, whose ID is `diary`, so we can get a list of the child nodes representing the individual entries as follows:

```
var entries=$("diary").childNodes;
```

The `$()` function resolves DOM nodes from their ID. We've already seen it in action several times in this book, and we'll be formally introduced in chapter 11. `childNodes` is a standard DOM property, but unfortunately `$()` returned one of those pesky pseudo-Arrays, so we can't invoke `each()` on it as it is. Let's modify our statement, then:

```
var entries=$A($("diary").childNodes);
```

`$A()` does its magic, and `entries` now points to a real Array object. Removing the expired entries is now a simple matter:

```
entries.each(
  function(node){
    var expiryDate=node.expires;
    var now=new Date();
    if (expiryDate<now){  Element.remove(node); }
  }
);
```

`Element.remove()` removes a DOM element from the page without fuss. Of course, if we felt like it, we could apply a Scriptaculous Effect such as Puff, Fade, or BlindUp instead, to make sure the user noticed that the diary was being tidied up.

It's worth noting that `$A()` is not just for DOM elements. Any object that supports a `toArray()` method can also be passed to `$A()`. Most notably, the String object type supports `toArray()` under Prototype, returning an Array of characters generated by the built-in `String.split()` function that we covered in section 10.2.5.

So, the host of powerful methods that we saw in sections 10.3 and 10.4 can be used with collections of DOM elements, if we do a little preparation. That's certainly good news, but there's still more! At the start of this chapter, we noted that in JavaScript any object could be used as an associative array. Prototype provides mechanisms for treating Objects as Arrays, with all the elegance and power that we've seen so far. In the next section, we'll look at these features in more depth.

10.5 Working with Hashes and ObjectRanges

As we noted at the outset of this chapter, every programming language worth its salt supports two basic types of array: the numerically indexed array, and the associative array. JavaScript has taken the slightly unusual route of supporting associative arrays through the core Object type, as we saw in chapter 10. We've covered the numerical Array type in depth here, both in its native form, and in the support provided by Prototype.js. However, we aren't quite through with Prototype's support for data structures. In this final section, we'll look at two other object types provided by Prototype: the Hash and the ObjectRange.

10.5.1 Using the Hash object

The Hash object provides a set of additional functionality for objects that work like associative arrays. Like the Enumerable object that we saw in section 10.4, Hash is a free-floating set of functions that can be mapped onto a variety of objects. In Ruby terminology, it is a mixin.

Hash introduces a much smaller group of functions than Enumerable. Let's look at each of them in turn. But first, we'll see how to create a Hash object.

Creating Hashes with $H

In this section, we'll introduce another of Prototype's A-list functions, whose status is denoted by the brevity of the name. In the previous section, we saw how we could turn a variety of objects into Arrays using $A(). A similar function, called $H(), converts objects into Hashes. When $H() is invoked on an object, it adds all the Hash methods to the object. It also applies the Enumerable methods that we described in section 10.4, allowing us to reuse the entire set of functionality described previously on objects other than Arrays. As with $A(), invoking $H() on an object that is already a Hash will simply return it unchanged. Snippet 10.36 shows off a little of what $H() can do for us.

Snippet 10.36

```
var obj={
  name: "Tree Frog",
  size: "small",
  colour: ['green','red'],
  toes: "pobbly"
};

var hash=$H(obj);
show("tree frog",
  hash.collect(
    function(value){ return value; }
  )
);
```

First off, we defined a plain old JavaScript object, holding various bits of information on a type of frog (well, why not?). Once we ran the object through $H(), we were able to use any of the Enumerable methods on it. Here, we simply used collect() to return the value that we were given, as we're curious to see

tree frog
1. name,Tree Frog
2. size,small
3. colour,green,red
4. toes,pobbly

what value the Enumerable iterator passes when working with an associative array. As you can see from the results, it returns an Array containing two elements, the key and the value, for each call of the iterator. In fact, it also maps the key and value to the named properties key and value, so we can read the element either as an Array or as an Object.

Now let's see what we can do with some of the more advanced Enumerable methods. First, let's filter our object, to list only the properties that have four letters in their names. Snippet 10.37 shows how it's done.

Snippet 10.37

```
var frog=$H({
  name: "Tree Frog",
  size: "small",
  colour: ['green','red'],
  toes: "pobbly"
});

show("tree frog (selected)",
  frog.findAll(
    function(pair){ return pair.key.length==4; }
  )
);
```

We've invoked $H() inline this time, and changed the variable, but it's still the same old frog. We can use findAll() to pull out the properties we're interested in. To aid readability here, we've renamed the argument to the iterator as pair, and we've referred to its elements by name rather than numerical index.

tree frog (selected)
1. name,Tree Frog
2. size,small
3. toes,pobbly

pair.key is the property name, and pair.value is the property value. Remember too, that the iterator function will accept a third argument—the numerical index—but we're not going to use it, so we omit it here.

Note, however, that the result is returned as an Array of little pair objects/arrays, and not as an Object with the same kind of structure that we passed in. If we want to return an Object that is easier to work with, we can use inject(), as described in snippet 10.30, and create an initially empty memo object that we populate via the iterator. Snippet 10.38 shows us how to do this.

Snippet 10.38

```
var frog=$H({
  name: "Tree Frog",
  size: "small",
  colour: ['green','red'],
  toes: "pobbly"
});

var result=frog.inject({},
  function(newFrog,pair){
    if (pair.key.length==4){
      newFrog[pair.key]=pair.value;
    }
    return newFrog;
  }
);

show("new Frog", result);
```

The first argument to `inject()` is the memo, which in our case is an empty Object declared using JSON. Within the iterator function, we refer to this as `newFrog`, and examine the `pair.key length` property before deciding whether or not to add to the memo.

OK, that's enough fun for now. Let's stop there with the standard Enumerable methods. The Hash object also provides a few methods of its own, so let's look at them briefly.

Iterating a Hash using keys() and values()

The standard Enumerable iterators work with the Hash contents in key-value pairs, which, for the most part, is a convenient way to work. Sometimes, though, we just want to iterate through the keys, or through the values. `Enumerable.pluck()`, as described in section 10.4.3, could solve this problem for us, but the Hash object has baked in a couple of useful methods, called `keys()` and `values()`, that do the job for us. They're very straightforward to use, as snippet 10.39 demonstrates.

Snippet 10.39

```
var frog=$H({
  name: "Tree Frog",
  size: "small",
  colour: ['green','red'],
  toes: "pobbly"
});

show("keys", frog.keys());
show("values", frog.values());
```

The `keys()` and `values()` methods return simple Arrays, which can then be iterated over or manipulated further.

There's one more method that we want to look at before we're done, so let's take a look at it now.

Manipulating Hashes with toQueryString()

We've spent most of this chapter in a happy abstract world of data structures. Let's briefly poke our heads up above the parapet and remember that we're writing code for web applications. It's a common feature of the web app to send information back to the server, and this is commonly sent as a querystrings, either in the URL or request body (see appendix A). Querystring are composed of key-value pairs, and they require a bit of special treatment to encode the value data.

Hash provides a `toQueryString()` method that makes it easy to create querystrings. In snippet 10.40, we're going to serialize our frog object in preparation for sending the information back to the server.

Snippet 10.40

```
var frog=$H({
  name: "Tree Frog",
  size: "small",
  colour: ['green','red'],
  toes: "pobbly"
});

show("query string", frog.toQueryString());
```

> **query string**
> name=Tree%20Frog&size=small&colour=green%2Cred&toes=pobbly

That concludes our exploration of the Hash object. In the following section, we'll look at the final feature in this chapter, the ObjectRange.

10.5.2 Using the ObjectRange

The ObjectRange is the last object, in Prototype's gallery of array-like types, that has access to the Enumerable methods. The ObjectRange provides a quick way of representing ranges of values, usually integers.

ObjectRange can be instantiated directly by its constructor, but Prototype also provides the `$R()` function as a shortcut. `$R()` takes three arguments, the start and end of the range, and an optional Boolean flag indicating whether or not the range includes the end value. Snippet 10.41 shows how to use the Object-Range to calculate the squares of all integers up to 6.

Snippet 10.41

```
var ints=$R(1,6);
show("squares",
  ints.collect(
    function(value){ return value*value; }
  )
);
```

> **squares**
> 1. 1
> 2. 4
> 3. 9
> 4. 16
> 5. 25
> 6. 36

We could achieve the same result by simply declaring an Array, `[1,2,3,4,5,6]`, and invoking `collect()` on that. We have saved ourselves a bit of typing, though, and the ObjectRange will scale extremely well. Imagine if we wanted to calculate all squares up to 1000, for example!

That concludes our survey of Prototype's support for Arrays, and our exploration of the core language features that Prototype provides. We'll conclude our exploration of Prototype in the next chapter, with a look at the support it offers for working within the web browser environment. In chapter 12, we'll revisit what we've learned in this section of the book, in the context of a real application.

10.6   *Summary*

We've covered a lot of ground in this chapter, and worked our way through one of the most complex and powerful subsystems of the Prototype libraries.

We began by looking at the plain Array object provided by the core language, in section 10.2. The JavaScript Array object is powerful in its own right, able to extend and truncate itself, operate as a stack, and insert an arbitrary number of members at any point. In section 10.3, we saw how Prototype extended the Array object to provide a few convenient extra methods.

Although Prototype does extend the Array prototype directly, it also provides a lot of capabilities indirectly through the Enumerable object, which we addressed in section 10.4. The Enumerable object's methods employ the concept of iterator functions, effectively exploiting the capabilities of functions that we covered in chapter 9.

By providing a lot of Array-like functionality in a separate object, rather than bolting it directly onto Array, Prototype opens that functionality up to other Array-like objects too, such as the Hash. In section 10.5, we saw how the Hash provides a more Array-like wrapper around the associative array-like nature of the base JavaScript object, and allows us to work with any object using the iterator function approach.

This chapter concludes our rather thorough detour through the JavaScript language fundamentals. We hope that with this solid grounding in the core language under your belt, you'll be capable of reading the Prototype and Scriptaculous code bases more easily, and be able to employ the same techniques in your own code.

In the next chapter, we'll return to our example application and apply some of what we've learned in the last few chapters. At the same time, we'll explore some of the support that Prototype offers for working with the web browser.

Back to the Browser

We've spent several happy chapters exploring the workings of the JavaScript language. Now it's time to remind ourselves that we're using JavaScript to develop web applications. All of our lovely code is going to be running inside a web browser, and that means we'll be using the browser-specific features of the Java-Script interpreter to get things done.

We've already seen in part 2 of the book how Scriptaculous can provide us with a lot of browser user interface (UI) elements out of the box. However, there are times when we'll want to manipulate the browser UI at a lower level. The standard way of interacting with the page contents is through the Document Object Model, or DOM. Scripting the DOM is notoriously verbose and tedious, but fortunately the Prototype library provides a number of helpers to make things easier.

In this chapter, we'll look at how Prototype helps us to work with the browser, rather than struggling against it. But first, we'll cover a few of the basic DOM methods, to help us see where Prototype's extensions are coming from.

11.1 A crash course in DOM methods

In order to quickly explore the DOM, we're going to modify the Scratchpad application from chapters 8–10 and add a bit more markup into the output pane. The modified Scratchpad application used in this chapter can be found in the download for the book as scratchpad/ps-dom-sandbox.html. Listing 11.1 shows the HTML markup that we've added to the page.

Listing 11.1   HTML markup for DOM exercises

```
<div id='a'>
  <div id='b' secret-attribute='hello world'>
    <ul id='list'>
      <li>one</li>
      <li>two</li>
      <li>three</li>
    </ul>
  </div>
  <img src='images/dscn0433.thumb.jpg'></img>
  <div id='c'>this is DOM node c</div>
</div>
```

The markup in listing 11.1 simply declares a few standard HTML elements, including DIVs, an unordered list, and an image. Figure 11.1 shows the way the markup appears in the browser. It's nothing fancy, but it gives us a way to work with our example snippets.

Programmatically, we can interact with this markup as a tree structure. Most modern browsers provide tools for viewing the current document as a DOM tree, either as core functionality or as part of a plug-in. Figure 11.2 shows our Scratchpad in the Mozilla DOM inspector.

To run the snippets in this chapter, run the Scratchpad application, either from a web server or directly off the filesystem (Internet Explorer may warn you about "active content" if you do the latter). Copy the snippet you want to run to the text area, and click on "run the code." To run another snippet, reload the Scratchpad application and copy the next snippet.

Figure 11.1 Result of the added HTML markup in the Scratchpad applications

In a classic web application, the server sends us a ready-to-go user interface as a web page. When we're writing Ajax apps, we will intercept server responses in our code, and update the user interface programmatically. To do this, we need to interact with the DOM.

We can interact with the DOM in two main ways. First, we can read the DOM and move around the tree to access elements. This will allow us to find elements within the user interface, in order to modify them. Second, we can manipulate

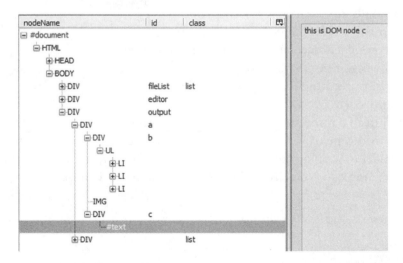

Figure 11.2 DOM tree underlying the added HTML elements, as viewed in the Mozilla DOM inspector

the tree, adding, moving, and removing nodes. This will allow us to add UI elements, remove or hide others, or otherwise modify the UI. When working with the HTML document, we're generally concerned with altering the DOM, but being able to traverse the tree is a prerequisite to that, so we'll look at it first.

11.1.1 Traversing the tree

Take a look at listing 11.1, and you'll see that we've added ID attributes to many of our items. Within an XML-like document, every ID should be unique, although web browsers are very lenient in parsing HTML and won't enforce this rule. The incentive to sticking to this rule in your own documents is that the document object (which represents the current page) has a useful method for getting references to DOM elements by their ID, as illustrated in snippet 11.1.

Snippet 11.1

```
var el=document.getElementById("b");
highlight(el);
```

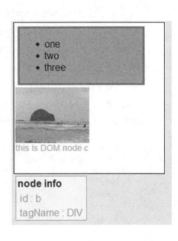

As you can see, the `highlight()` method in our Scratchpad application draws a thick red border around the highlighted element and adds a small information block to the output window.

In general, it's a good idea to provide a unique ID for every element that you want to be able to manipulate in your code. When generating content on the server, database primary keys often make a good choice, along with a short description, giving rise to IDs of the form "stock_1234". In our simple markup, we've taken a minimalist approach.

Having acquired a reference to one node in the tree, we'll commonly want to look at other nodes nearby. Snippet 11.2 shows how to get from a node to its immediate children. We may need to do this in order to inspect a set of buttons in a toolbar, for example, or rows in a table, in the UI of our Ajax app.

Snippet 11.2

```
var el=document.getElementById("b");
var children=el.childNodes;
$A(children).each(
  function(el){ highlight(el); }
);
```

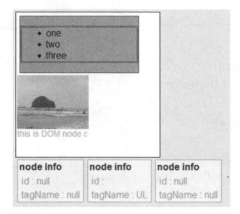
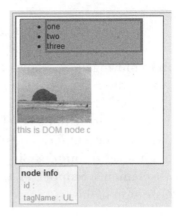

We've presented two versions of the visual output for this snippet, as Firefox (left) and Internet Explorer (right) yield different results. The reason for this is that Firefox (rather pedantically) treats whitespace as text nodes. Because we've formatted our HTML nicely with indents and carriage returns, the <UL> element is surrounded by bits of whitespace. Internet Explorer takes a more pragmatic approach and ignores these.

It's also worth pointing out that the childNodes property does not return a genuine JavaScript Array, but an array-like object. Although it responds to the length property and square braces syntax, it doesn't have all the lovely extensions to the Array prototype that we discussed in chapter 10. We therefore use the $A() function to turn it into a real Array so that we can use each().

Finally, a word of caution. DOM elements in Internet Explorer also support a property called children, which is an alias to childNodes. If you use the children property (and the name is more intuitive), your code won't run on other browsers.

Being part of a tree structure, a DOM element can have from zero to many children, but it always has only one parent node. Snippet 11.3 illustrates the use of the parent property. If we have a reference to a DOM element representing a button on a panel, for example, we may receive a UI event on that button and wish to respond by modifying the entire parent panel—minimizing, maximizing, or removing it.

Snippet 11.3

```
var el=document.getElementById("b");
highlight(el.parentNode);
```

In addition to moving up and down the tree, we can move sideways, traversing the siblings of the current node using `nextSibling` and `previousSibling`. In practice, this is generally not as useful as traversing up and down the tree, but it can be useful when iterating through a set of buttons, list items, or other grouped UI elements. Snippet 11.4 provides a simple demonstration of this.

Snippet 11.4

```
var el=document.getElementById('list');
highlight(el.firstChild.nextSibling);
```

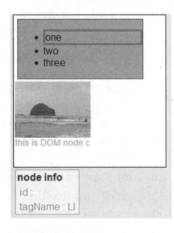

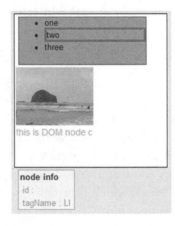

Again, we've provided screenshots of Firefox (left) and Internet Explorer (right) side by side, as the results differ. Firefox has evaluated the `firstChild` of the node as a piece of whitespace, and the next sibling as the first element. Internet Explorer, however, only sees the `<LI>` tags, and so evaluates `firstChild.nextSibling` as the second list item.

Clearly, we need a way of getting around this pesky whitespace issue when working with child nodes. One solution is outlined in Snippet 11.5.

Snippet 11.5

```
var el=document.getElementById('list');
highlight(el.getElementsByTagName("li")[0]);
```

The `getElementsByTagName()` method recurses through the entire subtree below a node, returning all DOM elements whose tag name matches the argument. Provided we know the basic structure of the document, this allows us to bypass the whitespace in both browsers. It can also be useful in retrieving collections of elements, such as all the `<LI>` tags under the `<UL>` tag. Note that, like `childNodes`, it returns a pseudo-array, so if you want to use Prototype Array methods on the result, use `$A()` first.

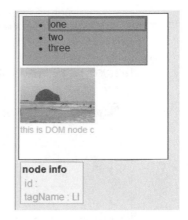

This completes the first part of our crash course in the JavaScript DOM. We've seen how to find our way around a DOM in this section. Typically when we do this, it is a precursor to identifying the elements that we wish to modify, so in the next section we'll look at the functionality that is at our disposal for modifying the UI using DOM.

11.1.2 Modifying the tree

We've seen how to inspect the existing document in the previous section, but we can also use DOM methods to build entirely new nodes that we can then add to the main document. The DOM defines several types of nodes, but the most useful two are the Element, which represents an HTML or XML tag, and the Text, which represents the contents of a node. Hence, the simple HTML fragment,

```
<p>Hello, world</p>
```

is represented in the DOM as two nodes, an Element node representing the `<p>` tag, with a Text node representing the "Hello, world" text as its child.

Snippet 11.6 shows how we can create DOM nodes programmatically.

Snippet 11.6

```
function domNode(id,tag,caption){
  var node=document.createElement(tag || "div");
  node.setAttribute("id",id);
  if (caption){
    var txtNode=document.createTextNode(caption);
    node.appendChild(txtNode);
  }
  return node;
}

var list=document.getElementById('list');
var li=list.getElementsByTagName("li");
```

```
var newli=domNode("new","li","new list item");
list.appendChild(newli);
highlight(newli);
```

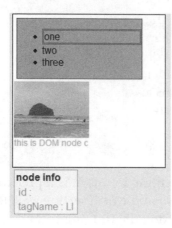 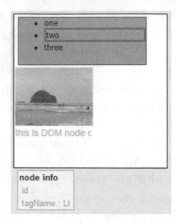

Creating the elements with their accompanying text is tedious, so, even in a simple example like this one, we've written a helper function to take the strain. We stitch the nodes together using the appendChild() method. As soon as a node is added to the main document, it becomes visible, so we assemble the entire fragment first, and then append it to the list. Similarly, calling the opposite method, remove-Child(), will remove the child element from the document permanently. (When hiding a part of the UI, it's more usual to use CSS than to modify the DOM directly.)

Where the node being appended to already has children, the new node is attached at the end. Snippet 11.7 shows the use of a second method to insert new nodes at arbitrary points in the group of children.

Snippet 11.7

```
function domNode(id,tag,caption){
  var node=document.createElement(tag || "div");
  node.setAttribute("id",id);
  if (caption){
    var txtNode=document.createTextNode(caption);
    node.appendChild(txtNode);
  }
  return node;
}

var list=document.getElementById('list');
var li=list.getElementsByTagName("li")[1];

var newli=domNode("new","li","new list item");
```

```
list.appendChild(newli);
highlight(newli);

var newli2=domNode("new2","li","another new list item");
list.insertBefore(newli2,li);
highlight(newli2);
```

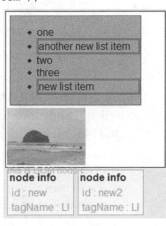

To use `insertBefore()`, we need to resolve the child element marking the insertion point, as well as the parent node. There is no `insertAfter()` method, but a combination of `insertBefore()` and `nextSibling` will do the trick.

Snippet 11.8 illustrates the final method for inserting and removing individual elements from the DOM: `replaceChild()` allows us to replace one child element with a new element. As we can see in the output, the list item labeled "two" has disappeared entirely.

Snippet 11.8

```
function domNode(id,tag,caption){
  var node=document.createElement(tag || "div");
  node.setAttribute("id",id);
  if (caption){
    var txtNode=document.createTextNode(caption);
    node.appendChild(txtNode);
  }
  return node;
}

var list=document.getElementById('list');
var li=list.getElementsByTagName("li")[1];

var newli=domNode("new","li","new list item");
list.replaceChild(newli,li);
highlight(newli);
```

DOM methods for creating and manipulating individual nodes are all very well, but when creating a real UI, we will typically want to assemble tens, if not hundreds, of DOM elements. Doing so programmatically would be tedious. Fortunately, there is a much terser shortcut that we can use to create more complex content, which is illustrated in snippet 11.9.

Snippet 11.9

```
var el=document.getElementById("list");
el.innerHTML="<h3>Some New Markup</h3>"
  +"<p>Brought to you "
  +"<ul><li>simply!</li>"
  +"<li>concisely!</li>"
  +"<li>without fuss!</li>"
  +"</ul>by innerHTML!!</p>";
```

Using the `innerHTML` property, we can quickly assemble content as HTML and pass it to the browser's native rendering engine for transformation into DOM elements. The `innerHTML` property is not part of the standard DOM and was initially introduced in Internet Explorer, but it's now supported by all major browsers.

That concludes our review of the DOM manipulation methods that are provided by default. We've encountered cross-browser issues and a tendency toward verbosity. Let's see now how Prototype makes working with the DOM altogether more pleasant.

11.2 Prototype and the DOM

DOM methods that we saw in section 11.1 allow us to manipulate the user interface of our Ajax app programmatically, but the experience of using the DOM is not always a pleasant one. DOM methods tend to be verbose and not suitable for developing large, complex UIs.

Prototype's focus throughout is on making the life of the Ajax developer easier. It's no surprise, then, that several modules relate to working with DOM elements. In this section, we'll show you a number of features that will make it easier to work with the UI of your Ajax app. We'll begin with a look at a set of simple functions that make working with the DOM more convenient.

11.2.1 Simple helper functions

In the previous section, we saw that the first step in most interactions with DOM was to use `document.getElementById()`. It is an extremely useful function, with an unfortunately long name.

Realizing this, the authors of Prototype gave us a function with a much shorter name: `$()`. Yes, `$` is a legal name for a function in JavaScript, and although it might look like a mixed-up version of Perl or PHP, `$('list')` is an invocation of the $() function. Snippet 11.10 shows us the terse way of referencing a DOM element.

Snippet 11.10

```
var el=$("list");
highlight(el);
```

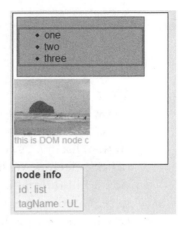

Simply for its brevity, $() is useful, but it also does several things that `document.getElementById()` doesn't. Snippet 11.11 shows off the full power of this function.

Snippet 11.11

```
var el=$("list");
var els=$(el,"a","b");
els.each(
  function(el){ highlight(el); }
);
```

The first thing that we did in this snippet is resolve the list, as before. In the second call to $(), we passed in three arguments, one of which is a resolved DOM element, the others being strings. If $() is called with more than one argument, it will resolve each argument individually and return the results as an Array—and that's a real Array, with all the Prototype extensions, such as `each()`, ready to use! If we want to get a programmatic reference to several elements at once—all the buttons on a panel, for example—this is an efficient and easy way to do it.

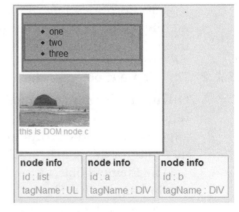

The fact that the first argument is a DOM element is not a problem. The `document.getElementById()` method translates a string into a DOM element, and it won't accept any other argument type. $() is slightly different, as it ensures that a DOM element is resolved. The majority of Prototype and Scriptaculous functions use $(), so Elements (discussed in the next section), Effects, and the drag-and-drop system all accept either DOM nodes or strings when working with DOM.

In the previous section, we also came across the `getElementsByTagName()` method. As of version 1.5, Prototype also provides a power-user equivalent of this function, called $$(). Snippet 11.12 illustrates its use.

Snippet 11.12

```
var els=$$("#list li");
els.each(
  function(el){ highlight(el); }
);
```

The argument that we passed in to $$() is a CSS selector expression, in this case specifying <li> tags that are children of a tag with an ID of list item. $$() supports a wide range of CSS selectors. We don't have space to provide a full tutorial on the types of selectors here, but there are many good resources for CSS on the web and in print. $$() returns all matching elements as an array.

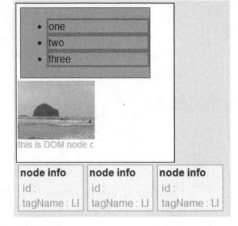

Together, $() and $$() provide a flexible means for locating DOM elements. Prototype also provides a lot of functionality for modifying the DOM. We'll begin to address that in the next section, with the Element object.

11.2.2 *The Element object*

Often, the first thing that we'll want to do, once we've acquired a programmatic reference to a DOM element, is to modify that element in some way, changing its appearance or other properties. The Element object contains a number of useful methods for doing that.

The Element object is a mixin-style object, similar to the Enumerable object we saw in chapter 10. That is, it is a standalone object defining a number of static functions, and these functions are also applied to the prototype of a built-in object, to enhance it with additional functionality. In the case of the Element object, its functionality is applied to the prototype of the built-in Element class—that is, to every DOM element. The functionality that Element provides can therefore be accessed in two ways, either as a static call to the Element class itself or as a direct method of a DOM node.

Let's look at a concrete example using our Scratchpad application. Element defines three methods for hiding and showing a DOM node by modifying the CSS display property: hide() hides the element, show() shows it, and toggle() flips it between the hidden and shown states. Snippet 11.13 demonstrates the use of these, using both syntaxes. Run each line in snippet 11.13 separately without reloading the Scratchpad application.

Snippet 11.13

```
Element.hide("b");
Element.show("b");
$("b").hide();
$("b").show();
```

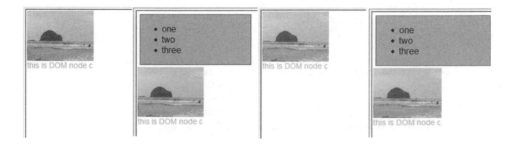

The code in snippet 11.13 hides and shows the element containing the ordered list twice. The first time around, we called the methods of Element directly, passing in a reference to the DOM node as an argument. This argument is resolved using $(), so it can be either a string, as here, or a programmatic reference to a node.

The second time, we resolved the DOM element directly using $() and called `hide()` and `show()` as methods of that object. We didn't need to pass in the argument this time, as Prototype performed the necessary plumbing behind the scenes to ensure that the DOM element was passed in as an argument to the `Element.hide()` and `show()` methods. If you want to examine the gory details on how it does this, take a look at the Element.extend.cache object; if you want to just enjoy being able to call the methods in two different ways, that's fine too!

The preceding methods simply hide or show the target DOM element. To remove a DOM element from the page, you can use the `Element.remove()` method, which, like all the other methods of Element, can be called either as a static method on Element, like this:

```
Element.remove("myNode")
```

or as a method on the DOM element itself, like this:

```
$("myNode").remove()
```

In snippet 11.9, we saw the power of the `innerHTML` property to quickly add new content to the DOM. The Element object provides a couple of useful methods to enhance this, called `update()` and `replace()`.

The update() method is essentially a straight synonym for innerHTML, but with one crucial difference. Setting the innerHTML property to a string that includes <script> tags will not result in the script being executed. update() works around this so that <script> tags are evaluated, as snippet 11.14 illustrates.

Snippet 11.14

```
function makeContent(method){
    return "<h3>Some New Markup</h3>"
    +"<p>Brought to you "
    +"<ul><li>simply!</li>"
    +"<li>concisely!</li>"
    +"<li>without fuss!</li>"
    +"</ul>by "+method+"!!</p>"
    +"<script>alert('hello "+method+"');</script>";
}

$("list").innerHTML=makeContent("innerHTML");
$("c").update(makeContent("Element.update()"));
```

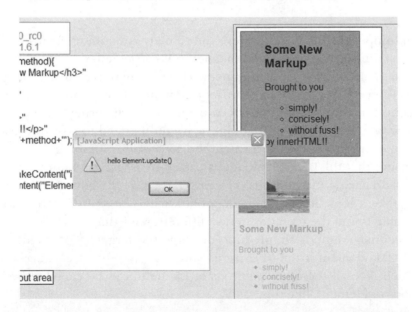

The makeContent() function simply generates some HTML markup similar to that in snippet 11.9, but it adds in a script tag that states the method used to add the content to the element. When we use innerHTML, the script tag is ignored, but when we use update(), the alert message appears.

The `update()` method adds the specified content inside the specified element; `replace()`, in contrast, removes the target element, adding the content in its place. Snippet 11.15 illustrates the difference.

Snippet 11.15

```
function makeContent(method){
  return "<h3>Some New Markup</h3>"
  +"<p>Brought to you "
  +"<ul><li>simply!</li>"
  +"<li>concisely!</li>"
  +"<li>without fuss!</li>"
  +"</ul>by "+method+"!!</p>"
  +"<script>alert('hello "+method+"');</script>";
}

$("b").replace(makeContent("Element.replace()"));
```

We've reused our `makeContent()` function from the previous code snippet. The element with `id=b` is the gray box containing the list, which has been completely removed by the `replace()` operation. Internet Explorer DOM elements have an `outerHTML` property that operates in a broadly similar fashion to `replace()`, but Mozilla browsers have never taken this up, so use of `outerHTML` is far less prevalent than `innerHTML`.

The Element object also contains a number of useful ways of working with CSS class definitions. In the plain old web browser environment without Prototype, we can modify the CSS styling of a DOM element in two ways: setting the `className` property to apply predefined CSS classes, or modifying values of the Element's style object to get finer-grained control. Let's look at each of these in turn.

A CSS class is assigned to a DOM element via the class attribute in HTML, or via the `className` attribute in JavaScript. In most cases, we assign a single named CSS class, but it is possible to assign several CSS classes to an element simply by separating the names with spaces. Suppose we defined one CSS class to increase the font size of a DOM element,

```
.big{
  font-size: 1.5em;
}
```

and a second one to draw a thick black border and increase the font weight,

```
.bold{
  border: solid black 3px;
  font-weight: bold;
}
```

If we assigned a `className` of "big bold" to an element, it would be styled by both CSS classes, appearing, well, big and bold. Secondary CSS classes of this type can be very useful for setting elements as visually highlighted, disabled, or invisible, for example.

Unfortunately, the standard DOM provides no way of managing the CSS elements as a list. Prototype's Element object fills that gap with `addClassName()` and `removeClassName()` methods, whose usage is illustrated in snippet 11.16. Run each of the pairs of code lines in Snippet 11.16 separately. (The previously mentioned CSS styles `big` and `bold` are declared in the Scratchpad application, so this snippet will run in there without modification.)

Snippet 11.16

```
Element.addClassName("b","big");
$("b").addClassName("bold");

show("b's classnames",$A($("b").classNames()));
show("b is bold?",$("b").hasClassName("bold"));

$("b").removeClassName("big");
show("b is big?",$("b").hasClassName("big"));
```

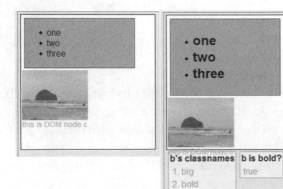
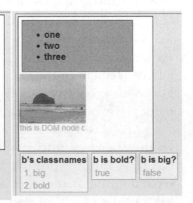

This snippet illustrates four methods of the Element object. The `classNames()` method returns a list of CSS classes operating on the node; `addClassName()` and `removeClassName()` allow easy modification of this list, making it easy for us to add `big` or `bold` to the DOM Element without interfering with existing CSS classes operating on that node; and `hasClassName()` allows us to query whether a DOM element possesses a given CSS class. As with all other methods of the Element object, we can call them via the Element object or as methods on a DOM element. We've mixed and matched the two usages here, to emphasize this.

Predefined CSS styles are useful, but in other situations, we will typically want to modify the styling of an element at a finer granularity, using the `style` property. To alter the size of a DOM element, for example, we might write this:

```
domElement.style.height="400px";
domElement.style.width="500px";
```

If we want to set several properties at once, this style can become cumbersome. Prototype's Element object provides a couple of useful methods for reading and writing from the `style` property more easily, as snippet 11.17 shows.

Snippet 11.17

```
$("b").setStyle(
  { width: "300px", border: "solid #ddd 4px" }
);

show("styles of 'b'",
  {
    width:  Element.getStyle("b","width"),
    height: $("b").getStyle("height"),
    border: $("b").getStyle("border")
  }
);
```

The screenshot for this snippet was taken when running the Scratchpad under Mozilla Firefox. The textual output of the style properties may differ in different browsers. Internet Explorer will report the border as `#ddd solid 4px`, but it's simply a different way of describing the same RGB color.

The `getStyle()` method takes a single style property's name as its argument and returns the value of that property. `setStyle()`

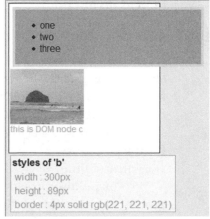

is rather more ambitious, taking an object as its argument, allowing multiple `style` attributes to be set in a single method call.

In snippet 11.4, we encountered a cross-browser compatibility issue resulting from the treatment of whitespace. We figured out some workarounds in snippet 11.5 by searching the DOM explicitly by node type using `getElementsByTag-Name()`. Prototype provides a different solution to this problem by providing the `cleanWhitespace()` method as part of the Element mixin. Snippet 11.18 is a prototype-based reworking of snippet 11.4, which produces identical—and intuitive—results across browsers, highlighting the second list item.

Snippet 11.18

```
var el=$('list');
el.cleanWhitespace();
highlight(el.firstChild.nextSibling);
```

This concludes our review of the Element object. Element, as the name suggests, provides us with methods that make it simple to style individual elements in the UI. While we could achieve the same effects using the DOM directly, we would end up writing much more code, and we'd have much greater scope for introducing errors.

Frequently, we'll want to modify the relationship between DOM elements, as well as modify the elements themselves. In the next section, we'll look at the Insertion name space, which provides methods to help us do just this.

11.2.3 *Insertion objects*

In section 11.1.2, we saw how to insert elements into the DOM using `append-Child()` and `insertBefore()`. These methods allow for flexible placement of elements, but they require DOM elements as arguments. If we're going to add new content to the document, creating these nodes can be an arduous task. We also saw the power of `innerHTML` to quickly and painlessly create new content, and how Prototype's `Element.update()` and `Element.replace()` extend the power of `innerHTML` a little.

Prototype also provides a set of objects under the Insertion namespace that give us the best of both worlds, allowing us to construct content as HTML strings and still place it precisely where we want it in an existing document.

Snippet 11.19 shows the first of the Insertion objects, Insertion.Top, in action.

Snippet 11.19

```
new Insertion.Top("list","<p>let's count to three!</p>");
```

In a single line of code, we can resolve the DOM element and add new content of arbitrary complexity. The Insertion.Top object takes two arguments. The first is a reference to a DOM node, which can be either a direct programmatic reference or an ID; internally, Insertion objects use $() to resolve the first argument. The second object is the HTML to be added.

This style of object, in which existing elements in the document are modified, should be familiar from the Scriptaculous effects, controls, and drag-and-drop systems. Prototype and Scriptaculous very rarely create new DOM elements directly.

Insertion.Top has a counterpart, Insertion.Bottom, which adds content at the end of an element (effectively the same as appendChild(), but accepting an HTML string). We can also use Insertion objects to place content relative to existing elements. Snippet 11.20 shows us how.

Snippet 11.20

```
var el=$$("#list li")[1];
highlight(el);
new Insertion.Before(el,"<p>look ma, we're counting!!</p>");
new Insertion.After(el,"<p>look ma, we're still counting!!</p>");
```

Insertion.Before() and Insertion.After() insert the new content as a sibling of the element passed in as the first argument. Here, we've used $$() to resolve a reference to the second list item (which we've highlighted), and then inserted some extra content before and after it.

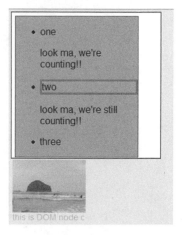

Insertion makes it easy for us to stitch new elements into a document, which is a prerequisite for adding new controls to a UI, for example. Again, Prototype has provided us with new ways of using existing DOM functionality, with vastly improved ease of use. In the next section, we'll look at the Position object, which allows us to manipulate DOM elements in other ways.

11.2.4 *The Position object*

Like the Insertion object, the Position object acts as a namespace for a number of useful functions. Where Insertion was concerned with manipulating the structure of the DOM, Position is concerned with the visual layout of elements. Snippet 11.21 shows us the basic information that the Position object can give us about elements within a page.

Snippet 11.21

```
new Insertion.Bottom(
  document.body,
  "<div id='abs'>hello!</div>"
);

var abs=$("abs");
show("absolute element",
  {
    "real offset" : Position.realOffset(abs),
    "cumulative offset" : Position.cumulativeOffset(abs),
    "positioned offset" : Position.positionedOffset(abs)
  }
);

var rel=$("b");
highlight(rel);
show("relative element",
  {
    "real offset" : Position.realOffset(rel),
    "cumulative offset" : Position.cumulativeOffset(rel),
    "positioned offset" : Position.positionedOffset(rel)
  }
);
```

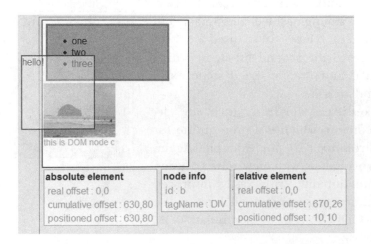

At the start of this snippet, we created an extra DOM element, which we added to the page using an Insertion object. The CSS styling for this element gives it an absolute position. That is, it is positioned exactly on the page relative to the top-left corner of the document, and it isn't controlled by the browser's layout engine. The default CSS position is relative, which means that the browser manages the layout. The CSS styling also specifies a 50 percent opacity. The new element can be seen overlaying the original markup, with the image and list showing through it.

The Position object has a number of methods for querying the position of a DOM element. The `realOffset()` method returns the offset resulting from any scrolling of the page, or of any elements on the path between this node and the document root. If no scrolling elements are present or parents or grandparents of this element, `realOffset()` will return 0 for both coordinates.

The `positionedOffset()` method returns the offset of this element relative to its immediate container. For relatively positioned objects, this will be the offset from the immediate parent node. For absolutely positioned elements, this will be the position relative to the entire document. The `cumulativeOffset()` method returns the offset of this element from the top of the document root regardless of the positioning type, iterating up the document tree to the root in the case of relatively positioned elements.

Our snippet has requested all three offset positions from the newly created element, and from the gray element housing the list, which is highlighted. As there are no scrolling regions, the `realOffset` for both is 0 along both coordinates. The `positionedOffset` and `cumulativeOffset` are the same for the absolutely positioned element, but are radically different for the relatively positioned one. Within the coordinate space of its immediate parent (that is, the `positionedOffset`), the element is only ten pixels from the origin. Relative to the entire document, however, it is over 600 pixels to the left, and 26 pixels from the top.

In different situations, being able to access both coordinate spaces are useful. The Position object gives us a simple cross-browser way of getting this information. However, it provides additional functionality beyond this basic capability, which we'll examine in snippet 11.22.

Snippet 11.22

```
new Insertion.Bottom(
  document.body,
  "<div id='abs'>hello!</div>"
);

var abs=$("abs");
```

```
var pos=Position.cumulativeOffset($("c"));
show(
    "node c within transparent area?",
    Position.within(abs,pos[0],pos[1])
);
```

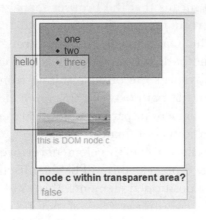 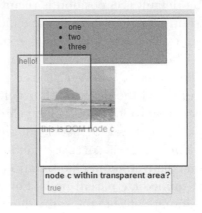

Once again, we've added the absolutely positioned semiopaque element, which overlaps the existing content. Because of rendering differences between the two browsers (Firefox on the left, Internet Explorer on the right), the new element overlaps DOM node *c* in one browser but not the other. Using `Position.within()`, we can programmatically detect this.

`Position.within()` takes three arguments. The first is a DOM element; the second and third are coordinate points, relative to the entire document. `Position.within()` returns `true` or `false` depending on whether the point lies within the DOM element, the position of which is calculated using `cumulativeOffset()`. Optionally, scrolling offsets can be taken into account or ignored.

The `cumulativeOffset()` method allows us to calculate the layout of absolutely and relatively positioned elements in a common coordinate system. On top of this, the Position object provides the `absolutize()` and `relativize()` methods for switching a DOM element between the two positioning types without altering its position on the page. (This is a very useful feature for the drag-and-drop system, for example.) Snippet 11.23 shows these methods in action. In this snippet, we're modifying the same element several times, so we've taken more than one screenshot, as indicated in the comments. To recreate the effect, copy the snippet code into the Scratchpad in stages, and then run the code.

Snippet 11.23

```
var el=$("b");
highlight(el);

Element.setStyle( el,
  {top: "100px", left: "100px" }
);
//screenshot 1 taken here

Position.absolutize(el);
//screenshot 2 taken here

Element.setStyle( el,
  {top: "100px", left: "100px" }
);
//screenshot 3 taken here
```

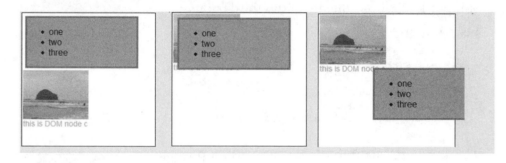

In snippet 11.23, we're operating on the element containing the list again. Initially, it's relatively positioned, so when we set its top and left style properties, it didn't move (as shown in the leftmost image). this is correct behavior for CSS.

We then made the element absolute, using Position.absolutize(). This effectively removed it from the calculated layout, making the image and subsequent content slide up behind it (as in the center image). The list element itself stayed where it was.

When we tried to set the top and left style properties again, the element responded (as seen in the rightmost image). Since it is absolutely positioned, it can be moved around the page.

Let's take a look now at the final method of the Position object, clone(). Position.clone() will set the size and position of one DOM element to match another. Snippet 11.24 shows it at work.

Snippet 11.24

```
var el=$("a");
var el2=$("b");

Position.clone(el,el2);
```

The `clone()` method takes two arguments. The first is the element to copy, and the second is the target element. In this case, the source is the top-level element in our markup, and the target is the gray element containing the list. CSS margins prevent an exact match, but the overlap is close.

`clone()` accepts an optional third argument, which contains the extra configuration information. Snippet 11.25 shows the use of this third parameter.

Snippet 11.25

```
var el=$("a");
var el2=$("b");

Position.absolutize(el2);
Position.clone(el,el2,
  { setHeight: false, offsetTop: 80, offsetLeft: 0 }
);
```

The third argument to `clone()` accepts six possible options: `setLeft`, `setTop`, `setWidth`, and `setHeight` are Boolean elements, and will determine whether the element is cloned or resized when it moves; `offsetTop` and `offsetLeft` take numerical values, and allow us to offset the cloned element from its source. In the snippet, we elected not to modify the height, and to offset the height by 80 pixels. As a result, only the width of the target has been modified, and it has been positioned below the top of the source.

That concludes our review of the Position object, and of Prototype's support for the DOM. So far, we've looked at ways of modifying the elements that are displayed on a page. This, of course, is only half of the job of building a user interface, the other half being the interactive behavior that we assign to the on-screen elements. In an Ajax app, interactivity is provided by the JavaScript event model. In the next section, we'll see what Prototype can do for JavaScript events.

11.3 *Extending the Event object*

Interactivity is the core differentiator between Ajax/DHTML web apps and classic web documents. The event-handling system that allows JavaScript code to respond to user input is at the heart of this.

Unfortunately, event handling using JavaScript in the web browser has suffered from a rather checkered history. As a legacy of the development of browsers, most modern systems provide two ways of working with mouse and keyboard events. The simple model allows a single event handler to be attached to each element. The more complex W3C standard, based on the Observer pattern, allows multiple event handlers to register for notification when an event occurs. While this standard is superior in principle, different browsers support the W3C model in widely different ways, making cross-browser event handling much more difficult under the W3C approach than using the simple model.

Prototype's Event object provides a cross-browser wrapper around the W3C/Observer-based approach, through the `Event.observe()` method. Snippet 11.26 shows it in use, adding some interactive feedback on mouse movements to the output panel of the Scratchpad.

Snippet 11.26

```
Event.observe(
  "output",
  'mousemove',
  function(event){
     var el=Event.element(event);
     el.innerHTML=Event.pointerX(event)+" x "+Event.pointerY(event);
  }
)
```

`Event.observe()` takes three arguments. The first is a reference to the DOM element to which the event handler should be attached—either a direct reference to a DOM node, or an ID, thanks to `$()`. The second argument defines the type of event, and the third is a callback function that takes an Event object as an argument when it is invoked.

In this case, the snippet writes the current mouse coordinates into the element whenever the mouse moves over it. This allows us to demonstrate another feature of the Event object, the `pointerX()` and `pointerY()` methods. The built-in Java-Script Event object provides the mouse position under several coordinate systems under different browsers, but it doesn't offer a coordinate system relative to the top of the page under all browsers. Prototype fills in this gap for us.

The final enhancement that Prototype offers to the event-handling system relates to the event-handler functions themselves. When an event-handler function is passed to the browser, the browser later invokes it, and when it does so, it switches the context object to the DOM element that received the event (see chapter 9 for an explanation of function context objects). When writing simple code, this isn't much of a concern, but when we're wrapping up functionality in objects, it can be disconcerting to have object methods in which the variable this doesn't refer to the object itself.

In snippet 11.27, we have turned our mouse coordinate code from snippet 11.26 into a reusable object.

Snippet 11.27

```
MouseTracker=Class.create();
MouseTracker.prototype={
  initialize:function(name,el){
    this.name=name;
    this.el=$(el);
    this.setEvent();
  },
  setEvent:function(){
    Event.observe(
      this.el,
      'mousemove',
      function(event){
        var el=Event.element(event);
        el.innerHTML=this.name
          +" says "
          +Event.pointerX(event)
          +" x "
          +Event.pointerY(event);
      }.bindAsEventListener(this)
    );
  }
}

new MouseTracker("mighty mouse","output");
```

In the setEvent() method of our MouseTracker object, we create an anonymous function. Rather than just printing the coordinates of the mouse, we want to add the name of our object, which we would ordinarily reference as this.name. However, if the event handler is going to have its context switched, this.name won't resolve to what we want.

> mighty mouse says 697 x 254

We saw in chapter 9 that Prototype provided an extension to the Function prototype called bind(), which allowed us to determine our own context object. Here, we've used a specialist version of that called `bindAsEventListener()`, which allows us to write our event-handler code in a natural way, with `this` referring to our MouseTracker object.

The final piece of Prototype's DOM functionality is its support for HTML forms. We'll look at that in the next section.

11.4 Working with HTML forms

We can only get so far in an Ajax application by providing interactivity within the client-side UI. Sooner or later, we're going to need to communicate with the server. HTML forms are the backbone of server communication in most classic web applications; in an Ajax-based web application, there is more scope for other forms of interaction, but forms still play an important role.

The Form namespace in Prototype provides a lot of useful support for working with HTML forms, again, making it simpler and easier to get the job done. In this section, we've modified our Scratchpad application to include some Form elements in the output window. Run the modified Scratchpad application, which can be found in the download bundle as scratchpad/ps-form-sandbox.html. Listing 11.2 shows the additional HTML markup for this form.

Listing 11.2 HTML markup for test form

```
<form id='myForm'>
<div>
<table>
<tr>
<td>
What is your name?
</td>
<td>
<input type='text' name='name' id='name'>
</td>
</tr>
<tr>
<td>
What is your favorite color?
</td>
<td><select name='favColor' id='favColor'>
<option>blue</option>
<option>no, green</option>
<option>I mean red (I think!)</option>
</select>
</td>
</tr>
<tr>
```

```
<td colspan='2'>
<input type='checkbox' id='plate' name='plate'> Would you say no if it were
    handed to you on a plate?
</td>
</tr>
</table>
</form>
```

The simplest and most useful helper function that Prototype provides is, as always, the one with the shortest name. `$F()` allows us to read the value of a form element based on its ID attribute. Snippet 11.28 shows how it works.

Snippet 11.28

```
var results=[
  $F('name'),
  $F('favColor'),
  $F('plate')
];

show("form data",results);
```

The best feature of `$F()` is that it works across all form element types. Using the form elements themselves, we have a bewildering array of properties to choose from, including `value` for text inputs, `checked` for checkboxes, and an options array for drop-down lists. `$F()` provides a single point of entry that works for all form elements.

In a classic web application, HTML forms will typically be submitted and serialized as querystrings by the browser. In an Ajax application, we may well submit the form programmatically, after validation. To this end, Prototype provides a `serialize()` method that captures the current state of the form. Snippet 11.29 uses this in conjunction with the `Form.reset()` method to demonstrate the live nature of the querystring.

Snippet 11.29

```
show("form data",Form.serialize('myForm'));

Form.reset('myForm');

show("after reset", Form.serialize('myForm'));
```

What is your name?	
What is your favorite color?	blue ▾
☐ Would you say no if it were handed to you on a plate?	

form data
name=dave&plate=on&favColor=I%20mean%20red%20(I%20think!)

after reset
name=&favColor=blue

Note that form data has been automatically URL-encoded, making it suitable for POSTing to the server using an Ajax.Request object or a similar method. The checkbox element called `plate` is omitted from the querystring if it isn't checked.

It's worth pointing out that `serialize()` requires that the `name` attribute of form elements be set. `$F()`, in contrast, works on the `id` attribute, so if you're planning on using both, you'll need to set the `name` and `id` attributes, as we did in listing 11.2.

A more complex part of the Form package is the support for observers, both on individual form elements, and on the form as a whole. Snippet 11.30 shows how to set an observer on a single element.

Snippet 11.30

```
new Form.Element.Observer(
  "favColor",
  2,
  function(el,value){
    show($F("name")+" likes...",value);
  }
);
```

What is your name?	dave
What is your favorite color?	I mean red (I think!) ▾
☐ Would you say no if it were handed to you on a plate?	

dave likes...	**dave likes...**
no, green	I mean red (I think!)

The Form.Element.Observer takes three arguments. The first is the element to observe, the second is the frequency with which to check for changes, and the third is a callback function. The callback is invoked whenever the value of the form has changed; it passes in the element and the new value as arguments.

In snippet 11.30, we attached an observer to the drop-down list, which will display a message in the Scratchpad output window whenever the value changes. For drop-down elements, this is similar to setting an onchange event handler, but for text input elements, it allows us to capture input regularly, as the user types.

We can do the same for entire forms, setting up an observer to watch for any changes to any form element. Snippet 11.31 shows this at work.

Snippet 11.31

```
new Form.Observer(
  "myForm",
  2,
  function(el,value){
    show("form data set to...",value);
  }
);
```

Here, we're using a Form.Observer rather than a Form.Element.Observer, but the principle is the same. In fact, they share a common parent class, the Abstract.TimedObserver. In this case, the value passed in to the callback is the serialized form, which may be useful for periodic server-side validation. The element is the element that has changed.

If we want to observe all form elements individually, we can set a Form.Element.Observer on each element independently, as in snippet 11.32.

Snippet 11.32

```
Form.getElements('myForm').each(
  function(formEl){
    new Form.Element.Observer(
      formEl,
      2,
      function(el,value){
        show(el.id+" set to...",value);
      }
    )
  }
);
```

This snippet illustrates the useful `Form.getElements()` method, which returns an Array of all the elements in a form. Setting individual observers in this way gives us a fine-grained view of changes to the form.

That concludes our tour of Prototype's support for working with HTML forms, and its support for DOM programming in general. With Forms, as with the Element, Position, and Insertion namespaces, and the simple helper functions, the emphasis has been on identifying common programming tasks and making them easier. Because of the large number of methods and helpers that Prototype provides, we've confined ourselves to simple examples. In the next chapter, we'll see how some of these methods work in a real application.

11.5 Summary

Working with DOM is a broad subject, and the Prototype library tackles it very comprehensively. We've covered a lot of ground in this chapter, touching on several subsystems in the library.

We began by looking at the support for DOM manipulation, and we moved on through event handling and HTML forms. In all cases, Prototype not only provides easy-to-use cross-browser support for existing functionality, but also extends the reach of the developer by making more complex but common tasks easy to do.

In the field of DOM manipulation, $() not only reduces typing, but offers a more flexible set of arguments, and allows us to resolve multiple nodes at once. Similarly, $$() opens up the full power of CSS selectors. Element builds upon these basic helpers to provide a powerful set of general-purpose additions to the DOM for working with visibility, content, CSS styling, and more. The Position object offers a uniform coordinate space across browsers, but also provides useful methods for working with that coordinate space, such as checking for overlap and swapping object layout positioning between absolute and relative.

Event observers make the more powerful W3C event model usable, and Form observers enable easy validation and interactive form checking.

We've now concluded our review of Prototype, which we started in chapter 8. In the next part of the book, we'll apply our knowledge of Prototype and Scriptaculous by looking at how we can apply the libraries to a real application when we revisit the QuickGallery application that we introduced in chapters 2–4.

Part 4

Advanced Topics

This final part of the book contains a couple of chapters that round out our discussion of Prototype and Scriptaculous. Having spent parts 2 and 3 looking close-up at the details of the libraries, we now pan out to take another look at the bigger picture.

Chapter 12 returns to the QuickGallery application that we presented in chapters 2 through 4, and gives it a significant makeover, using several features from the Scriptaculous libraries. Along the way, we also showcase a number of Prototype's features and demonstrate how the two libraries can be put to work in a setting closer to a real-world project.

Chapter 13 brings the spotlight to bear on a facet of Prototype and Scriptaculous that we've been downplaying until now, namely Ruby on Rails. While the emphasis throughout this book has been on using these libraries alongside any server-side environment, be it Java, PHP, .NET, or whatever else, Rails, Prototype, and Scriptaculous have grown up together, and they have some very neat integration features. For those of you using Rails, this chapter will provide a handy reference on how to make Prototype and Scriptaculous even easier to use. And for those of you not using Rails, maybe it will provide inspiration on how to integrate the JavaScript libraries with your own server-side frameworks.

Prototype and Scriptaculous in Practice

12

This chapter covers

- Using Prototype and Scriptaculous in a production setting
- Formulating a drag-and-drop strategy
- Using the Scriptaculous in-place editor
- Writing your own Effects classes

In the previous two parts of the book, we covered Scriptaculous and Prototype with a fine-toothed comb and learned a lot about the details of the libraries. We're going to round off that knowledge in this chapter with an in-depth example of a moderately complex application.

Remember the QuickGallery application that we introduced in chapter 2, and Ajax-enabled in chapters 3 and 4? By the end of chapter 4, we had streamlined the navigation of the images on the filesystem by using Ajax, but it was still basically a file browser. Having the filesystem contents available over the Web is nice for remote access, but any desktop operating system would provide us with this sort of functionality anyway. Having seen what Prototype and Scriptaculous can do, we're going to add some new functionality that the average desktop file explorer doesn't have. This will give us a chance to see how Prototype and Scriptaculous perform in a real-world setting, and to encounter some of the design issues that you might come across in your own projects. Let's begin by sketching out the requirements for our extended functionality.

12.1 QuickGallery application requirements

In this chapter, we're going to use a number of the features of Scriptaculous and Prototype in something much closer to a real-world development project, so that we can see how they complement one another. We also want to illustrate the process of deciding when to make use of Prototype and Scriptaculous. Between them, they offer a dizzying array of rich features, and if we try to shoehorn everything into a single project just because it's there, we risk ending up with a mess. So the first step we need to take is to figure out what features our application actually requires. Then we can decide where our favorite libraries can assist us.

Let's consider what we want out of the Web 2.0 version of QuickGallery. Version 1 uses the filesystem to organize the images that it displays. This restricts it to a hierarchical classification, in which any image can belong to one and only one category. Hierarchical classifications are limited, and one of the common themes of the Web 2.0 world is looking at alternative ways of storing and retrieving information. Tagging resources is one commonly adopted approach. Virtual folders are another, with the selection being made either manually, or automatically by a search algorithm or similar query.

We want to make the selection and presentation of images more flexible for QuickGallery. The solution that we've adopted for this example is to allow the user to gather images together as slideshows, which will be played automatically and can be stored on the server and retrieved for replaying later. While putting together the slideshow, the user will also be allowed to add a caption underneath each slide. A picture may be worth a thousand words, but words and pictures combined are even more powerful, whether you're simply reporting on a weekend trip or vacation, or baring your soul with some Web 2.0 high art.

The requirements for our extensions to QuickGallery are as follows, then:

- A slideshow can be composed of an arbitrary number of images, taken from any number of filesystem folders.
- Each slide in the slideshow can have a caption as well as an image.
- The slideshow can be edited within the application—slides can be added, deleted, and reordered, and captions can be modified.
- Slideshows can be saved to the server, and be easily retrieved.

There are two fairly separate pieces of functionality involved here. First, we need a slideshow editor. Secondly, we need a slideshow player. We'll begin by developing the editor in the next section.

12.2 Building the slideshow editor

We've already outlined the basic requirements for the slideshow editor. Before we begin implementing it, we need to figure out how the user interface is going to work. First, we need to establish the layout of the modified app, which we'll do next.

Developing a layout is only half of establishing a web app design. The key to the success of our app will be how easy it is to use, so we'll need to understand how the workflow operates and how the user interacts with the app. Only then can we turn to the third task, which is figuring out how to implement the design.

12.2.1 Modifying the page layout

Let's begin by reviewing the layout of the QuickGallery application as it was at the end of chapter 4. We've sketched out a simple representation of the page layout in figure 12.1.

The UI is composed of three main areas. The breadcrumb trail and subfolder list provide easy navigation around the filesystem, and the thumbnail area provides previews of the contents of the current folder. The thumbnail area will automatically expand to fit the number of thumbnail images in the folder. We deliberately chose to do this so that the UI elements themselves would not need to scroll. In a folder containing lots of images, the thumbnail region will simply expand beyond

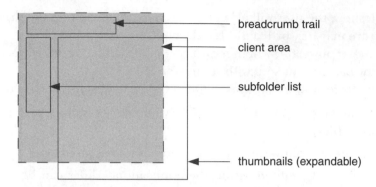

Figure 12.1 Layout of version 1 of QuickGallery. We allowed the thumbnails region to expand to accommodate all thumbnails and to resize with the client window.

the browser window's client area (that is, the body of the browser in which the HTML is rendered). We can continue to allow the thumbnail region to expand in this way, provided all additional controls are situated to the top or left.

Because we are enhancing QuickGallery in this chapter, we will need to add several new UI elements to support the extra functionality. First, we'll need to list all the slideshows that are stored on the server. Second, we'll need a toolbar or menu to perform some of the actions, such as saving and playing slideshows. We've decided to add these elements along the left side, as shown in figure 12.2.

As part of our modification to the application, we've decided to constrain the thumbnail region to a fixed size. We'll provide it with its own scroll bars if the thumbnails in a folder won't otherwise fit. Why have we done this? The reason is that we still have several other UI elements to add, as illustrated in figure 12.3.

When composing a slideshow, we'll want to be able to roam freely across the file-system, using the existing functionality. We therefore need a separate UI element to

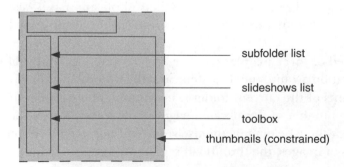

Figure 12.2 Modifying the left side to incorporate additional elements

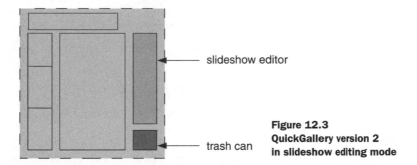

slideshow editor

**Figure 12.3
QuickGallery version 2
in slideshow editing mode**

trash can

provide a view of the slideshow in progress. This will need to be large enough to accommodate thumbnail images and reasonably large captions. We can't, therefore, fit it into the top or left areas without getting crowded. We've decided to add it to the right side of the UI, and to place a trash can underneath it for disposing of unwanted elements in the slideshow.

Because the slideshow editor and trash can will take up a lot of room, we've chosen to make the application modal, allowing us to show or hide the elements on the right side, and to expand or shrink the thumbnail area to fit the available space.

We can implement most of these changes in CSS. Listing 12.1 shows the additional CSS classes that we've defined to support our revised layout.

Listing 12.1   Additions to images.css to support the QuickGallery v2 layout

```
#images{
  top: 35px;
  left: 185px;
  width: 600px;
  height: 600px;
  overflow: auto;
  overflow-x: hidden;
  border: solid #888 1px;
}
#SlideshowName{
  top: 35px;
  left: 595px;
  width:150px;
  height: 30px;
  margin: 2px;
  font-size: 11px;
}
#slides{
  top: 71px;
```

```
    left: 595px;
    width: 150px;
    height: 458px;
    overflow: auto;
    overflow-x: hidden;
    align: center;
    background-color: #888;
}
#trash{
    top: 544px;
    left: 595px;
    width: 148px;
    height: 90px;
    background-color: #444;
    background-image: url(../icons/edittrash.png);
    background-repeat:no-repeat;
    border: solid black 2px;
}
.hidden{
    display: none;
}
```

The element with ID images, referenced by the first rule in listing 12.1, has had width and height added. These represent the dimensions in normal mode. When we flip to slideshow editing mode, we'll have to programmatically reset the width, as we'll see later. The overflow styles are set to allow vertical scroll bars only. If we allowed horizontal scroll bars, it would interfere with drag and drop in this layout, as we'll see later. The majority of the remaining CSS classes simply represent the new elements that we've discussed.

Note that we've provided a CSS class called hidden, which we can apply and unapply to hide or show the editor components. Listing 12.2 shows the code that switches the application from normal browsing to slideshow editing mode.

Listing 12.2   Initializing the UI

```
initUI:function(htmlContent){
  this.body.innerHTML='';
  Element.removeClassName(this.body,"hidden");          ❶ Remove hidden
  Element.removeClassName('trash',"hidden");               CSS class
  Element.removeClassName('SlideshowName',"hidden");
  Element.hide('closeup');
  Element.show('images');     ❷ Reduce thumbnail
  Element.setStyle(      ⤶        area width
    'images',
    { width: "396px" }
```

```
);
if (htmlContent){
  this.loadContent(htmlContent);
}
this.initDragDrop();
if (this.name && this.name.length>0){          ❸ Use existing
  $('SlideshowName').value=this.name;              name
}else{
  new Effect.Pulsate(
    'SlideshowName',                           Notify user with
    {                                        ❹ Pulsate effect
      duration: 2,
      beforeStart:function(){
        $('SlideshowName').value='please provide a name';
      },
      afterFinish:function(){
        var txtBox=$('SlideshowName');
        txtBox.value='';
        txtBox.focus();
      }
    }
  );
}
},
```

All functionality related to the slideshow has been coded into a separate file called slideshow.js, from which listing 12.2 and several subsequent listings are taken. The file defines an object called SlideShow with several methods. The initUI() method is responsible for revealing the extra elements when we go into editing mode. We use methods of the Element object, as discussed in chapter 11, to remove the CSS class hidden ❶ and to resize the thumbnail area ❷.

We can enter edit mode in two ways: we can create a brand new slideshow, or we can reopen an existing slideshow. Slideshows are stored by name, and we provide a text box immediately above the editor, in which the slideshow's name is shown. If we open an existing slideshow, the name is already determined, so we just quietly enter it into the text input box ❸. If, however, the name is not known, we will need the user to provide a name before the slideshow can be saved. We need to draw their attention to the text box, and Scriptaculous comes to our aid here with the Pulsate effect ❹.

That's all the code that we need to manage our layout. To display the Quick-Gallery application, specify the URL as http://localhost/album/slideshow/ (assuming you've installed QuickGallery under the web server root in a directory

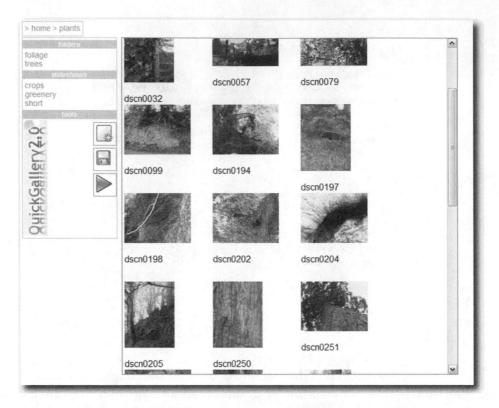

Figure 12.4   Screenshot of QuickGallery v2 in normal browsing mode. The slideshow editor components are hidden, and the thumbnail area is expanded to full size.

called album. Full setup instructions are provided in appendix D). Figure 12.4 shows QuickGallery v2 in normal browsing mode. Figure 12.5 shows the changes to the UI when we enter slideshow editing mode, while browsing the same folder.

Now that we have a static layout for our application, we need to consider interactivity. Building slideshows by browsing through images is an activity that seems well-suited to a drag-and-drop interaction model. Because Scriptaculous makes drag and drop so easy, as we saw in chapter 7, we'll go for it. In the next section, we'll define an interaction model for editing slideshows using drag and drop, and then we'll implement it using the Scriptaculous features we discussed in chapter 7.

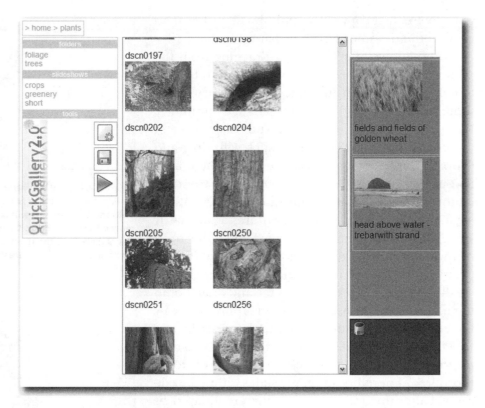

Figure 12.5 Screenshot of QuickGallery v2 in slideshow editing mode. The thumbnail area has been squeezed horizontally to make room for (top to bottom) the slideshow-name text box, the main editor, and the trash can

12.2.2 Defining a drag-and-drop strategy

OK, so we want to use drag and drop. We need to figure out what sorts of operations we want to allow.

First, we want to be able to drag thumbnails from the main thumbnail window onto the slide editor panel on the right, as illustrated in figure 12.6. There are two key characteristics to this operation. First, it's one way. We don't want to allow images from the slideshow to be dragged onto the thumbnail area—we aren't looking to create a general-purpose Ajax file manager here! Second, when we drag a thumbnail onto the slideshow editor, we

Figure 12.6 Drag operation 1—we want to be able to drag thumbnails from the main viewer onto the slide show editor. When dropped, a copy is created.

want to create a copy of the thumbnail, rather than remove the thumbnail from its parent folder.

Although we aren't allowing dragging from the editor to the thumbnail area, we do want to be able to delete images from the slideshow, in case we drag something in by accident, or just change our minds. We could add a delete button next to each image in the editor, but we've chosen to stick with drag and drop, and to provide a trash can below the editor. So our second drag-and-drop operation is from the editor to the trash can, as illustrated in figure 12.7.

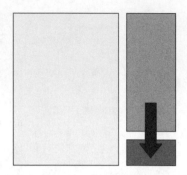

Figure 12.7 Drag operation 2—if a slide from the editor is dragged onto the trash can, it will be removed from the editor. Ordinary thumbnails from the main panel don't interact with the trash can.

The rules for this interaction are, again, fairly straightforward. Elements dragged onto the trash can will disappear from the editor, and won't reappear in the trash can. If we want to reverse a deletion, we simply browse back to the image and drag it onto the editor again. Also, the trash can is only for use by the editor pane, not the main thumbnail area.

The final drag-and-drop operation that we want to perform is to allow the slideshow in progress to be reordered. Therefore, dragging slides within the editor will alter the order in which they are dislayed, as shown in figure 12.8.

Putting everything together, we've defined a fairly complex drag-and-drop model here that will allow our users to create and edit slideshows in a fluid and intuitive way. If we were to code this ourselves using the raw DOM event model, we would

Figure 12.8 Drag operation 3— slides can be reordered within the editor using drag and drop

have set ourselves quite a task, but, fortunately, Scriptaculous has done a lot of the hard work for us already. In the next section, you'll see just how easy it can be to implement drag and drop, even for a reasonably complex interaction model such as the one that we've described here.

12.2.3 *Implementing drag and drop*

We chose to adopt drag and drop as the primary interaction model for building and editing slideshows in our QuickGallery v2 app because of its intuitive nature. In the previous section, we defined the details of the interaction model, in terms of which on-screen elements can be dragged, and which containers or drop zones are allowed to receive them. The rules that we came up with are nontrivial. Further, they will only apply when the app is running in editing mode, as opposed to the file browsing mode provided by version 1, and still supported in version 2.

We will wrap up all the slideshow functionality in a SlideShow object. We'll define a method that initializes the drag-and-drop capabilities, which is shown in listing 12.3, and we'll figure out when to call it as we proceed with the development.

Listing 12.3 Setting up drag and drop

```
initDragDrop:function(){          ❶ Enable
  Sortable.create(          ⤶        thumbnails
    'images',
    {
      tag: "div",                ❷ Exclude self from
      containment:[this.body],  ⤶  drop targets
      constraint: false,
      ghosting: true
    }
  );
                          ❸ Add editor as
                              drop target
  Droppables.add(    ⤶
    this.body,
    {
      onDrop:function(tile,target){
        if (tile.className=="slide"){ return; }  ❹ Duplicate
        this.createSlide(tile,target);    ⤶          thumbnail

      }.bind(this)
    }
  );
                    ❺ Add trash can
                        as drop target
  Droppables.add(    ⤶
    'trash',
    {
      onDrop:function(tile,target){
        if (tile.className=="slide"){
          tile.remove();
          if (this.trashEffect){
            this.trashEffect.cancel();          ❻ Reset
          }                                        or start
          this.trashEffect=new Effect.Pulsate(target);  effect
        }

      }.bind(this)
    }
  );

},
```

The initDragDrop() method takes care of the first two operations as described in the previous section. First, we made the thumbnail region into a Sortable ❶. Note that the containment option, which lists valid drop zones, contains only the slide-show editor ❷. Normally, Sortables will include themselves, allowing reordering of elements within the container. In this case, however, we don't have a use for reordering images within the thumbnail region, so we prevent it from happening. We don't need to define any callbacks for the Sortable, as the slideshow editor will take care of anything dropped onto it.

We defined two drag-and-drop interactions on the slideshow editor. First, it needs to accept slides from the thumbnails region, and second, it needs to allow sorting of its own members. We'll defer the second interaction until the next listing. Here, we register the editor as a simple drop zone ❸ and call a cre-ateSlide() method to duplicate the incoming thumbnail ❹. Note that in the callback we first check the CSS class name of the tile being dropped onto the target. We bail out of the method if the tile has come from the editor, because that is simply a sort operation, not the introduction of a new slide.

Finally, we register the trash can as a drop zone ❺. We want to provide notification when a slide is removed, and we've decided to stick with the Pulsate effect that we used earlier, to give visual consistency to our application. We want to have a maximum of one effect operating on the trash can at a time, so when we create the effect, we keep a reference to it and cancel any existing one before starting up another ❻. This technique can be useful when dealing with many effects. If you want to see what happens without canceling the effects, comment out the call to cancel() and then drag several slides quickly onto the trash. The results can be rather unpredictable!

The initDragDrop() method provides the interactivity to several parts of the UI. Unfortunately, as we browse the filesystem, we're continually refreshing the thumbnail component, which is an important part of our drag-and-drop system. We therefore need to call initDragDrop() whenever we browse to a new folder. Unfortunately, the event handlers for browsing between folders are located in a different JavaScript object, images.js. If we make calls from there to methods on our Slideshow object, our code starts to become tangled and tightly coupled. We need some sort of loosely coupled notification system.

Rather than write our own, we've made use of the Prototype Ajax Responder objects that we discussed in chapter 4. Any number of Ajax Responders can be registered with the Prototype Ajax stack, and they will be notified of incoming Ajax responses. Browsing between folders is accomplished using Ajax, so all we need to do is add a flag to the X-JSON header of the response, saying that this response is of type "folder," and we can define a responder to reset the drag-and-drop system once the new folder is loaded. We can do this in a few lines of code when initializing the SlideShow object, as follows:

```
Ajax.Responders.register(
  {
    onComplete:function(request,transport,json){
      if (json && 'folder'==json.action){
        this.initDragDrop();
      }
    }.bind(this)
  }
);
```

The `json` argument passed in to the callback represents the parsed X-JSON header. Note that `initDragDrop()` is a method of the SlideShow object, so we use `Function.bind()` to switch the context of the callback, as discussed in chapter 9. With this in place, `initDragDrop()` will be called automatically whenever the user browses to a different folder, and the thumbnails in that folder will be ready to drag onto the slideshow editor.

The final piece of the drag-and-drop puzzle is implementing the sorting of the slides in the slideshow. We do this by using `Sortable.create()`, as with the thumbnails, but we'll need to recreate the Sortable even more frequently; in fact, every time a new slide is added to the slideshow. We therefore haven't included that operation in `initDragDrop()`, but as part of the creation of the editable slide, as we'll see in the next section.

12.2.4 *Providing editable captions*

With the majority of the drag-and-drop functionality in place, we can now add and remove images from our slideshow. To complete the functionality required of the slideshow editor, we need to be able to sort the slide order and edit the captions on the slides.

In listing 12.3, we invoked a `createSlide()` method on the SlideShow object whenever a thumbnail was dragged onto the editor panel. Listing 12.4 shows the details of that method.

Listing 12.4   createSlide:function(tile,target){

```
var newSlide=Builder.node(       ◄───❶ Create new element
  "div", { className: "slide" }
);
newSlide.innerHTML=tile.innerHTML;    ◄─┐ ❷ Copy
target.appendChild(newSlide);            ┘   contents
```

```
var img=newSlide.getElementsByTagName("img")[0];        ❸ Remove close-
img.onclick=null;                                    ⟵⎯⎯⎯⎤    up capability
var caption=newSlide.getElementsByTagName("p")[0];
newSlide.fullSrc=img.src.replace("120","420");
newSlide.slideId=caption.firstChild.data;
new Ajax.InPlaceEditor(  ⟵⎯⎤    Enable caption
  caption,                    ❹  editing
  "echo.php",
  {
    rows:3,
    cols:36,
    submitOnBlur: true,
    okButton: false
  }                   ❺ Inform the
);                       server
new Ajax.Request(  ⟵⎤
  "thumbnail.php",
  {
    parameters: $H(
      {name: newSlide.slideId,path:currPath,size:"420"}
    ).toQueryString()
  }                   ❻ Enable slide
);                       sorting
Sortable.create(  ⟵⎤
  this.body,
  {
    tag: "div",
    containment:[this.body,'trash'],
    handle:'img',            ⟵⎯⎯⎯
    constraint: 'vertical',   ❼  Set drag-and-drop
    scroll: true                 handle
  }
);
this.body.scrollTop=this.body.scrollHeight;

},
```

There's a lot of activity going on when we add a new slide to the slideshow, so let's pick through it one step at a time. First, because we're duplicating the element, we need to create a new DOM element to house the duplicate ❶. The house style for Prototype and Scriptaculous tends not to favor DOM element creation, preferring to add behavior to existing elements, but in this case, creating the element programmatically is the right thing to do. Scriptaculous provides a utility object called the Builder that is somewhat easier to use than document.createElement().

Once we've got the duplicate object, we copy the contents across from the thumbnail using innerHTML ❷. This will copy over the visual elements, which we want, but also some behavior, which we don't. Specifically, we don't want to trigger a close-up display of the image when we click on the editor thumbnails, so we set the onclick handler to null ❸. We then add our own behavior to the caption, using the Scriptaculous InPlaceEditor ❹—we've already met this control in chapter 6. We don't have a lot of space in the editor UI, so we pass in some options that will allow the editor to submit when it loses focus, rather than requiring us to click on an OK button. Figure 12.9 shows the in-place editor in action.

When we run the slideshow, we're going to display the images at a larger predetermined size, using a server-side process similar to the one used to create the little thumbnail images (see listing 12.6). We therefore notify the server at this point that a 420-pixel thumbnail will be required ❺. We don't wait for an answer.

Our final task is to refresh the Sortable, so that the newly created slide is draggable within the editor. We use the Sortable.create() method for this ❻, setting the handle option to the <img> tag ❼. This means that only clicking on the image will trigger the drag, although the entire slide will be moved. Otherwise, clicking on the caption would trigger both drag and drop and the in-place editor.

To support the editor component, we need a couple of extra CSS rules. These are shown in listing 12.5.

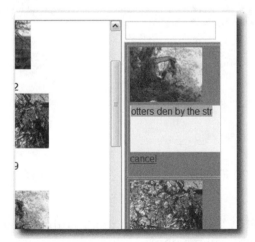

**Figure 12.9
Live editing of a slide captions, using
the InPlaceEditor**

Listing 12.5   CSS for editable slides

```css
#slides{
  top: 71px;
  left: 595px;
  width: 150px;
  height: 458px;
  overflow: auto;
  overflow-x: hidden;
  align: center;
  background-color: #888;
}
.slide{
  width: 160px;
  padding: 3px;
  margin-bottom: 2px;
  border: solid #bbb 1px;
}
```

Finally, listing 12.6 presents the PHP code that we use to generate the thumbnail images, using the GD library. Appendix C discusses the installation of the server-side components for these examples—our aim throughout this book is to focus on the client-side code. Similar image-manipulation libraries are available for other libraries.

Listing 12.6   thumbnail.php

```php
<?php
require('config.php');
require('thumbnail.inc.php');
$basename=$_REQUEST['name'];
$path=$_REQUEST['path'];
$size=$_REQUEST['size'];

ensure_thumbnail($basename,$path,$size);

?>
<h1>done</h1>
```

We've refactored the server-side PHP, breaking out the method that creates the thumbnails into a separate file, thumbnail.inc.php, which can be referenced from here and from the main images.php file that creates the thumbnail view of the current folder. Creating a thumbnail doesn't require any notifications to the client, so we don't bother sending back any X-JSON headers with this response.

We've now got a fully working slideshow editor that allows us to assemble, organize, and annotate images from the main gallery application. In order to satisfy our requirements, the next step is to provide the ability to save slideshows on the server, and to reload them later. Prototype and Scriptaculous will make light work of this task too, as we'll see in the next section.

12.3 Adding Ajax-based persistence

We've come a long way in this chapter in implementing the slideshow features of our next-generation QuickGallery application. However, without the ability to preserve our work on the server, our application isn't going to attract many users. In this section, we'll put this important piece of the jigsaw into place. First, let's consider how we're going to store the data.

12.3.1 Defining the persistence format

Thinking about the design of this application in the abstract, we have a number of choices as to how we could store a slideshow on the server. The crucial information that we need to capture is the path and name of each image, along with any caption that has been assigned to it, and the order of the slides.

We could define a simple XML or text format to store the data, and write some JavaScript to serialize the current slideshow into this format, followed by more code to parse the format back into a live slideshow editing session. If we were being thorough, we would probably want to parse the slideshow data on the server too, and ensure that it was valid before persisting it. If your Ajax app contains sensitive or important data, or a complex object model, we would urge you to follow these good practices.

However, we don't wish to get bogged down in this example by writing a lot of server validation code, nor additional JavaScript to convert between HTML and XML. We've therefore adopted a simpler persistence format; namely, the `innerHTML` of the live slide-editing panel. Let's walk through how it works. First, let's see what we need to do to save a slideshow.

12.3.2 *Saving a slideshow*

Any persistence solution requires two steps: persisting the data to storage, and restoring it. To save our slideshow as HTML, we need to pass the data down to the server, as shown in listing 12.7.

Listing 12.7   The saveSlides() method in JavaScript

```
saveSlides:function(){
  var snapshot=$('slides').innerHTML;
  new Ajax.Request(
    "saveSlides.php",
    {
      method: "post",
      contentType: "text/html",
      requestHeaders: ["X-SLIDENAME",this.name],
      postBody: snapshot
    }
  );
},
```

Getting a snapshot of the data is simply a matter of using the innerHTML property. We can then pass it to the server as a POST request using the Ajax.Request class, passing the HTML as the POST body. We also need to pass the name that we're going to save the slideshow as. We could add this into the POST body, but it's easier to pass it separately as a header, which we've called X-SLIDENAME. We also set the MIME type to text/html, for the sake of correctness.

Listing 12.8 shows the PHP code that parses this on the server.

Listing 12.8   saveSlides.php

```
<?php
require('../config.php');
require('slideshows.inc.php');

$allHeaders=apache_request_headers();
$slideName=$allHeaders['X-SLIDENAME'];
$postBody=$HTTP_RAW_POST_DATA;
if ($slideName!=null && $postBody!=null){
  $filename=$basedir.'/../slides/'.$slideName.'.slides';
  $filehandle=fopen($filename,'w');
  fwrite($filehandle,$postBody);
  fclose($filehandle);
}
```

```
$slideshows=list_slideshows();
if (count($slideshows)>0){
  $slideshow_list='"'.implode('","',$slideshows).'"';
}
$json='{ action:\'save\', slideshows:['.$slideshow_list.'] }';
header('X-JSON: '.$json);
?>
```

In PHP, we read the request headers using the `apache_request_headers()` array. If you're not running PHP on an Apache server, your mileage may vary here—consult your web server manual in case of problems, and have a look at appendix E for some useful hints. The raw POST data can be read from the `$HTTP_RAW_POST_DATA` variable. Because the POST body is not a URL-encoded querystring, as a request from an HTML form would be, the `$_REQUEST` and `$_POST` variables won't be populated.

If we successfully get the POST body and the slideshow name, we write the data to a file in the slides folder. We then list all the slideshow files in the folder, and construct a JSON header to pass back up to the client. We set the `action` property of this JSON object to save, so as not to trigger the client-side Ajax Responder that refreshes the drag-and-drop system.

The reason for passing a JSON header back here is to refresh the list of slides in the left side of the UI. If the slideshow we've just saved has been saved for the first time, it won't already be displayed there, and we might as well catch any updates by other users while we're at it. Listing 12.9 shows the code needed to register this Ajax Responder.

Listing 12.9 Updating the slides list

```
Ajax.Responders.register(
  {
    onComplete:function(request,transport,json){
      if (json && json.slideshows){
        SlideShow.showSlideshows(json.slideshows);
      }
    }
  }
);
```

There's not a lot to see here, as we delegate most of the action to a method of the SlideShow object. Listing 12.10 gives the lowdown on this.

Listing 12.10   SlideShow.showSlideshows()

```
showSlideshows:function(slideshows){
  if (slideshows.length==0){
    Element.hide("slideshows");
  }else{
    Element.show("slideshows");
    $("slideshows").innerHTML=slideshows.collect(
      function(slideshow){
        return "<div onclick='SlideShow.loadSlides(\""
                  +slideshow
                  +"\")'>"
                  +slideshow
              +"</div>";
      }
    ).join("");
  }
},
```

As you can see, showSlideshows() simply constructs some HTML markup for each saved slideshow, and adds it to the left panel. We've used Prototype's Array helpers here to collect markup for a clickable <DIV> tag for each slideshow. Collect() returns an Array, which we flatten to a String using the built-in join() method.

We've covered all the bases as far as saving our data to the server goes. Now let's look at what's involved in loading it up again.

12.3.3 *Loading content from the server*

We've saved the HTML markup for our slideshow from the editor panel onto the server. That's a good start, but the editor has added a lot of behavior on top of the HTML markup. When we reload the slideshow, we need to revive that behavior too.

The foundations for doing this have already been laid in the create() method that invokes the slideshow editor in the first place. Slideshow.initUI() takes an optional argument: a string of HTML content. When creating a new slideshow, this is ignored, but if it is present, it invokes a loadContent() method. Listing 12.11 shows how we use this to revive slideshows coming back from the server.

Listing 12.11 Loading a SlideShow in JavaScript

```
loadSlides:function(slideName){
  new Ajax.Request(
    "loadSlides.php",
    {
      postBody:                                          ❶ Create
        $H({slideName:slideName}).toQueryString(),  ⟵     query string
      onComplete:function(response){
        this.create(
          'slides',
          slideName,                          ❷ Read response
          response.responseText  ⟵               content
        );          }.bind(this)
      }
    );
  },
loadContent:function(htmlContent){
  this.body.innerHTML='';                ❸ Create tempo-
  var tmpDiv=Builder.node("div");  ⟵       rary node
  tmpDiv.innerHTML=htmlContent;
  tmpDiv.cleanWhitespace();
  $A(tmpDiv.childNodes).each(
    function(node){                 ❹ Create
      this.createSlide(node,this.body);  ⟵  slides
    }.bind(this)
  );
},
```

The first thing that we need to do when loading a slideshow from the server is to request the content using an Ajax request. In this case, the only information that we need to send with the request is the name of the slideshow to fetch. We can send this as a straightforward HTML form-style POST request, and use the Hash mixin object's toQueryString() method to encode the POST body for us appropriately ❶. The server will simply return the stored innerHTML as the response body, which we can read using the responseText property ❷. This invokes the create() method, with the HTML string as a third argument. This gets passed to initUI(), which has a short statement in it like this (see listing 12.2 for the full method):

```
if (htmlContent){
  this.loadContent(htmlContent);
}
```

Listing 12.11 shows the full implementation of loadContent(). We load the HTML into a temporary <DIV> element ❸ in order to parse it, and we iterate through the child nodes, thereby visiting every slide in the stored slideshow. In order to avoid the cross-browser issues associated with whitespace (discussed in chapter 11), we clean the whitespace from the element before iterating through the children.

Listing 12.4 showed the several steps required to introduce a new thumbnail into the slideshow editor, using the `createSlide()` method. Although we didn't see any connection to persistence when we wrote it, this method provides everything we need to revive our stored slideshows, one slide at a time ❹. Once every slide has been processed, the editor is fully active, and we can resume editing a slideshow from where we left off before saving it.

For completeness, listing 12.12 shows the simple PHP script required to retrieve the slideshow.

Listing 12.12   loadSlides.php

```php
<?php
require('../config.php');
$slideName=$_REQUEST['slideName'];
if ($slideName!=null){
  $filename=$basedir.'/../slides/'.$slideName.'.slides';
  if (file_exists($filename)){
    $filehandle=fopen($filename,'r');
    while (!feof($filehandle)) {
      echo fgets($filehandle);
    }
    fclose($filehandle);
  }
}
?>
```

There isn't a great deal going on here. Basically, we're constructing the filename, reading it, and emitting the contents to the response stream. `fgets()` is a curiously named method that returns the next line of an open file as a string. Because our Ajax request used a standard POST encoding this time, we can use the `$_REQUEST` variable rather than reading the raw POST body directly.

Our slideshow editor is now well on the way to completion. The final touch is simply to add a few buttons to the toolbar to help us drive it. We'll look at that in the next section.

12.4 Creating the toolbar

We've coded up the core functionality for the slide-show editor now, and made good use of features from both Prototype and Scriptaculous. Our task in this section is relatively simple, namely providing some buttons to allow the user to execute the functionality that we've written. Figure 12.10 shows a close-up of the expanded left panel, which now contains a list of saved slideshows and a toolbar, as laid out in figure 12.2. Because we're feeling pleased with the up-to-the-minute Web-2.0-ness of our application, we've also made space for a logo for our application, generated automatically by Alex P's Web 2.0 Logo Creator, complete with a little star to announce that we're fashionably in beta development stage!

Figure 12.10 Toolbar showing CSS styling of buttons on mouse-over. The tooltip is created automatically from the `title` attribute. Thanks again to David Vignoni for his wonderful Nuvola icon set.

The toolbar is relatively simple, with buttons for the tasks of creating a new slideshow, saving a slide-show, and playing a slideshow. To minimize use of space, we've simply provided an icon for each button, and added a mouse-over effect and a tooltip. Let's see how we did it.

The first step is to declare the HTML for the toolbar, which is shown in listing 12.13.

Listing 12.13 HTML for QuickGallery toolbar

```
<div id='toolbar'>
  <div style='float:left;padding-right:4px'>
    <img src='../icons/QuickGallery2.0BETA.png'>
  </div>
  <div style='float:right'>
  <div>
    <a class='btn' href='#' id='newSlideshow'
    title='make slideshow'>
      <img src='../icons/filenew.png' border='0'/>
    </a>
  </div>
```

```
<div>
  <a class='btn' href='#' id='saveSlideshow'
    title='save slideshow'>
    <img src='../icons/filesave.png' border='0'/>
  </a>
</div>
<div>
  <a class='btn' href='#' id='runSlideshow'
    title='run slideshow'>
    <img src='../icons/noatunplay.png' border='0'/>
  </a>
</div>
</div>
</div>
```

We've declared each button as an anchor tag (that is, <A>), with a CSS class of btn declared. Each button has a unique id, an href property that doesn't link to anywhere, and a title attribute. The title attribute will automatically generate our tooltip text. There are DHTML tooltip libraries available that allow programmatic generation of more complex tooltips, but in this case, the title attribute will suffice.

The CSS class is used to define the look of the button. Our modifications to the CSS are shown in listing 12.14.

Listing 12.14   CSS for QuickGallery toolbar

```
.btn{
  border: solid #aaa 1px;
  background-color: white;
  padding: 2px;
  width: 36px;
  height: 36px;
  display:block;
  text-decoration:none;
  color: #888;
  margin-top: 4px;
  margin-left: 6px;
}
.btn:hover{
  background-color: #adf;
  padding: 4px;
  color: #8a9;
  margin-top:6px;
  margin-left: 2px;
}
```

We chose an anchor tag rather than a DIV because we can apply the hover modifier in order to declare a change in appearance when the mouse passes over without having to write any JavaScript. Because we want to also define borders and a background color to the element, we needed to set the CSS display property to block. The default for an anchor tag is inline, in which case the border and background will not fully encompass the elements inside the button.

The second CSS rule defines the modifications to the look of the button when the mouse rolls over it. The hover modifier is recognized by very few tag types, notably anchor tags.

There are no onclick events defined for the buttons. We will add these in programmatically when the page has loaded up. To do this, we need to respond to the window.onload event. However, we've already defined a window.onload event in the images.js file for QuickGallery v1, like this:

```
window.onload=function(){
   ...
}
```

If we simply declare another window.onload() function, it will overwrite the first one, and our file browser will start to malfunction. We could combine the code for both the file browser and the slideshow into a single window.onload() function, but experience has taught us that creating such tight coupling between modules of code is generally bad news.

The solution is to use Prototype's Event observers. These allow us to attach multiple independent listeners to any element, including the window. Listing 12.15 shows the code for adding behavior to the buttons.

Listing 12.15   JavaScript for adding behavior to the QuickGallery toolbar

```
Event.observe(
  window,
  'load',
  function(){
    $('newSlideshow').onclick=function(){
      SlideShow.create('slides');
    }
    $('saveSlideshow').onclick=function(){
      SlideShow.saveSlides();
    }
    $('runSlideshow').onclick=function(){
      SlideShow.show();
    }
```

```
    $('SlideshowName').onblur=function(){
      SlideShow.name=this.value;
    }
  }
);
```

Event.observe() takes three arguments. The first is the element on which the event will fire, in this case the window. The second is the type of event to listen for, which in this case is a load event (we drop the "on" prefix when using Event.observe()). The third argument is the function to execute. Because each of our buttons has an id attribute, we can reference them using the $() function, and set the onclick properties programmatically. The SlideShow is a global object, so we can simply reference it directly and don't need to bind any functions to different contexts in this case. Note that while we're doing this, we also add the behavior to the slideshow-name text editor that sits on the top of the editor panel.

That's the toolbar implemented. We can now invoke our slideshow editor, and, when we're done, play the slideshow. Our final task is to implement the slideshow player, which we'll look at in the next section.

12.5   *Building the slideshow player*

We've now got a working slideshow editor program, and we can save our slideshows on the server and open them up again later. The final task to be done in implementing QuickGallery v2 is to provide a mechanism for playing the slideshows. We'll implement a simple slideshow player in this section, with the help of our favorite JavaScript libraries. Let's start by figuring out a user interface.

12.5.1   *Specifying a user interface*

We want the user interface for the slideshow player to operate separately from the main gallery, so we'll mask the main UI with a slightly transparent element that takes up the entire screen. We can place the slides in front of that backdrop element, along with any other UI elements that accompany them.

The UI for the slideshow will be very simple, as we only need to present a single image and caption at any one time. We can specify the layout using CSS, as we did for the slideshow editor. Listing 12.16 presents the new CSS classes required by the viewer.

Listing 12.16   CSS for slide viewer

```
#backdrop{
  background-color: #adf;
  opacity: 0.9;
  filter: alpha(opacity=90);
  position: absolute;
  top: 0px;
  left: 0px;
  width: 100%;
  height: 100%;
  text-align: center;
  padding-top: 240px;;
  font-size: 32px;
  color: #aaa;
}
#liveSlides{
  position: absolute;
  top: 25px;
  left: 25px;
  width: 735px;
  height: 520px;
  border: solid #888 2px;
  z-index: 100;
  background-color: white;
}
.liveslide{
  text-align: center;
}
.liveImage{
  margin: 25px;
  margin-bottom: 6px;
}
.liveCaption{
  font-size: 1.4em;
  color: #888;
  text-align: center;
  width: 685px;
  margin-left: 24px;
  margin-right: 24px;
}
```

backdrop is the DOM element that grays out the browsing and editing user interface when slides are being displayed. When the slideshow first starts, and the images are being preloaded, the backdrop may contain a message (see figure 12.11).

Figure 12.11 The `backdrop` DOM element presents a simple status message on top of the main UI while the slides load.

Once all slides are fully loaded, the `liveSlides` element is placed in front of the backdrop, as shown in figure 12.12. The remaining CSS classes provide styling for the image and caption that are displayed inside the slide viewer region.

For our first try at the slideshow player, we won't be looking at providing fine-grained control over the progress of the slideshow. We'll just let it run through the slides once and then stop. Hence, the only other control that we need to provide is a close button, which can be seen in the top-right corner in figure 12.12.

So, now that we know what we want, let's have a look at how to implement it.

12.5.2 *Implementing the slideshow player*

Given the requirements that we worked out in the previous section, our slideshow player simply needs a mechanism for taking control of a DOM element and modifying its appearance over time. The Scriptaculous Effects framework provides an ideal mechanism for this, and we're going to implement the slideshow player as a new subclass of Scriptaculous Effect.

Figure 12.12
Once the slides are loaded,
the `liveSlides` **slideshow**
element is made visible, on
top of the `backdrop`.

Listing 12.17 shows the full code for this subclass. Because the base Effect class already handles the scheduling and animation tasks, there isn't so much for us to do.

Listing 12.17   Effect.SlideShow class

```
Effect.SlideShow = Class.create();
Object.extend(                                    ❶ Subclass
  Object.extend(                                     base effect
    Effect.SlideShow.prototype,
    Effect.Base.prototype), {

  currentSlide: null,

  initialize: function(element,slides,opts) {
    this.element = $(element);
    var slideTools=$('slideTools');              ❷ Clear target
    this.element.innerHTML="";                      element
    this.element.appendChild(slideTools);
    Element.removeClassName(this.element,"hidden");
    this.slides=slides;
    var interval=
      (opts && opts.interval) ?                   ❸ Set transition
        opts.interval : 3;               ◁           interval
    var options=Object.extend(
      {
        duration: slides.length*interval,         ❹ Calculate total
        fps: (1/interval),                           duration
        transition:
```

```
            Effect.Transitions.linear  ←——  Default to linear
      },                                 ⑤   timing
      opts || {}
   );
   this.start(options);
},

 update: function(position) {
   var oldSlide=this.currentSlide;
   var len=this.slides.length;                ⑥  Compute
   var index=Math.floor(position*len);  ←——      current slide
   if (index==len){ index=len-1; }
   this.currentSlide=this.slides[index];
   if (this.currentSlide!=oldSlide){
     if (oldSlide){
       Element.remove(oldSlide);
     }                                    ⑦  Swap in
     this.element.appendChild                current slide
       (this.currentSlide);
   }
 }

});
```

You may recall from chapter 5 that the Scriptaculous Effects framework follows a well-designed class hierarchy, with a number of core effect types deriving from a base class, and further composite effects being built on top of the core types. The base class simply handles the business of repeatedly modifying the target element.

To implement the slideshow effect, we're going to subclass the Base effect directly ❶. To do this, we use Prototype's Object.extend() method, which we described in chapter 8. To provide a constructor function for our class, we then declare an initialize() method. In addition to passing in the target element (which, in our case, will be the main slideshow player element shown in figure 12.12), we pass in an array of DOM elements that represent the slides themselves. Our first action in the constructor function is to prepare the slideshow element by removing any content from the target element other than the stop button ❷.

Our Effect, like most classes in Prototype and Scriptaculous, will be called with an options object as an argument. The rest of the constructor function is taken up with preparing this options object before passing it to the start() method that we have inherited from the Base effect class.

Typically, effects are called with a fixed duration. In the case of our slideshow player, it seems more natural to express the duration as the interval between changing slides, given that the number of slides may vary considerably from one slideshow to another. We therefore ensure that a sensible default of 3 seconds is set for the interval if the option hasn't been overridden when an instance of the Effect is created. ❸, and automatically compute the total `duration` and frames per second (`fps`) properties ❹. Usually, the `fps` property is set to 25 frames per second to provide a smooth animation, but we override this with a much lower value, as the transitions in the slideshow are intended to be sudden and discontinuous. We also provide a different default transition ❺. Using the `linear` transition, each slide will have the same amount of time on screen, whereas under the default sinusoidal transition, more time would be allocated to the slides in the middle of the sequence.

With these options set, we can go ahead and call the `start()` method, which will begin the slideshow. The Effects framework will now handle most of the hard work for us. All we need to provide is an `update()` method, which will be called periodically to render each frame of the animation. The `update()` method takes a single argument, `position`, which tells us how far along the animation timeline we are, with a value of 0 indicating the start, and 1 indicating the end. We need to do a bit of simple math to convert this into an array index ❻, after which we can swap out the old slide for the new one ❼. Using the default `duration` and `fps` values that we calculated in the `initialize()` method, `update()` ought to be called only once for each slide, but we make a few checks anyway, in order to avoid swapping a slide in for itself.

This concludes our implementation of the Effect.Slideshow object. We now have a fully functional generic player that can run through a series of slides in order. We now need to write some glue code to tie this into our editor. We'll take on that task next.

12.5.3 *Launching the player*

Now that we have a ready-to-use slideshow player object, we simply need to marshal the arguments needed to construct one. The starting point for this is the `show()` method of the SlideShow object, which is invoked by the third button on the toolbar. Listing 12.18 shows the code responsible for preparing and starting up the slideshow player.

Listing 12.18 Launching the slideshow player

```
show:function(){
  this.slideData=$A(
    $("slides").childNodes        ❶  Collect slide
  ).collect(                           data
    function(node){
      var imgSrc=node.fullSrc;
      var caption=node.getElementsByTagName
        ("p")[0].firstChild.data;
      return {
        imgSrc: imgSrc,
        caption: caption
      };
    }
  );
  this.slideData.loadCount=0;
  this.slideData.liveCount=0;
  this.showBackdrop();              ❷  Iterate through
  this.slideData.each(                 raw data
    function(slide){
      slide.loaded=false;
      slide.image=new Image();
      slide.image.src=slide.imgSrc;
      slide.image.onload=function(){  ❸  Assign image
          this.slideLoaded(slide);        onload function
      }.bind(this);
      slide.div=Builder.node(
        "div",
        { src: slide.imgSrc,        ❹  Create DOM
          className: "liveslide"        element
        }
      );
      slide.div.innerHTML=          ❺  Populate DOM
        "<img src='"                    element
        +slide.imgSrc
        +"' class='liveImage'/>"
        +"<br/>"
        +"<p class='liveCaption'>"
        +slide.caption
        +"</p>";
    }.bind(this)
  );
},

slideLoaded:function(slide){
  slide.loaded=true;
  this.slideData.loadCount++;
  this.showBackdrop();
  if (this.slideData.loadCount
    ==this.slideData.length){
```

```
      this.effect=new Effect.SlideShow(        ❻ Create slideshow
        "liveSlides",                             player
        this.slideData.pluck("div")
      );
    }
  },
                                        ❼ Update backdrop
showBackdrop:function(){        ←┐        element
  Element.removeClassName
    ("backdrop","hidden");
  if (this.slideData.loadCount<this.slideData.length){
    $('backdrop').innerHTML
      ='loading: '
      +this.slideData.loadCount
      +' of '
      +this.slideData.length;
  }else{
    $('backdrop').innerHTML='loaded';
    $('stopShow').onclick=function(){
      if (this.effect){
        this.effect.cancel();
      }
      Element.addClassName("liveSlides","hidden");
      Element.addClassName("backdrop","hidden");
    }.bindAsEventListener(this);
  }
}
```

There's quite a bit to do in translating from the editor session to the arguments needed for the live slideshow. The Effect.SlideShow object that we've created in listing 12.17 expects an array of DOM elements ready for display. We can't simply pass the child nodes from the slide editor, as they contain small thumbnail images and behavior such as the in-place editor that we don't want during display.

The show() method of the SlideShow object does most of the heavy lifting in assembling the array of slides. First, it iterates over the child nodes of the editor panel ❶. This gives us another opportunity to apply Prototype's Array functionality, using both $A() and the Array.collect() method. The iterator function that we pass to collect() returns only the bare data for each element; that is, the image to display and the caption text. We store this array as a property of the SlideShow object, because we'll need to refer to it in other methods.

Having extracted the information, we also put it to immediate use in building up the DOM elements for each slide. We iterate over the slideData array that we've just created ❷, adding several extra properties to each element. The biggest complication is that the actual images that are going to be displayed during the slideshow haven't been loaded into the browser yet. The editor has ensured that the images exist on the server (see listings 12.4 and 12.6), but we want to make sure that they're loaded before the slideshow begins. For each element of the `slideData` array, we create an Image object, which we will use to preload the larger display images for each slide that we generated on the server in listing 12.4. The image data will load asynchronously, so we attach an `onload` event handler to each image ❸. This will be invoked on our behalf when the image data for each slide has loaded. The `onload` callback on the Image object is similar in operation to the `onSuccess` and `onFailure` handlers of the Ajax.Request class and its children. We'll return to the callback shortly, but while the Image data is loading, we have other things to do.

As well as preloading the image, we need to build the DOM element for each slide. We do this in two stages, first creating an empty DOM element using the Builder object ❹, and then populating it using `innerHTML` ❺. And that's our work done for the `show()` method.

Interestingly, we haven't yet created an Effect.SlideShow object, so when is our slideshow display going to start? The answer to that question lies in the callbacks on the image loading, so let's look at the `slideLoaded()` method next.

The `slideLoaded()` method will be called once for every image in the slideshow. As each image comes in from the server, we increment a counter and redraw the backdrop to display the loading message with the current count, as per figure 12.11. When the count of loaded slides equals the size of the `slideData` array, we know that all slides are loaded, and only then do we create the slideshow display ❻. The effect expects a simple array of DOM elements, and our `slideData` array holds a rich mix of data on each element by now, including the caption and image URL, the loaded Image object, and the slide itself. With a minimum of effort, we can extract the slides from this complex array using the `Array.pluck()` method. As soon as the effect is created, it will bring up the slideshow display in front of the backdrop and start the show.

The final block of code in listing 12.18 is the `showBackdrop()` method, which brings up the backdrop and updates the status message throughout the loading process ❼. The final time it is called, the backdrop text will display the message "loaded", but we won't see this, as the slideshow display will be sitting in front of it.

That's it! We now have a complete working slideshow system built on top of the original QuickGallery application. We've written a lot of additional code to implement it, and wrestled with a few tricky concepts along the way. However, we've been able to introduce an enormous amount of extra functionality in a very short space of time, including a smooth drag-and-drop user interface for editing our slides, and a straightforward display system. Scriptaculous has made a lot of functionality possible in a few lines of code, allowing us to focus on the workflow of our application rather than on UI mechanics. Prototype has had a good workout too, making a lot of small-scale activities more pleasant and straightforward to code.

We'll conclude this chapter with a quick code review, in which we'll present the client-side code as a whole, and then pick out several features that have benefited from the use of the libraries.

12.6 *Putting it all together*

We've presented most of the code for the QuickGallery v2 application throughout this chapter as we went along. In the interests of completeness, though, we're listing the complete client-side code here. We won't run through all of the PHP code on the server in detail, as much of it is concerned with simple topics such as filesystems and image manipulation, which aren't core to this book. None of the server-side code relies especially on PHP, and it could have just as easily been written in any modern server-side language, such as Java, C# or VB.Net, Python, Perl, or Ruby. The full PHP code is available in the download bundle from the website for this book at manning.com, and appendix C contains instructions for setting up a PHP development system if you want to run the application for yourself.

Let's look over the client-side code. We'll start with the HTML. Listing 12.19 provides the full HTML code for the application, with markup added since version 1 in bold.

Listing 12.19   index.html

```
<html>
<head>
<title>QuickGallery 2.0beta</title>
<link rel='stylesheet' type="text/css" href="images.css"/>
<script type='text/javascript' src='lib/prototype/prototype.js'></script>
<script type='text/javascript' src='lib/scriptaculous/scriptaculous.js'></
   script>
<script type='text/javascript' src='lib/images.js'></script>
<script type='text/javascript' src='lib/slideshow.js'></script>
```

The preceding line is where we add the extra JavaScript library containing the slideshow-related code. Because this is largely a separate piece of functionality, we've decided to keep it in a separate file from the code supporting the file-browsing functionality.

```
</head>
<body>

<div id='title' class='box'>
</div>

<div class='box' id='closeup'>
<img id='closeup_img'></img>
</div>

<div id='sidebar' class='box'>
  <div class='sidebartitle'>folders</div>
  <div id='folders' class='sidebarcontent'> </div>
  <div class='sidebartitle'>slideshows</div>
  <div id='slideshows' class='sidebarcontent'> </div>
  <div class='sidebartitle'>tools</div>
  <div id='toolbar'>
    <div style='float:left;padding-right:4px'>
      <img src='../icons/QuickGallery2.0BETA.png'>
    </div>
    <div style='float:right'>
    <div>
     <a class='btn' href='#' id='newSlideshow' title='make slideshow'><img
src='../icons/filenew.png' border='0'/></a>
      </div>
      <div>
       <a class='btn' href='#' id='saveSlideshow' title='save slideshow'>
         <img src='../icons/filesave.png' border='0'/>
       </a>
      </div>
      <div>
       <a class='btn' href='#' id='runSlideshow' title='run slideshow'>
         <img src='../icons/noatunplay.png' border='0'/>
       </a>
      </div>
    </div>
  </div>
</div>
```

We've wrapped the old folders sidebar up in a new top-level element, along with
all the markup needed to support the slideshows list and the toolbar. We're only
defining document structure here. We'll add interactivity in the JavaScript.

```
<div id='images' class='box'>
</div>

<input type='text' id='SlideshowName' class='box hidden'></input>

<div id='slides' class='box hidden'>
</div>
```

```
<div id='trash' class='box hidden' title='drag images here to remove from
   slideshow'>
</div>

<div id='backdrop' class='hidden'>
</div>

<div id='liveSlides' class='hidden'>
  <div id='slideTools' style='float:right'>
    <div id='stopShow'><img src='../icons/exit.png'></div>
  </div>
</div>

</body>
</html>
```

Finally, the preceding bare-bones elements act as placeholders for the new functionality. And that's it for the HTML.

Several new top-level entities were created for QuickGallery v2, such as the editor panels, toolbar, and slideshow display. We declared most of these elements in the HTML file, and styled them in the CSS. Note that many of the new elements in the HTML are not going to be seen at the same time, and are hidden from view initially through the CSS hidden class. We define this, and many other new CSS classes, in the images.css file, which is shown in listing 12.20. Once again, new code is in bold.

Listing 12.20 images.css

```
*{
  font-family: Arial, Helvetica;
}
.box{
  position: absolute;
  border: solid #adf 1px;
  background-color: white;
  padding: 4px;
  display: block;
}
#title{
  top: 5px;
  left: 5px;
  height: 18px;
  font-size: 14px;
  color: #8af;
}
#tools{
  top: 35px;
```

```
    left: 5px;
    height: 18px;
    width: 170px;
    font-size: 12px;
    color: #79f;
    float: right;
}
#sidebar{
    top: 35px;
    left: 5px;
    width: 170px;
    padding-left: 0px;
    padding-right: 0px;
}
.sidebartitle{
    background-color: #adf;
    color: white;
    font-size: 12px;
    font-weight: bold;
    text-align: center;
    width: 170px;
}
.sidebarcontent{
    font-size: 14px;
    width: 160px;
    padding: 4px;
    color: #8af;
}
#toolbar{
    border-top: solid #adf 1px;
    padding-top: 2px;
    font-size: 14px;
}
```

The preceding additional CSS rules support the sidebar and its constituent elements.

```
#images{
    top: 35px;
    left: 185px;
    width: 600px;
    height: 600px;
    overflow: auto;
    overflow-x: hidden;
    border: solid #888 1px;
}
#closeup{
    top: 35px;
    left: 185px;
}
.img_tile{
```

```
    float: left;
    width: 160px;
    height: 160px;
}

#SlideshowName{
    top: 35px;
    left: 595px;
    width:150px;
    height: 30px;
    margin: 2px;
    font-size: 11px;
}
#slides{
    top: 71px;
    left: 595px;
    width: 150px;
    height: 458px;
    overflow: auto;
    overflow-x: hidden;
    align: center;
    background-color: #888;
}
.slide{
    width: 160px;
    padding: 3px;
    margin-bottom: 2px;
    border: solid #bbb 1px;

}
#trash{
    top: 544px;
    left: 595px;
    width: 148px;
    height: 90px;
    background-color: #444;
    background-image: url(../icons/edittrash.png);
    background-repeat:no-repeat;
    border: solid black 2px;
}
```

The preceding elements support the slideshow editor component.

```
#backdrop{
    background-color: #adf;
    opacity: 0.9;
    filter: alpha(opacity=90);
    position: absolute;
    top: 0px;
    left: 0px;
    width: 100%;
```

```
       height: 100%;
       text-align: center;
       padding-top: 240px;;
       font-size: 32px;
       color: #aaa;
   }
   #liveSlides{
       position: absolute;
       top: 25px;
       left: 25px;
       width: 735px;
       height: 520px;
       border: solid #888 2px;
       z-index: 100;
       background-color: white;
   }
   .liveslide{
       text-align: center;
   }
   .liveImage{
       margin: 25px;
       margin-bottom: 6px;
   }
   .liveCaption{
       font-size: 1.4em;
       color: #888;
       text-align: center;
       width: 685px;
       margin-left: 24px;
       margin-right: 24px;
   }
```

The preceding CSS rules define the look of the slideshow viewer.

```
   .hidden{
       display: none;
   }
   .btn{
       border: solid #aaa 1px;
       background-color: white;
       padding: 2px;
       width: 36px;
       height: 36px;
       display:block;
       text-decoration:none;
       color: #888;
       margin-top: 4px;
       margin-left: 6px;
   }
   .btn:hover{
       background-color: #adf;
```

```
    padding: 4px;
    color: #8a9;
    margin-top:6px;
    margin-left: 2px;
}
```

Most of the CSS changes add new classes and rules to accommodate the new UI elements. Only the #images rule has been modified, to set a fixed size and internal scrolling on the thumbnail region, as discussed in section 12.2.1.

The main part of the application, though, is the JavaScript. QuickGallery v2 has two main JavaScript files: images.js handles the file-browsing functionality present in version 1, with a few modifications, and slideshow.js contains the new functionality that has been the main subject of this chapter. We'll begin with images.js, which is presented in listing 12.21 with the new code in bold.

Listing 12.21 images.js

```
var ui={};
var currPath="/";
Ajax.Responders.register(
  {
    onComplete:function(request,transport,json){
      showBreadcrumbs();
      showFolders(json.folders);
      if (json.count!=null){
        if (json.count>0){
          Element.show(ui.images);
        }else{
          Element.hide(ui.images);
        }
      }
    }
  }
);

Event.observe(
  window,
  'load',
  function(){
    ui.title=$('title');
    ui.closeup=$('closeup');
    ui.closeupImg=$('closeup_img');
    ui.folders=$('folders');
    ui.images=$('images');
    Element.hide(ui.closeup,ui.folders);
    load();
```

```
        }
    );
```

We replaced the original `window.onload` declaration with a Prototype event observer here.

```
function load(newPath){
    if (newPath!=null){ currPath=newPath; }
    new Ajax.Updater(
        "images",
        "images.php?path="+currPath,
        {
            method: "GET",
            evalScripts: true,
            onComplete: function(){
                Element.hide(ui.closeup);
            }
        }
    );
}

function showBreadcrumbs(){
    var crumbs=currPath.split("/");
    var crumbHTML=" &gt; <span onclick='load(\"/\")'>home</span>";
    for(var i=0;i<crumbs.length;i++){
        var crumb=crumbs[i];
        if (crumb.length>0){
            var path=subpath(currPath,"/",i);
            crumbHTML+=" &gt; <span onclick='load(\""+path+"\")'>"+crumb+"</span>";
        }
    }
    ui.title.innerHTML=crumbHTML;
}

function subpath(str,delim,ix){
    var all=str.split(delim);
    var some=all.findAll(
        function(v,i){
            //alert("i="+i+", ix="+ix+", v="+v+", result: "+(i<=ix));
            return (i<=ix);
        }
    );
    return some.join(delim);
}

function showFolders(folders){
    if (folders.length==0){
        Element.hide(ui.folders);
    }else{
        var folderHTML="";
        for (var i=0;i<folders.length;i++){
```

```
      var folder=folders[i];
      var path=(currPath=="/") ? "/"+folder : [currPath,folder].join("/");
      folderHTML+="<div onclick='load(\""+path+"\")'>"+folder
        +"</div>";
    }
    Element.show(ui.folders);
    ui.folders.innerHTML=folderHTML;
  }
}

function showCloseup(imgSrc){
  Element.hide(ui.images);
  Element.show(ui.closeup);
  ui.closeupImg.src=imgSrc;
}
```

Yes, we have displayed all of the changes in bold. The fact is, we've had to change very little in images.js while implementing the new functionality, as we've been able to make use of various library features, such as the Ajax.Responders, to decouple interactions between the two sets of functionality. The only change we did make was to replace a window.onload declaration with a Prototype event observer, which in itself was done to decrease coupling between the two files.

Finally, the complete listing for slideshow.js is shown in listing 12.22.

Listing 12.22 slideshow.js

```
Event.observe(
  window,
  'load',
  function(){
    $('newSlideshow').onclick=function(){
      SlideShow.create('slides');
    }
    $('saveSlideshow').onclick=function(){
      SlideShow.saveSlides();
    }
    $('runSlideshow').onclick=function(){
      SlideShow.show();
    }
    $('SlideshowName').onblur=function(){
      SlideShow.name=this.value;
    }
  }
);

Ajax.Responders.register(
  {
```

```
        onComplete:function(request,transport,json){
          if (json && json.slideshows){
            SlideShow.showSlideshows(json.slideshows);
          }
        }
      }
    }
  );
```

First, we do a few miscellaneous set-up jobs, such as adding interactivity to the toolbar elements and setting up the Ajax responder that refreshes the drag-and-drop system when we move to a new folder in the filesystem.

Next, we start to define the SlideShow object, which orchestrates the main workflow.

```
    var SlideShow={

      create:function(el,name,htmlContent){
        this.body=$(el);
        this.name=name;
        this.initUI(htmlContent);
        Ajax.Responders.register(
          {
            onComplete:function(request,transport,json){
              if (json && 'folder'==json.action){
                this.initDragDrop();
              }
            }.bind(this)
          }
        );
      },

      initUI:function(htmlContent){
        this.body.innerHTML='';
        Element.removeClassName(this.body,"hidden");
        Element.removeClassName('trash',"hidden");
        Element.removeClassName('SlideshowName',"hidden");
        Element.hide('closeup');
        Element.show('images');
        Element.setStyle(
          'images',
          { width: "396px" }
        );
        if (htmlContent){
          this.loadContent(htmlContent);
        }
        this.initDragDrop();
        if (this.name && this.name.length>0){
          $('SlideshowName').value=this.name;
```

```
      }else{
        new Effect.Pulsate(
          'SlideshowName',
          {
            duration: 2,
            beforeStart:function(){
              $('SlideshowName').value='please provide a name';
            },
            afterFinish:function(){
              var txtBox=$('SlideshowName');
              txtBox.value='';
              txtBox.focus();
            }
          }
        );
      }
    },

    initDragDrop:function(){
      Sortable.create(
        'images',
        {
          tag: "div",
          containment:[this.body],
          constraint: false,
          ghosting: true
        }
      );
      Droppables.add(
        this.body,
        {
          onDrop:function(tile,target){
            if (tile.className=="slide"){ return; }
            this.createSlide(tile,target);

          }.bind(this)
        }
      );

      Droppables.add(
        'trash',
        {
          onDrop:function(tile,target){
            if (tile.className=="slide"){
              tile.remove();
              if (this.trashEffect){
                this.trashEffect.cancel();
              }
              this.trashEffect=new Effect.Pulsate(target);
            }
```

```
        }.bind(this)
      }
    );

  },
```

The preceding set of methods allow us to initialize the user interface and switch on the drag-and-drop functionality.

```
loadContent:function(htmlContent){
  this.body.innerHTML='';
  var tmpDiv=Builder.node("div");
  tmpDiv.innerHTML=htmlContent;
  tmpDiv.cleanWhitespace();
  $A(tmpDiv.childNodes).each(
    function(node){
      this.createSlide(node,this.body);
    }.bind(this)
  );
},

createSlide:function(tile,target){
  var newSlide=Builder.node("div", { className: "slide" } );
  newSlide.innerHTML=tile.innerHTML;
  target.appendChild(newSlide);
  var img=newSlide.getElementsByTagName("img")[0];
  img.onclick=null;
  var caption=newSlide.getElementsByTagName("p")[0];
  newSlide.fullSrc=img.src.replace("120","420");
  newSlide.slideId=caption.firstChild.data;
  new Ajax.InPlaceEditor(
    caption,
    "echo.php",
    {
      rows:3,
      cols:36,
      submitOnBlur: true,
      okButton: false
    }
  );
  new Ajax.Request(
    "thumbnail.php",
    {
      parameters: $H(
        {name: newSlide.slideId,path:currPath,size:"420"}
      ).toQueryString()
    }
  );
  Sortable.create(
    this.body,
    {
```

```
        tag: "div",
        containment:[this.body,'trash'],
        handle:'img',
        constraint: 'vertical',
        scroll: true
      }
    );
    this.body.scrollTop=this.body.scrollHeight;

},

showSlideshows:function(slideshows){
  if (slideshows.length==0){
    Element.hide("slideshows");
  }else{
    Element.show("slideshows");
    $("slideshows").innerHTML=slideshows.collect(
      function(slideshow){
        return
          "<div onclick='SlideShow.loadSlides(\""
          +slideshow
          +"\")'>"
          +slideshow
          +"</div>";
      }
    ).join("");
  }
},

loadSlides:function(slideName){
  new Ajax.Request(
    "loadSlides.php",
    {
      postBody: $H({slideName:slideName}).toQueryString(),
      onComplete:function(response){
        this.create('slides',slideName,response.responseText);
      }.bind(this)
    }
  );
},

saveSlides:function(){
  var snapshot=$('slides').innerHTML;
  new Ajax.Request(
    "saveSlides.php",
    {
      method: "post",
      contentType: "text/html",
      requestHeaders: ["X-SLIDENAME",this.name],
      postBody: snapshot
    }
```

```
    );
  },
```

Then, in the preceding methods, we define the code that allows us to save and reload entire slideshows on the server.

```
show:function(){
  this.slideData=$A($("slides").childNodes).collect(
    function(node){
      var imgSrc=node.fullSrc;
      var caption=node.getElementsByTagName("p")[0].firstChild.data;
      return { imgSrc: imgSrc, caption: caption };
    }
  );
  this.slideData.loadCount=0;
  this.slideData.liveCount=0;
  this.showBackdrop();
  this.slideData.each(
    function(slide){
      slide.loaded=false;
      slide.image=new Image();
      slide.image.src=slide.imgSrc;
      slide.image.onload=function(){
          this.slideLoaded(slide);
      }.bind(this);
      slide.div=Builder.node("div",
        { src: slide.imgSrc, className: "liveslide" }
      );
      slide.div.innerHTML=
        "<img src='"
        +slide.imgSrc
        +"' class='liveImage'/>"
        +"<br/>"
        +"<p class='liveCaption'>"
        +slide.caption
        +"</p>";
    }.bind(this)
  );
},

slideLoaded:function(slide){
  slide.loaded=true;
  this.slideData.loadCount++;
  this.showBackdrop();
  if (this.slideData.loadCount==this.slideData.length){
    this.effect=new Effect.SlideShow(
      "liveSlides",
      this.slideData.pluck("div")
    );
  }
},
```

```
showBackdrop:function(){
  Element.removeClassName("backdrop","hidden");
  if (this.slideData.loadCount<this.slideData.length){
    $('backdrop').innerHTML='loading: '
      +this.slideData.loadCount
      +' of '
      +this.slideData.length;
  }else{
    $('backdrop').innerHTML='loaded';
    $('stopShow').onclick=function(){
      if (this.effect){
        this.effect.cancel();
      }
      Element.addClassName("liveSlides","hidden");
      Element.addClassName("backdrop","hidden");
    }.bindAsEventListener(this);
  }
}

};
```

The slideshow itself is defined as a separate class. The SlideShow object's final set of methods (the preceding ones) defines how to launch the slideshow viewer, which we are going to implement next.

```
Effect.SlideShow = Class.create();
Object.extend(Object.extend(Effect.SlideShow.prototype,
  Effect.Base.prototype), {

  currentSlide: null,

  initialize: function(element,slides,opts) {
    this.element = $(element);
    var slideTools=$('slideTools');
    this.element.innerHTML="";
    this.element.appendChild(slideTools);
    Element.removeClassName(this.element,"hidden");
    this.slides=slides;
    var interval=(opts && opts.interval) ? opts.interval : 3;
    var options=Object.extend(
      {
        transition: Effect.Transitions.linear,
        duration: slides.length*interval,
        fps: (1/interval)
      },
      opts || {}
    );
    this.start(options);
  },
```

```
update: function(position) {
  var oldSlide=this.currentSlide;
  var len=this.slides.length;
  var index=Math.floor(position*len);
  if (index==len){ index=len-1; } //if position=1.0 exactly
  this.currentSlide=this.slides[index];
  if (this.currentSlide!=oldSlide){
    if (oldSlide){ Element.remove(oldSlide); }
    this.element.appendChild(this.currentSlide);
  }
}

});
```

We implement the slideshow player as a Scriptaculous Effect, thus getting a lot of the scheduling of the animation for free.

That concludes our exploration of QuickGallery v2, and our demonstration of how Prototype and Scriptaculous make it easy—even fun—to create a reasonably complex user interface and blur the boundaries between web and desktop apps a little.

12.7 Summary

Our aim in this chapter was to revisit a lot of the techniques that we've discussed throughout this book, and to see how they work alongside one another in something close to a production setting. As you can see, QuickGallery has made significant leaps forward with version 2, and we haven't even had to work up a sweat.

The star of the show in this example is clearly Scriptaculous. While we aren't in a position to cause the serious online photo sites, like Flickr, to lose any sleep, we've created a fluid workflow and an uncluttered user interface with relatively little effort on our part, utilizing techniques such as drag and drop and inline editing, and prebuilt components and frameworks such as the Controls and Effects packages. We've made use of all the main components of Scriptaculous here.

We covered the Effects package in chapter 5. Here, we've thrown in effects as simple one-liners to notify the user of changes, and we've also implemented an entirely new effect class ourselves. The in-place editor that we reviewed in chapter 6 as part of the Controls package has also eased our development effort considerably. Finally, the drag-and-drop system that we covered in chapter 7 has had a thorough workout, as we combined several droppables and sortables to create a comprehensive drag-and-drop-based workflow for our application.

Along the way, Prototype has also done a great deal of work for us. We've made use of a range of object creation techniques, as discussed in chapter 8. At the simple end, we created and manipulated ad hoc objects created using JSON syntax in listing 12.18. In the middle ground, we encapsulated a great deal of behavior and state in the SlideShow object itself, which we created as a singleton. For a finale, we used Prototype's inheritance mechanisms to subclass the Effects classes when creating the slideshow viewer.

Working with objects introduces interesting scope issues, and we've bound more functions and created more closures in this chapter than we care to count. Fortunately, the `Function.bind()` method that we discussed in chapter 9 has helped to keep our code clean and readable, and has prevented us from getting bogged down in these issues.

We've also made significant use of the Array methods provided by Prototype, which we covered in chapter 10. We've used them to swiftly flip between pure data structures and DOM elements, and to generate lists of links for the UI. Although we only used a small handful of the methods covered in chapter 10, it made a big difference to our coding.

The DOM-based helpers from chapter 11 also came in useful in many places, in manipulating DOM elements with multiple CSS classes, and resizing and reorganizing the UI.

Finally, we should note how easy it was to make simple Ajax calls to the server using Ajax.Request, and also to organize the application code in a modular fashion through the use of the Ajax responders that we encountered in chapter 4. We decided at the end of that chapter to adopt the content-centric approach, noting the limitation of that approach in more complex applications, and how the X-JSON headers provided a way around that limitation. Our application has increased a great deal in complexity in this chapter, and our decision to use the X-JSON headers has proven to be a good one.

We've covered the theory and practice of most of the corners of the Prototype and Scriptaculous libraries. We hope we've persuaded you to give them a try in your own Ajax applications, of whatever flavor.

There's one more chapter left in this book, in which we'll cover a natural ally of these libraries that we've been ignoring up to now. We firmly believe that Prototype and Scriptaculous make great partners with just about any server-side technology, but they have enjoyed a very close relationship with the Ruby on Rails software stack. In chapter 13, we'll look at how Prototype and Scriptaculous integrate with Rails.

13

Prototype, Scriptaculous, and Rails

This chapter covers

- Understanding the Rails approach to generating JavaScript on the server
- Using the Rails Ajax helpers to work with Prototype and Scriptaculous
- Accessing Scriptaculous's advanced features from Rails
- Using Rails RJS templates to solve the multiple-update problem, and for other advanced techniques

Our main aim in this book has been to explore Prototype and Scriptaculous as standalone JavaScript libraries, independent of any server-side technologies. In our opinion, these libraries can increase your productivity in developing Ajax solutions with any server-side stack. However, there is no getting away from the fact that both Prototype and Scriptaculous are strongly allied with the Ruby on Rails framework. As a result of this alliance, they have been designed to play well with Rails in several ways, and in this chapter, we're going to explore the key features that Rails provides that make the use of Prototype and Scriptaculous even smoother.

This isn't the time or place to provide a full discussion of the Ruby on Rails framework—there are already very good books providing depth of coverage in that area. However, for those who have never come across Rails, here's a brief description from the rubyonrails.org website:

> Rails is a full-stack framework for developing database-backed web applications according to the Model-View-Control pattern. From the Ajax in the view, to the request and response in the controller, to the domain model wrapping the database, Rails gives you a pure-Ruby development environment. To go live, all you need to add is a database and a web server.

We're going to assume a working knowledge of Rails, and concentrate on integrating Prototype and Scriptaculous.

If you're already developing Rails projects, this chapter will show you a number of shortcuts and useful tricks that will allow you to leverage the knowledge that you've already gained. If you're working with other software stacks, this chapter will be less relevant to you, unless you're developing or extending your current framework and want to see how the Ruby guys make life easier for themselves.

13.1 Generating JavaScript

Everything that Rails provides by way of Prototype and Scriptaculous integration is based around one technique—generating JavaScript. That's right, Rails will write your JavaScript for you! Congratulations. You're done. Give yourself a holiday!

OK, so it's not quite that easy. It's true that many of the techniques and features you've already seen in this book can be achieved without writing as much as a line of JavaScript, but unfortunately that doesn't mean you'll be putting your feet up. You are going to be writing Ruby code instead. And the good news is that you'll still need to know many of the details of the Scriptaculous and Prototype libraries that we've covered in the previous twelve chapters.

So why would we want to switch programming languages in this way? Isn't adding an extra layer of code that writes code just confusing things? Well, there are three main benefits to this approach:

- better integration with the Rails framework and your Rails application
- cleaner source code
- no need to switch languages

That may sound persuasive, but you can judge for yourself by taking a look at how it works. Let's get straight down to an example.

13.1.1 *Hello World, Prototype, and Rails style*

There's nothing like a nice simple example to get things going, and there's nothing like "Hello World" for a nice simple example. To warm up, we're going to use Rails to create a simple app that prints out that well-loved phrase. We'll fetch the text from the server using Ajax.

Rails follows the Model-View-Controller pattern. To start, create a new Rails application and add a controller class, HelloController, by running the following "rails generator" command from the directory of the Rails application:

```
ruby script/generate controller hello
```

Next, we'll define a method in our controller class that outputs the text for us:

```
class HelloController < ApplicationController
  def say_hello
    render :text => "Hello World"
  end
end
```

For simplicity, we've passed the text as a parameter to the render() method, rather than creating an entirely trivial view template. If the content were a bit more complex, we would probably use a partial page template.

Next, we'll create a view that contains an HTML starting page and the Java-Script needed to make the Ajax call. Create a file, app/views/hello/index.rhtml, containing the following:

```
<html>
<head><%= javascript_include_tag :defaults %></head>
<body>
<p><%= link_to_remote "Click Me",
 :url => { :action => 'say_hello' },
 :update => 'display' %></p>
<p id='display'></p>
</body>
```

That's right, there isn't so much as a `<script>` tag in sight, let alone any Java-Script. We can see what looks like a hyperlink defined by a `link_to_remote` method. In fact the `link_to_remote` method creates both a hyperlink and the necessary JavaScript to make an Ajax call to the server.

To run the Rails application, start the WEBrick server included with the Rails installation:

```
ruby script/server
```

Point your browser at http://localhost:3000/hello, and you will see a page with a "Click Me" link. Clicking the link will cause the "Hello World" message to appear on the page.

The `link_to_remote` method is what Rails calls a "helper" method. Helpers are simply methods we can use in our views to quickly and easily generate fragments of HTML or JavaScript. A large library of helpers is provided with Rails, including many helpers for working with Prototype and Scriptaculous. In the next section, we'll take a look at Rails helpers in more detail.

13.1.2 *Introducing Rails helpers*

As we've seen in the previous section, helpers are simple Ruby calls that can be embedded into your view templates to generate fragments of HTML or JavaScript for you. For example, embedding the following Ruby code,

```
<%= link_to "click here", :controller => 'c', :action => 'some_action' %>
```

will generate a simple HTML link:

```
<a href="/c/some_action">click here</a>
```

A good deal of the Prototype and Scriptaculous integration in Rails is provided as helpers just like this one. Our Hello World example contains two helpers. The first, `javascript_include_tag`, generates the required script tags, ensuring that the Prototype and Scriptaculous libraries are available. You can use this helper to include any JavaScript file you like, but when you pass the `:defaults` argument as we just did, it generates five standard script tags:

```
<script src="/javascripts/prototype.js" type="text/javascript"></script>
<script src="/javascripts/effects.js" type="text/javascript"></script>
<script src="/javascripts/dragdrop.js" type="text/javascript"></script>
<script src="/javascripts/controls.js" type="text/javascript"></script>
<script src="/javascripts/application.js" type="text/javascript"></script>
```

You should recognize the first four as including Prototype and three parts of Scriptaculous. The final script tag includes application.js, which is the standard place in Rails for you to put your own application-specific JavaScript library.

It's easy to forget the `javascript_include_tag` and then wonder why nothing is working. So it's a good idea to add it to every page, using Rails' global layout feature. Just add the following line in the HTML `head` section of app/views/layouts/application.rhtml:

```
<%= javascript_include_tag :defaults %>
```

That won't guarantee it is available everywhere, because any page in Rails is free to override the global layout. But by default every page will now have Prototype and Scriptaculous included. With the whole application now Ajax-enabled, we're ready to get into some code.

The only other helper in our Hello World example is `link_to_remote`. Sound familiar? It's the Ajaxified version of plain old `link_to`, which we just saw. Let's have a look at the JavaScript that gets generated by this helper. Here's the Ruby code again,

```
<%= link_to_remote "Click Me", :url => { :action => 'say_hello' },
                               :update => 'display' %>
```

and here's the generated JavaScript that the browser will see:

```
<a href="#"
   onclick="new Ajax.Updater(
     'display',
     '/hello/say_hello',
     {asynchronous:true, evalScripts:true}
   );
   return false;">Click Me</a>
```

Note that the generated JavaScript has been reformatted by hand here, and throughout this chapter, to improve legibility. The `link_to_remote` helper has generated a simple JavaScript link, which, when clicked, creates a Prototype Ajax.Updater, just like the ones we were coding by hand in chapter 4.

The important part to notice is the way the parameters to `link_to_remote` appeared at the appropriate places in the generated JavaScript. The first parameter became the content of the link, just as with `link_to`. The `:url` hash was used to generate the target URL for the Ajax.Updater (the options are documented in detail in the Rails `url_for` helper method—see http://api.rubyonrails.com). The `:update => 'display'` parameter determined that the first parameter to Ajax.Updater (that is, the ID of the DOM node to be updated) was `'display'`.

Hopefully, this gives you a taste for why you would use helpers rather than coding the JavaScript by hand. You get to stick to one language, which helps to keep your source code cleaner and alleviates the burden of switching back and forth between two syntaxes. Second, notice how the URL is specified in terms of the actions and controllers that make up your application. You don't need to worry about how this maps to a URL, as the helper will make the conversion for you. This is just one example of the way JavaScript helpers give you a tighter integration between your Rails application and the JavaScript that runs inside the browser. The helper tag is generally a fair bit shorter than the generated JavaScript too.

Now that you've got a taste for helper tags in Rails, we're going to work our way through the full set of JavaScript-based helpers, and see how they match up with Prototype and Scriptaculous.

13.2 *Ajax helpers*

Now that we're familiar with the concept of generating JavaScript from Ruby helpers, let's take a look at some more helpers provided by Rails. We're going to start with a group of helpers that are extremely useful in any kind of Ajax programming.

These helpers are all essentially similar: they provide a means to trigger an Ajax call in response to some kind of client-side event, and to update the page using the result returned by the server. The client-side events that trigger the Ajax call are listed in table 13.1.

Table 13.1 Ajax helpers and the client-side events that trigger them

Ajax helper	Triggered by
link_to_remote	Link clicked
form_remote_tag	Form submitted
submit_to_remote	Form submitted
observe_field	Value of a specific form field changed
observe_form	Value of any field in a given form changed
periodically_call_remote	Polls the server at regular intervals
remote_function	Programmer-defined trigger
update_element_function	Programmer-defined trigger

The last three helpers are different from the others in that they can be used in any context where JavaScript is allowed. For example, you could use remote_function in an onkeypress event handler (it generates just the new Ajax.Updater code, without any surrounding HTML).

When you use any of these helpers, there are three main ways you will want to configure them:

- You will always provide the URL to which the Ajax request will be sent.
- You will usually want to provide details about which part of the page should be updated by the response text.
- You will sometimes want to provide extra snippets of JavaScript to be executed at particular points in the request cycle. For example, you could apply a highlight effect to the updated content.

Because these options are common to all the Ajax helpers, there is a standard way of configuring them. In the following section, we'll see how to set these options in Ruby.

13.2.1 *Standard configuration options*

The standard configuration options are made available as a set of keyword parameters, which are available to all of the Ajax helpers. Let's look at each in turn.

Setting the URL

All of these Ajax helpers support the :url parameter. As we've seen, this parameter defines the URL that the Ajax call is sent to. You can pass a raw URL as a string, or, more typically, as a hash identifying the URL by controller, action, and ID. Here's an example:

```
:url => { :controller => "person", :action => "home", :id => 12 }
```

Note that any other items you put in that hash will become parameters in the URL's query string.

Controlling the page update

There are two parameters used to configure the way the page is updated. A DOM element ID is provided with the :update parameter, along with, optionally, the :position parameter to control where the new content appears relative to that element.

The :update parameter's value can be either a string containing a single ID, or a hash containing two IDs, like this:

```
:update => { :success => 'people', :failure => 'error_message' }
```

As you might guess, this allows you to have a different node updated in the case of an error. Success and failure are determined by the HTTP status code. Anything in the range 200–299 is a successful response, and any other status code is an error, such as "403 forbidden." (See appendix A for more details on HTTP.)

Note that on the server, you can control the HTTP status returned by your action by using the `:status` parameter to the `render` method, like this:

```
render :text => "You are not allowed...", :status => 403
```

If the `:position` parameter is not given, the current content of the element you specify will be entirely replaced. If it is given, the new content will be inserted into the page without replacing anything already there. The value of the `:position` parameter controls where the content is inserted, relative to the element identified by `:update`. The choices are outlined in table 13.2.

Table 13.2 Values for the `:position` parameter

Value of `:position`	Response text is inserted ...
before	Just before the opening tag of the element
top	Just after the opening tag of the element
bottom	Just before the closing tag of the element
after	Just after the closing tag of the element

Adding JavaScript callbacks

Finally, each of the Ajax helpers can have custom snippets of JavaScript executed at particular points in the Ajax request cycle. It is very common to use this feature to apply a Scriptaculous effect to the updated portion of the page. Here's how:

```
<%= link_to_remote "Click Me", :url => { :action => 'say_hello' },
    :update => 'display',
    :success => "new Effect.Highlight('display')"
%>
```

Here we've triggered a nice highlight effect to help our users spot all these seamless updates we're slipping in. (Later in this chapter, we'll look at how to use another Rails helper to create that `Effect.Highlight` call, keeping the code entirely JavaScript-free.) In this example, we've used the `:success` callback, so the script fragment we provided is executed on successful completion of the Ajax call.

The full set of callback parameters are listed in table 13.3. You might recognize them as the various states of the XMLHttpRequest object.

Table 13.3 Callback parameters

Callback parameter	Script fragment runs ...
:loading	When the response *starts* to return from the server.
:interactive	When the user can interact with the (incomplete) response. This isn't really meaningful in an Ajax context, but there it is.
:loaded	When the response *completes* loading.
:success	On completion of the request if the HTTP status is not an error (i.e., only if it is in the 200–299 range).
:failure	On completion of the request if the HTTP status is an error (i.e., only if it is outside the 200–299 range).
:complete	After the success or failure callback, regardless of the HTTP status.

13.2.2 A tour of Ajax helpers

The parameters we've seen so far are common to all of the Ajax helpers. Let's now take a brief look at each individual helper in turn. We'll review some of the additional parameters they support, as well as the code that they generate. This won't be an exhaustive reference, but rather a discussion of the more useful features and how they can be used.

link_to_remote

We've already had a look at the link_to_remote helper. By way of a recap, let's just compare the server-side Ruby code that we'd write in our .rhtml file with the generated JavaScript that the browser will see.

Additional parameters
None

Server-side Ruby and HTML code

```
<%= link_to_remote "Click Me", :url => { :action => 'say_hello' },
                               :update => 'display' %>
```

Generated JavaScript code

```
<a href="#"
   onclick="new Ajax.Updater('display',
                             '/hello/say_hello',
                             { asynchronous:true, evalScripts:true });
           return false;">Click Me</a>
```

Clearly the helper is more compact, showing just the salient options and hiding details such as the asynchronous option. This extra clarity is a typical benefit of these helpers, as we'll see.

form_remote_tag

The `form_remote_tag` helper works in just the same way as the non-Ajax `form_tag` helper: it creates a form tag. The difference is that this form tag will have an `onsubmit` handler that will intercept the regular form submission and do an Ajax call instead. In your controller, the form parameters will be available in the usual manner (via the `params` hash).

A clever feature of this helper is that the form will automatically fall back to a "normal" (non-Ajax) form if the browser does not have JavaScript enabled. By default, this regular form submission will go to the same URL as the Ajax call. In your controller, you can detect whether a particular request was made via Ajax or regular form submission by using the following code:

```
def my_action
  if request.xml_http_request?
    # handle Ajax request
  else
    # handle regular form submission
  end
end
```

Typically the server will do much the same thing either way, but it will return a different response. In the Ajax case, an HTML fragment may be returned, whereas in the non-Ajax case, an entire page will be rendered.

Note that `form_remote_tag` is used slightly differently than the other helpers because it generates both the opening and closing form tags. In the following example, note the use of `<%` rather than `<%=`, and the `do` and `end` keywords.

Additional parameters
```
:html
```

This parameter allows custom HTML attributes to be placed on the form tag. For example, you could use it to choose between GET and POST for the non-Ajax fallback.

Server-side Ruby and HTML code
```
<% form_remote_tag :url => { :controller => 'c', :action => 'a' },
                   :update => 'my-node',
                   :html => { :method => 'GET' } do %>
    <!-- body of the form here -->
<% end %>
```

Generated JavaScript code
```
<form action="/c/a"
      method="GET"
      onsubmit="new Ajax.Updater('my-node',
                                 '/c/a',
                                 { asynchronous:true,
```

```
                                         evalScripts:true,
                                         parameters:Form.serialize(this)});
               return false;">
   <!-- body of the form here -->
</form>
```

Note that all the magic is in Prototype's `Form.serialize()` method, as discussed in chapter 11. `Form.serialize()` emulates a normal POST body made from an HTML form, and the Ajax.Updater handles the retrieval and rendering of the HTTP response.

observe_field

The `observe_field` helper triggers an Ajax call automatically whenever the value of a specified form field changes. The way you use it is to first create the form field with a given ID, and then use the `observe_field` helper, referring to that ID as the first parameter, like this:

```
<input type='text' id='text1'>
<%= observe_field 'text1', :url => ... %>
```

There are two options for how the change is detected. If you provide a frequency (in seconds) using the `:frequency` parameter, the form-field's value is checked periodically for a change. If you do not provide a frequency, the JavaScript event mechanism will be used instead. By default, this means an `onchange` event handler will be added to the form field in question.

The value of the form field is sent in the Ajax call as the entire body of the post. This means that you will receive this value in your controller not using the usual `params` hash, but using `request.raw_post`.

Additional Parameters
`:frequency`

The frequency with which the field should be checked for changes. Omit this parameter to use event-based observation instead.

`:function`

Providing this parameter means the helper doesn't use Ajax at all. Instead, the specified JavaScript snippet is executed when the change occurs. Be careful—the name is slightly confusing. This needn't be a function at all. It is simply a snippet of JavaScript, similar to the callbacks we've already seen.

Server-side Ruby and HTML code

```
<%= observe_field "text1",
                  :url => "/my/url",
                  :frequency => 2,
                  :update => "some-div" %>
```

Generated JavaScript code

```
<script type="text/javascript">
//<![CDATA[
  new Form.Element.Observer('text1',
                            2,
                            function(element, value) {
                                new Ajax.Updater('some-div',
                                        '/my/url',
                                             { asynchronous:true,
                                               evalScripts:true,
                                               parameters:value })
                            })
//]]>
</script>
```

Note how, again, this single helper is actually using a useful combination of two entirely separate Prototype objects. This time `Form.Element.Observer` and `Ajax.Updater` are combined into a useful whole.

observe_form

The `observe_form` helper is identical to `observe_field`, except that the ID of an entire form is provided rather than just a single form field. Each field of the form will be observed for changes. When any change occurs, the entire form will be submitted in the same manner as with `form_remote_tag`.

Additional parameters

Same as for `observe_field`.

Server-side Ruby and HTML code

```
<%= observe_form "form1",
                 :url => "/my/url",
                 :frequency => 2,
                 :update => "some-div" %>
```

Generated JavaScript code

```
<script type="text/javascript">
//<![CDATA[
  new Form.Observer('form1',
                    2,
                    function(element, value) {
                        new Ajax.Updater('some-div',
```

```
                                         '/my/url',
                                         { asynchronous:true,
                                           evalScripts:true,
                                           parameters:value })
                        })
    //]]>
    </script>
```

Once again, we see that the real work is all in Prototype. The only difference between the two observer helpers is that `observe_field` generates a call to new Form .Element.Observer, while `observe_form` generates a call to new Form.Observer.

periodically_call_remote

The `periodically_call_remote` helper sets up a simple periodic Ajax call polling the server with the same URL at regular intervals. This is particularly useful when your page contains live data that changes regardless of what the user is doing.

Additional parameters
```
:frequency
```

This is the frequency in seconds of the call. The default frequency is 10 seconds.

Server-side Ruby and HTML code
```
<%= periodically_call_remote :frequency => 10,
                             :url => "/my/url",
                             :update => "some-div" %>
```

Generated JavaScript code
```
<script type="text/javascript">
//<![CDATA[
  new PeriodicalExecuter(function() {
                        new Ajax.Updater('some-div',
                                         '/my/url',
                                         { asynchronous:true,
                                           evalScripts:true })
                        },
                        10)
//]]>
</script>
```

There's a pattern emerging here, isn't there? This time, the PeriodicalExecuter and the Ajax.Updater are combined to create the required functionality. The astute reader may notice that the same effect could be achieved using the Ajax.PeriodicalUpdater that we discussed in chapter 4. In this case, we suspect that Rails hasn't quite caught up with some of Prototype's more recent changes. Whatever the case, the generated code does what we need.

remote_function

The `remote_function` helper really does nothing more than generate a call to Ajax.Updater. It can be used anywhere JavaScript is valid. A typical use would be in a JavaScript event handler, such as an `onchange`, like this:

```
<select id='menu'
        onchange='<%= remote_function :update => "abc",
                                      :url => "/somewhere",
                                      :with => "$F('menu')" %>'>
  <option>Choice 1</option>
  <option>Choice 2</option>
</select>
```

Note the `:with` parameter, which is passed a string containing a JavaScript expression specifying the parameters for the XMLHttpRequest. The value of this expression becomes the POST body of the Ajax request and can be accessed in the controller using `request.raw_post`. In this example, we're using Prototype's `$F()` function to get the current selection in the menu.

Additional parameters
`:with`

This is a JavaScript expression used to provide the body of the Ajax request.

Server-side Ruby and HTML code
```
<%= remote_function :update => "abc",
                    :url => "/somewhere",
                    :with => "$F('menu')" %>
```

Generated JavaScript code
```
new Ajax.Updater('abc',
                 '/somewhere',
                 { asynchronous:true,
                   evalScripts:true,
                   parameters:$F('menu') })
```

The important point to notice is that the generated code is JavaScript only, with no surrounding HTML. That's exactly what we want, because we use this helper in JavaScript contexts, such as inside an `onchange` attribute.

That's about it for the Ajax helpers, but support for Prototype and Scriptaculous in Rails goes a lot further than that. We'll continue by taking a look at some of the more advanced features, which package up these lower-level building blocks and provide ready-to-go application-level functionality, such as autocompletion, and in-place editing.

13.3 *Scriptaculous helpers*

We covered the core details of the Scriptaculous library in chapters 5 through 7. The three main components of Scriptaculous were the visual effects library, the controls, and the drag-and-drop system.

Unsurprisingly, Rails support for Scriptaculous follows the same pattern, and we can break down our coverage of the Scriptaculous helpers along similar lines. We'll begin our exploration of Scriptaculous integration into Rails by looking at the visual effects package.

13.3.1 *Creating visual effects*

The `visual_effect` helper is designed to be used with the callback parameters we've seen on various other helpers. For example, here's a very typical Ajax delete button written as a Ruby fragment inside an .rhtml page:

```
<%= link_to_remote "Delete", :url => { :action => "delete",
                                       :id => person.id }
                   :success => visual_effect(:fade, "person")
%>
```

This will apply a fade effect to the element with ID `person` on successful completion of the Ajax call. So we've fulfilled our promise made at the start of this chapter—that we would see a way to include visual effects while still keeping our code entirely JavaScript free.

In addition to choosing an effect and specifying the element to be affected, extra parameters can be used to customize the effect, as shown in the following two code samples.

Server-side Ruby and HTML code
```
visual_effect(:fade, "person", :duration => 0.5)
```

Generated JavaScript code
```
new Effect.Fade("person", { duration:0.5 });
```

Remember that different subclasses of visual effects can accept different options in the JavaScript options object. Any options passed to `visual_effect` on the Ruby tier that are not otherwise understood will be passed through to the options object.

This single helper function is, then, sufficient to enable access to the entire Effects package from the .rhtml file. We can specify any type of effect and pass any type of option to it, including both the standard options on the base effect, such as `duration`, `from`, and `to`, and the more exotic configuration objects operating on specific effects. The only things that `visual_effect` can't do for us is compose effects or create new subclasses on the fly, and these tasks are probably too complex to address within an automated code-generation system.

13.3.2 *Implementing in-place editors*

In-place editing is a term for a user interaction where a read-only part of a web page changes at a click to an editable field. Any changes to the content are immediately sent to the server via Ajax. It's a nice way to keep your pages uncluttered, yet make everything easily editable without forcing users to go to a separate editing page. We introduced the Scriptaculous in-place editor in chapter 6, and used it to allow editing of the slide captions in our QuickGallery app in chapter 12.

The combination of Scriptaculous and Rails makes it so easy to add this functionality that it almost comes for free. As an example, assume you've got a Person model with a name field. We're going to provide in-place editing for that name.

Server-side Ruby controller class

```ruby
class PersonController < ApplicationController
  in_place_edit_for :person, :name
  def show
    @person = Person.find(params[:id])
  end
end
```

Server-side Ruby and HTML code

```
<html>
  <head><%= javascript_include_tag :defaults %></head>
  <body>
    Name: <%= in_place_editor_field :person, :name %>
  </body>
</html>
```

This is all it takes! That's actually a fully working implementation of in-place editing; just add the Person model as previously described.

OK, so what did we just do? Let's start with the view. The single `in_place_editor_field` helper was all we needed. This helper takes two parameters: the name of the instance variable containing the model object (`:person`), and the name of the field we want an editor for (`:name`).

The HTML created by that helper is as follows:

Generated HTML and JavaScript

```html
<span class="in_place_editor_field"
      id="person_name_1_in_place_editor">Tom</span>
<script type="text/javascript">
```

```
//<![CDATA[
  new Ajax.InPlaceEditor('person_name_1_in_place_editor',
                         '/person/set_person_name/1')
//]]>
</script>
```

All the real work is done by Scriptaculous, using Ajax.InPlaceEditor, but the Rails helper has been kind enough to automatically generate a unique identifier for us. The identifier includes the instance variable name, the field name, and the ID of the model object, so it's a pretty safe bet it will always be unique.

The next thing to notice is the URL being passed to Ajax.InPlaceEditor:

```
/person/set_person_name/1
```

Rails will route this URL to the set_person_name action on our controller. If you look again at the source code for the controller, you might guess that this action has been automatically added to our controller by the call to in_place_edit_for. Rails is writing our code for us at both the client end and the server end!

For the curious, the action added to our controller is very simple, looking something like this:

Generated server-side Ruby code
```
def set_person_name
  Person.find(params[:id]).update_attribute(:name, params[:value])
end
```

Note that the use of update_attribute means that ActiveRecord's validation facility is bypassed. If you need validation, you'll need to write your own action (set_person_name in this example).

The in_place_editor_field helper supports a variety of options, but the ones you will commonly need are :rows and :cols, which determine the size of the edit box. If you specify a value of :rows greater than 1, it automatically switches to using an HTML text area rather than a single-line input field.

Who would have thought that working with these controls could get even more painless? The other main control in the Scriptaculous controls subsystem is the autocompleter. We'll see in the next section how Rails integrates that for us.

13.3.3 *Adding autocomplete features*

Why make your users type too much when your app could be doing the typing for them? That's the thinking behind the increasingly popular autocomplete feature. The idea, in brief, is that as you type into a search field, Ajax calls are happening behind the scenes to find matches for the term you've typed so far. Those matches are presented in a drop-down list, so you can either stop typing and click one, or keep typing just long enough to get to the particular item you're searching for. This is a really nice icing-on-the-cake feature.

Once again, Scriptaculous provides an out-of-the-box implementation that's trivial to use, as we saw in chapter 6. And once again, Rails makes it utterly trivial to add to your app.

Let's continue with the Person theme from the last section. We'll assume there's a Person model that has a name field. We're building a page where people can be searched for by name, and, naturally, we'd like autocompletion.

Server-side Ruby controller class

```ruby
class PersonController < ApplicationController
  auto_complete_for :person, :name
end
```

Server-side Ruby and HTML code

```
<html>
  <head><%= javascript_include_tag :defaults %></head>
  <body>
    Name: <%= text_field_with_auto_complete :person, :name %>
  </body>
</html>
```

As you can see, the general setup is very similar to that for in-place editing. A single declaration in the controller sets up the server-side support, and a single helper in the view creates the magic text field.

Let's have a look at the generated HTML:

Generated HTML and JavaScript

```
<style>
<!-- The helper generates a small stylesheet here,
     which we've omitted for clarity -->
</style>
<input id="person_name" name="person[name]" size="30"
  type="text" />
<div class="auto_complete" id="person_name_auto_complete"></div>
<script type="text/javascript">
//<![CDATA[
  var person_name_auto_completer =
      new Ajax.Autocompleter('person_name',
                             'person_name_auto_complete',
                             '/hello/auto_complete_for_person_name',
                             {})
//]]>
</script>
```

The helper has generated all four components required for a working autocomplete text field: a small stylesheet, the input field, an empty DIV ready to be populated with the search results, and finally the `script` tag, which instantiates the Ajax.Autocompleter from Scriptaculous.

The inclusion of the stylesheet along with everything else is rather bad style, but fortunately it can be disabled. If you want to neaten things up a bit, first use `text_field_with_autocomplete` as shown earlier, and paste the style rules from your browser's view-source window into an appropriate CSS file—probably public/stylesheets/application.css. Now add the `:skip_style` option to the helper, like this:

```
<%= text_field_with_auto_complete :person, :name, {}, :skip_style => true %>
```

Note that empty hash! This is needed, because the helper takes two distinct sets of options and `:skip_style` belongs to the second set.

Finally, you've probably noticed that apart from the autocomplete functionality, the text field doesn't actually do anything. That's OK—it's up to you to build this into a working feature for your app. In our case, we wanted to perform a search, so the next step might be to add a Find button that would take the value from the text field and retrieve and display the person. That's left as an exercise for the reader.

So, we've seen how Rails integrates the Effects and Controls packages from Scriptaculous effortlessly. The final major piece of Scriptaculous is the drag-and-drop system, for which Rails provides a set of helpers too. We'll examine these in the next section.

13.3.4 *Implementing drag and drop*

We introduced Scriptaculous's drag-and-drop system in chapter 7, and saw how powerful it could be in a real-world application in chapter 12.

If you remember, Scriptaculous's drag-and-drop system operates in two layers. At the simple level, it supports draggable objects that can be moved around the page, and droppable objects that can receive the draggables. We can build our own drag-and-drop user interfaces directly on top of these. We can also create higher-level Sortable components, in which all child elements of a container are drag-and-drop enabled, allowing them to be dynamically reordered, or dragged from one container to another.

You won't be surprised by now to be told that Rails supports all of these things from the comfort of our .rhtml file. We'll work through these systems in order, starting with the draggables and droppables, and then moving on to the more complex Sortables.

Creating draggables and droppables

Rails provides two useful helpers that make it very easy to access Scriptaculous's basic drag-and-drop functionality. The style of these helpers is similar to the `observe_field` helper we looked at earlier, in that you first create an element with a particular ID, and then you use the appropriate helper to attach behavior to that element.

Server-side Ruby and HTML code

```
<html>
  <head><%= javascript_include_tag :defaults %></head>
  <body>
    <style>
      .box     { border: thin solid black; width: 100px;
                 margin: 10px; padding: 10px; }
      .big.box { width: 200px; height: 200px; }
    </style>

    <div class="box" id="drag">Drag Me!</div>
    <%= draggable_element "drag" %>

    <div class="big box" id="drop1">Drop here</div>
    <%= drop_receiving_element "drop1",
      :url => { :action => "dropped", :target => 1 } %>

    <div class="big box" id="drop2">Or here</div>
    <%= drop_receiving_element "drop2",
      :url => { :action => "dropped", :target => 2 }  %>

  </body>
</html>
```

In the preceding code, we've thrown in a stylesheet for good measure, as things can get a bit confusing without one. The parts that we're interested in, though, are the `draggable_element` and `drop_receiving_element` helpers. These are the Rails wrappers that wrap the Scriptaculous drag-and-drop support.

The `draggable_element` helper is trivial, providing just a thin veneer over the Scriptaculous Draggable object that we saw in chapter 7.

Server-side Ruby and HTML code

```
<%= dragabble_element "drag" %>
```

Generated JavaScript code

```
<script type="text/javascript">
//<![CDATA[
new Draggable("drag", {})
//]]>
</script>
```

There's a little more to `drop_receiving_element`, and the `:url` parameter gives us the clue. This helper has built-in support for Ajax. A callback is attached to the drop target that makes an Ajax call when an element is dropped. Here's the generated HTML.

Server-side Ruby and HTML code

```
<%= drop_receiving_element "drop1", :url => { :action => "dropped",
                                              :target => 1 } %>
```

Generated JavaScript code

```
<script type="text/javascript">
//<![CDATA[
Droppables.add(
  "drop1",
  { onDrop: function(element) {
              new Ajax.Request(
                '/demo/dropped?target=1',
                { asynchronous:true,
                  evalScripts:true,
                  parameters: 'id=' +
                              encodeURIComponent(element.id) })
          }
  })
//]]>
</script>
```

You can also see that the DOM ID of the element that was dropped is passed to the server as a POST parameter `id`. Note that in addition to the `:url` parameter, the other standard Ajax-helper parameters are also supported, such as `:update` and `:position`.

Customizing drag and drop

In chapter 7, we saw that a number of parameters are supported by `new Draggable` and `Droppables.add` to customize the drag-and-drop behavior. You'll be glad to hear that the Rails helpers also support these parameters. As with the `visual_effect` helper, all extra parameters to the Ruby method are passed through to the options object in the JavaScript code. For example, here's how to get the dragged item to revert to its original position after dropping:

Server-side Ruby and HTML code

```
<%= dragabble_element "drag", :revert => true %>
```

Generated JavaScript code

```
<script type="text/javascript">
  //<![CDATA[
  new Draggable("drag", {revert:true})
  //]]>
</script>
```

The `draggable_element` and `drop_receiving_element` helpers support all of the same parameters as their Scriptaculous counterparts, Draggable and Droppable.

We can now write our own low-level drag-and-drop routines. What can Rails offer us if we want to work with the big gun of Scriptaculous drag and drop, the Sortable object? We'll look at that in the next section.

Making list elements sortable

We've seen in chapters 7 and 12 how easy Scriptaculous makes it to turn a simple list into a drag-and-drop sortable list. It will come as no surprise that Rails provides a helper to make it just that little bit easier. Here's an example Rails view with a sortable list:

Server-side Ruby and HTML code

```
<html>
  <head><%= javascript_include_tag :defaults %></head>
  <body>
    <ul id='list'>
      <li id="item_1">Apples</li>
      <li id="item_2">Oranges</li>
      <li id="item_3">Pears</li>
      <li id="item_4">Bananas</li>
    </ul>
    <%- sortable_element "list", :url => { :action => 'reorder' } %>
  </body>
</html>
```

The style is becoming very familiar–an element in the page is referred to by its ID in order to upgrade it with some special functionality. In this case, the bulleted list is made sortable via the `sortable_element` helper.

As you might have guessed, `sortable_element` supports Ajax much like the `drop_receiving_element` in the previous section. The `:url`, `:update`, and `:position` parameters, familiar from `link_to_remote`, can be used to define an Ajax call that will be triggered whenever the ordering of items is changed.

One thing that can trip you up with sortables is the IDs on the individual items. These must be given, and they must follow the format we've used here:

```
<item-name>_<item-id>
```

Rails will use these IDs to map the UI elements to the data model when fielding the Ajax call. In a Rails app, it would be typical to generate these IDs using the actual ActiveRecord IDs of the model objects. For example, here is a list of people with appropriate ID attributes. We are assuming the instance variable `@people` holds an array of Person model objects, and that the Person model has `id` and `name` attributes.

Server-side Ruby and HTML code

```
<ul>
  <% for person in @people %>
    <li id="person_<%= person.id %>"><%= person.name %></li>
  <% end %>
</ul>
```

Let's have a quick look at the HTML generated by the `sortable_element` helper:

Server-side Ruby and HTML code

```
<%= sortable_element "list", :url => { :action => 'reorder' } %>
```

Generated JavaScript code

```
<script type="text/javascript">
//<![CDATA[
  Sortable.create(
    "list",
    { onUpdate: function() {
                  new Ajax.Request(
                   '/demo/reorder',
                    { asynchronous:true,
                      evalScripts:true,
                      parameters:Sortable.serialize("list") })
                }
    })
//]]>
</script>
```

Unsurprisingly, the generated code calls `Sortable.create()`. The interesting part is that an `Ajax.Request` has been declared on the Sortable's `onUpdate` callback. This is what gives us the Ajax call every time the list ordering is changed. Also note the use of `Sortable.serialize()` to generate the POST parameters for the Ajax call.

Let's have a quick look at the parameters returned by `Sortable.serialize`. (The easiest way to do this is to look at the XMLHttpRequest trace in Firebug's console—you are using Firebug, right? If not, run, don't walk, to your favorite search engine and type "firebug"!) However you get there, you should see that `Sortable.serialize` is returning something along these lines:

```
list[]=1&list[]=3&list[]=2&list[]=4
```

This is an unusual looking query string, until you understand how this is interpreted by Rails. Have a look at the entry added to the Rails log file (log/development.log) when you reorder the list. You should see the parameter hash generated by the Ajax call:

```
{ "list"=>["1", "3", "2", "4"], "action"=>"reorder", "controller"=>"demo" }
```

When Rails sees multiple parameters with the same name, and that name ends with [], it groups all the values into an array such that the ordering is preserved. We now have an array of the IDs of our sortable items, indicating the order they are now in. Perfect!

There's an interesting point here. So far we've seen various ways that Rails provides support for Scriptaculous. Now we see that the story goes a little deeper. Not only does Rails have support for Scriptaculous, but Scriptaculous has features, such as `Sortable.serialize()`, that specifically support Rails.

That concludes our coverage of the Scriptaculous helpers, and the support for Prototype and Scriptaculous that is available from within the .rhtml file. The story doesn't end here, though. Recently, Rails has added another set of features to support Ajax, called RJS templates. As the lead developer of these features is none other than Sam Stephenson of Prototype, we'll see that our favorite JavaScript libraries feature prominently here too. We'll investigate these in a minute, but first, let's stop to consider what we've seen so far.

13.4 *To JavaScript or not to JavaScript*

With all this effort put into keeping your views free of JavaScript, you might get the impression that Rails developers think JavaScript is evil. Not at all. In fact, any nontrivial Ajaxified web app is bound to need custom JavaScript. What can get very nasty though, is too much mixing of languages. Your view templates already consist of Ruby embedded in HTML; having JavaScript inside Ruby inside HTML is a mess we recommend you don't get into.

As a rule of thumb, if you need custom JavaScript, define a function in your public/javascripts/application.js and call it from your page. Try to limit your .rhtml files to HTML and Ruby. If you do need a snippet of JavaScript, and the provided helpers won't do, consider writing a custom helper for the job. It's very easy: just add a method to app/helpers/application_helper.rb that returns your JavaScript as a string.

OK, let's move on now to look at the recent developments in Rails 1.1 that directly support the use of Ajax, Prototype, and Scriptaculous.

13.5 *The next level: RJS*

RJS is a new kind of view template added to Rails in version 1.1. RJS gives us a very easy and powerful mechanism for doing advanced Ajax, by generating JavaScript dynamically on the server and sending it to the browser in response to an Ajax call. RJS integrates so smoothly with your Ruby code, it almost feels like you've got an object reference directly from the server to the browser's DOM document.

The name comes from the .rjs file extension. In the same way that a .rhtml file is a template for a dynamically generated HTML page, a .rjs file is a template for dynamically generated JavaScript. The big difference is that while a .rhtml file is basically an HTML file with embedded Ruby "scriptlets" (the <%= . . . %> tags), a .rjs file contains nothing but Ruby code. Rails employs some clever Ruby tricks to convert this Ruby code into JavaScript before sending it to the browser.

Before we dive into the details, let's have a look at the motivation for adding this facility.

13.5.1 *The multiple-update problem*

The traditional approach to Ajax in Rails is as follows:

- Client makes an Ajax request in response to some event.
- Application logic executes on the server, probably querying or updating the database.
- The server returns a fragment of HTML.
- The client renders this HTML fragment in the section of the page that needs updating.

There's an inherent limitation here—we're assuming only one part of the page needs updating. We can see this assumption baked right in to Ajax.Updater—you pass it the ID of a single element that needs updating. The same limitation is in all of the Ajax helpers we've seen—they all provide the :update parameter to specify the ID of a single element to be updated. This is probably the most commonly hit limitation of the Ajax helpers.

There's really only so far you can go with Ajax development before you hit the need to update two parts of the page at once. The classic example is when you have some kind of summary information on the page. For example, you have a list of items in a shopping cart, along with an Ajax-powered button to add another item. The button might look like this:

```
<%= link_to_remote "Add to Cart", :url => { :action => "add_item" },
                       :update => "cart",
                       :position => "bottom" %>
```

But what of the shopping cart summary? Typically, we'll have a line at the bottom of the cart, or in a sidebar, reading something like "12 items. Total: $29.40". When we add a new item to the cart, that total needs to change too.

We've already encountered this problem in chapter 4, with our QuickGallery application, where we needed to update the subfolders list and breadcrumb trail along with the main thumbnail area. We developed two solutions to the issue using hand-coded JavaScript. The first was to write inline `<script>` tags in the content, which the browser ignores but Prototype strips out and parses. The second was to make use of the Ajax.Responders and X-JSON header introduced in Prototype 1.5.

However, in this chapter we're using Rails, not hand-coded JavaScript. Rails' RJS system provides a wrapper around Prototype's support for multiple updates. By way of a sneak preview, here's a snippet of the RJS code that would solve our multiple-update problem:

```
page.insert_html :bottom, :cart, :partial => "item", :object => @cart
page.replace_html :summary, :partial => "summary", :object => @cart
```

That's an RJS script telling the browser to update two DOM nodes, which results in rendering two corresponding partial page templates. Is this magic? Surely updating the DOM and rendering partials take place on either side of the client/server divide, maybe thousands of miles apart? This seems too good to be true!

Let's retreat from magical incantations for a moment and take refuge in something familiar—good old Hello World.

13.5.2 *Hello from RJS*

In this simple example, we're going to use the RJS system to update a DOM element with the phrase "Hello from RJS!". To do this, we need to first create a view for the application. This will be a standard .rhtml file; that is, HTML with embedded Ruby helpers.

Rails view template (app/views/hello/index.rhtml)

```
<html>
<head><%= javascript_include_tag :defaults %></head>
<body>
  <%= link_to_remote "Say Hello", :url => { :action => "say_hello" } %>
  <div id="display"></div>
</body>
</html>
```

So far, everything looks familiar enough. Note the `link_to_remote` helper, which will generate an Ajax request in the emitted JavaScript. You may have noticed that the `link_to_remote` call lacks the `:update` parameter. We'll see why shortly. Next, let's add a controller to provide a `say_hello()` method for the URL of this request to map onto.

Rails controller (app/controllers/rjs_hello_controller.rb)

```
class RjsHelloController < ApplicationController
  def say_hello
  end
end
```

We simply need to declare the method in the controller. Our view template doesn't need access to any dynamic data, so the method doesn't need to do anything. Normally, at this point, we'd move on to generate a .rhtml partial, but here we're going to do something slightly different, and add a .rjs template file instead.

Rails RJS template (app/views/rjs_hello/say_hello.rjs)

```
page.replace_html "display", "Hello From RJS!"
```

That's it—click on the link and voila!

OK, so what happened? The first thing to notice is that the RJS script is a view. It lives in the same place as a traditional .rhtml view, but it has a .rjs file extension. Rails uses the extension to decide how to handle the template. If Rails finds a template with a .rhtml extension, any embedded scriptlets will be processed, and the resultant HTML will be sent to the client. If the template has a .rjs extension, Rails processes the file differently. The RJS is executed as a Ruby script, with a special page object in scope: a JavaScriptGenerator.

Before we see how the script works, let's take a look at the output, either by examining the XMLHttpRequest trace in the Firebug console, or simply by pointing the browser at http://localhost:3000/rjs_hello/say_hello. You should see the following JavaScript:

Generated JavaScript code

```
try {
  Element.update("display", "Hello from RJS!");
} catch (e) {
  alert('RJS error:\n\n' + e.toString());
  alert('Element.update(\"display\", \"Hello from RJS!\");');
  throw e
}
```

The single line in our RJS template got translated to a call to `Element.update()`, and the whole thing was wrapped up in some helpful error handling.

Clearly, this JavaScript was evaluated in order to get our "Hello" message onto the page, but when and how? As was mentioned earlier, the `link_to_remote` helper that triggered the RJS has no `:update` parameter. This means Rails generated an Ajax.Request rather than an Ajax.Updater, and no part of the page is going to be automatically updated with the response text. What's happening is that the content type of the Ajax response is set to `text/javascript`. Prototype is detecting this and automatically evaluating the script.

Let's get back to the RJS template itself, which is just this single line:

```
page.replace_html "display", "Hello From RJS!"
```

That call to `page.replace_html` looks like an operation to update the DOM document. In fact, it's not. To be accurate, this call generates JavaScript that will update the page, when it is evaluated by the browser. It's either a subtle distinction, or an enormous one, depending on your mood. Think of the page object as a kind of buffer, accumulating a JavaScript script. Each time you invoke one of its operations, it adds some JavaScript to the buffer. The result of the RJS template is the final script that the page object has accumulated.

Hopefully, by now it makes sense that RJS is a new kind of view template. It's a template that, when rendered, gives you JavaScript instead of HTML.

13.5.3 *Multiple updates and RJS*

Now that you've seen how you can update a single element in RJS, it's pretty clear that updating two or more is not going to be a problem—just call `page.replace_html` as many times as necessary.

The next part of our solution to the multiple-update problem concerns where all this dynamically added HTML is coming from. In our previous example, we passed a simple "Hello From RJS" string to the `replace_html` method. That's not going to scale up well. What we want is the ability to keep all our HTML tidily in partial page templates. Support for exactly this is built right into `page.replace_html`. Upgrading the Hello From RJS example to use a partial page template, would give us the following:

Rails partial view template (app/views/demo/_hello.rhtml)
```
<b><i>Hello World!</i></b>
```

Rails RJS template (app/views/demo/say_hello.rjs)
```
page.replace_html :display, :partial => "hello"
```

The RJS we have already seen as a sneak preview should now make sense:

Rails RJS template
```
page.insert_html :bottom, :cart, :partial => "item", :object => @cart
page.replace_html :summary, :partial => "summary", :object => @cart
```

The only new thing here is `page.insert_html`, which takes a position as its first parameter, and inserts the new content. It is the RJS equivalent of passing a `:position` parameter to the standard Ajax helpers. Just as with the familiar `render()` method, the `:partial` parameter specifies a partial page template to use, and the `:object` parameter passes an object into the template for rendering.

Let's also recall the "Add to Cart" link from our shopping cart example. Here is the non-RJS version again:

Rails view template fragment (non-RJS version)
```
<%= link_to_remote "Add to Cart", :url => { :action => "add_item" },
                   :update => "cart",
                   :position => "bottom" %>
```

Now that we're using RJS, we need to make a small change. We're not using traditional single-update Ajax, so the `link_to_remote` call should not have `:update` or `:position` parameters.

Rails view template fragment (RJS version)
```
<%= link_to_remote "Add to Cart", :url => { :action => "add_item" } %>
```

Hopefully, these simple examples have illustrated how RJS operates. So far, we've looked at a few of the methods it supports, such as `insert_html` and `replace_html`. In the next section, we'll take a deeper look at the capabilities of the JavaScript-Generator object.

13.5.4 A tour of RJS

The `replace_html` and `insert_html` methods on the page object are extremely useful by themselves. RJS doesn't stop there though. Let's take a quick tour of the other features provided by RJS. Remember, RJS is nothing but a mechanism for generating JavaScript, so we're essentially looking at the different kinds of JavaScript statements we can create, and the various ways of doing so.

Using element proxies

Prototype often provides more than one way of doing the same thing. For example, in chapter 11, we saw that the Element object's methods could be called either as static methods, or as methods on the DOM nodes themselves, which use

Element as a mixin. So, for example, `Element.hide('x')` and `$('x').hide` are equivalent. The latter form is just a bit more compact and has a more object-oriented feel.

This OO-style is also available in RJS, like this:

Rails RJS
```
page[:x].hide
```

There's something clever going on here, using a bit of dynamic Ruby magic. The expression `page[:x]` yields something called an element proxy. Any method call we make on this proxy results in the equivalent JavaScript call being added to the generated script. It's completely generic—you can call any method that you know will be available when the JavaScript runs:

Rails RJS
```
page[:x].how_clever
```

Generated JavaScript code
```
$('x').howClever()
```

Notice that the proxy even converts between Ruby's underscore convention and JavaScript's camel-case convention, making the Ruby programmer feel that little bit more at home!

Prototype and Scriptaculous add a rich set of very useful methods to the Element class, so there's suddenly a great deal we can do with RJS, just using this one generic feature—element proxies. For example, we can create visual effects:

Rails RJS
```
page[:summary].visual_effect "highlight", :duration => 0.5
```

Generated JavaScript code
```
$("display").visualEffect("highlight", {"duration": 0.5});
```

Here we see that the element proxy also knows how to convert between Ruby and JavaScript conventions for keyword parameters.

Using class proxies

Many of the features built in to Prototype and Scriptaculous are exposed as class methods rather than instance methods. A common example is the Form class, which provides methods like `Form.enable()`, `Form.disable()`, `Form.focusFirst-Element()`, etc. Using a similar trick to the element proxy, RJS makes all such methods available directly from Ruby. Here's an example:

Rails RJS
```
page.form.disable "myform"
```

Generated JavaScript code
```
Form.disable("myform")
```

The general form is `page.<class-name>.<method-name>`. Any method call on the page object (as long as it is not already a defined method, such as `replace_html`) will generate a class proxy, and any method call on this class proxy will add the equivalent JavaScript method call to the generated script.

Working with collections

One of the most impressive features of RJS is its ability to work very easily with entire collections of elements. This support leverages Prototype's `$$()` function, which we covered in chapter 11. Using `$$()`, you get to select the elements you want to work on using CSS selectors.

Let's start with a quick example, which hides every element in a certain CSS class:

Rails RJS
```
page.select(".myclass").each do |e|
  e.hide
end
```

Once again, it seems too good to be true! A lot of the support for this style of programming is actually in Prototype itself, rather than RJS. You can see this in the generated JavaScript, which turns out to be very similar to the Ruby code:

Generated JavaScript code
```
$$(".myclass").each(function(value, index) {
  value.hide();
});
```

As we remarked in chapter 10, Prototype's Array extensions follow the Ruby Enumerable mixin quite closely. While this helps to make the Ruby programmer more comfortable when hand-coding JavaScript, we can see here that it also eases the job of the JavaScript generator considerably. The `page.select()` method takes a CSS selector and returns yet another magical proxy. And once again, the proxy is completely dynamic, so you can use any method supported by Prototype's Enumerable type.

Adding arbitrary JavaScript

If all of these clever generic tricks still don't get you the JavaScript you need, there is a last resort—you can add any JavaScript you like to the generator, simply by passing a string to the << method, like this:

Rails RJS
```
page << "x = myFunction(1, 2, 3);"
```

As was explained previously, the page object maintains a buffer of generated JavaScript. The << operator simply allows you to append text directly to this buffer.

Now that you have seen the capabilities of the JavaScriptGenerator object, let's take a look at another way of accessing this object.

13.5.5 *Rendering RJS inline*

Sometimes the RJS you need is so short that it seems a headache to have to put it in a separate RJS file. In these situations, you might want to include the RJS directly in the controller. The :update parameter to render gives you just this:

Rails controller code
```
def my_action
  ...
  render :update do |page|
    page[:some_div].visual_effect :fade
  end
end
```

Of course, it can be argued that this is bad style, in that it mixes view logic with controller logic, but it's a handy option, especially when you're trying a quick experiment.

All in all, we can see that RJS templates offer a powerful means for generating JavaScript on the server tier. Of course, we could just write all that code directly in JavaScript—the real magic comes from the fact that RJS integrates the server tier and client-side scripting into a seamless whole. You have access to database data, server-side HTML templates, and client-side user-interface code all in one place. The Rails community has an overarching goal for Ajax: "as easy as not to." With RJS they've taken a giant step closer to that goal.

13.6 *Summary*

That concludes our whistle-stop tour of Ruby on Rails, and specifically of how it integrates Prototype and Scriptaculous quite neatly. While the emphasis throughout the rest of this book has been on hand-written JavaScript utilizing Prototype's and Scriptaculous's power, we've seen in this chapter an alternative approach to using these libraries, in which control of the entire client-side code base is handed over to the server.

When "writing" our JavaScript code in Ruby, it's remarkable how closely the server-side code mimics the client-side code that we would have written if we really were writing the JavaScript ourselves. The Prototype idiom of providing extensible options objects as constructor arguments fits perfectly with Ruby's ability to add named parameters to method calls. Looking at the JavaScript libraries in this way, we can see how closely the development of Prototype and Scriptaculous have followed Rails, and vice versa, creating a powerful synergy between the three.

As we remarked at the outset of this chapter, using Rails to write all your Java-Script in Ruby doesn't mean that you don't need to understand how the Java-Script works. If you're a hardcore Ruby fan who has snuck straight to this chapter, we urge you to go back and read the rest of the book, and to discover the full power of Prototype and Scriptaculous. Even if we can't persuade you to write any JavaScript, understanding the details of the libraries will greatly improve your ability to work with them.

HTTP Primer

> "Excuse me, sir. Might I have a copy of *Great Expectations* by Charles Dickens?"
>
> "Why certainly, sir! Here it is straight-away."

While perhaps a tad on the formal side, this simple verbal interaction represents a real-world example of a request for something, followed by a response that satisfies that request. Such simple interactions are the heart and soul of the HTTP protocol—the standard protocol on which the World Wide Web depends.

So what the Dickens does Dickens have to do with the Web? Let's find out.

A.1   Why should we care about HTTP?

Yes, why? After all, between the browsers and the server-side libraries available to us, we never really have to know what's going on beneath the surface, do we?

When a form is submitted, or a link is clicked, the browser takes care of creating and sending the request to the server. And when the response is returned, the browser interprets it and acts accordingly on our behalf. Server-side mechanisms, such as PHP or the Servlet and JSP mechanisms of J2EE, take care of parsing the request in order to make its information (cookies, parameters, headers, and so on) available to our server-side code via a tidy API. Such facilities also create and send the response on our behalf using an equally tidy API. So why bother learning anything about the guts of HTTP at all?

Well first, it's always a good idea to have a sound base of knowledge on the lower-level workings of the mechanisms that we are using. Having a good understanding of how the tools and packages we rely upon do their job makes it much easier for us to ensure that we are using them effectively. Additionally, such fundamental knowledge can be put to good use when diagnosing problems that arise when things don't go quite the way we'd planned.

But even beyond that, using Ajax through XMLHttpRequest exposes us to more of the underbelly of the Web than we were ever forced to confront when merely using links and forms in HTML pages.

So let's take a bit of a look at the back alleys of the Web, and see what makes it tick.

A.2   What is HTTP?

Simply put, HTTP (Hypertext Transfer Protocol) is a text-based protocol for transferring data across the Internet. It is the basis for World Wide Web communications, where clients send requests to servers, which return responses to the clients, all using a lower-level protocol: TCP/IP (Transmission Control Protocol/ Internet Protocol).

Conventionally, servers listen on port 80 for HTTP requests, though it is possible to configure the use of other ports. Port 8080 is frequently used as an alternative port for active content serving, such as by servlet engines.

Be aware that we will only be exploring the tip of the iceberg in this appendix—the tip that is most important to us as web developers. For more details, consult the HTTP 1.1 specification itself, which is available at http://www.w3.org/ Protocols/rfc2616/rfc2616.html.

Two very important aspects of HTTP—at least as far as web developers are concerned—are that requests are made for the delivery of resources, and that HTTP is a stateless protocol. Let's explore what those aspects mean for web developers.

A.2.1 Resources and URLs

"Why did the chicken cross the road?" This tired old joke may have many punch lines, but the answer to a similar question, "Why did the client make a request," has only one: "To access a resource."

While we may be conditioned by our Web experience to think of resource as files, be they HTML, image data, plain text, zip archives, or any other file type, resources are really a varied lot. You may not think of server-side state as a resource, but as far as HTTP concepts are concerned, it's as concrete a resource as an image file of your favorite pet.

In practical terms, something is always returned to the client (which is sometimes termed the user agent) as a response to the request. It may be a direct response, such as a requested document, or an indirect response, such as a document containing the results of an operation.

A direct response simply returns a resource that was requested: the aforementioned pet photo, for example, or an HTML document, or perhaps even a CSS stylesheet. The request asks for the pet photo or other resource, and the response provides it.

In an indirect response, the returned response is a result of the actual satisfaction of the request, not the resource itself. For example, the request could have been to perform an action that causes a database to be updated, perhaps supplying some data to go with the request. The response would return the results of that action; perhaps an HTML page denoting success or failure, but at minimum a status code is always returned.

In either case, the resource to be accessed is identified by a Universal Resource Locator, more affectionately known as a URL. A URL identifies the protocol to be used, the server to be contacted, and the specific resource that is to be accessed on that server.

A typical URL is of this form:

```
protocol://server-domain/resource
```

Here's a simple example:

```
http://www.bearbibeault.com/index.html
```

This specifies that the HTTP protocol is to be used to access a resource named index.html on the server identified by the domain name www.bearbibeault.com.

It is beyond the scope of this book to describe how domain names are used to locate servers on the Internet, but if you are interested, do a search on the term "Domain Name System" or "DNS."

We also stated that HTTP was stateless. Let's find out what is meant by that.

A.2.2   *Statelessness*

"No man is an island, entire of itself." What John Donne wrote in 1624 may be true of a human being, but it's not applicable to HTTP requests.

HTTP is termed a stateless protocol because every request/response cycle is "an island unto itself." The HTTP protocol makes no provisions for the server to recognize multiple requests from the same user agent as having any relation to each other, or to remember any data from one request to the next.

So how can we use HTTP to create web applications? If we can't retain any sort of state across multiple requests, it will be difficult to get anything but the most simple tasks accomplished.

Many web servers come to our aid in this regard, overcoming this obstacle by providing the concept of a session. Sessions allow state to be retained on the server across multiple requests; sessions are identified by a unique key (usually termed the session ID) that is passed back and forth between the client and server. The exact mechanism for maintaining a session is specific to each web server, though frequently cookies are used to maintain the session ID across multiple requests.

Up to this point, we've talked about requests as if they are of a single type. But actually there are a handful of different types of requests that can be made to a server. Let's find out a bit more about that.

A.3 *What are the request types?*

Chances are that when you think of a request to the server, you think of obtaining a resource from the server; "give me Dickens," for example. But that's only one of the possible types of requests that can be made.

There are actually eight different types of requests that a user agent can make of a server. Each of these types is distinguished by the method specified for the request (sometimes also termed the verb). These methods specify the type of operation that is to be applied to the resource identified in the URL. The eight methods are briefly described in table A.1.

Table A.1   The HTTP request methods

Method	Description
GET	Asks for a resource to be returned as the response. This is likely the most common type of request made on the Internet.
HEAD	Similar to GET except that only the metadata associated with the resource is returned. This is useful for finding out information about a resource without having to actually download the entire resource.
POST	Sends data to the server to be processed by the target resource. Generally the resource is a program or other execution unit that processes the data and returns the results of that processing as its response.
PUT	The opposite of GET, used to upload a resource to the server.
DELETE	Causes the specified resource to be deleted from the server.
TRACE	Usually used as a diagnostic tool; causes the request to be echoed back to the user agent.
OPTIONS	Returns information about the capabilities of the web server with regards to the specified resource.
CONNECT	Reserved for use with a proxy that can dynamically switch to being an SSL tunnel.

Of these request types, only the GET, POST, and HEAD methods are common on the Web; the remainder have little to no broad support across different browsers.

As Ajax developers, we have a little more say in requests that are sent from the client via XMLHttpRequest, but even so, browser limitations and inconsistencies between the various implementations of Ajax prevent us from going whole-hog with regards to the generation of requests, as we will examine soon. We'll see a tool that will tell us more about these limitations in section A.5.3.

For now, let's concentrate on how HTTP requests are formatted for transmission to the server.

A.4 What are the formats of HTTP messages?

We've already stated that an HTTP cycle consists of the user agent sending a request message to the server, and receiving a response message back. In this section, we'll look at the actual formats of these messages.

Even though the browser, or the XMLHttpRequest object in the case of Ajax, usually takes care of formatting these messages on our behalf, understanding their format is helpful in using these mechanisms effectively, or for diagnosing problems when things blow up in our faces.

HTTP is a simple text-based protocol. Messages are formatted from text characters without any binary encoded data. Within each message, all lines must be terminated with a CRLF pair (a carriage return character, followed by a line feed character). The textual nature of the messages makes them easy to create, read, and interpret. But even so, the formats of the messages, as outlined in the next few sections, must be rigidly followed for the messages to be considered valid.

Let's take a look at the request message.

A.4.1 The request message format

The format of a request message is rather straightforward. It and consists of the following elements:

- An opening line identifying the method, resource, and protocol being used. Each of these fields must be separated from the next with a space character.

- Zero or more header lines consisting of the name of the header, a colon, at least one whitespace character, and the value of the header.

- A blank line.

- An optional request message body whose interpretation depends upon the method being employed.

Pretty simple stuff, considering how much work it gets done!

Let's take a look at a sample GET request message (the notation `<crlf>` is used to denote the CRLF pair of characters):

```
GET /some/path/to/a/folder/whatever.html HTTP/1.1<crlf>
Host: www.bearbibeault.com:80<crlf>
User-Agent: Fred's Nifty-Wifty Browser V1.0beta<crlf>
<crlf>
```

This request asks the server to get the specified resource, an HTML file in this case, using the HTTP 1.1 protocol. It then includes two headers. The `Host` header is mandatory for the HTTP 1.1 protocol, and it specifies the Internet resource host and port number of the resource being requested. It is used whenever there is an ambiguity that cannot be resolved merely by inspecting the URL. All other headers are optional, but it is considered good form to at least include a `User-Agent` header to identify the program making the request.

Headers can span multiple lines if need be, by starting continuation lines with at least one whitespace character. The blank line separating the headers from the body content must be present even if the body is empty, as it is in this case.

GET requests send no data to the server; at least not as part of the request message. Query parameters are the only means to send data to the server during a GET.

For POST requests, things get more interesting. The body of a POST is expected to be a list of name-value pairs specifying the data to be processed by the resource. Each value is separated from its name with an equal sign character (=), and each data pair is separated from the next with an ampersand (&).

Because special characters within the data (including the equals and ampersand characters used to separate fields) would cause confusion to any software responsible for parsing this data, the names and values composing the data fields must be URL encoded. Luckily, the browser handles this for us when performing a form submission, but when building up the body content of a POST message (or creating the query string for a GET) we hold the responsibility for ensuring that the data is properly encoded.

The encoding of special characters is fairly simple. Some characters have a direct replacement; for example, space characters are represented by the plus sign. Other characters do not have a direct replacement, and their encoding consists of the percent character (%) followed by the hexadecimal ASCII value for the character. When operating under JavaScript control, the global functions `encode-URI()` and `encodeURIComponent()` come to our aid, preventing us from having to encode the elements by hand. (On a Java server, check out the java.net.URLEncoder class for a helping hand.)

As an example of this encoding scheme, let's say that we wanted to POST data values with names: "a 1", b 2", and "c 3", whose respective values are "Me & I", "Me and I", and "Me + I". Note that all the values and names have some non-alphanumeric characters that require encoding. Properly formatted and encoded, the body content for the POST message to pass these parameters would be as follows:

```
a+1=Me+%26+I&b+2=Me+and+I&c+3=Me+%2B+I
```

Notice how the non-alphanumeric characters (ampersand, equals, plus, and spaces) have been encoded so as not to interfere with the punctuation characters used to format the data fields.

Simple enough! But surely the response, where large amounts of data might be transferred, is more complicated? Let's see.

A.4.2 *The response message format*

The format of a response is similarly straightforward. It consists of the following:

- An opening line identifying the protocol used, a response status code, and a reason string
- Zero or more header lines consisting of the name of the header, a colon, at least one whitespace character, and the value of the header
- A blank line
- Any data being returned whose interpretation depends upon the method being employed

Except for the first line, it's almost identical in format to a request message. But while the format of the headers may be the same, the types of headers sent back differ from those that make sense for a request message.

Here is a minimal response message (omitting a bunch of headers that a server might usually include):

```
HTTP/1.1 200 OK<crlf>
Content-type: text/html<crlf>
Content-length: 55<crlf>
<crlf>
<html><crlf>
  <body><crlf>
    Hi there!<crlf>
  </body><crlf>
</html><crlf>
<crlf>
```

The status codes that can be returned (as the second item in the first line) are defined by the HTTP specification and are too numerous to list here. These are some of the most commonly seen status codes and their customary reason strings:

- 200 OK
- 403 Forbidden
- 404 Not Found
- 500 Internal Server Error

Note that the reason strings are considered customary. Servers and server-side software units are free to return any reason string that they feel is appropriate. For example, an attempt to access a protected resource could result in this status line:

```
HTTP/1.1 403 Hey buddy! What kind of tomfoolery are you trying to
pull?
```

The status code, reason string, response headers, and body content are all of very great interest to us as Ajax developers, as they are the results returned to us when an Ajax request completes. In the next section, we'll take a look at how XMLHttpRequest exposes us to HTTP in ways that HTML forms and links do not.

A.5 *What's the Ajax connection?*

Confined in the tight little box of anchor tags and forms, the non-Ajax web developer doesn't have a whole lot of leeway when it comes to generating requests, and pretty much none when dealing with responses. A link created with the HTML anchor tag always results in a GET request, and the method attribute of the form tag allows only the specification of GET or POST (anything else usually results in the browser submitting a GET). And just completely forget about setting request headers!

But web developers who have Ajax as part of their application development toolbox have a bit more say in the matter. First, let's take a look at generating requests.

A.5.1 *Generating requests with Ajax*

The power of the XMLHttpRequest object gives a greater degree of control over the requests that we can send to a server. With Ajax requests generated via XMLHttpRequest, we can set request headers to our heart's content; something we are powerless to do with form submissions or links.

We also have a somewhat limited means to create request messages with any of the valid request method types—limited because the support for methods other than GET or POST is inconsistent across implementations of XMLHttpRequest (or equivalent) in the various browsers. Firefox appears to be the implementation with the broadest support for HTTP methods.

Using the Prototype Ajax.Request object in a capable browser, such as Firefox, we could make an Ajax request to a server-side resource using the DELETE method as shown in listing A.1.

Listing A.1 Making a request to the server using Ajax

```
new Ajax.Request(
  '/the/server/side/resource',
  {
    method: 'delete',
    requestHeaders: [
      'x-headerName1', 'headerValue1',
      'x-headerName2', 'headerValue2'
    ],
    postBody: Form.serialize(document.someForm)
  }
);
```

This bit of code creates and sends a request message to the server specifying a resource via the URL of the first parameter, and within the options hash it specifies the method, request headers, and POST body to send.

Unlike in the method attribute of an HTML form element, we have some freedom to specify other request methods. Here, we specified delete; something we cannot do with an HTML form. But, as mentioned earlier, some browsers will not allow methods such as DELETE to be specified and will silently substitute a supported method type; usually GET. Be aware of these limitations when coding your applications. (See section A.5.3 for a tool that can help you uncover any limitations in browsers that you are planning to support.) Also note that when specifying request methods to a Prototype Ajax.Request instance, method names must be lowercased, even though they will eventually be uppercased in the request message.

In listing A.1, we also supplied some custom request headers. Again, this is something we cannot do with an HTML form or anchor element.

And finally, we supplied a POST body to be sent as the content of the message. However, it won't do us much good in this case—Prototype will only send the value of the postBody option as the message body if the method type is post. That makes sense, if you think about it, and it is consistent with the intentions of HTTP.

As you can see, XMLHttpRequest gives us more power to control requests than is available through conventional HTML elements. But where it really gives us some muscle is in dealing with responses. Let's take a look at how Ajax grants us access to the innermost secrets of responses.

A.5.2 *Getting responses via Ajax*

Without Ajax and XMLHttpRequest, web developers don't have a great deal to do with responses. After the browser generates a request, it receives the response and reacts to that response according to the information provided by the response headers.

Quite commonly, the content type of the response will identify the response as an HTML document, and the browser will display the document. Other content types and "content dispositions" are possible that could result in other activities, such as processing an XML document using an XSLT stylesheet, downloading a zip file to the filesystem, or even launching a PDF attachment in a reader program. But in all of these cases, the browser is in control, and we, as web developers, aren't included in the festivities.

All that changes with Ajax. With the XMLHttpRequest object (or its use though a facility such as Prototype), we initiate the request, and we receive the response. Or more accurately, XMLHttpRequest receives the response and makes it available to us to process in any manner that we deem appropriate.

Table A.2 shows the methods and properties of XMLHttpRequest that allow us to gain access to the inner workings of the response. Using these properties and methods, we can react to the response in any manner that we desire; the browser doesn't get to bully us out of the picture in this case!

Table A.2 XMLHttpRequest response-revealing methods and properties

Method/Property	Description
`responseText`	After a successful request/response cycle, this contains the response text.
`responseXML`	After a successful request/response cycle, this contains an XML DOM obtained by automatically parsing the response body as an XML document. It is only valid if the content-type header of the response is `text/xml`.
`status`	This contains the status code for the response.
`statusText`	This contains the reason message for the response.
`getAllHeaders()`	This returns all the response headers in a string. If you want to get at individual headers, you'll need to do some parsing.
`getHeader(name)`	This returns the value of the named response header.

Those who have already read through the chapters in this book will by now be familiar with the concept of a lab page. In order to demonstrate how Ajax allows us to more intimately deal with requests and responses, a lab page has been set up for this appendix. Let's see it in action.

A.5.3 *The Request Message Lab Page*

In the sample code for this book, you will find a folder named appa and within it an HTML file named lab-requests.hmtl. This lab page allows us to experiment by specifying various methods, headers, and parameters for a request, and then viewing the aspects of the returned response.

Because we require an active server-side component in order to be able to examine the attributes of the request and generate an appropriate response, this page must be served by a JSP-capable web server. To make setting up this page and its supporting code as a web application as easy as possible, the structure of the folders and files rooted at the appa folder already conform to rules for a Servlets 2.4-compliant web application. All you need to do is declare a web application context with its document base at the appa folder. If you do not already have a servlet-capable web server set up on your system, see appendix C for instructions on obtaining and installing Tomcat. Don't worry, it's free and it's easy!

Once you have set up the server and have the web application running, open the page and you should see a display as shown in figure A.1.

This page is divided into four panels:

- The upper left panel, labeled Request Information, is where you will specify the attributes of the requests to be generated.
- The upper right panel shows the options applied to an Ajax.Request instance used to generate a request message to the server.
- The lower right panel shows the details of the response to the Ajax request.
- The lower left panel, labeled Form Results, shows the response received as a result of submitting a request using a traditional form submission.

Operating this page is simple: use the controls in the Request Information panel to specify the details for a request message to be passed to a server-side resource. This server-side resource consists of a JSP page that inspects the incoming request and generates an HTML page containing the information garnered from the request.

In the Request Information panel, you can specify the HTTP method to be applied to the request. Additionally, you can specify up to three custom request headers and three request parameters by supplying a name and a value for each in the provided text boxes.

When you click the Apply button, two requests are generated: an Ajax request, and a "traditional" form submission. The traditional request is generated by adding any parameter names and values that you specified as hidden input elements

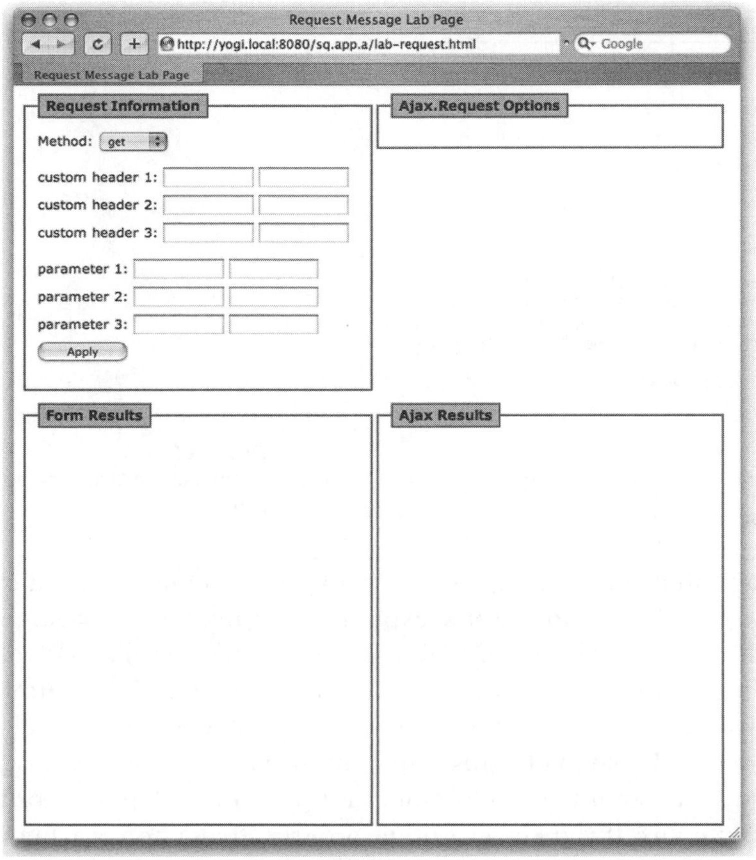

Figure A.1   The layout of the Request Message Lab Page

to a form that is submitted to an `<iframe>` element in the Form Results panel. The result will be something like what you can see in figure A.2.

This subpage shows a timestamp (so it's easy to tell when it's been updated) and information gathered from the request, such as the method, querystring, headers, and parameters.

The corresponding Ajax Request is generated using the Prototype Ajax.Request class, and the options assembled and passed to this object are displayed in the Ajax.Request Options panel. When the response is returned, the onSuccess callback function gathers information from the XMLHttpRequest instance (using the methods and properties outlined in table A.2) and displays it in the Ajax Results panel.

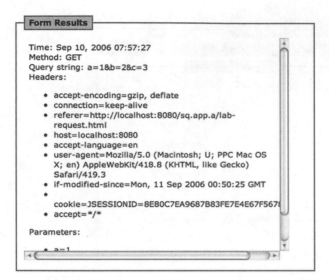

**Figure A.2
Results of the traditional form
submission**

The entire page after a sample request pair has been submitted is shown in figure A.3. You're now ready to conduct some experiments using this lab page.

You should experiment with this lab page using any browser that you think your users might employ, as each browser's implementation of XMLHttpRequest (or equivalent) varies slightly in its treatment of request generation. At minimum, testing on Internet Explorer, Firefox, and Safari will cover the vast majority of Internet users. If you want to be even more thorough, throw Opera, Mozilla, and Netscape into the mix. If you know of other browsers that a nontrivial portion of your customers will be using, try those out too.

As a suggestion, here are some exercises you should try using this page:

- With no headers or parameters specified, run through the various method types and inspect the results. You may be surprised how differently the various browsers act when confronted with method types other than GET or POST.

- Specify custom headers and see how they are reflected in the requests generated via Ajax.

- Specify parameters and see how they are passed differently between GET and POST operations. How do they behave when the method is something other than GET or POST?

- Try any other combinations you can think of that are pertinent to the types of activities you are planning to implement in your applications.

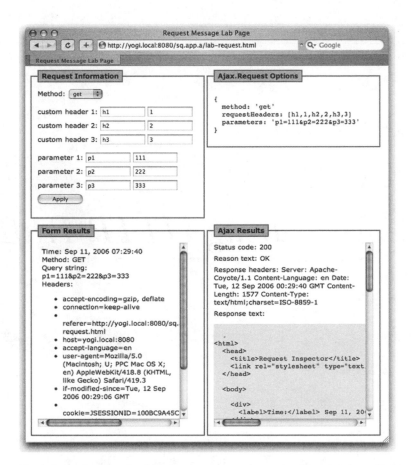

Figure A.3   Results of submitting a request pair: one traditional and one Ajax

Hopefully this appendix has given you a good overview of how HTTP plays into your use of Ajax. Understanding what goes on under the covers is a good first step to knowing how to use the power of Ajax to its best advantage, and to help you figure out just what's going on when things go awry. Like they sometimes do!

Measuring HTTP Traffic

In chapters 3 and 4, we developed several different prototypes of the Ajax-powered QuickGallery application. As part of the decision-making process for picking the one that we would carry forward for development into version 2, we measured the HTTP traffic generated by each, and presented some graphs.

Being able to measure and present data on web traffic with an application can be extremely useful. We used it to evaluate alternative designs for an app. It can also be used when planning a new release of a program to measure the load that different versions of an application place on the network.

In this chapter, we're going to share our HTTP measuring toolkit with you, and show you how to generate graphs of the types we showed in chapter 4. We've relegated this to an appendix because it isn't directly concerned with Prototype and Scriptaculous, but we hope you'll find it useful.

There are three phases to the process. First, we need to capture the raw data. Second, we need to parse it, and generate summary reports. Third, we need to present the data. We'll begin by looking at the raw data capture.

B.1 *Capturing HTTP traffic data*

In the simplest of situations, HTTP traffic passes directly between your web browser and the web server (figure B.1). It is sometimes the case that your requests are routed through one or more proxy servers that may filter or block sites, or cache responses locally to reduce network load (figure B.2).

If we want to watch and record the HTTP traffic, we can attempt to do so in the browser, on the server, or, if we're using one, at the proxy server. All three are possible, in fact, with the recording of web server logs being the most common. Web server logs will typically provide a record of each request made to the server, the

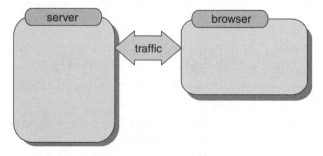

Figure B.1   HTTP traffic passing directly between the browser and web server

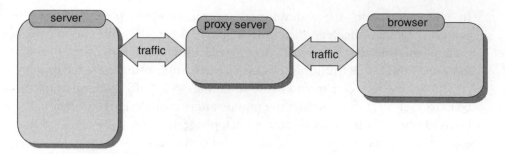

Figure B.2 HTTP traffic passing between the browser and web server via a proxy

resource fetched, the outcome of the response, and the size of the response content in bytes.

We have chosen not to use web server logs for two main reasons. The first is that the size of the response content is only part of the story. As we saw in appendix A, HTTP traffic is composed of a request and a response, each of which may have headers and a body. If our app is sending infrequent, bulky updates, the majority of the traffic will be response headers, but if the data is primarily being sent from browser to server, or if lots of small, chatty exchanges are being made, request body or headers could dominate.

The second reason for not measuring data on the server is that it limits us to measuring our own web sites. The tools presented here can be used to gather information about any site that one is able to see. Our primary aim in developing these tools was to measure our own applications, but flexibility is nice to have.

We've used two different open-source tools to measure our traffic. One of these is built into the client, and the other is a standalone application that functions as a proxy. Let's look at them each in turn.

B.1.1 Mozilla LiveHTTPHeaders

The Mozilla web browsers, the most popular of which is Firefox, can have their functionality enhanced through an extension system. LiveHTTPHeaders is an extension for Mozilla that presents details on HTTP traffic from the browser in a GUI interface within the browser's sidebar (see figure B.3).

The LiveHTTPHeaders extension can be obtained from the following URL: http://livehttpheaders.mozdev.org/installation.html. Once installed, it allows details on HTTP traffic to be recorded and displayed as a sidebar. The full headers for both request and response are recorded. Using the context menu (that is, the right-click menu), it is possible to save the transcript of a session as a text file.

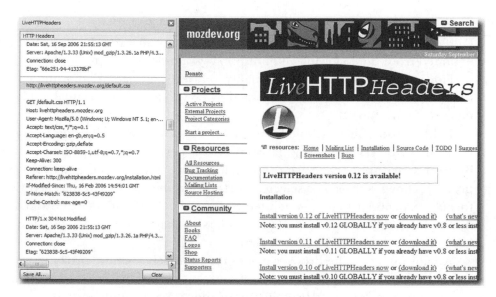

Figure B.3 **LiveHTTPHeaders extension within the Firefox web browser**

In terms of our classification of recording points, LiveHTTPHeaders is embedded in the web browser, as illustrated in figure B.4. As such, it can only record traffic when the client is a Mozilla browser.

The chances are that Firefox is available for your operating system, but you may not wish to use Firefox, or your app might not run on the Mozilla browsers. In such cases, we need to look at ways of recording HTTP traffic via a proxy, which we'll do in the next section.

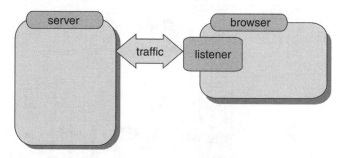

Figure B.4 **LiveHTTPHeaders captures traffic from within the browser**

B.1.2 *Microsoft Fiddler*

Fiddler is an open-source tool developed by Microsoft's Eric Lawrence. It can be obtained from the following URL: http://www.fiddlertool.com/fiddler/.

Fiddler provides similar functionality to LiveHTTPHeaders, allowing individual requests and responses to be inspected as raw text, in hexadecimal, and even as images (figure B.5).

Fiddler also offers a whole lot more for the power user, allowing the proxying of traffic to be scripted using JavaScript, and permitting you to mimic different browser signatures, shape bandwidth, and more. Most importantly for our purposes, it allows sessions, or selected parts of sessions, to be saved as text files in a format very similar to that generated by the LiveHTTPHeaders extension for Firefox. Fiddler differs from LiveHTTPHeaders in that it runs independently of the browser, as a proxy server (figure B.6).

An advantage of the browser extension approach over the proxy server is that the extension can be loaded and configured as part of the browser. When using a proxy, the browser must be told where the proxy is, and be told to direct its requests through it. Fiddler makes this as painless as possible when using Internet Explorer, automatically modifying the Windows Internet settings to use Fiddler as a proxy whenever Fiddler is started, and unsetting them when Fiddler closes.

This has led some to assert that Fiddler can only be used with Internet Explorer. This is untrue. For other browsers, it is simply necessary to set the proxy

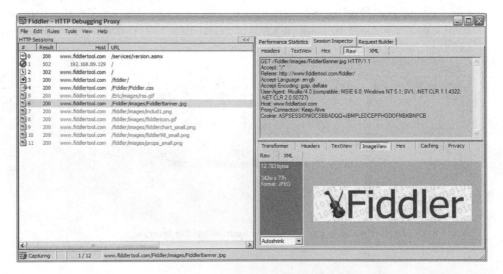

Figure B.5   Fiddler provides a number of views on both requests and responses in an item of HTTP traff

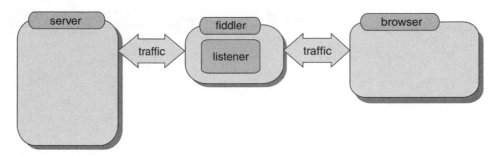

Figure B.6   Fiddler works as a proxy server, and intercepts traffic between client and server

configuration to point to Fiddler manually. By default, it runs on port 8888. It is even possible to run the Fiddler proxy on a different machine than the web browser, allowing Fiddler to work with non-Windows browsers.

Fiddler can save data in a number of formats. To save in the format we require, select the items you wish to save from the left-hand list, and select Save from the right-click menu. Choose the "Headers only" option.

We've now seen two ways of capturing raw HTTP traffic in a readable text format. The data that LiveHttpHeaders and Fiddler produce is, however, rather too verbose to make easy reading. In the next section, we'll present a simple program that can parse LiveHTTPHeaders and Fiddler output files, and generate concise reports on the traffic.

B.2 Parsing HTTP traffic data

Using LiveHTTPHeaders and/or Fiddler, we can capture rich details of an HTTP session. The headers can tell us the size of a request and response body, what mime types are used, and other useful details. And, as the full headers are recorded, we can also measure the size of the header data in bytes.

We couldn't find a program that generated this sort of information for us, so we wrote our own. Listing B.1 presents the code for a simple Python script that reads in a text file generated by LiveHTTPHeaders or Fiddler, and outputs a CSV file that can be imported into a spreadsheet. The Python script can be found in the download code that accompanies this book.

Listing B.1   httpmetrics.py

```python
import sys
import string
import time
import re

class TrafficParser:

  def __init__(self,infile):
    self.traffic=[]
    self.request={}
    self.response={}
    self.threshold=100000       ❶ Set file-size
    self.file=open(infile,"r")       threshold
    try:
      while(1):
        self.parse()
    except StopIteration:
      self.file.close()

  def parse(self):
    f=self.file
    line=f.next()
    if line[0:3]=="GET":
      self.parseRequest(line)
    elif line[0:4]=="POST":
      self.parseRequest(line)
    elif line[0:4]=="HTTP":
      self.parseResponse(line)
    elif self.isDelimiter(line):
      self.storeCurrent()

  def isDelimiter(self,line):
    return (line[0:4]=="----")

  def storeCurrent(self):
    if len(self.response)>0:
      self.traffic.append({"request":self.request,"response":self.response})

  def parseRequest(self,line):
    self.request={}
    self.response={}

   [self.request['verb'],self.request['url'],self.request['protocol']]=line.
   split(" ",2)
    self.parseHeaders(line,self.request)

  def parseResponse(self,line):
    self.response={}
```

```
  [self.response['protocol'],self.response['statusCode'],self.response['sta
tusMsg']]=line.split(" ",2)
    self.parseHeaders(line,self.response)

def parseHeaders(self,line,owner):
  owner['headers']={}
  bytecount=0
  while len(line.strip())>1:
    line=self.file.next()
    header=line.split(":",1)
    if len(header)==2:
      owner['headers'][header[0].strip()]=header[1].strip()
      bytecount+=len(line)
    elif self.isDelimiter(line):
      break
  owner['headers']['Header-Size']=str(bytecount)
  if self.isDelimiter(line):
    self.storeCurrent()

def report(self,urlRegex=0):
  print "url,response status,mime type,timestamp,request headers,request
 content,response headers,response content"
  mimeHistogram={}
  cumReqHdrLen=0
  cumRespHdrLen=0
  cumReqConLen=0
  cumRespConLen=0
  currUrl=None
  currStatus=None
  currMimetype=None
  currTimfl-0.0
  regex=0
  if urlRegex:
    regex=re.compile(urlRegex)
  for t in self.traffic:
    req=t['request']
    resp=t['response']
    url=req['url']
    status=resp['statusCode']
    mimetype="--"
    if resp['headers'].has_key('Content-Type'):
      mimetype=resp['headers']['Content-Type']
    timstr=resp['headers']['Date']
    timtup=time.strptime(timstr,'%a, %d %b %Y %H:%M:%S %Z')
    timfl=time.mktime(timtup)
    reqConLen="0"
    respConLen="0"
    reqHdrLen=req['headers']['Header-Size']
    if req['headers'].has_key("Content-Length"):
      reqConLen=req['headers']['Content-Length']
```

```
          respHdrLen=resp['headers']['Header-Size']
          if resp['headers'].has_key("Content-Length"):
            respConLen=resp['headers']['Content-Length']
          if regex:
            if regex.search(url):
              if currUrl!=None:
                print
string.join([currUrl,currStatus,currMimetype,str(currTimfl),str(cumReqHdr
Len),str(cumReqConLen),str(cumRespHdrLen),str(cumRespConLen)],",")
              currUrl=url
              currStatus=status
              currMimetype=mimetype
              currTimfl=timfl
              cumReqHdrLen=0
              cumRespHdrLen=0
              cumReqConLen=0
              cumRespConLen=0
            cumReqHdrLen+=int(reqHdrLen)
            cumRespHdrLen+=int(respHdrLen)
            cumReqConLen+=int(reqConLen)
            cumRespConLen+=int(respConLen)
          else:
            print
string.join([url,status,mimetype,str(timfl),reqHdrLen,reqConLen,respHdrLe
n,respConLen],",")
          if int(respConLen)<self.threshold:
            if mimeHistogram.has_key(mimetype):
              mimeHistogram[mimetype]+=int(respConLen)
            else:
              mimeHistogram[mimetype]=int(respConLen)

    if currUrl!=None:
      print
string.join([currUrl,currStatus,currMimetype,str(currTimfl),str(cumReqHdr
Len),str(cumReqConLen),str(cumRespHdrLen),str(cumRespConLen)],",")
    print
    print "mime type,total response content length"
    for k in mimeHistogram.keys():
      print k,",",mimeHistogram[k]

infile=sys.argv[1]
tp=TrafficParser(infile)                    ❷ Define significant
tp.report("\.(php|html)")        ←┘           file types
```

This is not a Python programming book, and the program is a utility rather than
an example, so we won't run through it line by line. In broad terms, it parses the
file line by line, recognizing the start of requests and responses, and pulling the

information out of them into a structured data set. Once all the data is parsed, it then iterates through the data and generates two summary reports.

The program can be told to ignore traffic where the response is greater than a specific size ❶. By default, this is set to 100,000 bytes, or roughly 100 KB. We introduced this feature specifically for QuickGallery, to allow us to ignore the large digital camera images in our data set.

The first report selects significant URLs from the traffic list, and lists out the traffic associated with them. The significance of the URL is determined by whether it matches a regular expression, which we have set by default to match URLs containing either .html or .php ❷. You may wish to tune this if you're working with other server languages. Insignificant rules by these criteria include CSS files, JavaScript, and images. These are typically secondary resources that will be loaded as a side effect of a new page or Ajax request, rather than being requested directly by the user. Figure B.7 shows a typical structure of such a report.

A1	▼	ƒx	un					
	A	B	C	D	E	F	G	H
1	url	response status	mime type	timestamp	request headers	request content	response headers	response content
2	/dave/album/images_datacentric.html	200	text/html;	1146860710	1753	0	1370	37280
3	/dave/album/imagedata.php?path=/	200	text/xml; c	1146860710	446	0	235	205
4	/dave/album/imagedata.php?path=//animals	200	text/xml; c	1146860719	3758	0	2763	725439
5	/dave/album/imagedata.php?path=	200	text/xml; c	1146860721	446	0	235	204
6	/dave/album/imagedata.php?path=/plants	200	text/xml; c	1146860722	11118	0	8396	115907
7	/dave/album/imagedata.php?path=/plants/foliag	200	text/xml; c	1146860724	1182	0	797	7548
8	/dave/album/imagedata.php?path=/plants	200	text/xml; c	1146860725	446	0	235	847
9	/dave/album/imagedata.php?path=/plants/trees	200	text/xml; c	1146860726	3390	0	2492	712466
10								

Figure B.7   Summary report of traffic generated by each significant item of HTTP traffic

The second report totals up all the traffic for the session by mime type, as shown in figure B.8.

The two reports are written to standard output, one below the other. They can easily be piped into a file, like this:

```
python httpmetrics.py MyFiddlerSession.txt > MyFiddlerSession.summary.csv
```

10		
11	mime type	total response content length
12	image/jpeg	177004
13	text/html; charset=UTF-8	433
14	text/html; charset=iso-8859-1	311
15	application/x-javascript	36120
16	text/xml; charset=utf-8	2773
17	text/css	416
18		
19		

**Figure B.8
Summary of traffic by
mime type**

If you're running Unix (including Mac OS X), the chances are that you already have Python installed. If you're running Windows, you can install Python from http://www.python.org—the installer is simple to use, and it should add Python to your system path so that it is accessible from your Command Prompt.

Whatever operating system you're using, we're assuming that you're in the directory containing both the Python script and the HTTP session data file. If this isn't the case, you can pass absolute or relative paths.

The final step to generating the report is to create a graph. The Python script outputs files with comma-separated values, which can be read by your favorite spreadsheet program. We generated the graphs in chapter 4 using Microsoft Excel, but OpenOffice Calc will do a good job too. Spreadsheet programs are simple to use, so we won't go into any great detail here.

That's it for this appendix. We hope that you find this tool useful in keeping an eye on your web applications. In the next two appendices, we'll cover the steps needed to run the example code presented in this book.

Installing and Running Tomcat 5.5

In order to address the needs of a variety of server-side systems, some of the chapters in this book use Java Servlets and JavaServer Pages (JSP) as their back-end mechanism. In order to run the examples for these chapters, it is necessary to set up an application server that is Servlets 2.4 and JSP 2.0 capable.

But not to fear! The free and easily obtained Tomcat 5.5 server is a snap to set up, and requires no knowledge of Java to do so. This appendix will walk you through obtaining and setting up your Tomcat server.

This, of course, assumes that you have Java, itself, installed upon your system. If not, please visit the Sun site for details on installing Java 1.5 for your operating system. (This is also a not-too-arduous task).

C.1 *Obtaining and unpacking the distribution*

You can download Tomcat 5.5 from the Apache Tomcat site at http://tomcat.apache.org/download-55.cgi (see figure C.1). Version 5.5.20 is the latest stable build at the time of this writing, but you'll probably want to grab the most recent 5.5 version that is available.

For Windows, you'll want to grab the Core.zip file (avoid the Windows executable—it does a much deeper installation than is needed for simply running the examples). For Mac OS X and other Unix systems, download the Core .tar.gz file. Be sure to avoid the pgp and md5 links—you don't need encrypted downloads.

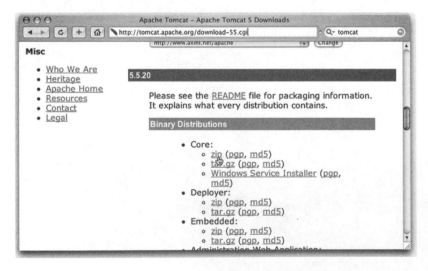

Figure C.1 Downloading the core Tomcat 5.5 distribution

Choose a location to unpack the .zip or .tar distribution:

- On Windows, you should avoid any folders with spaces in their names, so I usually unpack the distribution right to C:\.

- On Mac OS X, a typical location to place such installations is in the /Library folder. You can also choose the /Applications folder if you like, but many people like to reserve the /Applications folder for GUI applications.

- On other Unix systems, the typical location is the /usr/local folder. You could also use this folder on OS X, but /Library is more typically used on that platform, as it makes the files accessible via the GUI Finder.

Using the appropriate program (WinZip is a popular choice on Windows), unpack the folder to the desired location. On Mac OS X, you should just be able to double-click on the downloaded .tar file.

This will create a folder hierarchy rooted at a folder named apache-tomcat-5.5.20. We will refer to this folder as CATALINA_HOME in the remainder of this appendix, and this is the environment variable name that Tomcat will use to refer to this location.

In case you were wondering, "Catalina" was the code name for Tomcat 4, and it just sort of stuck.

C.2 Setting up JAVA_HOME

In order to let Tomcat know where your Java implementation is located, you need to set up the JAVA_HOME environment variable. Depending upon how you installed Java previously, this might already be defined. If so, just skip along to the next section.

On Windows, if you're using Cygwin as your shell, you can set up the environment variable as you would any other in your .bash_profile script. Otherwise, you'll need to use the Windows Control Panel to set up JAVA_HOME as a system-level environment variable (Control Panel > System > Advanced > Environment Variables).

Set the value of the variable JAVA_HOME (case is important!) to point to the root folder of your Java installation. On my XP system, that folder is C:\jdk1.5.0_06. On my OS X box, its value is set to /System/Library/Frameworks/JavaVM.framework/Versions/1.5.0/Home.

On Unix systems (which includes Mac OS X), set up the environment variable in the startup script for your particular shell (e.g., .bash_profile for the bash shell).

C.3 *Setting up the application contexts*

In J2EE parlance, a *context* is a self-contained web application. A single application server can load and service many such contexts, keeping requests to each context separate through the use of a unique prefix in the URL of each request. This prefix is known as the context path.

When a context is defined to the server (we'll see how to do that in just a bit), it is assigned a unique context path and the location on the filesystem that serves as its "root" or document base.

Let's say that one context is defined with a context path of /abc (context paths always start with a slash), and another with /xyz. If each has a file named index.jsp at the root folder (document base), the respective URLs would be the following:

```
http://someserver.com:8080/abc/index.jsp
http://someserver.com:8080/xyz/index.jsp
```

Note that the context path prefixes are used to let the server know which web application is to be accessed. These URLs also assume that the default Tomcat port of 8080 is being used.

Setting up the contexts is easy. All that you need to do is create a small XML file that defines the context, and drop it into the appropriate folder in the Tomcat installation.

Chapter 6 requires an application server in order to use the code samples, so we'll use the code for that chapter as an example. Let's assume that you have downloaded and unpacked the code for this book onto your filesystem at C:\sq-examples. Within the expanded folders, find the folder named chap6. This folder is already set up to be a self-contained, working web application.

We'll assign the name /sq.chap.6 to the context for the chapter 6 application. To define the context, create a file named after the context, sq.chap.6.xml for example, and within it place a single line (case matters):

```
<Context path="/sq.chap.6" docBase="c:/sq-examples/chap6"/>
```

The value of the docBase attribute should be set appropriately for wherever you put the expanded chap6 folder on your filesystem. The preceding example assumes a Windows installation.

Drop this file into the $CATALINA_HOME/conf/Catalina/localhost folder. Repeat this for any other chapter examples that require a J2EE server.

C.4 Starting Tomcat

Start the Tomcat server by executing a script that you will find in the $CATALINA_HOME/bin folder. For Windows, use the startup.bat script, and for Unix (including Mac OS X) use startup.sh. When it comes time to shut down, you'll find the corresponding shutdown scripts in this same folder.

To make sure that Tomcat is up and running (after giving it a few seconds to get on its feet, of course), open a browser and enter this URL:

```
http://localhost:8080/
```

You should see the Tomcat welcome page displayed, as shown in figure C.2.

If you do not see this page, go back and check your work. Unless you made a typo in the context files, or failed to set up the JAVA_HOME environment variable correctly, there's really no reason that Tomcat should not be up and running at this point.

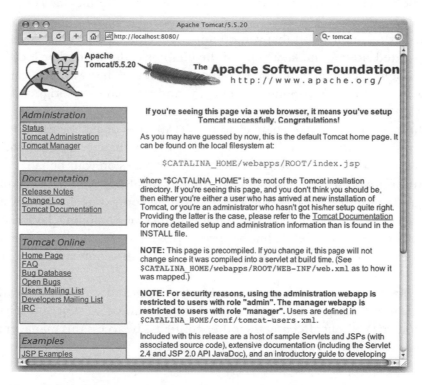

Figure C.2   The Tomcat welcome page—success!

The URL for the chapter 6 web application will then be

```
http://localhost:8080/sq.chap.6/
```

The :8080 in the URL specifies the port that Tomcat is running on. It must be specified in the URL as shown; otherwise the default of port 80 is used. You can change the port that Tomcat runs on, if you'd like, in the $CATALINA_HOME/ conf/server.xml file, but it is recommended that you leave it at 8080 to avoid any conflicts with other servers (such as Apache) unless you have a really good reason to change it. Just remember to include the :8080 in your URLs.

If all you want to do is run the example applications, that's all there is to it. If you plan on making changes to the example applications, read on to the next section.

C.5 *Managing Tomcat contexts*

If you are planning to make changes to the web applications supplied as examples to this book, you may need to stop and restart contexts after making certain types of changes.

First, it is recommended that you do not change the applications as they have been provided. Rather, make a copy of the chapter code in another location on your filesystem and create another context for them. That way, you can make changes to your heart's content in the copy, and still have the original code to look back to as a reference.

In the copy, if you make changes to the HTML files or JSP pages, you do not need to restart anything. Tomcat will detect any such changes and automatically serve up the new HTML files, or retranslate the JSP pages on your behalf.

However, if you make a change to the deployment descriptors (web.xml), or change and recompile servlets, the web application context needs to be restarted to pick up those changes. The specific mechanics of compiling Java classes is beyond the scope of this book, but be sure to place the resulting class files in the proper location under the WEB-INF/classes folder for the context you are making changes within.

Note that you do not need to stop and restart Tomcat itself. Tomcat provides a built-in context-management application that you can use to stop and start individual contexts without affecting the other contexts. To access this manager application, use your browser to access the following URL:

```
http://localhost:8080/manager/html/
```

Oops! It wants you to log in, as shown in figure C.3.

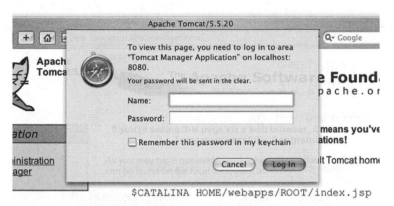

Figure C.3   Not just anyone can use the manager application

While it may seem a nuisance at the moment, this level of security is quite necessary. After all, you don't want just anyone to access the manager application, giving them the ability to stop and start your web applications, do you?

In order to gain access to the manager application, you will need to set up a privileged Tomcat user whose credentials you will use to log into the app. It's actually quite simple: open the file $CATALINA_HOME/conf/tomcat-users.xml in any text editor. You will see the contents of the file, as shown in listing C.1.

Listing C.1   The initial tomcat-users.xml file

```xml
<?xml version='1.0' encoding='utf-8'?>
<tomcat-users>
  <role rolename="tomcat"/>
  <role rolename="role1"/>
  <user username="tomcat" password="tomcat" roles="tomcat"/>
  <user username="both" password="tomcat" roles="tomcat,role1"/>
  <user username="role1" password="tomcat" roles="role1"/>
</tomcat-users>
```

To this file, add this line to the end of the role elements:

```xml
<role rolename="manager"/>
```

Next, add the following line to the end of the user elements, substituting a username and password of your choosing:

```xml
<user username="wallace" password="gromit" roles="manager"/>
```

Finally, save the file.

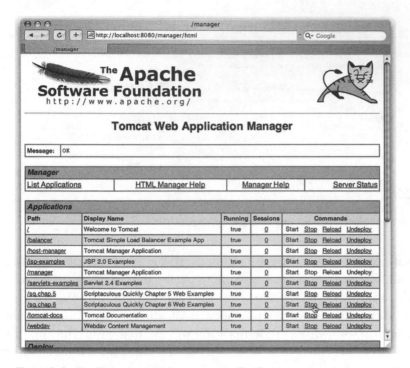

Figure C.4   The Tomcat context-manager application

Shut down and restart Tomcat, and when it's back up and running, go to the manager URL again. Enter the username and password you specified in the users file when prompted. After logging in, you will see the manager application, as shown in figure C.4.

With this application, you can easily and quickly stop and start individual application contexts (via the Stop and Start links for each) whenever you make a change requiring a restart.

You're now ready to dig into those examples!

Installing and Running PHP

In keeping with our assertion that Scriptaculous and Prototype can play well with a range of server-side technologies, we've developed the examples for this book in more than one server-side language. In appendix C you saw how to set up Apache Tomcat to run the Java-based examples. In this appendix, we'll look at installing PHP, the server language we used to build the back end for our QuickGallery applications in chapters 2–4 and 12.

PHP is a general-purpose scripting language originally designed to run on Unix-based systems, although it can now run on Windows too. It is probably the most commonly used scripting language on the Web, and certainly most Unix-based ISPs and web-hosting solutions will offer PHP as standard. You might therefore like to run QuickGallery on your hosted web site, in which case PHP will already be installed for you. The instructions here apply primarily to installing PHP on your own development machines, in order to play with our example applications.

D.1 System requirements

PHP is an extensible system and suffers from rather poor separation of the modules from the core product. Further, the core system can be configured in more than one way. As a result, installs of PHP differ widely from one machine to another.

We've written our example code to be as undiscriminating as possible, and to run on a wide variety of PHP installations. However, in order to get the job done, we've had to lay down a few requirements, so here they are.

D.1.1 PHP version

PHP version 5 is the latest version of the language, but version 4 is still commonly in use in many places. We've run our example code against versions 4 and 5 of PHP without encountering any issues. It may even work on version 3, but we can't offer any guarantees.

D.1.2 Web server

PHP most commonly runs as a module of the Apache Web Server, but it can run with other web servers, such as lighttpd and Microsoft's IIS. We've only tested our code on the Apache Web Server, and in one place we do use a function, which according to the documentation may be Apache-specific, to read an HTTP request header. We don't know that it will break on other systems, but you're on your own.

We've successfully run the application on both Apache 1.3 and Apache 2.0 systems.

D.1.3 Operating system

PHP can run on most operating systems. We've tested the code on Windows 2000, Windows XP, Mac OS X 10.4, and Ubuntu Linux (both the Breezy Badger and Dapper Drake versions). Ubuntu happens to be the Linux distro that I'm using this week, and installing the system on any other distro should be a simple matter. If you're running anything other than these OSs, we assume that you know what you're doing!

D.1.4 Libraries

Because we generate thumbnail images on the fly, we require a version of PHP that is compiled with the GD graphics libraries. This is the biggest stumbling block that you're likely to face in getting the application running on your system.

The simplest ways to get it working are to use a prepackaged bundle of PHP with GD built in, or to install GD using a package manager. We managed to do it without too much effort or loss of temper, and still had time left over to write this book! In the following section, we'll show you how to do it too.

D.2 Installation

Your machine may already have PHP installed on it. If so, the preinstalled PHP may or may not be up to the job of running our example applications. There are many ways of installing PHP on any operating system. In this appendix, we're going to assume that you're only doing this because you have to, and we'll show you the quickest way to get it done.

We're going to cover installing on Linux, Windows, and Mac OS X separately, as the last-effort methods we came up with varied across the operating systems.

D.2.1 Installing PHP on Linux

As we said, we used Ubuntu Linux version 6.06 (Dapper Drake) to test our installation of QuickGallery. Ubuntu has an incredibly easy and pleasant package management system, with GUI front-ends available (Synaptic if you're using Gnome, Adept if you're using KDE). Dependencies between packages are resolved automatically, so you need only select a few top-level packages for installation.

The easiest route is to install the packages php5 and php5-gd, which are in the main Dapper repositories. These will automatically pull in the supporting web server packages (Apache 2), and the underlying image manipulation libraries required by GD. If you require PHP4, you'll need to fetch the packages from the

Ubuntu Universe repository, but the principles are the same. Figure D.1 shows the Adept package manager browsing available php4 packages.

Once installed, the web server can be started and stopped from the script / etc/init.d/apache2. To start Apache, open a console and type this line:

```
sudo /etc/init.d/apache2 start
```

To shut down the web server, type this:

```
sudo /etc/init.d/apache2 stop
```

Apache will start and stop automatically when you switch your machine on and off, so there's normally no need to do this manually. If you do it manually, Apache will prompt you for your password. This is because the sudo command executes a command that requires super-user privileges. Ubuntu relies entirely on sudo to perform admin tasks, and doesn't create a super-user account by default. The password you need to enter is your own, not the super-user's.

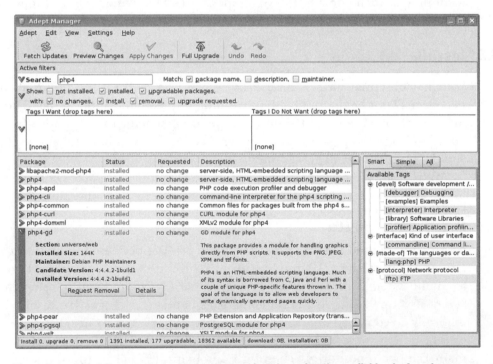

Figure D.1 Adept Package Manager for Ubuntu Linux browsing the available php4 packages

The root web folder can be found in /var/www. We also like to set up a sites directory in our home folder, into which we can drop all our web applications. To create such a folder, execute the following commands in a console (substitute your own username if you're not called dave!):

```
cd /home/dave
mkdir sites
cd /var/www
ln -s /home/dave/sites dave
```

The location /var/www/dave now points at your sites folder. If you unzip the QuickGallery code into the sites folder, it will create, for example, a /home/dave/sites/album/slideshow/ folder containing the version 2.0 code. To view this app in a browser, simply visit the URL:

```
http://localhost/dave/album/slideshow/
```

You may need to edit the configuration file and set folder permissions before everything works. We'll look at that in section D.3.

If you're using a different Linux distro, it should be easy to adapt these instructions. Mandriva, Suse, and Fedora all support dependency-resolving package managers these days, and the /var/www root web folder seems to be a near-universal standard these days. If in doubt, use the appropriate support channels for your distro. If you're having trouble working with your distro's package manager, you might like to look at the prebundled XAMPP for Linux (see the Mac OS X instructions in the next section, and adapt them to your tastes).

D.2.2 Installing PHP on Mac OS X

As of version 10.4 (Tiger), Mac OS X ships with Apache 1.3 installed by default. PHP version 4 is bundled in with this, although you need to uncomment a couple of lines in the httpd configuration file in order to activate it. However, this version of PHP doesn't support GD, and we couldn't figure out an easy way to add it in.

Mac OS X, by default, doesn't contain any large packaging system for third-party applications. If you like Debian Linux-style software repositories, you might like to try Fink or MacPorts (previously DarwinPorts). If you already use one of these, you may prefer to use them to install PHP and GD, but the overhead of setting up Fink or DarwinPorts is rather high for playing around with examples from a web development book.

At this point, we encountered XAMPP, a prebuilt bundled installation of Apache 2.0, PHP, Perl, the MySQL database, and other goodies necessary for a LAMP development environment. Conveniently for us, the PHP that comes with XAMPP is bundled with a range of useful, nonstandard extensions, including the GD libraries.

XAMPP is supported on Mac OS X 10.3 or above. The most recent release at the time of writing is 0.6, which is only supported on Intel-based Macs—if you're using a PowerPC Mac, you'll need to use an older release of XAMPP. Version 0.4 carries a warning stating that it is "less stable" than XAMPP for Linux or Windows, but we ran QuickGallery on a PowerPC-based Mac Mini using XAMPP 0.4 during our testing.

XAMPP can be found at http://www.apachefriends.org/, and the latest version of the installer for Mac OS X is at http://www.apachefriends.org/en/xampp-macosx.html. Older versions of XAMPP for Mac OS X can be found on SourceForge at http://sourceforge.net/project/showfiles.php?group_id=61776&package_id=140453. We proceeded to SourceForge and grabbed the tar.bz2 file. The only downside here is that the download is large, roughly 43 MB.

By default, our Firefox browser drops all downloads onto the desktop, so once the file had downloaded, we opened up a terminal window and typed in the following:

```
cd ~/Desktop
bunzip2 xampp-macosx-0.5.tar.bz2
cd /Applications
tar xvf ~/Desktop/xampp-macosx-0.5.tar
```

This simply installs the binaries for XAMPP. To start them up requires super-user privileges, and Mac OS X, like Ubuntu, uses the sudo system to allow ordinary users to execute privileged commands, rather than providing a root user.

Before bringing XAMPP up, make sure that the built-in Apache 1.3 install is turned off (use sudo apachectl stop), and execute the following command in a terminal window:

```
sudo /Applications/xampp/xamppfiles/mampp start
```

This will produce a few lines of output, after which the various parts of XAMPP will run in the background, until it is shut down with the following command:

```
sudo /Applications/xampp/xamppfiles/mampp stop
```

The web root folder can be found in /Applications/xampp/htdocs. Under Mac OS X, a Sites folder will already be present in your home directory, and this can be hooked up to the XAMPP web server as a symbolic link, like so (again, substitute your own name if you aren't called dave):

```
ln -s /Users/dave/Sites /Applications/xamppp/htdocs/dave
```

A folder called album in your Sites folder will now be visible in the web browser as http://localhost/dave/album.

That's all we need to do to install the PHP examples on the Mac OS X operating system. Figure D.2 shows XAMPP being launched in a terminal on Mac OS X, and serving up the QuickGallery application.

In the next section, we'll turn our attention to Windows.

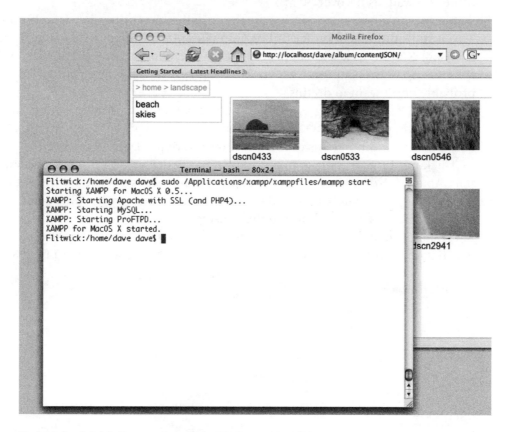

Figure D.2   QuickGallery running under XAMPP on Mac OS X

D.2.3 *Installing PHP on Windows*

Windows doesn't ship with a package management system by default. If you're using Cygwin, the Unix emulation layer for Windows, the installation of Apache, PHP, and GD can be performed in a very straightforward way. If you use Cygwin, we'll assume that you don't need much hand-holding, and let you get on with it.

If you're not using Cygwin, we recommend XAMPP again. XAMPP on Windows even comes with a little GUI app for starting and stopping the servers. Go to the XAMPP site at http://www.apachefriends.org/en/xampp-windows.html and downloaded the installer.exe program via SourceForge. (Make yourself a cup of coffee while you wait, as it's over 30 MB.)

Once you've downloaded it, run the installer, accepting the default options. This installs the system under C:\Program Files. At the end of installation, it offers to install XAMPP as a service, in which case the web server, database server, etc., will start up when your machine boots. If you're only using it to run our apps, you probably don't want to do this.

If XAMPP isn't running as a service, start it from the Start menu, under apache-friends > xampp > CONTROL XAMPP SERVER PANEL. This will bring up the GUI for launching the components of XAMPP, shown in figure D.3.

Clicking the Start button ought to bring a service up—in our case, we want to start Apache. Note that the XAMPP control panel isn't very good at reporting on errors. If Apache fails to start, the Admin button next to it will remain grayed out; no messages will be shown in the console.

The most common cause for Apache failing to start is that port 80 is already in use. If you are running another web server, remember to switch it off first. XAMPP

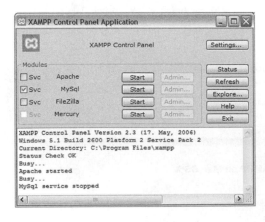

Figure D.3
The XAMPP control panel
under Windows

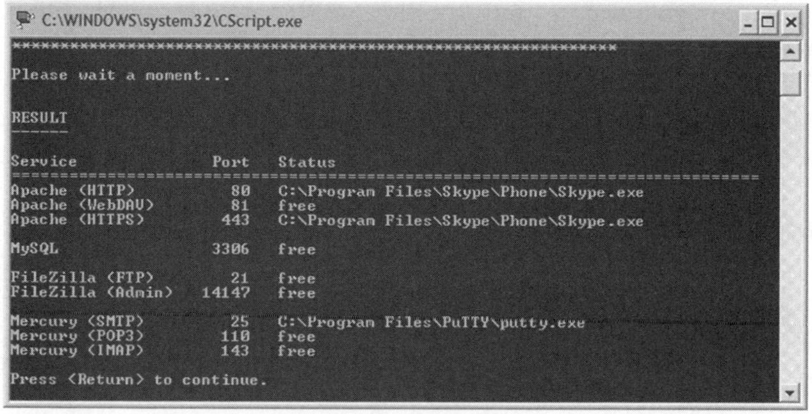

Figure D.4 Output of the XAMPP port-checker program

provides a useful utility under C:\Program Files\xampp called xampp-port-check.exe, which will scan all the ports required by XAMPP and report on the processes that are currently using them. Figure D.4 shows the output of running the port checker on my machine.

As you can see, port 80 has been reserved by Skype, the IM and VoIP program. On investigating, I discovered that, although Skype normally runs over a high-numbered port, it has an option to fall back to port 80 or 443 if the high-numbered port is blocked by a firewall. This option is turned on by default, but when I unchecked it and restarted Skype, Apache was able to start up correctly. Many instant messenger systems will use this technique to keep connections open within corporate networks, so be prepared to do a bit of detective work if Apache won't start, and make good use of the port-checker utility.

On Linux and Mac, we created symbolic links from the web root folder to our home directories. On Windows, Explorer shortcuts aren't really part of the filesystem, so it wasn't possible to create a link from C:\Program Files\xampp\htdocs to my development copy of the code. The simplest thing to do is just to copy the top-level folder into XAMPP's htdocs directory, at which point the magic URL, http://localhost/album/slideshow/, began to work, as with the other platforms. If you really want the web server to serve pages from another location, you can manually modify the httpd.conf file, and add extra `<Directory>` directives. The httpd.conf file can be found in C:\Program Files\xampp\apache\conf.

XAMPP is not intended for production use, but rather for coders who need to get a simple, hassle-free development environment up quickly. As such, it suits our purposes (and hopefully yours!) for running the QuickGallery code from this book. If you know your way around Apache and PHP already, you should find that QuickGallery runs easily enough on your existing installation too.

Whatever your platform, we now have PHP up and running, and a copy of the demo code installed. The final task is to configure QuickGallery for the peculiarities of the operating system being used. We'll look at that in the next section.

D.3 Configuring QuickGallery

Throughout the book, we've developed various versions of QuickGallery. For ease of deployment, every version is bundled together in a single zip file, sharing the same set of image data. Further, there is a single configuration file shared by all versions of the app that sets the paths on the local system.

So, now that you have PHP installed, simply unzip the zip file into your web server's filesystem, change the configuration files, and you're ready to go. Figure D.5 shows what the expanded filesystem ought to look like.

Once the files are unzipped, you'll need to edit the config.php file. This lists the paths on the filesystem where QuickGallery can expect to find the images that it will display. The three variables are listed in table D.1.

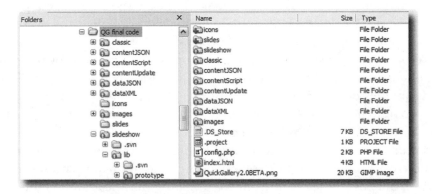

Figure D.5   Expanded QuickGallery demo code, with shared folders for images, icons, and slides, and a shared configuration file (config.php). The HTML, CSS, PHP, and JavaScript for each version of the app live in their own subfolders.

Table D.1 Configuration variables for QuickGallery

Variable	Description
$basedir	The absolute path to the root directory of the folders containing the images on the server filesystem. The directory and all subdirectories must be readable and writeable by the web server.
$img_pre_path	The prefix to attach to the server host when constructing a URL for the images. This is typically the path to the $basedir relative to the web root folder.
$slides_dir	A directory into which slideshow data is stored, used by QuickGallery v2 only. The directory must be writeable.

The config file in the download zip file is shown in listing D.1.

Listing D.1   config.php

```
/* uncomment for standard Linux setup
$basedir='/home/dave/sites/album/images';
$slides_dir='/home/dave/sites/album/slides';
$img_pre_path='/dave/album/images';
*/

/* uncomment for standard Mac setup
$basedir='/Users/dave/Sites/album/images';
$slides_dir='/Users/dave/Sites/album/slides';
$img_pre_path='/dave/album/images';
*/

/* uncomment for standard Windows XAMPP setup
$basedir='c:/Program Files/xampp/htdocs/album/images';
$slides_dir='c:/Program Files/xampp/htdocs/album/slides';
$img_pre_path='/album/images';
*/

$thumb_max=120;
?>
```

The config file contains three commented-out configurations, for Linux, Mac OS X, and Windows, based on the instructions given in previous sections of this appendix. If you're on a Unix system and you've followed a standard install according to our instructions, you should only need to uncomment only one of these blocks, and change the username from dave to your own user account name. If you've installed to a different location, you'll need to modify the paths. If you're on Windows, note that PHP allows you to express file paths using Unix-style forward slashes. We recommend you do this, as the PHP code sometimes needs to interchange between filesystem paths and URLs, and the latter can only be written with forward slashes.

Once the configuration file has been edited, you can point your browser at the top-level page for the QuickGallery install. You should see a home page like that shown in figure D.6.

The page provides a short overview of the various versions of QuickGallery, listed by book chapter. The icons act as clickable links to launch each of the examples. Enjoy your exploration of our example code, and direct any questions to us at www.manning.com/crane3.

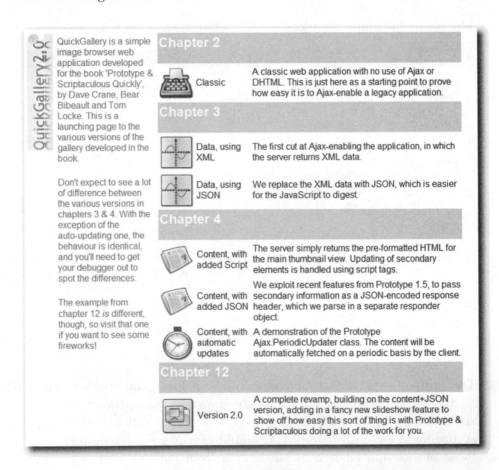

Figure D.6 Home page for the QuickGallery examples. Click on the icons to launch the examples. Have fun!

Porting
Server-Side Techniques

Ajax is essentially a client-side technology, and Prototype and Scriptaculous are client-side libraries. This gives us the luxury of being able to present code that will run against any server-side language. We've tried to emphasize this point by presenting the necessary supporting server-side code in a number of languages, but we realize that we can't please everyone. We've emphasized Java and PHP over .NET and Ruby in this book, and that choice was essentially arbitrary.

Most of the time, writing server-side code for Ajax is pretty much the same as writing server-side code for any web application. We're still using HTTP, after all, and we don't need to show you how to read querystring parameters in the programming languages that you're already familiar with. However, when using Ajax, we have better control over the low-level details of HTTP, allowing us to create requests that don't look quite the same as those originating from a classic web app. We therefore need to handle these requests a little differently on the server.

To assist in the translation of our coding techniques to languages other than the ones that we covered in detail so far, we're going to point out a few of the less common things that we've done, and show how to make them work in the language of your choice.

E.1 Reading request headers

Using the XMLHttpRequest object, we can add any arbitrary header to a request, and on the server, we can read these headers. We did this in chapter 12 in Quick-Gallery version 2, in the `saveSlides()` method. Normally, we'd pass this sort of information as a CGI parameter rather than a header, but in this case, we wanted to use the entire POST body to send a complex chunk of data (we'll see in section E.3 how to read the body of such a request). An alternative would have been to send a multipart request, but building the request this way was easier.

Here's the code for creating the Ajax.Request object:

```
new Ajax.Request(
  "saveSlides.php",
  {
    method: "post",
    contentType: "text/html",
    requestHeaders: ["X-SLIDENAME",this.name],
    postBody: snapshot
  }
);
```

The requestHeaders option that we've specified will add a header called X-SLIDE-NAME to the request, which we will read to find out what name to save the slideshow as on the server. So, how do we pick out the header when the request hits the server?

E.1.1 *PHP*

In PHP, there is no definitive way to do this. However, the majority of PHP installations run on top of the Apache HTTPD web server, and in this case, request headers can be accessed as an associative array.

Let's look at the code that we used in QuickGallery:

```
$allHeaders=apache_request_headers();
$slideName=$allHeaders['X-SLIDENAME'];
```

First, we get a reference to the request headers as an array, using apache_request_headers(). Then we can simply read the value that we want out of that array.

E.1.2 *Java Servlet API*

When working with the Java Servlet API, whether in a servlet or a JSP, we'll receive the request as a javax.servlet.http.HttpServletRequest object. This object has methods for interrogating the headers by name, so we can write our example simply like this:

```
String slideName = request.getHeader("X-SLIDENAME");
```

In this case, request is a reference to the HttpServletRequest. If you're using a JSP page, the request variable will be automatically set for you. If you're using a servlet, the request will be referenced by whatever name you've set in the arguments to the doGet() or doPost() method.

E.1.3 *.NET*

In .NET, the incoming request will be represented as a System.Web.HttpRequest object. The headers can be read from the Headers property as a NameValueCollection object. So, in C#, we might write this:

```
String slideName=Request.Headers.Get("X-SLIDENAME");
```

Note that many commonplace headers are also represented as specialized properties in the HttpRequest object, as well. ContentType provides direct access to the MIME type (that is, the Content-type header), and similar properties are available for Content-length, Accept-types, and so on.

The API presented earlier is a standard part of the .NET API, so whether you're using VB.NET, Boo, JScript.NET, or IronPython, the calling semantics will be the same.

E.1.4 Ruby on Rails

When using Ruby on Rails, we interact with the CGI interface through the Action-Controller part of ActionPack. ActionController defines an abstract base class, ActionController::AbstractRequest, which is subclassed by the CgiRequest (used in production) and the TestRequest (used in testing). Inside the controller code, the request object is referenced by the name request.

The AbstractRequest provides specialized methods for retrieving headers, such as the MIME type and the accepts string.

To access the full set of HTTP headers in production, the CgiRequest object provides a property called env, which returns the hash of environment variables for the request. So, to read our custom header, we would write the following in the controller code:

```
slidename=request.env["X-SLIDENAME"]
```

We've now covered the business of reading custom headers sent from the browser. We might also want to return custom headers to the browser, so we'll look at that next.

E.2 Adding response headers

When the server returns a response, we often want to add headers to it. Most commonly, we will want to set the Content-type header, to specify the MIME type of the response. This is important, for example, when returning XML from the server. If the MIME type is not set to a suitable value, the responseXML property of the XHR object will return null, even if the body of the response is valid, well-formed XML. Also, when we're using Prototype's Ajax.Request object, setting the response MIME type to text/javascript will cause the response to be automatically evaluated for us.

It is worth noting, in all languages, that response headers must be set early on, before any data from the response body has been sent out. Some server-side systems will permit buffering of the response on the server, allowing headers to be set after the first part of the response is written, but it's best not to rely on this capability, and to always write any headers before the body.

E.2.1 *PHP*

To set a response header in PHP, we call the `header()` function. To set the response MIME type to `text/xml`, for example, we would write this:

```
header("Content-type: text/xml; charset=utf-8");
```

Note that we've specified the UTF-8 character set here, as part of the MIME type too. This is not necessary, unless you're expecting to deal with nonstandard internationalized characters in your data.

E.2.2 *Java Servlet API*

When writing a servlet, we are provided with a javax.servlet.http.HttpServletResponse object as an argument to `doGet()` or `doPost()`, along with the request object. The response object can be modified, and we can add headers using the `addHeader()` or `setHeader()` methods. `setHeader()` will ensure that a header name isn't duplicated, whereas `addHeader()` allows for duplicates.

So, to set the content type of the response to denote XML, we would write the following:

```
response.setHeader("Content-type","text/xml; charset=utf-8");
```

Here, `response` is the name of the response object passed in to `doGet()` or `doPost()`.

E.2.3 *Java Server Pages*

When writing a JSP page, we can specify the MIME type directly in the JSP page directive, as follows:

```
<jsp:directive.page
  contentType="text/xml; charset=utf-8"
  import="java.util.*"
/>
```

Note that the directive must appear at the start of the page, and it may contain several attributes. Here, we've added an `import` statement as well, to allow us to use the Java Collections API in the page.

The `contentType` attribute is obviously only applicable to setting the `Content-type` header. To set an arbitrary response header in the JSP, we can use the `addHeader()` or `setHeader()` methods described in section E.2.2. In a JSP page, the variable name response is automatically applied to the HttpServletResponse object.

E.2.4 .NET

.NET provides a System.Web.HttpResponse class to match the HttpRequest class that we looked at in section E.1.3. The request and response objects are similar in many ways, and HttpResponse offers specific properties for common headers such as ContentType, and a general-purpose headers property that returns a NameValueCollection.

The MSDN documentation states about the Headers property that "this property supports the ASP.NET infrastructure and is not intended to be used directly from your code." However, we can use it to pass extra header information if we need to.

To set the content type of our response, we need simply write this:

```
Response.ContentType="text/xml; charset=utf-8";
```

E.2.5 Ruby on Rails

In Rails, if we want to set headers, we should do so in the controller rather than in the view. From here, we have full access to the array of headers. To set the MIME type of a response, we might write this:

```
class MyAjaxController < ApplicationController

def index
  headers["Content-type"] = "text/xml; charset=utf-8";
  ...
  render(:layout=>false)
end
```

We can set any response header in this way. Note that we end the controller method by calling render() with layout set to false, to prevent any additional decoration of our output.

E.3 Reading a POST request body

In a classic web application, the only POST requests that we will receive come from HTML forms. The browser creates these requests for us, with URL-encoded querystrings in the body, and the appropriate MIME type set automatically. Most server-side frameworks are built around the assumption of receiving form-like data, and they will provide APIs for presenting the request body as a series of key-value pairs.

When we're using Ajax, we have a lot more freedom about how we shape our request bodies, and we may wish to send XML or JSON data in the body, for example. When saving the slideshow data in QuickGallery version 2 (see chapter 12), we sent a large chunk of HTML as the request body.

Server-side APIs invariably provide a way to read the raw request body, as well as the parsed set of key-value pairs from a querystring, but it's generally less well known. Here's how to do it in the most common server-side languages.

E.3.1 PHP

PHP provides a special variable to read the raw data as a string:

```
$postBody=$HTTP_RAW_POST_DATA;
```

E.3.2 Java Servlet API

The Java Servlet API is slightly less straightforward. If we don't want to read the response as a set of key-value parameters, we need to read the POST body of the request as a stream.

We can choose whether to use a binary java.io.InputStream, or a character-based java.io.Reader. Because the POST body is always character-based, a Reader is the simpler option:

```
StringBuffer rawPostData=new StringBuffer();
try{
  BufferedReader reader=new BufferedReader(request.getReader());

  String line=reader.readLine();
  while(line!=null){
    rawPostData.append(line);
    rawPostData.append("\n");
    line=reader.readLine();
  }
}catch (IOException ioex){
}
String rawPost=rawPostData.toString();
```

First, we create a StringBuffer object in which to assemble the content as it arrives. We then get the Reader from the request, and wrap it in a BufferedReader. We can continue to read from the Reader, one line at a time, until the entire request has been read, at which point we convert the StringBuffer to a String.

E.3.3 .NET

Like the Java API, the .NET System.Web.HttpRequest class allows us to read the raw POST body via an input stream. The semantics differ slightly from the Java, but the principle is the same.

```
Stream stream=Request.InputStream;
long length=str.Length;
byte[] data=new byte[length];
```

```
stream.Read(data, 0, length);

// Convert byte array to a text string.
String rawPost="";
for (int i=0;i<length;i++){
  rawPost+=data[i].ToString();
}
```

We get the total length of the stream beforehand, and read it into an array of bytes in a single read. We can then convert these bytes to a string.

E.3.4 Ruby on Rails

Reading the raw POST data in Ruby on Rails is very straightforward, as the abstract base request class provides us with a raw_post method. The code is as follows:

```
rawPost=request.raw_post
```

E.4 Summary

As we noted at the outset, most of the server code that we write for an Ajax application will be very similar to what we'd write for a classic app, at least as far as the low-level mechanics of handling the HTTP requests and responses are concerned. However, because of the greater flexibility of the XMLHttpRequest object, when compared to traditional hyperlinks and HTML forms, we've sometimes done things in the example server code for this book that won't look so familiar.

In the examples for the book, we've had to pick a specific server-side language for implementation. This appendix has demonstrated how to do the less-common operations on the HTTP stack for a range of other languages, allowing you to use the techniques that we've demonstrated in the language of your choice.

index

MORE TITLES FROM MANNING

Ajax in Action
    by Dave Crane and Eric Pascarello
        with Darren James
    ISBN: 1-932394-61-3
    680 pages
    $44.95
    October 2005

Ajax in Practice
    by Dave Crane, Jord Sonneveld
        and Bear Bibeault
        with Ted Goddard, Chris Gray
        and Ram Venkataraman
    ISBN: 1-932394-99-0
    450 pages
    $44.99
    April 2007

For ordering information go to www.manning.com

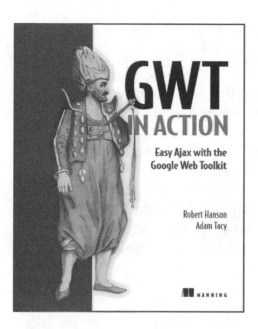

GWT in Action
  Easy Ajax with the Google Web Toolkit
  by Robert Hanson and Adam Tacy
  ISBN: 1-933988-23-1
  600 pages
  $49.99
  June 2007

GWT in Practice
  by Robert Cooper and Charles Collins
  ISBN: 1-933988-29-0
  450 pages
  $44.99
  August 2007

For ordering information go to www.manning.com

MANNING EBOOK PROGRAM

All ebooks are 50% off the price of the print edition!

In the spring of 2000 Manning became the first publisher to offer ebook versions of all our new titles as a way to get customers the information they need quickly and easily. We continue to publish ebook versions of all our new releases, and every ebook is priced at 50% off the print version!

Go to www.manning.com/payette to download the ebook version of this book and have the information at your fingertips wherever you might be.

MANNING EARLY ACCESS PROGRAM

Get Early Chapters Now!

In 2003 we launched MEAP, our groundbreaking Early Access Program, to give customers who can't wait the opportunity to read chapters as they are written and receive the book when it is released. Because these are "early" chapters, your feedback will also help shape the final manuscript.

Our entire MEAP title list is always changing and you can find the current titles at www.manning.com